The Clinical Management of Early Alzheimer's Disease

A Handbook

Edited by

Reinhild Mulligan
University Hospitals of Geneva

Martial Van der Linden
University of Geneva

Anne-Claude Juillerat
University Hospitals of Geneva

NEW YORK AND HOVE

First published by
Lawrence Erlbaum Associates, Inc., Publishers
10 Industrial Avenue
Mahwah, NJ 07430

This edition published 2013 by Psychology Press

Psychology Press
Taylor & Francis Group
711 Third Avenue
New York, NY 10017

Psychology Press
Taylor & Francis Group
27 Church Road, Hove
East Sussex BN3 2FA

Psychology Press is an imprint of the Taylor & Francis Group, an informa business

First issued in paperback 2013

Cover design by Kathryn Houghtaling Lacey

Library of Congress Cataloging-in-Publication Data

The clinical management of early Alzheimer's disease : a handbook / edited by Reinhild Mulligan, Martial Van der Linden, Anne-Claude Juillerat.
p. cm.
Includes bibliographical references and index.
ISBN 0-8058-3370-6 (alk. paper)
1. Alzheimer's disease. 2. Alzheimer's disease—Patients—Care. I. Mulligan, Reinhild. II. Van der Linden, Martial. III. Juillerat, Anne-Claude.
[DNLM: 1. Alzheimer Disease—therapy. 2. Alzheimer Disease—diagnosis. WT 155 C6414 2003]
RC523 .C575 2003
616.8'3106—dc21 2002017867
CIP

ISBN 978-0-805-83370-6 (hbk)
ISBN 978-0-415-65231-5 (pbk)

Contents

Foreword

After some two million years of human evolution, an unprecedented demographic process has begun. Large numbers of people are remaining alive until a late age. Since the Middle Pleistocene, this has never happened before. The consequence is that millions of human brains are now surviving to the stage when neurodegenerative events start to manifest themselves. And these brains are the biological basis of their owners' mental life, owners who now constitute as much as one fifth of some populations. Within this group of elderly persons, a sizeable fraction have some degree of cognitive decline. For some, this decline is progressive. The personal and social consequences are profound. The economic and health care consequences now threaten the wealthiest of countries.

In the health care of the elderly, much attention has rightly been given to the care of persons with fully established dementias. Not nearly so much attention has been directed at milder and incipient states of cognitive decline. Yet from the viewpoint of population health, this group is just as deserving. They are numerically far greater than the numbers of people with dementia, their cognitive decline is associated with nontrivial disablement in daily life, and their impairment is believed to be at a stage when interventions may have some chance of slowing degeneration and protecting the person's functional capacity.

Here, then, is an area of need that calls for a range of scientific efforts toward treatment and prevention: in neuropharmacology, neuropsychology, behavioral treatments, and psychosocial interventions. The advances achieved in each of these need then to be applied through professional and community resources. Drs. Mulligan, Van der Linden, and Juillerat have a full recognition of this, but they also reveal their awareness of the need for this diversity of resources to work together. Indeed, that is a primary motive in their organizing and editing this handbook. It is all very well to have an array of highly trained expertise within a community, but that is for naught if the experts do not work in harmony with each other, with administrators, and, above all, with their consumers. Where complementarity is highly valued, the performance of such teams flourishes. The editors want to help achieve that.

Between these two covers, there is assembled a body of information, ideas, and perspectives that make *The Clinical Management of Early Alzheimer's Disease* an exceptionally rich resource for those who work for the health and well-being of older persons. It is professionally and scientifically nonpartisan because it carries contributions from many disciplines. And it balances the need for evidence-based treatments with the need for compassion. As a contribution to the health care of the elderly, it is a book that should itself age well!

—Scott Henderson

Preface

This book is divided into two parts. The first part deals with clinical and cognitive aspects of Alzheimer's Disease (AD) crucial for the diagnosis of early dementia and related disorders, reviewing recent research findings in this area. The second raises the important issue of appropriate and optimal management in the early stages of the disease.

The complex question of how to evaluate the costs of chronic diseases, such as AD, for a society is addressed in Chapter 1; in particular the impact of medical treatment and care strategies in the very early stages of AD are discussed. Important points raised in this chapter are the unclear relationship between type and amount of expenditure on care and the patient's and caregiver's welfare. Many methodological issues related to the cost analysis of dementia still remain unresolved and further studies are needed to help health professionals in their choice of treatment and care utilization.

Guidelines for screening and the clinical evaluation of dementia in primary health care are proposed in Chapter 2. Clinical features and diagnostic criteria of the most frequent dementias are described and suggestions are made about which patients should be referred to specialists for further investigations. A basic laboratory workup is recommended and indications for neuroimaging proposed. The impact of methods developed for cognitive psychologists on neuropsychological assessment is discussed in Chapter 3. In contrast to traditional neuropsychological formulations, new approaches showed that AD can selectively impair specific cognitive systems or processes while sparing others, that factors allowing an optimization of cognitive performance may be identified, and that there is an important heterogeneity in both the nature and the progression of deficits. These findings have greatly influenced the practice of assessment and rehabilitation in AD. Moreover, it was also demonstrated that—beyond the observed heterogeneity—certain types of deficits, such as deficits in executive function and episodic memory, are prevalent in the initial stages of the disease and that the identification of these deficits could contribute to the early diagnosis of AD. Clinical assessment of dementia at a specialist level is discussed in Chapter 4, with an emphasis on the contribution of different disciplines and techniques to the diagnosis of early AD, or other types of dementias. The roles of the primary care physician and their collaborators are analyzed vis-à-vis both the diagnostic procedure and the establishment of management plans adapted to the specific needs of patients and families. A more detailed description of the role of the memory clinics in the United Kingdom in Chapter 5 demonstrates common goals and a similar approach to the evaluation of dementia. The choice of neuropsychological tests might vary depending on cultural differences and resource allocations, but there seems to be an overall consensus on the domains of cognition to be investigated.

The development, properties, clinical efficacy, and limitations of acetlylcholinesterase inhibitors, currently the only available pharmacological treatment of AD, are described in Chapter 6. Important new approaches to treatment, such as attempts to target the main underlying pathology of the disease—amyloid formation—are presented, and a critical appraisal of the current state of knowledge about immunization against AD are also discussed. Based on findings from the most recent major studies, Chapter 7 deals with clinical and theoretical aspects of the comprehensive assessment of behavioral and psychiatric symptoms of AD and proposes guidelines for their pharmacological treatment. Although the more disturbing behavior problems usually appear in the more advanced stages of the disease, symptoms such as anxiety, depression, and sleep impairment are a frequent challenge for treatment in the early stages.

Identification and adequate treatment of these problems represent an important aspect of the management of early AD. Complementary to pharmacological approaches, it is possible to develop psychological interventions that take into account the heterogeneity of factors underlying behavior problems. Chapter 8 presents an empirical approach to these problems including a holistic assessment of case profiles and an analysis of the patient's relationships. The chapter also deals with conceptual issues, selection of management options and comments on intervention techniques. Chapter 9 is devoted to neuropsychological rehabilitation in early AD. In the first part, the chapter describes the various and complex aspects of pre- and post-rehabilitation neuropsychological assessment such as how to understand the nature of cognitive, mood, and behavioral dysfunctions, how to examine the impact of these deficits on daily life activities and how to identify the preserved abilities and optimization factors that could be exploited for intervention; how to receive informed treatment consent from the patient and family members; and how to evaluate the outcome of rehabilitation. In the second part, the three main goals of rehabilitation of cognitive problems in early AD are presented and illustrated: facilitating performance by using optimizing factors, teaching specific knowledge by using techniques that tap preserved cognitive systems, and structuring the patient's environment and providing external cognitive aid. Finally, the chapter closes with a discussion of the role of day-care centers as ideal structures for the rehabilitation of patients with early AD.

The exploration of patients' everyday activities is also important for diagnosis and management and should primarily aim to reduce their handicap in day-to-day living. Chapter 10 analyzes problems in the assessment of these activities in AD patients and critically reviews the usefulness of current evaluation techniques and theoretical models developed to understand functional impairment in brain-damaged or AD patients. Comprehensive management of AD must also encompass the patients' caregivers. Their crucial role at different stages is discussed in Chapter 11. The need for a flexible but structured setting for caregiver and patient is emphasized, thus allowing the caregiver to promote, maintain, and generalize the use of optimizing factors, external aids, or preserved abilities. Chapter 12 addresses the important issue of the caregivers' burden and underlines the need for interventions to promote their well-being. Different interventions—based on theoretical models of stress and coping—are described that aim to enhance their abilities to cope with the demands of caring.

The different contributions to this book show that substantial progress has been made in diagnosing and characterizing early AD, as well as in understanding the consequences of the disease for daily life and the well-being of caregivers. Pharmacological treatment is now available to stabilize cognitive deficits and to treat psychiatric and behavioral problems. In addition, the efficacy of various neuropsychological interventions for both patients and caregivers has been demonstrated. However, important problems remain unresolved and need further investigation. Some of the more pressing issues concern the questions of how to introduce neuropsychological interventions on a large scale into caregiving systems, how to integrate neuropsychological and pharmacological interventions to improve treatment efficiency, and how to include patients' needs, values, and preferences in the assessment and intervention program. We hope that this book will stimulate research interest in these domains.

Last but not least, we would like to thank all the contributors of the chapters. To collaborate with authors from different parts of the world has been a challenging and stimulating experience. We are also indebted to Susan Milmoe at Lawrence Erlbaum Associates for making this project possible and to Erica Kica for her invaluable help with the organization and editing of the book.

—Reinhild Mulligan
—Martial Van der Linden
—Anne-Claude Juillerat

List of Contributors

Stéphane Adam, Neuropsychology Unit, University of Liège, Bvd du Rectorat, 3 (B33), 4000 Liège, Belgium.

Michael Bird, Centre for Mental Health Research, Australian National University, Canberra ACT 0200, Australia.

Fabienne Collette, Neuropsychology Unit, University of Liège, Bvd du Rectorat, 3 (B33), 4000 Liège, Belgium.

Francine Fontaine, Service de Psychologie, Institut Universitaire de Gériatrie de Montréal, 4565, ch. Queen-Mary, Montréal, Quebec, H3W 1W5, Canada.

Serge Gauthier, McGill Centre for Studies in Aging, 6825 LaSalle Blvd., Verdun, Quebec, Canada, H4H 1R3.

Marie Gendron, Research Centre, Institut Universitaire de Gériatrie de Montréal, 4565, ch. Queen-Mary, Montréal, Quebec, H3W 1W5, Canada.

Ezio Giacobini, Department of Geriatrics, University Hospitals of Geneva, Rte de Mon-Idée, 1226 Thônex, Switzerland.

Panteleimon Giannakopoulos, Department of Psychiatry, Clinic of Geriatric Psychiatry, University Hospitals of Geneva, 2, chemin du Petit-Bel-Air, 1225 Chêne-Bourg, Switzerland.

Brigitte Gilbert, Service de Psychologie, Institut Universitaire de Gériatrie de Montréal, 4565, ch. Queen-Mary, Montréal, Quebec, H3W 1W5, Canada.

Gabriel Gold, Department of Geriatrics, University Hospitals of Geneva, 3, chemin du Pont-Bochet, CH–1226 Thônex, Genève, Switzerland.

François Herrmann, Department of Geriatrics, University Hospitals of Geneva, CH–1226 Thônex, Genève, Switzerland.

Eli J. Jaldow, Neuropsychiatry and Memory Disorders Clinic, King's College, University of London, St. Thomas' Hospital, London, SE1 7EH, Great Britain.

Anne-Claude Juillerat, Memory Clinic, Department of Geriatrics, University Hospitals of Geneva, 69, rue des Vollandes, 1207 Geneva, Switzerland.

Michael D. Kopelman, Neuropsychiatry and Memory Disorders Clinic, King's College, University of London, St. Thomas' Hospital, London, SE1 7EH, Great Britain.

Louise Lévesque, Research Centre, Institut Universitaire de Gériatrie de Montréal, 4565, ch. Queen-Mary, Montréal, Québec, H3W 1W5, Canada.

Thierry Meulemans, Neuropsychology Unit, University of Liège, Bvd du Rectorat, 3 (B33), 4000 Liège, Belgium.

Jean-Pierre Michel, Department of Geriatrics, University Hospitals of Geneva, 3, chemin du Pont-Bochet, CH–1226 Thônex, Genève, Switzerland.

Karine Morasse, Service de Psychologie, Institut Universitaire de Gériatrie de Montréal, 4565, ch. Queen-Mary, Montréal, Québec, H3W 1W5, Canada.

Reinhild Mulligan, Memory Clinic, Department of Geriatrics, University Hospitals of Geneva, 69, rue des Vollandes, 1207 Geneva, Switzerland.

Juliana Onwumere, Neuropsychiatry and Memory Disorders Clinic, King's College, University of London, St. Thomas' Hospital, London, SE1 7EH, Great Britain.

Philippe H. Robert, Memory Center, Clinic of Psychiatry and of Medical Psychology, Centre Hospitalier Universitaire de Nice Sophia Antipolis, 30, Avenue de la Voie Romaine, 06002 Nice, France.

Martial Van der Linden, Cognitive Psychopathology Unit, University of Geneva, FPSE, 40, Bd Pont d'Arve, 1205 Geneva, Switzerland.

Dina Zekry, Department of Geriatrics, University Hospitals of Geneva, CH–1226 Thônex, Genève, Switzerland.

1

Sociodemographic and Economic Aspects

Jean-Pierre Michel
Gabriel Gold
François Herrmann
Dina Zekry
Reinhild Mulligan
Panteleimon Giannakopoulos
University Hospitals of Geneva

"Dementia is certainly one of the most dramatic medical and economic challenges that our society will face in the coming years"
—Souêtre et al., 1995

Dementia is a superordinant category of illness that includes all conditions causing loss of cognitive abilities in an individual who was previously intellectually normal (or was functioning at a higher level) and that are not accounted for by an acute illness causing delirium (Geldmacher & Whitehouse, 1996). Dementia is a slowly progressive, currently incurable, long-lasting disease (Whitehouse, 1997) that ranks very high in the global burden of diseases. In 1994, the incidence of dementia was the ninth most frequent among all disorders (959,000 cases per year) in the United States, and its prevalence ranked eighth (7,082,000 cases; Murray & Lopez, 1997). In most industrialized countries the prevalence of Alzheimer's Disease (AD), the most common dementing disorder, varies between 6% and 8% of persons older than 65. In every decade after the sixth, the number of patients suffering from AD approximately doubles (Katchaturian & Radebaugh, 1998), with an estimated 30% of the population older than 85 years of age affected by it (Ritchie & Kildea, 1995). AD and other degenerative dementias have a drastic impact on the lives of patients and on family members who serve as caregivers for these patients (Cayton, 1993; Coon & Edgerly, 1999). Moreover, dementia induces enormous health care costs, which will increase more rapidly in an aging society (Meerding, Bonneux, Polder, Koopmanschap, & van der Maas, 1998). In the United States, the annual direct costs of treating AD were estimated to be $21 billion in 1991 (Ernst & Hay, 1994) and $29.8 billion in 1998 (Menzin, Lang, Friedman, Neumann, & Cummings, 1999). In the Netherlands in 1994, dementia ranked third in total health care costs (5.6% with 7.4% for women and 2.9% for men), first in the 65–84 age group (9.5%), and first in the over 85 age group (22.2%; Meerding et al., 1998). In the early stages of the disease, major costs stem from the loss of patient's and caregiver's productivity and from family out-of-pocket expenses (Schumock, 1998). In the advanced stages of the disease, costs are mainly linked to long-term and institutional care (Menzin et al., 1999). Until now, escalating health care costs were for care and not for cure (Meerding et al., 1998) of an increasing number of affected people (Katchaturian & Radebaugh, 1998). The expected impact of new drug developments may result in not only an improvement of the patient's cognitive functioning and quality of life but also a reduction in the time spent by caregivers, a delay in nursing home placement, and a reduction of indirect costs (Schumock, 1998). But the current goal is to obtain rapidly a 5-year delay in the onset of the disease, which could reduce the number of patients by 50% (Katchaturian & Radebaugh, 1998). For these reasons, the economic evaluation of AD and related dementia will play an increasingly influential role in clinical and resource allocations in the coming years. Physicians and other health care professionals should familiarize themselves with techniques of cost-effectiveness analysis (Neumann, Herrmann, Berenhaum, & Weinstein, 1997), and this is the aim of this chapter.

DEMENTIA COSTS: HOW TO UNDERSTAND ECONOMIC ANALYSIS

Pharmacoeconomics is a new area of health economics that emerged in the late 1970s, arising from concerns about the relative effectiveness and costs of different drugs (Bootman, Townsend, & McGhan, 1996; Spilker, 1996). The term *pharmacoeconomics* may have first been used in 1986 in reference to postmarketing drug research. Pharmacoeconomics dealt first with preventive strategies, such as immunization and screening programs, and later with the treatment of acute illnesses, such as antibodies use in burn patients and antibiotic use for different types of infections (Whitehouse, 1997). Until a few years ago chronic conditions such as dementia suffered from a lack of both theoretical and empirical developments in this field (Whitehouse, 1997). However, the use of "dementia costs" as key words for Medline research now allows us to identify more than 800 papers published in peer reviewed journals in the last 5 years that are devoted to economic considerations of AD.

Researchers must consider both societal and specific payer's perspectives. From the societal perspective, all relevant costs are included. From the perspective of the specific payer (e.g., patients, families, insurance companies, municipality, county), various selected costs are included or excluded (Winblad, Hill, Beermann, Post, & Wimo, 1997).

Three main types of analysis can be identified (see Table 1.1).

The economic burden analysis of a disease (i.e., cost of illness) is estimated by counting all relevant costs of a particular disease to a society, without any consideration as to which care strategies are used. This kind of

TABLE 1.1

Various Types of Cost Analysis Applied to Dementia

Type	*Description*
Economic burden	
Cost of illness (Winblad et al., 1997)	Description of all relevant costs of a particular disease (dementia) to a society. Care strategies are not evaluated.
Costs of various care strategies	
Cost description (Drummond, Stoddart, & Torrance, 1987)	Analysis of the costs of one type of treatment/care strategy; no comparison with alternative types of treatment/care strategies.
Cost analysis	Comparison of the costs of different therapies/care strategies; not taking into account the effects.
Trade-off analysis between care costs and defined or supposed outcomes	
Cost-minimization analysis (CMA)	Comparative cost analysis of two treatments/care strategies estimated to have the same effects.
Cost-benefit analysis (CBA)	Analysis of all costs achieved by one treatment/care strategy with good outcome; same monetary unit.
Cost-effectiveness analysis (CEA)	Analysis of all costs achieved by one treatment/care strategy with good outcome; nonmonetary unit.
Cost-utility analysis (CUA; Torrance, 1987)	Analysis of all costs of a therapy/care strategy with a single important outcome, such as quality of life.
Pharmacoeconomics	Could be part of types II and III analysis.
Cost consequence	Outcomes and costs of a specific treatment are measured together in the same indirect mathematical analysis.

Note: Adapted from Wimo et al. (1997). Costs of dementia and dementia care: A review. *International Journal of Geriatric Psychiatry, 12.* Also adapted from Winblad et al. (1997). Issues in the economic evaluation of treatment for dementia: Position papers from the international working group on harmonization of dementia drug guidelines. *Alzheimer Disease and Associated Disorders, 11.*

analysis is very complicated and is valuable only for social and health policy discussions (Winblad et al., 1997).

Cost analysis of various care strategies includes cost description and cost analysis. Cost description analysis is an economic analysis of only one type of treatment or care, without making any comparisons with alternative types of treatment or care (Drummond, Stoddart, & Torrance, 1987). Cost analysis compares different therapies/treatments but does not compare the effect of these treatments. A large majority of economic studies of dementia care are of this type, and many have their origin in a local project or program. Home care costs (Dellasega & King, 1996; Rice et al., 1993; Souêtre et al., 1995; Stommel, Collins, & Given, 1994), day care costs or intermediate care alternatives (Knapp, Wilkinson, & Wigglesworth, 1998; Wimo, Ljunggren, & Winblad, 1997; Wimo, Mattson, Krakau, Eriksson, & Nelvig, 1994a, 1994b; Wimo et al., 1997), nursing home costs (Ernst & Hay, 1994; Fries, Mehr, Schneider, Foley, & Burke, 1993; Ljunggren & Brandt, 1996; Rovner, Steele, Shmuley, & Folstein, 1996), and special care units (Holmes, Ory, & Teresi, 1994; Volicer et al., 1994) have been analyzed differently. Four methodological strategies were used: Detailed cost analysis, average costs, longitudinal cost analysis of patients' care, and cost comparison with other types of care.

Trade-off analysis between care costs and defined or supposed outcomes include cost-minimization, cost-benefit, cost-effectiveness and cost-utility analyses. Cost-minimization analysis (CMA) compares the costs with a final recommendation of the use of the cheaper, assuming equivalent effects of the two treatments or care strategies. This type of analysis fulfills criteria for complete health economic studies. However, it is currently rarely used and is recommended for future studies. Cost-benefit analyses (CBA) and cost-effectiveness analysis (CEA) correspond respectively to the same monetary and nonmonetary analysis of all costs linked to a therapy/care strategy with an expected precise outcome. CEA shows the relationship between all resources used and the health benefit achieved (i.e., the effects) of one intervention (Neuman et al., 1997, 1999). CEA is a possible solution for evaluating informal care (shadow price method) and for considering the patient's quality of care (Busschbach, Brouwer, van der Donk, Passchier, & Rutten, 1998). Cost-utility (CUA) analysis considers the cost of a care treatment/strategy, considering one single important outcome, such as the patient's quality of life (Torrance, 1987). CUA shows the relationship between weights or utility weights (quality-adjusted life years or quality) for particular outcomes and quality of life (Albert et al., 1996). The use of generic scales could allow comparison with other diseases (Winblad et al., 1997).

Pharmacoeconomics, in the strictest sense, could be part of the previous types of analyses. However, pharmacoeconomics also includes cost-consequences analysis, which corresponds to consumer preferences/satisfaction (with an indirect mathematical analysis) of outcome and costs of a specific treatment/health service (Whitehouse, 1997). For example, the cost-effectiveness of the new dementia drugs (acetylcholine esterase inhibitors, AchE I) includes not only the price of the drug but also its ability to stabilize or improve the patient's and caregiver's quality of life and reduce caregiving costs (Ernst & Hay, 1994; see Table 1.2). This kind of analysis is complex because it must include data and costs that vary constantly, such as delay of institutionalization, reduction in number of hours of informal caregiving required by the patient, improvement of quality of life for patients and caregivers, and that need to be compared with societal trends and progress (Souêtre et al., 1995).

The importance of cost analysis was recently stressed by Winblad et al. (1997), who published a position paper of the international working group on harmonization of dementia drug guidelines. The understanding of these various types of cost analysis is fundamental for physicians and other health care professionals who wish to influence clinical policy and resource allocation (Neumann et al., 1997).

DEMENTIA COSTS: PROBLEMS OF ANALYSIS

Regardless of the type of cost analysis used in a study, other important considerations have to be taken into account:

TABLE 1.2

Different Types of Variables and Costs Considered in a Cost-Effectiveness Analysis of AD Treatment

All Resources Used	*Health Benefits Achieved*
Health care resources	*Effectiveness of interventions*
Diagnostic tests	Change in patient's global and cognitive functioning
Medications	Years of life gained
Efforts to monitor and treat side effects	Quality of life
Acute hospital care	
Physician's services	
Home health care	
Nursing home	
Nonhealth care resources	
Support from paid services	
Time spent by unpaid family members	

Note: Adapted from Neumann et al. (1997). Methods of cost-effectiveness analysis in the assessment of new drugs for AD. *Psychiatric Services, 48.*

Variability of Study Design

Sound demographic statistics must be attained to have a precise idea of the prevalence of dementia in a study population. Even more important, valuable diagnostic criteria and dementia severity scales have to be applied to the study population (Winblad et al., 1997). The increasing number of vulnerable elderly (i.e., those over 85 years) and the probable increase of disease duration (e.g., baby boomers are better educated and healthier, hence they live longer with the disease) will probably change the actual prospective calculation of care costs for demented patients (Katchaturian & Radebaugh, 1998)

Too few prospective longitudinal studies over a long period of time have been published. The same is true for population-based studies with a health economic approach, in which both total costs and costs of different care alternatives are studied (Whitehouse, 1997). Prolongation or compression of morbidity of a country's population could widely modify data interpretation. An analysis based on pharmacoeconomics should cover the entire survival period of study groups along the disease course, taking into account changing parameters such as modification of care needs, modification of care structures, and concurrent diseases/disabilities (Winblad et al., 1997).

Randomized studies, standardized studies, or both, that allow transnational comparisons could be useful. Differences among countries related to heath care system organizations, financing, patient payment, and taxation levels make comparisons across countries difficult. Moreover, the meaning of care concepts (e.g., care levels and staff categories, such as staff numbers and staff competence) and care alternatives (e.g., physical factors, such as buildings and equipment) as well as currency exchange rates and consumer price indexes must be taken into account (Winblad et al., 1997). Complex ethical issues should also be considered: If age-based rationing becomes a guiding force in health care expenditures of some countries, surely AD patients will be the most vulnerable.

Inconsistent Use of Terminology

The poor quality control of studies is also linked to a nonagreement on the essential definitions of costs (see Table 1.3). The costs linked to organization and operating within the health sector can be divided into direct and indirect costs (Drummond et al., 1987; Winblad et al., 1997). Direct costs include direct medical costs, such as outpatients' care visits (e.g., with general practitioners [GP], specialists, physiotherapists, occupational therapists), laboratory investigations, diagnostic tests, drug costs, home care and social services, hospitalization, residential care, and nursing home care (with consideration of the staff number versus staff competence

TABLE 1.3

Composition of Overall Costs

Cost Type	*Description*
Costs within the health sector	
Direct medical costs	Outpatients care visits
	Laboratory investigations
	Diagnostic tests
	Drug costs (international differences)
	Home care/social services
	Hospitalization
	Residential care (international differences)
	Nursing home care (international differences, staff number vs. competence, human vs. technical equipment)
Direct non-medical costs	Rent, heat, food, electricity
	Out-of-pocket expenses
	Patient/family input into treatment
	Informal care
Indirect costs	Comorbidity
	Drug side effects
	Costs of production losses (i.e., time lost from work)
Intangible costs	Psychic costs (pain and suffering)
Externally borne costs	
Community indirect costs	Costs of production loss (i.e., time lost from work)
	Community planning

Note: Adapted from M. Drummond et al. (1987). *Methods for the Economic Evaluation of Health Care Programmes,* Oxford, UK: Oxford University Press, and from Windblad et al. (1997) Issues in the Economic Evaluation of Treatment for Dementia: Position Paper From the International Working Group on Harmonization of Dementia Drug Guidelines, *Alzheimer Disease and Associated Disorders, 11.*

and staff composition versus technical equipment). Direct non-medical costs include rent for housing, electricity, heat, food, out-of-pocket expenses, and patient and family input into treatment.

Indirect costs are essentially related to production loss (i.e., time lost from work; Drummond et al., 1987), but they also include costs caused by the following unpaid informal care; behavioral and psychiatric disturbances (Nagaratnam, Lewis-Jones, Scott, & Palazzi, 1998); comorbidity; and drug side effects.

Intangible costs correspond to psychic costs, such as pain and suffering. They generally are excluded of any cost analysis. Costs borne externally by the health sector patients and their families (e.g., community planning, road modification) have to be added to direct and indirect costs. They are also generally excluded of any cost analysis.

Need for a Better Care Categorization

The poor quality control of studies is also linked to discrepancies between the significance and composition of formal and informal care.

Formal care can be care by health professionals or care by paid persons, whatever their professional competence. To simplify matters for cost analysis, it is possible to consider formal care as the equivalent of paid care (Fox, 1997).

In contrast, informal care usually means unpaid care (Fox, 1997). Spouses or female relatives (e.g., daughter, daughter-in-law) provide the vast majority of long-term care. There are two different methods of evaluating informal costs. The replacement cost method values each informal care hour at the equivalent hourly wage of a professional. The second method estimates the caregiver's cost in having to give up paid employment or in passing up the opportunity for career advancement (Knapp et al., 1998). Large differences in cost estimation caused the application of one or the other method of calculation.

Controversy About Outcome Measures

The first major step of any economic evaluation is to measure the magnitude of the therapeutic/care strategy effects. For this purpose, it is necessary to translate any outcome assessment into defined effects (Winblad et al., 1997).

To assess cognitive treatment effects, scores of simple psychometric tests are generally compared over time. However, these methods are not adequate for evaluating the nature and type of patients' needed care (Winblad et al., 1997).

On the other hand, repeated measurements of activities of daily living (ADL) and instrumental activities of daily living (IADL) appear useful and evaluate noncognitive effects. The evaluation and the interpretation of the demented patient's or caregiver's quality of life raise multiple and difficult questions (Albert et al., 1996). How can one measure quality of life—a subjective feeling of well-being with multidimensional components—in demented patients? What links exist between quality of life and dementia itself? Are these links different in other diseases? Is it possible to evaluate the health-related quality of life? Is there any clinical significance of quality-adjusted life years calculations? What is the relationship between a patient's quality of life and a caregivers' quality of life (Whitehouse, 1997)?

Problems of Funding

Studies funded by drug companies themselves can have important conflicts of interest.

DEMENTIA COSTS: MAIN RESULTS OF ECONOMIC RESEARCH

As demonstrated in the first two parts of this chapter, economic evaluation of dementia is not only difficult to conduct but also difficult to analyze. Because of the publication of several position and harmonization papers (Whitehouse, 1997; Winblad et al., 1997), a better approach to evaluating dementia costs is now emerging (Table 1.4).

Historical Studies of Dementia Costs

Methodological differences, lack of consensus on the exact components of direct and indirect costs, as well as difficulties in transnational comparisons explain the wide discrepancies among the early cost evaluations. Direct medical costs vary, ranging from $12,000 per demented patient living at home to $2,300 per institutionalized patient (Hu, Huang, & Cartwright, 1986). The direct medical costs were estimated at less than a quarter of the total costs in a few U.S. studies (Hay & Ernst, 1987; Huang, Cartwright, & Hu, 1988), less than half the total costs in Italian publications (Trabucchi, Govoni, & Bianchetti, 1994), and more than two thirds the total costs in a French short-term survey (Souêtre et al., 1995). These variations in results triggered a more focused approach to the cost evaluation of dementia.

Consideration of the Dementia Stages

Dementia severity increases the total cost. The time between the first symptom and the first medical consultation is 1.5 years (Trabucchi et al., 1994). At this early stage of the disease, costs are essentially linked to diagnostic procedures and include various direct medical costs (Souêtre et al., 1995; Trabucchi et al., 1994). Severely demented patients need more third-party caregiving (e.g., housework, care of the person, surveillance) or institutionalization. This explains why indirect costs are much more important than direct costs during the final stages of dementia (Souêtre et al., 1995; Trabucchi et al., 1994). For each MMSE decrease of one point, the cost increase is 4% (Trabucchi, Ghisla, & Bianchetti, 1996). Moreover, concomitant diseases, behavioral disturbances, and psychiatric symptoms interact significantly with costs (Albert et al., 1998).

TABLE 1.4

Examples of Analysis of the Economic Burden of Dementia and Cost Descriptions and Cost Analysis of Various Care Strategies

Economic Burden

Inclusion Criteria
- Number of demented patients in the study population
  (Hay & Ernst, 1987; Huang et al., 1988)
- Cognitive impairment, dementia, or AD
  (Smith, Shan, Wright, & Lewis, 1995)
- Severity of dementia
  (Wimo, Karlsson, Sandman, Corder, & Winblad, 1996)
- Comorbidity analysis
  (Manton, Corder, & Clark, 1993)

Care Organization
- Cost categories inclusion
  (Hay & Ernst, 1987; Huang et al., 1988; Ernst & Hay, 1994)
- Volunteer care involvement
  (Gray & Fenn, 1993)
- Day/cost in residential settings
  (Gray & Fenn, 1993)

Cost Analysis
- Comparison with total cost of illness
  (Rice, Hodgson, & Kopstein, 1985)
- Comparison with hip fracture costs
  (Schneider & Guralnik, 1990)

Costs of Various Care Strategies

Home Care: Two Methodological Approaches
- Costs of a typical day of home care
  (Rice et al., 1993; Stommel et al., 1994)
- Longitudinal cost analysis of a home care dementia population, which could include use of institutional care
  (Weinberger et al., 1993)

Four Other Methodological Considerations

- Degree of dementia
  (Dellasega & King, 1996; Souêtre, 1995)
- Family members care = included or not as a cost?
- Family members care = paid or unpaid work?
  (Rice et al., 1993; Stommel et al., 1994)
- Gross or net costs?
  (Weinberger et al., 1993)

Day Care (DC): Two Methodological Approaches

Analysis of the cost of a day-care unit
(Keys & Szpak, 1983; Panella, Lilliston, Brush, & McDowell, 1984; Sands & Belman, 1986)

Longitudinal analysis of costs of day-care patients (inclusion of costs from other care resources)
(Engedal, 1989; Wimo et al., 1990, 1994a)

Other Methodological Considerations

Various settings (hospital, apartment, bungalow, ...)

Degree of dementia

Definition of control groups
(Engedal, 1989; Wimo et al., 1990, 1994a)

Intermediate Care Alternatives:
Group living and residential care (six to nine demented patients live together in one part of home for the aged or in a nursing home, which is staffed around the clock):
Three Methodological Approaches

Analysis of the cost of a group-living unit
(Sands & Belman, 1986; Wimo et al., 1994b)

Longitudinal analysis of costs of group-living patients
(Wimo et al., 1995)

Cost comparison with other types of care
(Knapp et al., 1998; Wimo et al.,1995)

Nursing Home Care: Two Methodological Approaches

Detailed analysis of the costs of all activities in which demented patients are involved
(Coughlin & Liu, 1989; Ernst & Hay, 1994; Fries et al., 1993; Hay & Ernst, 1987; Ljunggren & Brandt, 1996; Rovner et al., 1996)

Average costs of all nursing home patients

Comparison With Other Types of Care

Special care units (SCU)

Average costs of all SCU patients
(Holmes et al., 1994; Volicer et al., 1994)

Comparison with other types of care

Family Care

Out-of-pocket expenditures

Value of contribution: paid or unpaid

Note: Adapted from Wimo et al. (1997). Costs of Dementia and Dementia Care: A Review. *International Journal of Geriatric Psychiatry, 12.*

EXPRESSION OF INFORMAL COSTS AS A MULTIPLE OF FORMAL COSTS

Large regional variations in the availability of paraprofessional home care explains the wide differences in the use of hours of care received by demented patients. For example, a recent study conducted out in New York City found that half of demented patients have only informal care (7.2 hours per day), one quarter of them have only formal care (9.8 hours per day), and one third get both kinds of care (14.6 hours per day; Albert et al., 1998). Mean costs linked to informal care are a multiple of formal costs in several countries: 1.4 in Italy (Cavallo & Fattore, 1997), 1.7 in France (Souêtre et al., 1995), 1.9 and 2.3 in the United States (Ernst & Hay, 1994; Huang et al., 1988) and 3.0 in the United Kingdom (Nuttall, Blackwood, & Bussell, 1993). The more important implication of formal care for severely demented patients living in the community is more a supplementation of informal care than a substitution of it (Albert et al., 1998). This last finding suggests that the increased availability of formal services does not encourage inappropriate use of formal care or substitution of formal services with informal care (Albert et al., 1998). The consequence of this increased need of care is a cost increase. A retrospective analysis using U.S. administrative claims data—a 10% random sample of 62,450 recipients over age 60—proved that the cost of care for a demented patient is approximately $7,700 more per year than that of a matched compared cohort. A greater use of nursing homes primarily explained these results (Menzin et al., 1999).

No matter the impressive economic data collected to demonstrate the financial burden of dementia in health care expenditures, it is essential to stress the intangible costs linked to the family's burden. The changing nature of family composition and the increasing participation of women in the workforce are important factors to be considered in the future (Cavallo & Fattoré, 1997).

Nursing Home Care and Dementia Costs

Institutionalization is the largest component of cost, accounting for 84% of the costs for people with severe dementia (Hux et al., 1998). Nursing home care represents 71% of U.S. long-term care expenditures, which reached $90.9 billion in 1995 (U.S. Congress General Accounting Office, 1997, 1998). Among the 1.56 million nursing home residents, 48% were estimated to have some form of dementia (Krauss & Altman, 1998). The residential costs of patients with AD and other degenerative dementias in the United States reached $30.9 billion in 1995, of which $19.7 billion was devoted to AD patients (it is estimated that AD patients in nursing homes make up 492,400 of the residents; Katzman, Lasker, & Bernstein, 1986; Leon & Moyer, 1999).

Other Residential Costs: Assisted Care Facilities as a Substitute for Nursing Homes

To face the institutionalization costs of demented patients, staffing patterns of nursing homes could be differentiated (Leon & Moyer, 1999). In this trend, assisted care facilities (ACF) are promoted. ACFs combine housing and supportive services designed to provide care to individuals who require assistance with the tasks of daily living but who do not need the level of skilled nursing care provided in nursing homes (U.S. Congress General Accounting Office, 1997). Several recent studies have shown that ACF costs were lower than nursing home costs (Leon, Neumann, & Hermann, 1998; Lewin, 1996; Mollica & Snow, 1996; U.S. Congress General Accounting Office, 1997).

Managed Care Costs

In the United States, the high prevalence of dementia coupled with total costs of up to $195,000 for each case of AD (Schumock, 1998) create significant clinical and financial incentives for managed care plans to improve the care of demented patients (Gutterman, Markowitz, Lewis, & Fillit, 1999). Managed care for individuals with dementia has three main issues: promotion of high-quality cost-effective health care, reduction of inappropriate use of medication and service, and amelioration of patients' outcomes and quality of life (Clouse, 1994; Fillit, Kopman, Cummings, & Appel, 1999). Regardless of the type of health care organization (HMO), it appears that people diagnosed with dementia have 1.5 to 1.9 higher health care use and costs than enrollees without dementia ($p < .001$) (Gutterman et al., 1999; Weiner, Powe, Weller, Shaffer, & Anderson, 1998). The difference in the results of these two studies is related to the adjustment for level of comorbidity. In both studies, the higher costs for demented cases are linked to in-patients expenses (two thirds of the costs; Gutterman et al., 1999; Weiner et al., 1998).

The Impact of New Medications

The expected positive impact of AD symptomatic treatment was an improvement of cognitive functioning, a reduction in caregiving time, a reduction of indirect costs, and a delay of nursing home placement (Schumock, 1998). The lack of long-term data on resource use and drug efficacy led various authors to apply theoretical models to forecast the real impact of the latest anticholinesterase inhibitors on the course of AD. A decision analytic model predicts a possible reduction of $9,250 per patient if treatment with tacrine is used from the time of diagnosis (Schumock, 1998). A modeling approach based on disease progression and estimated by MMSE scale decline intervals attests that the greatest long-term cost savings is obtained from the treatment of mild AD (MMSE > 20). If a patient's life expectancy is lower than 2 years, cost savings are greater by prioritizing patients with moderate AD (20 > MMSE > 11) (Fenn & Gray, 1999). In an incremental cost-effectiveness theoretical model, comparing the impact of donepezil with that of no treatment on quality-adjusted life years gained, drug costs appeared partially offset. The model predicts that for mild AD the drug will pay for itself in terms of cost offset (Neumann et al., 1999). However, the positive impact of these results is attenuated by the application of a Markov model, estimating the 5-year cost-effectiveness of the adjunction of donepezil (5 mg/d) to the usual care in the management of patients with mild to moderate AD (10 < MMSE < 26) in Canada (O'Brien et al., 1999). The overall cost savings reached CA$882 per patient using donepezil. Patients not receiving donepezil are predicted to spend 2.21 years of the 5-year study in nonsevere dementia, whereas a treated AD patient will spend 2.41 years in nonsevere dementia. Thus, the delay gained by treatment seems to be very short (O'Brien et al., 1999).

CONCLUSIONS

Projections for 1997–2007 by the U.S. Health Care Finance Administration show an increase of 80% in total health care expenditures (to over $2 trillion annually). A parallel increase of over $148 million if nursing home health care expenditures is predicted. From the U.S. government's perspective, these costs would threaten budgetary stability (Health Care Finance Administration, 1997). Ironically, there is no evidence that this substantial resource consumption is associated with a better outcome or an improve- ment in patients' and families' quality of life.

Considerable effort has to be made to cope with the problems of dementia. This effort should consist of the following measures:

- Basic research focused on the cause of the disease has to be strengthened.
- Epidemiological research should concentrate on predictive models of disease progression, institutionalization, and survival (Alloul, Sauriol, & Kennedy, 1998).
- Preventive strategies to delay the onset of the disease and the disability process have to be promoted (Souêtre et al., 1995).
- Drug intervention to slow or delay the course of the disease must be prescribed immediately after early diagnosis (Gottlieb, 1999).
- Aggressive support for caregivers must be implemented (Gottlieb, 1999).
- New models of caring for dementia sufferers have to be developed to reduce the period of dependency (Katchaturian & Radebaugh, 1998).

- New models of financing have to be implemented because the current system is hopelessly inadequate (Katchaturian & Radebaugh, 1998).

ACKNOWLEDGMENTS

The authors gratefully thank E. Giacobini and B. Grab for valuable advice and careful revision of the text.

REFERENCES

Albert, S. M., Del Castillo-Castaneda, C., Sano, M., Jacobs, D. M., Marder K., Bell, K., Bylsma, F., Lafleche, G., Brandt, J., Albert, M., & Stern, Y. (1996). Quality of life in patients with AD as reported by patients proxies. *Journal of the American Geriatrics Society, 44,* 1342–1347.

Albert, S. M., Sano, M., Bell, K., Merchant, C., Small, S., & Stern, Y. (1998). Hourly care received by people with AD: Results from an urban community survey. *Gerontologist, 38,* 704–714.

Alloul, K., Sauriol, L., & Kennedy, W. (1998). Alzheimer's disease: A review of the disease, its epidemiology and economic impact. *Archives of Gerontology and Geriatrics, 27*(3), 189–221.

Bootman J. L., Townsend, R. J., & McGhan, W. F. (1996). *Principles of pharmacoeconomics* (2nd ed.). Cincinnati, OH: Harvey Whitney Books.

Busschbach, J. J., Brouwer, W. B., van der Donk, A., Passchier, J., & Rutten, F. F. (1998). An outline for a cost-effectiveness analysis of a drug for patients with Alzheimer's disease. *Pharmacoeconomics, 13*(IPt.1), 21–34.

Cavallo, M. C., & Fattore, G. (1997). The economic and social burden of AD on families in the Lombardy region of Italy. *Alzheimer Disease and Associated Disorders, 11*(4), 184–190.

Cayton, H. (1993). The social consequences of dementia. In G. K. Wilcock (Ed.), *The management of Alzheimer's disease* (pp. 151–158). Petersfield, UK: Wrightson Biomedical Publishing.

Clouse, J. C. (1994). Pharmacoeconomics: A managed care perspective. *Topics in Hospital Pharmacy Management, 13*(4), 54–59.

Coon, D. W., & Edgerly, E. S. (1999). The personal and social consequences of AD. *Genetic Testing, 3*(1), 29–36.

Coughlin, T. A., & Liu, K. (1989). Health care costs of older persons with cognitive impairments. *Gerontologist, 29*(2), 173–182.

Dellasega, C., & King, L. E. (1996). The psychogeriatric nurse in home health care: Use of research to develop the role. *Clinical Nurse Specialist, 10*(2), 64–68.

Drummond, M., Stoddart, G. L., & Torrance, G. E. W. (1987). *Methods for the economic evaluation of health care programmes.* Oxford, UK: Oxford University Press.

Engedal, K. (1989). Day care for demented patients in general nursing homes. Effects on admission to institutions and mental capacity. *Scandinavian Journal of Primary Health Care, 7*(3), 161–166.

Ernst, R. L., & Hay, J. W. (1994). The U.S. economic and social cost of AD revisited. *American Journal of Public Health, 84,* 1261–1264.

Fenn, P., & Gray, A. (1999). Estimating long term cost savings from treatment of AD. A modelling approach. *Pharmacoeconomics, 16*(2), 165–174.

Fillit, H., Kopman, D., Cummings, J., & Appel, F. (1999). Opportunities for improving managed care for individuals with dementia: Part 1—The issues. *The American Journal of Managed Care, 5*, 309–315.

Fox, P. J. (1997). Service use and cost outcomes for persons with AD. *Alzheimer Disease and Associated Disorders, 11*(Suppl. 6), 125–134.

Fries, B. E., Mehr, D. R., Schneider, D., Foley, W. J., & Burke, R. (1993). Mental dysfunction and resource use in nursing homes. *Medical Care, 31*, 898–920.

Geldmacher, D. S., & Whitehouse, P. J. (1996). Evaluation of dementia. *The New England Journal of Medicine, 335*, 331–336.

Gottlieb, G. L. (1999). Cost analysis, policy development and AD. *The American Journal of Geriatric Psychiatry, 7*, 297–299.

Gray, A., & Fenn, P. (1993). Alzheimer's disease: The burden of illness in England. *Health Trends, 25*(1), 31–37.

Gutterman, E. M., Markowitz, J. S., Lewis, B., & Fillit, H. (1999). Cost of AD and related dementia in managed care. *Journal of the American Geriatrics Society, 47*, 1065–1071.

Hay, J. W., & Ernst, R. L. (1987). The economic costs of Alzheimer's disease. *American Journal of Public Health, 77*, 1169–1175.

Health Care Finance Administration. (1997). *Projections for national health care expenditures, 1997–2007.* Washington, DC: Health Care Finance Administration, USPHS.

Holmes, D., Ory, M., & Teresi, J. (1994). Special dementia care: Research policy, and practice issues. *Alzheimer Disease and Associated Disorders, 8*(Suppl. 1), 5–13.

Hu, T. W., Huang, L. F., & Cartwright, W. S. (1986). Evaluation of the cost of caring for the senile demented elderly. *The Gerontologist, 26*(2), 158–163.

Huang, L. F., Cartwright, W. S., & Hu, T. W. (1988). The economic cost of senile dementia in the United States. *Public Health Report, 103*(1), 3–7.

Hux, M. J., O'Brien, B. J., Iskedjian, M., Goeree, R., Gagnon, M., & Gauthier, S. (1998). Relation between severity of Alzheimer's disease and costs of caring. *Canadian Medical Association Journal, 159*, 457–465.

Katchaturian, Z. S., & Radebaugh, T. S. (1998). AD: Where are we now? Where are we going? *Alzheimer Disease and Associated Disorders, 12*(Suppl. 3), 24–28.

Katzman, R., Lasker, B., & Bernstein, N. (1986). *Accuracy of diagnosis and consequences of misdiagnosis of disorders causing dementia.* Washington, DC: U.S. Government Printing Office.

Keys, B., & Szpak, G. (1983). Day care for Alzheimer's disease: Profile of one program. *Postgraduate Medicine, 73*, 245–250.

Knapp, M., Wilkinson, D., & Wigglesworth, R. (1998). Economic consequences of Alzheimer's disease. *International Journal of Geriatric Psychiatry, 13*, 531–543.

Krauss, N., & Altman, B. (1998). *Characteristics of nursing home residents 1996* (Agency for Health Care Policy and Research MEPS Research findings No. 5, AHCPR Pub. No 99–00006). Rockville, MD: U.S. Government Printing Office.

Leon, J. L., & Moyer, D. (1999). Potential cost savings in residential care for Alzheimer's disease patients. *Gerontologist, 39*, 440–449.

Leon, J. L., Neumann, P., & Hermann, R. (1998). Health related quality of life and health service utilisation for mild, moderate and severely impaired AD patients: A cross sectional study. *Neurology, 50*, A320.

Lewin, V. H. I. (1996). *National study of assisted living for the frail elderly: Literature review update* (Report prepared for HHS/ASPE, Contract No. DHHS–100–94–0024). Research Triangle Park, NC: Research Triangle Institute.

Ljunggren G., & Brandt, L. (1996). Predicting nursing home length of stay with resource-based classification system. *International Journal of Technology Assessment in Health Care, 12*(2), 72–79.

Manton, K. G., Corder, L. S., & Clark, R. (1993). Estimates and projections of dementia-related service expenditures. In R. Suzman, B. Singer, & K. Manton (Eds.), *Forecasting the health of the oldest old* (pp. 43–68). New York: Springer-Verlag.

Meerding, W. J., Bonneux, L., Polder, J. J., Koopmanschap, M. A., & van der Maas, P. J. (1998). Demographic and epidemiological determinants of healthcare costs in the Netherlands: Cost of illness study. *British Medical Journal, 317*(7251), 111–114.

Menzin, J., Lang, K., Friedman, M., Neumann, P., & Cummings, J. L. (1999). The economic cost of AD and related dementia to the California Medicaid Program ("Medi-Cal") in 1995. *The American Journal of Geriatric Psychiatry, 7*, 300–308.

Mollica, R. L., & Snow, K. I. (1996). *State assisted living policy 1996* (Report prepared for HHS/ASPE, Contract No. DHHS-100-94-0024). Portland, ME: National Academy for State Health Policy.

Murray, C. J., & Lopez, A. D. (1997). *Summary: The global burden of disease*. Cambridge MA: Harvard University Press.

Nagaratnam, N., Lewis-Jones, M., Scott, D., & Palazzi, L. (1998). Behavioural and psychiatric manifestations in dementia patients in a community: Caregiver burden and outcome. *Alzheimer Disease and Associated Disorders, 12*, 330–334.

Neumann, P. J., Herrmann, R. C., Berenhaum, P. A., & Weinstein, M. C. (1997). Methods of cost-effectiveness analysis in the assessment of new drugs for AD. *Psychiatric Services, 48*, 1440–1444.

Neumann, P. J., Hermann, R. C., Kuntz, K. M., Araki, S. S., Duff, S. B., Leon, J., Berenbaum, P. A., Goldman, P. A., Williams, L. W., & Weinstein, M. C. (1999). Cost-effectiveness of Donepezil in the treatment of mild or moderate AD. *Neurology, 52*, 1138–1145.

Nuttall, S. R., Blackwood, R. J. L., & Bussell, B. M. H. (1994). Financing long-term care in Great Britain. *Journal of the Institute of Actuaries, 121*(Part 1), 1–68.

O'Brien, B. J., Goeree, R., Hux, M., Iskedjian, M., Blackhouse, G., Gagnon, M., & Gauthier, S. (1999). Economic evaluation of Donepezil for the treatment of AD in Canada. *Journal of the American Geriatrics Society, 47*, 570–578.

Panella, A. J., Lilliston, B. A., Brush, D., & McDowell, F. H. (1984). Day care for dementia patients: An analysis of a four-year program. *Journal of the American Geriatrics Society, 32*, 883–886.

Rice, D. P., Fox, P. J., Max, W., Webber, P. A., Lindeman, D. A., Hauck, V. W., & Segura, E. (1993). The economic burden of caring for people with Alzheimer's disease. *Health Affairs* 12(2), 164–176.

Rice, D. P., Hodgson, T. A., & Kopstein, A. N. (1985). The economic costs of illness: A replication and update. *Healthcare Financial Review, 7*(1), 61–80.

Ritchie, K., & Kildea, D. (1995). Is senile dementia "age related"or "aging related"? Evidence from a meta-analysis of dementia prevalence in the oldest old. *Lancet, 346*, 931–934.

Rovner, B. W., Steele, C. D., Shmuley, Y., & Folstein, M. F. (1996). A randomized trial of dementia care in nursing homes. *Journal of American Geriatrics Society 1996, 44*(1), 7–13.

Sands, D., & Belman, J. (1986). Evaluation of a 24-hour care system for Alzheimer's and related disorders (Contract report prepared for the Office of Technology Assessment, U.S. Congress).

Schneider, E. L., & Guralnik, J. M. (1990). The aging of America, impact of health care costs. *The Journal of the American Medical Association, 263*, 2335–2340.

Schumock, G. T. (1998). Economic considerations in the treatment and management of AD. *American Journal of Health-System Pharmacy, 55* (Suppl. 2), 17–21.

Smith, K., Shah, A., Wright, K., & Lewis, G. (1995). The prevalence and costs of psychiatric disorders and learning disabilities. *British Journal of Psychiatry, 166*(1), 9–18.

Souêtre, E. J., Qing, W., Vigoureux, I., Dartigues, J. F., Lozet, H., Lacomblez, L., & Derouesné, C. (1995). Economic analysis of Alzheimer's disease in outpatients: Impact of symptom severity. *International Psychogeriatrics, 7*(1), 115–122.

Spilker, B. (1996). *Adopting higher standards for quality of life trials. Quality of life and pharmacoeconomics in clinical trials* (2nd ed.). Philadelphia: Lippincott-Raven.

Stommel, M., Collins, C. E., & Given, B. A. (1994). The costs of family contributions to the care of person with dementia. *Gerontologist, 34*, 199–205.

Torrance, G. W. (1987). Utility approach to measuring health related quality of life. *Journal of Chronic Diseases, 40*, 593–600.

Trabucchi, M., Ghisla, K. M., & Bianchetti, A. (1996). CODEM: A longitudinal study on Alzheimer disease costs. In R. Becker & E. Giacobini (Eds.), *Alzheimer's disease: From molecular biology to therapy* (pp. 561–565). Boston: Birkhauser.

Trabucchi, M., Govoni, S., & Bianchetti, A. (1994). Socio-economic aspects of Alzheimer's disease treatment. In E. Giacobini & R. Becker (Eds.), *Alzheimer's disease: Therapeutic strategies* (pp. 459–463). Boston: Birkhauser.

U.S. Congress General Accounting Office. (1997). *Long term care—Consumer protection and quality-of-care issues in assisted living* (GAO Publication No. HEHS–97–93). Washington, DC: U.S. Government Printing Office.

U.S. Congress General Accounting Office. (1998). *Alzheimer's disease: Estimates of prevalence in the United States* (GAO pub. No. HEHS–98–16). Washington, DC: U.S. Government Printing Office.

Volicer, L., Collard, A., Hurley, A., Bishop, C., Kern, D., & Karon, S. (1994). Impact of special care unit for patients with advanced Alzheimer's disease on patient's discomfort and costs. *Journal of the American Geriatrics Society, 42*, 597–603.

Weinberger, M., Gold, D. T., Divine, G. W., Cowper, P. A., Hodgson, L. G., Schreiner, P., & George, L. K. (1993). Expenditures in caring for patients with dementia who live at home. *American Journal of Public Health, 83*, 268–341.

Weiner, M., Powe, N. R., Weller, W. E., Shaffer, T. J., & Anderson, G. F. (1998). Alzheimer's disease under managed care: Implications from Medicare utilisation and expenditure patterns. *Journal of the American Geriatrics Society, 46*, 762–770.

Whitehouse, P. J. (1997). Pharmacoeconomics of dementia. *Alzheimer Disease and Associated Disorders, 11* (Suppl. 5), 22–33.

Wimo, A., Mattsson, B., Kraku, I., Eriksson, T., Nelvig, A., & Karlsson, G. (1995). Cost-utility analysis of group living in dementia care. *International Journal of Technology Assessment in Health Care, 11*(1), 49–65.

Wimo, A., Karlsson, G., Sandman, P. O., Corder, L., & Winblad, B. (1996). Cost of illness due to dementia in Sweden. *International Journal of Geriatric Psychiatry, 12*, 857–861.

Wimo, A., Ljunggren, G., & Winblad, B. (1997). Costs of dementia and dementia care: A review. *International Journal of Geriatric Psychiatry, 12*, 841–856.

Wimo, A., Mattsson, B., Krakau, I., Eriksson, T., & Nelvig, A. (1994a). Cost-effectiveness analysis of day care for patients with dementia disorders. *Health Economics, 3*, 395–404.

Wimo, A., Mattsson, B., Krakau, I., Eriksson, T., & Nelvig, A. (1994b). The impact of cognitive decline and workload on the costs of dementia care. *International Journal of Geriatric Psychiatry, 9*, 479–489.

Wimo, A., Wallin, J. O., Lundgren, K., Ronnback, E., Asplund, K., Mattsson, B., & Krakau, I. (1990). Impact of day care on dementia patients-costs, well-being and relatives' views. *Family Practice, 7*, 279–287.

Winblad, B., Hill, S., Beermann, B., Post, S. G., & Wimo, A. (1997). Issues in the economic evaluation of treatment for dementia: position paper from the international working group on harmonization of dementia drug guidelines. *Alzheimer Disease and Associated Disorders, 11*, 39–45.

2

Clinical Aspects

Serge Gauthier
McGill University
McGill Center for Studies in Aging

COMMON MODES OF PRESENTATIONS

Screening for Cognitive Decline in an Asymptomatic Aging Individual

The least common mode of presentation of Alzheimer's Disease (AD) is poor performance on a brief cognitive test, such as the Mini Mental State Examination (MMSE; Folstein, Folstein, & McHugh, 1975) during routine screening of elderly persons in the community. The Canadian Consensus Conference on Dementia (CCCD; Patterson et al., 2001), after careful consideration of available evidence, has ruled against routine screening for cognitive impairment in the absence of memory or functional complaints from the patient or the family. On the other hand, health professionals should maintain a high index of suspicion for dementia in older people and follow up on concerns about functional decline and memory loss expressed by the patient, the family, or both, as observed during routine visits. These concerns are discussed in the following section.

Memory Complaints by the Patient

There are more individuals consulting their family practitioner and memory clinics regarding subjective memory complaints. They often come alone and report difficulties in remembering names of people, occasional word finding, and planning and executing more than one project at a time. Although depression, anxiety over age-associated memory decline, or fear of genetic predisposition toward AD are the common causes of such complaints, it is important to establish, with the help of a reliable informant, whether the patient has suffered an observable decline during the preceding 12 months and an interference in the performance of everyday activities (Morris et al., 1991). A positive answer to these questions triggers a full assessment for dementia. A negative answer can lead to reassurance and a follow-up in 1 year, after a baseline MMSE and clock drawing (Dastoor, Schwartz, & Kurtzman, 1991) for future reference. The majority of individuals with minimal cognitive impairment (MCI) will not progress toward dementia, but many will (up to 40% over 3 years, according to recent reports). There is currently a concerted research effort using randomized clinical trials to establish if alpha-tocopherol, cyclo-oxygenase 2 selective inhibitors, and cholinesterase inhibitors, such as donepezil, rivastigmine, or galantamine; delay conversion of MCI to AD (see chap. 6 of this book). Persons with MCI could thus be referred to memory clinics that enroll in such preventive studies.

Memory Complaints by the Family

The following is the most common mode of presentation for AD: the family (or close friends) initiate the visit and come with the patient, who may have little or no complaints from lack of insight into his or her condition. Although most patients do not object to questions being asked and answered truthfully in their presence, some do, and separate interviews may be required. As per the definition of dementia in DSM-IV (American Psychiatric Association, 1994), to diagnose dementia one must establish the presence of a decline in memory and at least one other intellectual domain, such as speech, praxis, gnosis, or executive functioning, that interfere significantly in social or occupational functioning (see Table 2.1).

A systematic history is thus required, with emphasis on performance at work (when applicable), in complex hobbies, and in instrumental tasks of daily living (IADL), such as handling money, completing household chores, using the telephone, going on an outing, and planning a meal.

TABLE 2.1

Diagnostic Criteria for Dementia of the Alzheimer's Type

Multiple cognitive deficits in 1) memory and 2) one or more of language, praxis, gnosis, and executive functioning
Significant impairment and decline in social or occupational functioning
Gradual onset and continuing cognitive decline
Not caused by other central nervous system or substance-induced conditions
Deficits not exclusively during the course of delirium and not better accounted for by depression or schizophrenia

Note: Adapted from American Psychiatric Association (1994). *Diagnostic and Statistical Manual of Mental Disorders* (pp. 142–143). Washington, DC: Author.

Structured scales for IADL, such as the Functional Activities Questionnaire (FAQ; Pfeffer, Kurosaki, Harrah, Chance, & Filos, 1982), may prove useful as a complement to office-based psychometric tests, such as the MMSE. Serial assessment of both cognition and functional abilities may be required to establish a gradual progression and confirm the diagnosis of dementia, but the pattern of progressive decline of memory for recent events over 1 year, followed within months by difficulty finding words or traveling alone in unfamiliar surroundings, errors in time orientation and word recall, and impaired copy of the pentagon on the MMSE is satisfactory for diagnosis of dementia of the Alzheimer type (AD). Such diagnosis is usually handled by the family practitioner, without the need for referral. Further refinement on this diagnosis can be made using National Institute of Neurological and Communicative Disorders and Stroke–Alzheimer's Disease and Related Disorders Association (NINCDS–ADRDA) criteria of probable or possible AD (McKhann et al., 1984; Table 2.2).

Cognitive Impairments Other Than Memory

Rarely, progressive aphasia may be the first and main complaint noted by both the patient and the informant. Although not all patients progress toward dementia, most will (Mesulam, 1982). Even more rarely, apraxia, acalculia, or visuospatial impairment will be so prominent as to suggest a

TABLE 2.2

Criteria for Clinical Diagnosis of AD

Probable AD if:

- dementia established by clinical examination and documented by a structured assessment tool;
- deficits in two or more areas of cognition;
- progressive worsening; no disturbance of consciousness;
- onset between 40 and 90;
- and absence of other brain or systemic disease that could account for the dementia.

Possible AD if:

- dementia with variations in the onset, presentation, or clinical course;
- in the presence of a second brain or systemic disorder sufficient to cause dementia;
- and in the presence of a single gradually progressive cognitive deficit in the absence of another identifiable cause.

Definite AD if:

- clinical criteria for probable AD;
- and histopathologic evidence obtained from brain biopsy or autopsy.

Note: Adapted from McKhann et al. (1984). Clinical diagnosis of Alzheimer's Disease: Report of the NINCDS-ARDRA workgroup. *Neurology, 34,* 940.

focal deficit secondary to stroke or brain tumor. With progression over time toward a more global dementia, most of these patients are ultimately diagnosed as possible AD or Pick's disease by a consulting neurologist (Pryse-Phillips & Galasko, 1999).

Noncognitive Complaints: Mood, Behavior, or Personality Changes

Some patients are brought to the medical professional by their families because of a cognitive decline associated with negative symptoms (e.g. lack of energy, excess or poor quality of sleep, lack of interest). Many of these patients have a combination of depression and dementia. There is no perfect scale to distinguish depression from dementia, and, when in doubt, it is recommended that physicians treat for depression using a low dose of one of the selective serotonin uptake inhibitors, such as sertraline, and reassess cognition and functional abilities at a follow-up examination. Patients may also present with disruptive behaviors reflecting halluci- nations, delusions, or exaggeration of previous personality traits, such as paranoia or jealousy (see chap. 7 of this book). These symptoms can be associated with early AD but can also suggest other conditions, such as Lewy body or frontotemporal dementias.

CLINICAL ASSESSMENT OF SUSPECTED DEMENTIA

Structured History With Patient and Informant

Once the possibility of dementia has been identified by self-complaints (rarely), family reports (most commonly), or direct observation, there is a need for a semistructured history, which may require the patient to make a separate visit to the family practitioner with a reliable informant (Gauthier, 1999a). As described by Bouchard and Rossor (1999), a general medical history is followed by careful neurological, neurobehavioral, psychiatric, nutritional, and drug histories. Finally, the family history may reveal relevant illnesses, such as depression, dementia, or Down syndrome, in first-degree relatives. Many patients with well-established AD often have a straightforward history of cognitive decline with impaired functional abilities for complex hobbies and IADL and good general health. They progress through predictable stages (Reisberg, Ferris, DeLeon, & Crook, 1982; see Table 2.3), and the family practitioner will be able to recognize the pattern of a typical AD patient. However, the clinical picture may be extremely heterogeneous in the early stages of the disease and might therefore require a multidisciplinary diagnostic workout.

TABLE 2.3

Global Deterioration Scale

Stage 1	No symptoms
Stage 2	Subjective complaints about memory; normal examination
Stage 3	Difficulty at work or complex hobbies, in speech, in travel through unfamiliar areas; difficulties detectable by family; subtle memory deficit on examination
Stage 4	Decreased ability to travel, handle complex finances, remember current events
Stage 5	Need assistance choosing clothes; disorientation to time and place; decreased recall of names of grandchildren
Stage 6	Needs supervision when eating and toileting; may be incontinent; disoriented to time, place, and persons
Stage 7	Needs total assistance; severe speech loss; incontinence; motor rigidity

Note: Adapted from Reisberg et al. (1982). The Global Deterioration Scale for assessment of primary degenerative dementia. *The American Journal of Psychiatry, 139,* p. 1337.

Structured Physical, Neurological, and Neuropsychological Examination

The physical examination focuses on the presence of risk factors for stroke, such as systolic hypertension, carotid bruits, and atrial fibrillation, in addition to the search for systemic illnesses, such as hypothyroidism. The neurologic examination aims to rule out evidence of increased intracranial pressure by examination of the fundi and documents evidence of focal deficits, such as asymmetric reflexes and unilateral grasp. It is useful to look for early signs of Parkinsonism, such as rigidity and gait disturbances. The patient with typical AD will have a normal physical and neurological examination, except for the mental status (Bouchard & Rossor, 1999).

An office-based psychometric test, such as the MMSE, can be performed in less than 10 minutes by the family practitioner. Although very useful in clinical practice (especially for follow-up exams for progression or response to treatment), such a psychometric test cannot be used as a diagnostic tool. Clock drawing may be useful as a complement to the MMSE in high-performing individuals. Formal neuropsychological assessment is required in mild cognitive impairment to achieve earlier diagnosis, either through a structured mental status examination (Strub & Black, 1993) or by referral to a neuropsychologist (see chap. 3 of this book).

Laboratory Tests

The diagnosis of AD is clinical, and there are few blood tests required of all patients with typical AD (see Table 2.4). Additional laboratory tests can be ordered on a case by case basis, depending on suspected or known concomitant disorders.

Although structural brain imaging using computer tomography (CT) is required to rule out certain causes of dementia, such as stroke, tumor, normal pressure hydrocephalus (NPH), and subdural hematoma, such a scan is not required of all patients presenting typical AD (see Table 2.5). The latter criteria would have reduced by two thirds the number of scans in a memory clinic (Freter, Bergman, Gold, Chertkow, & Clarfield, 1998) and thus reduced the cost of diagnosis quite substantially (Chui & Zhang, 1997; Gauthier, 1998).

A number of ancillary tests, including electroencephalography, evoked potentials, magnetic resonance and functional imaging, blood apolipoprotein E (apoE) and presenilin genotyping, spinal fluid tau and beta-amyloid

TABLE 2.4

Minimal Laboratory Workup Recommended in Typical AD

Complete blood count
Thyroid stimulating hormone
Serum electrolytes
Serum calcium
Serum glucose

Note: Adapted from Patterson et al. (2001). The recognition, assessment and management of dementing disorders: Conclusions from the Canadian Consensus Conference on Dementia. *Canadian Journal of Neurological Science, 28*(Suppl. 1), p. S–5.

TABLE 2.5

Indications for Computer Imaging in Dementia

Age less than 60
Rapid (1 to 2 months) unexplained decline in cognition or function
Duration of symptoms less than 2 years
Recent and significant head trauma
Unexplained neurologic symptoms, such as headaches or seizures
History of cancer
Use of anticoagulants or bleeding diathesis
Early urine incontinence and gait disorder
Any new localizing sign
Atypical cognitive symptoms or presentation

Note: Adapted from Patterson et al. (2001). The recognition, assessment and management of dementing disorders: Conclusions from the Canadian Consensus Conference on Dementia. *Canadian Journal of Neurological Science, 28*(Suppl. 1), p. *S–6.*

fragments, are considered inappropriate in the primary care setting until more evidence of clinical use is available (Patterson et al., 2001). Even in a research setting, none of the proposed biological markers has yet demonstrated the specificity and sensitivity required for use as standard adjunctive laboratory test to complement the clinical assessment in early AD (Growdon, 1998). Only apoE genotyping has been found to improve the specificity of the clinical diagnosis in symptomatic individuals (Mayeux et al., 1998), but it is not recommended for asymptomatic individuals (American College of Medical Genetics/American Society of Human Genetics Working Group on ApoE and Alzheimer Disease, 1995). Because genetic information may have a long-lasting impact on the asymptomatic children of persons who undergo genetic testing, the risks versus benefits of apoE genotyping in clinical practice should be carefully considered before its use outside structured genetic counseling clinics (Sadovnick & Lovestone, 1999).

When and Who to Refer

In many countries, there have been systematic efforts to reach family practitioners through continuous health education and to facilitate the recognition, diagnosis, and management of AD at the primary care level (Gauthier, Panisset, Nalbantoglu, & Poirier, 1997). This may require multiple office visits to obtain a clear picture of dementia and to determine whether the mode of presentation and clinical course are compatible with typical AD. Patients who do not follow this typical pattern (e.g. patients with early behavioral symptoms, Parkinsonian, or focal physical findings) could be referred to a memory clinic or to individual consultants in the fields of neurology, old-age psychiatry, or geriatric medicine. Other reasons for referral have been identified (see Table 2.6). Because of limited availability, genetic counseling resources should be used for families when AD appears to be genetically inherited in a dominant pattern, usually causing early onset of AD (ages 40 to 50).

DIFFERENTIAL DIAGNOSIS OF DEMENTIA

Alzheimer's Disease

Traditionally considered a diagnosis of exclusion, a positive diagnosis of AD is now possible in cases of gradual decline in cognition and functional autonomy, generally following the course outline in the Global Deterioration Scale (see Table 2.3). However, because it is now well established that there can be important variations in early symptoms and the course of the disease, atypical clinical presentations should not rule out further assessment. The diagnosis has been further refined as probable or possible (see Table 2.2). The clinical-pathological correlations using these criteria are high

TABLE 2.6

When to Refer a Patient With Dementia

Continuing uncertainty about diagnosis after initial assessment and follow-up
Request by patient or family for a second opinion
Presence of significant depression unresponsive to first line of therapy
Treatment problems or failure to improve with new AD medications
Need for additional help in patient management and caregiver support
Need to involve voluntary agencies and local service providers
When genetic counseling is indicated
When research studies into diagnosis and treatment are being carried out

Note: Adapted from Patterson et al. (2001). The recognition, assessment and management of dementing disorders: Conclusions from the Canadian Consensus Conference on Dementia. *Canadian Journal of Neurological Science, 28 (Suppl. 1), p. S–6.*

(Blacker, Albert, & Bassett, 1994) and have made possible multicenter, randomized clinical trials as well as etiological research specific for probable A. From a neuropsychological perspective, there is heterogeneity in the early stages (Caramelli et al., 1997), but a global deterioration in later stages.

Dementia With Lewy Bodies

This condition has attracted a lot of attention in the United Kingdom and has led to clinical and pathologic diagnostic criteria (see Table 2.7). The clinician may suspect this condition in a demented patient with unusual fluctuations, visual hallucinations, and early Parkinsonian signs. The interest in recognizing this condition is the marked sensitivity to neuroleptic drugs and the responsiveness to cholinesterase inhibitors (Aarsland, Bronnick, & Karlsen, 1999; see chap. 6 of this book).

TABLE 2.7

Diagnostic Criteria for Dementia with Lewy Bodies (DLB)

Progressive cognitive decline interfering with social or occupational functioning
One (possible DLB) or two (probable DLB) of:
fluctuating cognition with pronounced variations
recurrent visual hallucinations
spontaneous motor features of Parkinsonism

Note: Adapted from McKeith et al. (1996). Consensus guidelines for clinical and pathological diagnosis of dementia with Lewy Bodies (DLB): Report of the Consortium on DLB International Workshop. *Neurology, 47,* p. 1114.

Frontotemporal Dementia

A number of conditions with early and prominent neuropsychiatric symptoms have been regrouped under the term *frontotemporal dementia* (FTD), better known as Pick's disease, for which clinical and pathological criteria are available (see Table 2.8). These conditions usually involve women in their 50s and cause a heavy burden on their families, leading to early institutionalization. Verbal outbursts and inappropriate activity can distinguish AD from FTD (Mendez, Peryman, Miller, & Cummings, 1998).

TABLE 2.8

Diagnostic Criteria for Frontotemporal Dementia

Behavioral disturbances, including early loss of personal and social awareness
Affective symptoms, including emotional unconcern
Speech disorder, including reduction, stereotype, and perseveration
Physical signs, including primitive reflexes, incontinence, akinesia, and rigidity

Note: Adapted from Lund and Manchester Groups (1994). Clinical and neuropathological criteria for frontotemporal dementia. *Journal of Neurology, Neurosurgery, and Psychiatry, 57,* pp. 416–417.

Vascular Dementias

For many years thought to be the main cause of dementia through hardening of the arteries, the vascular dementias (VaD) are under intense study because of possible prevention through the control of risk factors. Clinical diagnostic criteria have been proposed (Chui et al., 1992; Roman et al., 1993; see Table 2.9), and there is renewed interest in strategic single infarcts and subcortical vascular dementia.

The diagnosis of VaD is suggested by a history of abrupt onset of neurological symptoms, a staircase pattern of decline, and focal neurological findings. These elements are captured in the Ischemic Scale (Hachinski et al., 1974; see Table 2.10). In clinical practice, many patients have a mixed

TABLE 2.9

Diagnostic Criteria for Vascular Dementia (VaD)

Decline in intellectual function sufficient enough to interfere with activities of daily life and not caused by the physical effects of stroke(s) alone
Evidence by history, physical, or neuroimaging examination of stroke(s)
Temporal relationship between dementia and cerebrovascular disease

Note: Adapted from Chui et al. (1992). Criteria for the diagnosis of ischemic vascular dementia proposed by the State of California Alzheimer's Disease Diagnostic and Treatment Centres. *Neurology, 42,* and from Roman et al. (1993). Vascular dementia: Diagnostic criteria for research studies. Report of the NINCDS-AIREN International Workshop. *Neurology, 43.*

TABLE 2.10
Ischemic Scale

Abrupt onset
Stepwise deterioration
Fluctuating course
Nocturnal confusion
Preserved personality
Depression
Somatic complaints
Emotional incontinence
Arterial hypertension
History of stroke
Associated atherosclerosis
Focal neurological symptoms
Focal neurological signs

Note: Adapted from Hachinski et al. (1974). Cerebral blood flow in dementia. *Archives of Neurology, 32,* p. 634.

pattern of AD with cerebrovascular disease, described as mixed dementia (Rockwood, 1997).

Subcortical Dementias

In addition to subcortical vascular dementia, there are conditions such as Parkinson's disease, progressive supranuclear palsy, Huntington's disease, and NPH, in which abnormal movements and gait impairment are evident at the onset of cognitive decline. These conditions rarely cause difficulties in terms of differential diagnosis, but they usually require referral to a specialist for advice on management.

ETIOLOGICAL HYPOTHESIS

This complex disease likely has multiple etiological factors. Inherited genetic mutations appear to be primary etiological factors in some patients on chromosomes 1, 12, 14, and 21 (Levy-Lahad, Tsuang, & Bird, 1998), whereas the apoE4 mutation on chromosome 19 increases the risk of AD, particularly in homozygotes (i.e., persons carrying the defective gene from both parents; Strittmatter, 2000). Other factors appear to positively and negatively modify these genetic risks (Canadian Study of Health and Aging Working Group, 1994). For instance, low education will accelerate the onset of AD symptoms, whereas long-term use of nonsteroidal anti-inflammatory drugs will delay them. Knowledge and modification of such risk factors, such as control of systolic hypertension, could lead to preventive approaches for AD.

The pathology of AD has been extensively described, including neuritic plaques, intraneuronal neurofibrillary tangles, acute-phase reactants, and inflammatory cells. The loss of synaptic connectivity from impairment of synaptic plasticity could be the earliest pathological change, followed by cell loss. This pathology first appears in the hippocampus and cortical cholinergic system (Geula, 1998). The role of beta-amyloid deposition versus tau hyperphosphorylation in the cascade of molecular events leading to neuronal death is hotly debated (see chap. 6 of this book).

These etiological hypotheses, primarily based on epidemiological and pathological data and modeling from transgenic mice expressing some of the molecular pathology of human AD, have led to experimental therapies, such as antioxidants, anti-inflammatory drugs, apolipoprotein E promotors, and eventually gamma-secretase inhibitors (Cummings, Vinters, Cole, & Khachaturian, 1998).

MEDICAL MANAGEMENT

Specific management issues will be discussed in the subsequent chapters. The first general steps include the recognition of dementia, an accurate diagnosis of AD, and treatment of concomitant disorders, such as depression, drug misuse, and metabolic or nutritional abnormalities that exaggerate cognitive impairment. An honest discussion about the diagnosis and prognosis of AD is also an important step in the global psychosocial management of a condition that will change significantly the well-being of many individuals with a family (Gauthier, 1999b).

Interested readers can study guidelines and consensus documents on diagnosis and management of AD issued by a number of professional associations and academic groups in recent years (Corey-Bloom et al., 1995; Costa, Williams, & Albert, 1996; Geldmacher & Whitehouse, 1996; Quality Standards Subcommitte of the American Academy of Neurology, 1994; Rabins & the Work Group on Alzheimer's Disease and Related Dementias, 1997; Small et al., 1997).

REFERENCES

Aarsland, D., Bronnick, K., & Karlsen, K. (1999). Donepezil for dementia with Lewy bodies: A case study. *International Journal of Geriatric Psychiatry, 14*, 69–74.

American College of Medical Genetics/American Society of Human Genetics Working Group on ApoE and Alzheimer Disease. (1995). Consensus statement: statement on use of apolipoprotein E testing for Alzheimer's disease. *The Journal of the American Medical Association, 27*, 1627–1629.

American Psychiatric Association. (1994). *Diagnostic and statistical manual of mental disorders* (4th ed.). Washington, DC: Author.

Blacker, D., Albert, M., & Bassett, S. S. (1994). Reliability and validity of NINCDS-ADRDA criteria for Alzheimer's disease. *Archives of Neurology, 51,* 1198–1204.

Bouchard, R., & Rossor, M. N. (1999). Typical clinical features. In S. Gauthier (Ed.), *Clinical diagnosis and management of Alzheimer's disease* (2nd ed., pp. 57–71). London, UK: Martin Dunitz.

Canadian Study of Health and Aging Working Group. (1994). The Canadian Study of Health and Aging: Risk factors for Alzheimer's disease in Canada. *Neurology, 44,* 2073–2080.

Caramelli, P., Poissant, A., Gauthier, S., Bellavance, A., Gauvreau, D., Lecours, A. R., & Joanette, Y. (1997). Educational level and neuropsychological heterogeneity in dementia of the Alzheimer type. *Alzheimer Disease and Associated Disorders, 11,* 9–15.

Chui, H. C., Victoroff, J. I., Margolin, D., Jagust, W., Shankle, R., & Katzman, R. (1992). Criteria for the diagnosis of ischemic vascular dementia proposed by the State of California Alzheimer's Disease Diagnostic and Treatment Centres. *Neurology, 42,* 473–480.

Chui, H. C., & Zhang, Q. (1997). Evaluation of dementia: A systematic study of the usefulness of the American Academy of Neurology's practice parameters. *Neurology, 49,* 925–935.

Corey-Bloom, J., Thal, L. J., Galasko, D., Folstein, M., Drachman, D., Raskind, M., & Lanska, D. J. (1995). Diagnosis and evaluation of dementia. *Neurology, 45,* 211–218.

Costa, P. P., Williams, T. F., & Albert, M. S. (1996). *Recognition and initial assessment of Alzheimer's disease and related dementias* (Clinical Practice Guideline Number 19, U.S. Department of Health and Human Services, Agency for Health Care Policy and Research Publication No. 97–0702). Rockville, MD: Agency for Health Care Policy and Research.

Cummings, J. L., Vinters, H. V., Cole, G. M., & Khachaturian, Z. S. (1998). Alzheimer's disease: Etiologies, pathophysiology, cognitive reserve, and treatment opportunities. *Neurology, 51*(Suppl. 1), 2–17.

Dastoor, D., Schwartz, G., & Kurtzman, D. (1991). Clock drawing: An assessment technique in dementia. *Journal of Clinical and Experimental Gerontology, 13,* 69–85.

Folstein, M. F., Folstein, S. E., & McHugh, P. R. (1975). Mini Mental State: A practical method for grading the cognitive state of patients for the clinician. *Journal of Psychiatric Research, 12,* 189–198.

Freter, S., Bergman, H., Gold, S., Chertkow, H., & Clarfield, A. M. (1998). Prevalence of potentially reversible dementias and actual reversibility in a memory clinic cohort. *Canadian Medical Association Journal, 159,* 657–662.

Gauthier, S. (1998). Costs of diagnostic procedures. In A. Wimo, G. Karlsson, & B. Winblad (Eds.), *Health economics of dementia* (pp. 269–273). West Sussex, UK: Wiley.

Gauthier, S. (1999a). *Alzheimer's disease in primary care.* London: Martin Dunitz.

Gauthier, S. (1999b). Managing expectations in the long-term treatment of Alzheimer's disease. *Gerontology, 45*(Suppl. 1), 33–38.

Gauthier, S., Panisset, M., Nalbantoglu, J., & Poirier, J. (1997). Alzheimer's disease: Current knowledge, management and research. *Canadian Medical Association Journal, 157,* 1047–1052.

Geldmacher, D. S., & Whitehouse, P. J. (1996). Evaluation of dementia. *The New England Journal of Medicine, 335,* 330–336.

Geula, C. (1998). Abnormalities of neural circuitry in Alzheimer's disease. *Neurology, 51*(Suppl. 1), 18–29.

Growdon, J. H. (1998). The Ronald and Nancy Reagan Research Institute of the Alzheimer's Association and the National Institute on Aging Working Group. Consensus report of the Working Group on: Molecular and biochemical markers of Alzheimer's disease. *Neurobiology of Aging, 19*, 109–116.

Hachinski, V. C., Iliff, L. D., Zilkha, E., Du Boulay, G. H., McAllister, V. L., Marshall, J., Russell, R. W., & Symon, L. (1974). Cerebral blood flow in dementia. *Archives of Neurology, 32*, 632–637.

Levy-Lahad, E., Tsuang, D., & Bird, T. (1998). Recent advances in the genetics of Alzheimer's disease. *Journal of Geriatric Psychiatry and Neurology, 11*, 42–54.

Lund and Manchester Groups. (1994). Clinical and neuropathological criteria for fronto-temporal dementia. *Journal of Neurology, Neurosurgery, and Psychiatry, 57*, 416–418.

Mayeux, R., Saunders, A. M., Shea, S., Mirra, S., Evans, D., Roses, A. D., Hyman, B. T., Crain, B., Tang, M. X., & Phelps, C. H. (1998). Utility of the apolipoprotein E genotype in the diagnosis of Alzheimer's disease. *The New England Journal of Medicine, 338*, 506–511.

McKeith, I. G., Galasko, D., Kosaka, K., Perry, E. K., Dickson, D. W., Hansen, L. A., Salmon, D. P., Lowe, J., Mirra, S. S., Byrne, E. J., Lennox, G., Quinn, N. P., Edwardson, J. A., Ince, P. G., Bergeron, C., Burns, A., Miller, B. L., Lovestone, S., Collerton, D., Jansen, E. N., Ballard, C., de Vos, R. A., Wilcock, G. K., Jellinger, K. A., & Perry, R. H. (1996). Consensus guidelines for the clinical and pathological diagnosis of dementia with Lewy bodies (DLB): Report of the consortium on DLB international workshop. *Neurology, 47*, 1113–1124.

McKhann, G., Drachman, D., Folstein, M., Katzman, R., Price, D., & Stadlan, E. M. (1984). Clinical diagnosis of Alzheimer's disease: Report of the NINCDS-ADRDA workgroup. *Neurology, 34*, 939–944.

Mendez, M. F., Peryman, K. M., Miller, B. L., & Cummings, J. (1998). Behavioral differences between frontotemporal dementia and Alzheimer's disease: A comparison on the BEHAVE-AD rating scale. *International Psychogeriatrics, 10*, 155–162.

Mesulam, M. M. (1982). Slowly progressive aphasia without generalized dementia. *Annals of Neurology, 11*, 592–598.

Morris, J. C., McKeel, D. W., Storandt, M., Rubin, E. H., Price, J. L., Grant, E. A., Ball, M. J., & Berg, L. (1991). Very mild Alzheimer's disease: Informant-based clinical, psychometric, and pathologic distinction from normal aging. *Neurology, 41*, 469–478.

Patterson, C. J., Gauthier, S., Bergman, H., Cohen, C. A., Feightner, J. W., Feldman, H., & Hogan, D. B. (2001). The recognition, assessment and management of dementing disorders: Conclusions from the Canadian Consensus Conference on Dementia. *Canadian Journal of Neurological Sciences, 28*(Suppl. 1), S3–S16.

Pfeffer, R. I., Kurosaki, T. T., Harrah, C. H., Chance, J. M., & Filos, S. (1982). Measurement of functional activities of older adults in the community. *Journal of Gerontology, 37*, 323–329.

Pryse-Phillips, W., & Galasko, D. (1999). Non-Alzheimer dementias. In S. Gauthier (Ed.), *Clinical diagnosis and management of Alzheimer's disease* (pp. 73–92). London: Martin Dunitz.

Quality Standards Subcommittee of the American Academy of Neurology. (1994). Practice parameters for diagnosis and evaluation of dementia (summary statement). *Neurology, 44*, 2203–2206.

Rabins, P., & the Work Group on Alzheimer's Disease and Related Dementias. (1997). Practice guidelines for the treatment of patients with Alzheimer's disease and other dementias of late life. *The American Journal of Psychiatry, 154,* 1–39.

Reisberg, B., Ferris, S. H., DeLeon, M. J., & Crook, T. (1982). The global deterioration scale for assessment of primary degenerative dementia. *The American Journal of Psychiatry, 139,* 1136–1139.

Rockwood, K. (1997). Lessons from mixed dementia. *International Psychogeriatrics, 9,* 245–249.

Roman, G. C., Tatemichi, T. K., Erkinjuntti, T., Cummings, J. L., Masdeu, J. C., Garcia, J. H., Amaducci, L., Orgogozo, J. M., Brun, A., Hofman, A., Moody, D. M., O'Brien, M. D., Yamaguchi, T., Grafman, J., Drayer, B. P., Bennett, D. A., Fisher, M., Ogata, J., Kokmen, E., Bermejo, F., Wolf, P. A., Gorelick, P. B., Bick, K. L., Pajeau, A. K., Bell, M. A., De Carli, C., Culebras, A., Korczyn, A. D., Bogousslavsky, J., Hartmann, A., & Scheinberg, P. (1993). Vascular dementia: Diagnostic criteria for research studies. Report of the NINCDS-AIREN International Workshop. *Neurology, 43,* 250–260.

Sadovnick, A. D., & Lovestone, S. (1999). Genetic counselling. In S. Gauthier (Ed.), *Clinical diagnosis and management of Alzheimer's disease* (pp. 355–365). London: Martin Dunitz.

Small, G. W., Rabins, P. V., Barry, P. P., Buckholtz, N. S., DeKosky, S. T., Ferris, S. H., Finkel, S. I., Gwyther, L. P., Khachaturian, Z. S., Lebowitz, B. D., McRae, T. D., Morris, J. C., Oakley, F., Schneider, L. S., Streim, J. E., Sunderland, T., Teri, L. A., & Tune, L. E. (1997). Diagnosis and treatment of Alzheimer's disease and related disorders. Consensus statement of the American Association for Geriatric Psychiatry, the Alzheimer's Association, and the American Geriatrics Society. *The Journal of the American Medical Association, 278,* 1363–1371.

Strittmatter, W. J. (2000). Apolipoprotein E and Alzheimer's disease. *Annals of the New York Academy of Sciences, 924,* 91–92.

Strub, R. L., & Black, F. W. (1993). *The mental status examination in neurology* (3rd ed.). Philadelphia: F.A. Davis Company.

3

Cognitive-Neuropsychological Aspects

Fabienne Collette
University of Liège

Martial Van der Linden
University of Geneva

Anne-Claude Juillerat
University Hospitals of Geneva

Thierry Meulemans
University of Liège

Alzheimer's disease (AD) is classically characterized by the progressive accumulation of deficits affecting several cognitive domains, almost without any specific neurological signs. Neuropsychological studies have long been guided by the concept of a generalized and homogenous impairment in AD patients. Consequently, neuropsychologists have searched for a typical cognitive AD profile ("the essence" of AD deficits). The adoption of cognitive psychology concepts and methods in the neuropsychological approach of AD has largely modified this point of view (see Van der Linden, 1994; Venneri, Turnbull, & Della Sala, 1996).

Indeed, it is now widely acknowledged that AD is not characterized by a global cognitive deterioration but that the disease can selectively impair specific cognitive processes or systems, while sparing others. In other words, preserved cognitive abilities may be observed in AD patients. Moreover, several studies have documented different factors allowing an optimization of cognitive performance in AD patients. Finally, a large number of studies have shown that both the nature of the defective processes and the impairment progression can vary considerably from one AD patient to another. Such heterogeneity can be seen both between cognitive functions (e.g., between language and visuospatial abilities) and within a particular cognitive domain.

All these changes in the neuropsychological conception of AD have clearly influenced assessment and rehabilitation practices.

THE HETEROGENEITY AND SPECIFICITY OF NEUROPSYCHOLOGICAL DEFICITS IN AD PATIENTS

The heterogeneity of patterns of decline in early AD patients has been illustrated in a recent study by Perry and Hodges (2000), who explored the longitudinal profile of 12 patients with questionable (very mild) AD. All subjects had Mini Mental State Examination (MMSE) scores (Folstein, Folstein, & McHugh, 1975) of 24 or greater at entry to the study and showed, on the clinical examination, impaired episodic memory as the only deficit (judged by no recall or minimal recall of a name and address after 5 minutes). An extensive neuropsychological battery, which examined five domains of cognition—episodic memory, attention and executive function, semantic memory, auditory-verbal short-term memory, and visuospatial function—was performed at entry and after a delay of 12 to 14 months. The results showed that at entry, even after subjects were given this extensive neuropsychological battery, 8 of the 12 subjects had only episodic memory deficits. After 12 months, three patients remained only amnesic, and the other patients with isolated memory disorders developed either semantic or attentional/executive deficits. Disorders in both of these cognitive domains preceded impairments in visuospatial function and auditory-verbal short-term memory. This typical pattern of neuropsychological changes is consistent with the common view concerning the progression of the disease, which is thought to affect initially the transentorhinal (or perirhinal) region before spreading into the hippocampal complex proper in the medial temporal lobe structure and, thereafter, the temporal lobes and basal forebrain (Braak, Braak, & Bohl, 1993; Van Hoesen, 1997). Thus, these data indicate that tests of attention and semantic memory appear to be the most sensitive markers of decline beyond the amnesic phase of early AD. However, the analysis of individual patterns of AD patients' performance demonstrated that semantic memory deficits may occur before impairment in attentional/executive processing, and the reverse pattern was also seen, suggesting heterogeneity in the cognitive evolution of AD.

More striking evidence illustrating both the selectivity and heterogeneity of deficits in AD came from a study conducted by Galton, Patterson, Xuereb, and Hodges (2000), in which the clinical and neuropsychological profile of 13 patients with pathologically proven AD was described. Four patients showed a typical neuropsychological pattern, with episodic memory deficits as the initial feature, and subsequent involvement of attentional, language, semantic memory, and visuospatial abilities. The other patients could be considered as demonstrating an atypical profile because their initial and major cognitive deficit did not affect episodic memory: six patients showed progressive (fluent and nonfluent) aphasia, one patient showed progressive visual dysfunction, and two patients showed progressive biparietal syndrome. There were no differences between the typical and atypical presentations with respect to age at presentation, length of illness, or in the length of time that symptoms were reported before presentation at the memory clinic. By the time of neuropsychological assessment, most, but not all, of the typical and atypical patients showed evidence of a more global cognitive impairment. Although the majority of patients had deficits in episodic memory, two patients did not present such an impairment. Thus, this study clearly demonstrated the large spectrum of AD presentations (see also Benson & Zaias, 1991; Berthier, Leiguarda, Stacksetin, Sevlever, & Taratuto, 1991; Green, Morris, Sandson, McKeel, & Miller, 1990; Greene, Patterson, Xuereb, & Hodges, 1996; Kobayashi, Hirota, Saito, & Utsuyama, 1987, for a presentation of AD cases with progressive occipitoparietal, biparietal, and aphasia syndromes).

In addition to multiple case studies, several group studies have also identified the existence of subgroups of AD patients, determined on the basis of their cognitive impairment profiles (for a review see Joanette, Belleville, Gely-Nargeot, Ska, & Valdois, 2000; Joanette, Ska, Poissant, & Bélant, 1992). For example, Martin et al. (1986) showed that a large proportion of AD patients had a cognitive impairment which did not affect all cognitive functions equally. More precisely, 60% of their AD patients had impairments that looked quite even across the different functions examined (language and visuospatial processes). Of the remaining patients, they isolated one subgroup with major deficits in language tasks but a relatively good performance in visuospatial tasks, whereas another subgroup of patients showed the reverse pattern. The authors also showed that the metabolic brain distribution in the three groups of patients was relatively consistent with neuropsychological findings: The patients with both language and visuospatial impairments showed temporal and parietal hypometabolism, bilaterally; those with impaired language processes and relatively spared visuospatial abilities exhibited greater hypometabolism in the left temporal regions relative to other cortical areas; and, finally, those with impaired visuospatial functioning and spared language abilities demonstrated greater hypometabolism in the right parietal region.

More recently, Fisher et al. (1996) confirmed the data obtained by Martin et al. (1986) using a larger, more representative group of AD patients. They identified three neuropsychological subgroups. The largest AD group was considered as global, with patients showing both language and visuospatial/constructional dysfunction. Patients in the second subgroup (left-hemisphere AD) displayed relatively spared visuospatial/constructional functioning but severe anomia. Members of the third subgroup (right-hemisphere AD) exhibited intact naming associated with borderline visuospatial/constructional functioning. In a subsequent study, the authors followed longitudinally some of the AD patients who were reliably classified into the three neuropsychological subgroups. They found that the neuropsychological domain that was initially more severely affected remained disproportionately impaired with the progression of the disease. This heterogeneity within a group in the presenting cognitive syndrome has been supported by other studies (Kanne, Balota, Storandt, McKeel, & Morris, 1998; Neary et al., 1986; Price et al., 1993). For example, Kanne et al. (1998) established, in 41 AD patients, three main cognitive factors corresponding to executive, memory, and visuospatial domains and observed a significant correlation between these factors and the relative distribution of AD pathology in frontal, temporal, and parietal regions, respectively. Interestingly, Price et al. (1993) especially showed that although episodic memory was affected in all patients, the memory deficit was mild when compared with language or visuospatial disorders in four cases.

An important heterogeneity in AD patients' performance has also been observed within a single cognitive domain. In fact, the typical pathology of AD, characterized by heterogeneous microstructural changes in the cortical architecture (see Boller, Forette, Khatchaturian, Poncet, & Chrysten, 1992), might facilitate the emergence of fine-grained dissociations (Venneri et al., 1996). Thus, in the memory domain, Baddeley, Della Sala, and Spinnler (1991) identified, in a sample of 55 AD patients, some cases in which deficits were predominant in long-term episodic memory or in short-term memory (with a relative sparing of long-term episodic memory); they also described cases with specific visual or verbal memory deficits. This variation does not seem to be the consequence of random fluctuation because no examples of nonsense syndromes were ever found with respect to the cognitive theory of memory (see also Ergis, Van der Linden, Boller, Degos, & Deweer, 1995, for similar results).

Such heterogeneity was also found within the working memory domain. Indeed, several group studies (e.g., Morris, 1984, 1987a, 1987b) indicated a normal functioning of the phonological loop (i.e., the working memory component that is specialized for the temporary storage of verbal material and that is composed of two subsystems: a phonological store and an articulatory rehearsal process; Baddeley, 1986), although other studies demonstrated the existence of deficits affecting either the phonological store or the articulatory rehearsal mechanism (Belleville, Peretz, & Malenfant, 1996; Hulme, Lee, & Brown, 1993). To assess the integrity of the different subcomponents of working memory, Belleville et al. (1996) performed a single-case analysis in a group of mildly impaired AD patients. The researchers showed that most of the patients had impairments affecting the central executive component of working memory (the attentional control system), whereas only half of the patients presented articulatory rehearsal mechanism, phonological store impairments, or both. More recently, Collette, Van der Linden, Bechet, and Salmon (1999) also reported an important heterogeneity in the working memory performance of AD patients. In particular, several cases of double dissociation were observed within the phonological loop system, with some patients showing deficits affecting the phonological store but not the articulatory rehearsal mechanism, and other patients displaying the reverse profile. The authors also found that a deficit can specifically affect a central executive function, with the phonological loop being spared. Finally, even though central executive impairments generally preceded phonological loop deficits, three patients showed deficits affecting the phonological loop, without any difficulties on the tasks assessing the central executive system.

The existence of dissociations between AD patients has also been revealed in the face recognition and visuospatial domains (Bruyer & Van der Linden, 1995; Cosslett & Safran, 1996; Della Sala, Muggia, Spinnler, & Zuffi, 1995; Franconie, Gely-Nargeot, Van der Linden, & Touchon, 1998). For example, using a multiple single case approach, Della Sala et al. (1995) found a double dissociation between tasks assessing familiar face recognition and tasks assessing unknown face discrimination, with 4 of the 30 patients showing a selective impairment in familiar face recognition and 2 patients showing the reverse pattern. More recently, Della Sala, Kinnear, Spinnler, and Stangalino (2000) revealed in a few AD patients a dissociation between object-color retrieval and both color sorting and color naming, supporting the notion of a separation of pure color processing from object-color knowledge.

With regard to language functions, it is commonly admitted that language deficits are observed in 8% to 15% of early AD patients and that syntactic and phonological processes are relatively preserved compared with lexico-semantic abilities (Emery, 1996). However, Ska, Joanette, Poissant, Bélant, and Lecours (1990) analyzed the language abilities of a group of mild AD patients and found that only half of the subjects had a performance compatible with this classical description. The other patients demonstrated impairment of syntactical abilities, phonological abilities, or both, in the absence of any gross impairment of semantic abilities. The heterogeneity of language deficits in AD has also been confirmed by Diesfeldt (1992), who demonstrated a double dissociation in the language performance of two AD patients: One of them showed intact phonological and syntactic processes along with an important semantic deficit, and the other patient displayed the reversed pattern.

An important variability has also been noted in the presentation and existence of anosognosia in AD (Agnew & Morris, 1998). Finally, concerning the executive control function, a common view considers that disorders affecting this domain are present in AD (see Duke & Kaszniak, 2000), but they are less prominent than the memory disorders and tend to become more pronounced later in the course of the illness. However, Johnson, Head, Kim, Starr, and Cotman (1999) recently identified a subgroup of patients with pathologically confirmed AD who, in the early stages of the disease, presented disproportionate deficits on tests of frontal lobe functioning and showed a greater-than-expected degree of neurofibrillary tangles in the frontal lobes. These results are similar to those of Binetti et al. (1996), who identified 7 of 36 mildly demented AD patients with severe impairments on frontal tests. As suggested by Johnson et al. (1999), further studies should be conducted to investigate executive processes using more specific tests and to determine precisely the relationships between executive dysfunction and frontal hypometabolism in AD.

THE PREVALENCE OF SOME TYPES OF COGNITIVE DEFICITS

Given the heterogeneity of cognitive disorders observed in AD patients, a search for cognitive predictors, which could allow early identification of individuals at risk for developing AD, appears to be useless. Indeed, only long and detailed neuropsychological examinations, exploring repeatedly the different cognitive functions with sensitive tasks, would contribute to early and reliable diagnosis.

However, several recent studies have suggested that beyond the observed heterogeneity, there exists a prevalence of certain types of deficits early in the disease. The identification of these deficits could therefore contribute to the early diagnosis of AD. More specifically, two types of impairment seem to be particularly frequent and occur early in the course of AD: executive (controlled) function and episodic memory impairments.

Executive function refers to various processes (e.g., inhibition, planning, shifting, updating) whose main purpose is to facilitate a subject's adaptation to novel situations, especially when action routines are not sufficient (Miyake, Friedman, Emerson, Witzki, & Howerter, 2000; Shallice, 1982). Episodic memory refers to long-term memory of events within specific spatiotemporal contexts (Tulving, 1983). This memory system is explored by means of explicit memory tests, such as recall or recognition, which require the deliberate recollection of specific episodes.

Executive Function and Attention Deficits

In a recent prospective study, Fabrigoule et al. (1998) suggested that preclinical deficits in early AD reflect the deterioration of a general factor, which might be interpreted as the disturbance of control processes. They administered a battery of seven neuropsychological tasks to 1,159 elderly subjects ages 65 years and older who showed no signs of dementia. From these subjects, 16 were classified 2 years later as having AD. The performance of these patients in the various cognitive tasks was inferior to that of normal elderly subjects. A principal component analysis coupled with a logistic regression showed that one factor explaining 45.3% of the variance in test performance constituted a good predictor of the risk to develop AD. The neuropsychological tasks loading on this factor were the digit symbol substitution test (Wechsler, 1981), the semantic verbal fluency task (Isaacs & Kennie, 1973), the multiple-choice form of the Benton Visual Retention Test (Benton, 1965), and the Zazzo's cancellation task (Zazzo, 1974). Fabrigoule et al. (1998) proposed that this factor represents a general factor corresponding to the controlled or executive aspects of the tasks used. More generally, in the line of Jorm's (1986) hypothesis, they suggested that the first stages of AD could be characterized by a relative deterioration of controlled processes, as opposed to the preservation of automatic ones. To summarize, these results indicate that although AD patients may differ in the extent to which they manifest certain aspects of their disease, they all share a common global cognitive impairment, interpreted as reflecting the operation of control processes (see Salthouse & Becker, 1998, for similar results). In the same perspective, a number of studies (Lafleche & Albert, 1995; Orgogozo, Fabrigoule, Rouch, Amieva, & Dartigues, 2000; Small, Herlitz, Fratiglioni, Almkvist, & Bäckman, 1997; Tierney et al., 1996) also showed that cognitive tasks that better discriminate AD from normal aging are those involving executive processes, such as the coordination of simultaneous mental activities, shifting abilities, or self-control activities (especially, the Trail Making Test, Part B [Reitan, 1979], the verbal fluency task, and the digit symbol substitution test).

However, the interpretation suggesting that early AD patients show impaired control (executive) processes along with spared automatic processes was based on a post hoc analysis of performance obtained on a series of multicomponent tasks, which were not specifically designed to assess executive functioning. In this context, we recently demonstrated the existence of executive impairments in a group of mild to moderate AD patients in several tasks assessing various executive processes, in particular the ability to divide attentional resources (dual task paradigm; Baddeley, Della Sala, Gray, Papagno, & Spinnler, 1997) and to manipulate information stored in working memory (alpha span task; Belleville, Rouleau, & Caza, 1998), the short-term preparation for a specific event (the delayed alternation task; Bhutani, Montaldi, Brooks, & McCulloch, 1992), the capacity to retrieve information in semantic memory (a phonemic fluency task; Perret, 1974), the inhibition capacity (the Hayling task; Burgess & Shallice, 1996), and the monitoring of self-generated responses (the self-ordered pointing task; Petrides & Milner, 1982).

In the alpha span task (Belleville et al., 1998), the capacity of the subjects to recall a number of items corresponding to their span level minus one is compared in two conditions: serial order recall (implicating only the temporary storage of information) and alphabetical order recall (implicating storage and manipulation of information). The decrease of performance for the serial to the alphabetical recall condition is considered to reflect the ability of the central executive to manipulate actively the information stored in working memory.

The dual task paradigm (Baddeley et al., 1997) compares the performance in a digit span task and in a cancellation task carried out separately to the performance when the two tasks are carried out simultaneously. Again, the decrease of performance from the single tasks to the dual task is considered to reflect the functioning of the central executive.

The delayed alternation task (Bhutani et al., 1992) requires the person to search for a target stimulus in one of two boxes placed in front of him or her; once the person has found the target, the examiner replaces the stimulus in the alternative location, out of sight of the person, who is then required to search again; whenever the subject successfully identifies the localization of the stimulus, its position is automatically reversed.

In the phonemic fluency task, the participant is given 120 seconds to generate aloud a list of words beginning with a target letter (letter *P*) but excluding proper names and variants of a same word.

In the Hayling test (Burgess & Shallice, 1996), the participant is presented with sentences in which the last word is missing; what this last word should be is strongly cued by the rest of the sentence. The task consists of two sections: In the initiation section of the test, the participant has to complete the sentence by supplying the missing word, and in the inhibition section, a word that makes no sense in the sentence context has to be produced by the subject.

The self-ordered pointing task (Petrides & Milner, 1982) consists in the presentation of a series of cards, one card at a time. The same set of 16 abstract designs is printed on each card, but the position of the designs varies randomly from card to card. The subject is required to point to a different design on each card successively presented.

The AD patients' performance was significantly impaired compared with control subjects on all tasks, confirming that executive deficits may be present in the first stages of the disease. Moreover, it was found that these executive deficits cannot be completely explained by dementia severity or the presence of a slowing down. Finally, a principal component analysis demonstrated that the performance of AD patients on the Hayling task, the delayed alternation task, and the verbal fluency task loaded on the same factor, reflecting inhibition processes. The performance on the alpha span task, the dual task paradigm, and the self-ordered pointing task loaded on another factor, presumably devoted to the coordination between temporary storage and processing functions. The existence of these two factors suggests that different components of cognition contribute to the performance of AD patients in executive tasks.

In two other studies (Adam, Van der Linden, & Juillerat, 1999; Collette, Van der Linden, Bechet, et al., 1999), we explored more directly the hypothesis that early AD patients exhibit executive dysfunction along with a preservation of automatic processes. The first study (Collette, Van der Linden, Bechet, et al., 1999) was based on Baddeley's (1986) working memory model and examined the integrity of the phonological loop and central executive components of working memory in a group of mild to moderate AD patients. Because phonological loop functioning is considered relatively automatic, whereas the central executive is involved in control processes, we hypothesized that AD patients in the first stages of the disease would exhibit impairments in tasks assessing the central executive with a preservation of the subcomponents of the phonological loop (phonological store and articulatory rehearsal mechanism).

The articulatory rehearsal mechanism was examined by comparing the span performance for short and long words, whereas comparing the span performance for phonologically similar and dissimilar words assessed the integrity of the phonological store. Moreover, the contribution of long-term memory to span performance was explored by comparing the span performance for words and nonwords. Finally, the two tasks used to evaluate the central executive functioning were the alpha span task (Belleville et al., 1998) and the dual task paradigm (Baddeley et al., 1997).

The results showed that, as a group, AD patients presented poor performance in all tasks assessing the phonological loop, the contribution of long-term memory to span performance, and the central executive. However, further analyses indicated that only the subgroup of patients with a low span performance and a more severe dementia (the span level of AD patients was related to the severity of the disease, as measured by the Mattis Dementia Rating Scale; Mattis, 1976) showed deficits affecting the different components of the phonological loop. On the other hand, both subgroups of more- and less-demented AD patients, with low and high span levels, showed deficits affecting central executive functioning and the contribution of long-term memory to span performance. Thus, these data indicate that high span level and less-demented patients have impairments involving executive processes as well as the integration of different types of information (especially information stored in long-term and working memory), whereas the low span level and more-demented patients showed deficits involving more basic and automatic processes. Globally, these results support Fabrigoule et al.'s (1998) view that there exists an early impairment of the control process in AD, whereas the automatic processes, such as those involved in phonological loop functioning, are affected later in the disease.

In the second study (Adam, Van der Linden, & Juillerat, 1999), we adopted the process dissociation procedure proposed by Jacoby (1991) to explore the contribution of automatic and controlled processes in early AD patients' performance on a memory task (a word-stem completion task).

The process dissociation procedure required subjects to perform two tasks, one inclusion and the other exclusion.

In the inclusion task, subjects were asked to complete a stem with a previously studied word (controlled retrieval processes, C) and, if they could not to do so, to give the first word that came to mind (automatic retrieval, A). Considering the independence of both retrieval processes, the performance in the inclusion condition can be described as follows: INCLUSION = C + A*(1 – C). In the exclusion task, the participants had to complete a stem with a word that was not presented during the earlier study phase (in other words, they were asked to avoid studied words). The performance in this exclusion condition can be described as follows: EXCLUSION = A*(1 – C).

Then, controlled processes (C) can be estimated by subtracting the probability of responding with a studied word in the exclusion task from the probability of responding with a studied word in the inclusion task (C = Inclusion – Exclusion).

Once an estimate of controlled processes (C) has been obtained, the contribution of automatic processes (A) corresponds to the probability to complete a stem with the studied word in the exclusion condition divided by 1 minus the probability to complete a stem with the studied word in the inclusion condition (A = Exclusion / (1 – C)).

The results revealed that the contribution of controlled processes to AD patients' memory performance was severely affected (and the deficit increased with the length of the retention interval), whereas the contribution of automatic processes was preserved (see also Knight, 1998; Koivisto, Portin, Seinela, & Rinne, 1998, for globally similar findings). These data confirm the existence of an automatic-control dissociation in early AD patients. Further studies using Jacoby's (1991) procedure should be conducted to determine whether AD patients present a similar dissociation in cognitive domains other than memory (for example in inhibition, Lindsay & Jacoby, 1994).

From a more general point of view, all these results can be replaced in the context of the studies suggesting that attentional deficits are not global in early AD but seem to affect tasks requiring more complex cognitive processes and not tasks involving more automatic processes. Indeed, the existence of attentional deficits in early AD is well established (for a review see Collette & Van der Linden, 2002a). However, it appeared that these deficits do not affect all the subcomponents of attention in the same way (see Gainotti, Marra, & Villa, 2001; Perry, Watson, & Hodges, 2002a).

Researchers who explored attentional functioning in early AD patients observed normal performance in sustained attention (i.e., the ability to detect a large number of items over a brief period of time; e.g., Lines et al., 1991), vigilance (i.e., the ability to stay alert for a prolonged period of time to detect relevant but very infrequent and irregular stimuli; e.g., Nebes & Brady, 1993), and alertness (i.e., the capability to enhance response readiness following a warning stimulus; e.g., Pate, Margolin, Friedrich, & Bentley, 1994).

However, deficits in selective attention (i.e., the ability to select or focus on a single input in the presence of competing inputs) were demonstrated in several studies. More precisely, although AD patients showed no impairments in engaging or focusing attention on the location or on an attribute of the stimulus, specific impairments in disengaging or reorienting attention were found (Oken, Kishiyama, Kaye, & Howieson, 1994; Parasuraman, Greenwood, Haxby, & Grady, 1992; Scinto et al., 1994). Moreover, other studies demonstrated that AD patients have specific selective attention impairments when the task requires to switch attention not only between different attributes of items (Foster, Berhmann, & Stuss, 1999; Haxby, Parasuraman, Gillette, & Raffaele, 1991) but also between different levels of perceptual organization within a single complex stimulus (Filoteo et al., 1992; Massman et al., 1993).

Another aspect of selective attention, namely inhibition processes, also appeared to be affected in AD. Inhibition is defined as a mechanism that actively suppresses task-irrelevant information. A related concept, interference, refers to the susceptibility of decreased performance in the presence of distracting stimuli. In fact, AD patients exhibited large sensitivity to interference, such as that measured by the Stroop Test (Simone & Baylis, 1997; Spieler, Balota, & Faust, 1996), as well as semantic inhibition deficits, such as that measured by the Hayling task (Collette, Van der Linden, & Salmon, 1999; Rouleau, Belleville, & Van der Linden, 2001). However, results appear less clear-cut when a negative priming paradigm was used to assess inhibition processes.

The negative priming effect occurs when participants are asked to provide some response to a given stimulus (the target), while at the same time ignoring an irrelevant stimulus. If the distractor on one trial (the prime trial) becomes the target in the next trial (the test trial), performance is usually hampered (as suggested by an increased response time or, sometimes, more errors). The dominant interpretation of this effect is that it indicates inhibitory attentional processes: In the prime trial, the representation of the distractor is inhibited, and, subsequently, when it is presented as a target in the test trial, additional processing time is required to overcome the inhibition generated in the previous trial.

Using this negative priming procedure, some studies found no inhibition impairments in AD patients (e.g., Danckert, Maruff, Crowe, & Currie, 1998; Langley, Overmier, Knopman, & Prod'Homme, 1998), whereas a deficit was observed in other studies (Rouleau et al., 2001).

Finally, tasks involving divided attentional abilities appear to be impaired in patients with AD. Divided attention has been frequently explored in AD patients using a dual task procedure that requires the subject to perform two tasks separately before performing both tasks simultaneously (it should be noted that dual task coordination is considered an important executive function; see Baddeley, 1986; Miyake et al., 2000). Deficits in dual task coordination were found in tasks requiring or not requiring storage of information (Baddeley, Bressi, Della Sala, Logie, & Spinnler, 1991; Baddeley, Logie, Bressi, Della Sala, & Spinnler, 1986; Nestor, Parasuraman, Haxby, & Grady, 1991), and even in relatively automatic dual tasks, such as talking while walking, which leads to a higher probability of falls (Camicioli, Howieson, Lehman, & Kaye, 1997). However, these studies did not specifically assess early or very early AD patients.

More recently, Perry et al. (2000) administered to a group of minimal (MMSE = 24 – 30) and mild (MMSE = 18 – 23) AD patients a battery of attentional tests aimed to assess different components of attention: sustained, divided, and selective attention and inhibition processes. Deficits in all tasks were found in the mild AD group, whereas minimal AD patients experienced difficulties with the selective attention and inhibition tasks but demonstrated normal performance in sustained and divided attention tasks. The evidence of normal divided attention in minimal AD patients is surprising because most of the studies using a dual task paradigm demonstrated impairment. However, it might be that the dual task used by Perry et al. (i.e., digit repetition and cancellation task) is not sufficiently sensitive in the early stage of AD (see also Greene, Hodges, & Baddeley, 1995). In a similar way, Rizzo, Anderson, Dawson, Myers, and Ball (2000) demonstrated that patients with mild AD performed significantly worse than control subjects on measures of sustained attention, divided attention, and selective attention. The divided attention task did not really assess dual coordination but required identification of two (central and peripheral) targets presented simultaneously. The existence of a decreased performance in sustained attention contradicts previous studies showing a preservation of this attentional component in mild AD patients. However, the sustained task used by Rizzo et al. consisted of the identification of a target among distractors, contrary to previous studies in which the to-be-detected items were presented in isolation. Consequently, the AD patients' deficits could be due to the selective attention aspects of the task.

Altogether, these studies confirmed that there exists in early AD a specific impairment affecting executive functioning as well as the control aspects of attentional processes. However, some cognitive and neuropsychological data have indicated that the executive function may not be a unitary system (Miyake et al., 2000; Shallice & Burgess, 1993). Rather, there seem to be several control functions, which are commonly labeled "executive" and which may operate quite independently. Recently, Miyake et al. (2000) administered a set of executive tasks to a large group of young subjects to examine the separability of three often postulated executive functions (shifting between mental sets or tasks, updating and monitoring of working memory contents, and inhibition of prepotent responses). Confirmatory factor analysis indicated that these three executive functions are moderately correlated with one another but are clearly separable, thus indicating both unity and diversity of executive functions. Moreover, structural equation modeling suggests that the executive tasks often used in cognitive and neuropsychological studies are not completely homogeneous in the sense that the three executive functions isolated (shifting, updating, and inhibition) contribute differentially to performance on complex executive tasks. For example, performance on the Wisconsin Card Sorting Test was related most strongly to the shifting function, whereas performance on the Tower of Hanoi was associated with inhibition processes. The only complex executive task that did not relate clearly to the three target executive functions was the dual task. This suggests the possibility that the simultaneous coordination of multiple tasks is an ability that is somewhat distinct from the three other executive functions explored in this study.

In this sense, it is possible that executive deficits in AD patients are not global in nature and that, at least in the early stages of the disease, there is some specificity of impairment (as already observed for attentional processes). From a clinical point of view, a better understanding of executive functioning in AD patients should lead to a selection of the best executive tasks that could be used as specific and accurate cognitive predictors of AD.

Episodic Memory Deficits

Episodic memory deficits (i.e., memory for events distinct in time and space) are a hallmark symptom of AD. Several hypotheses have been proposed to account for these deficits, which might affect encoding, storage, or retrieval, and which might result from attention/executive deficits, semantic difficulties, poor contextual memory, or metamemory problems (Van der Linden, 1989, 1994).

In addition, episodic memory disorders have consistently been demonstrated in preclinical AD (Collie & Maruff, 2000; Grober, Lipton, Hall, & Crystal, 2000; Hodges, 1998). These disorders in persons who will eventually develop AD have been found for both verbal (Tierney et al., 1996) and nonverbal materials (Small et al., 1997), as well as in different retrieval conditions, including free recall (Grober et al., 2000), cued recall (Bäckman & Small, 1998), and recognition (Small et al., 1997). In a recent prospective follow-up of a community-based cohort, with 3 and 6-year follow-ups of a population-based sample, Small, Fratiglioni, Vittanen, Winblad, and Bäckman (2000) confirmed that memory deficits are the first indicator of AD and that the diagnosis of AD is preceded by a long preclinical phase in which cognitive deficits are present (memory disorders being the most common). In addition, it appeared that the magnitude of the cognitive (memory) impairments remains relatively stable until shortly before clinical diagnosis. Similarly, in a 22-year prospective study of a community-based cohort, Elias et al. (2000) confirmed that the preclinical phase of detectable cognitive deficits precedes the appearance of probable AD by many years and that lower scores on measures of memory and abstract reasoning are the strongest predictors of probable AD when the initial assessment and the development of probable AD is long (10 years).

Bäckman, Small, and Fratiglioni (2001) also demonstrated that AD is characterized by a long preclinical period during which episodic memory deficits are detectable. Using data from a population-based study, they compared persons who developed AD ($n = 15$) with persons who were not demented ($n = 105$), 6 and 3 years prior to the diagnosis of dementia. Participants were administered episodic memory tasks (free recall and recognition of words) and working memory tasks (digit span, forward and backward). On recall and recognition tasks, the incident AD patients performed more poorly than the nondemented participants both 3 and 6 years before diagnosis. However, there was no evidence for an accelerated decline of episodic memory deficits from 6 to 3 years, suggesting that the memory deficit is characterized by an early onset followed by relative stability, at least until a few years before the AD diagnosis is confirmed. No group difference was observed in the digit span tasks. This lack of difference, particularly in the backward digit span task, is noteworthy, given that this test requires simultaneous storage and processing and thus presumably involves the contribution of the central executive component of working memory. According to Bäckman et al. (2001), this result may reflect that those prefrontal brain structures known to be critical to central executive functions (see Collette & Van der Linden, 2002b) are relatively preserved in the preclinical phase of AD. Alternatively, it could be argued that the backward digit span task does not sufficiently tax the executive (manipulation, updating, inhibition) processes (see Grégoire & Van der Linden, 1997).

Although evidence points to the usefulness of episodic memory tests in discriminating preclinical AD patients from normal elderly adults, it has also been suggested that not all episodic memory tasks are equally useful. Some studies suggested that delayed recall, and more specifically the comparison between immediate and delayed recall, is the best discriminatory measure available (Albert, 1996; Welsh, Butters, Hughes, Mohs, & Heyman, 1991, 1992). However, other investigators have found little or no evidence of abnormal delayed recall in AD patients, particularly when the effects of immediate recall have been adequately controlled (Chapman, White, & Storandt, 1997; Money, Kirk, & McNaughton, 1992; Robinson-Whelen & Storandt, 1992). For example, Chapman et al. (1997) showed that delayed recall of a prose passage does not appear to enhance the differentiation of very mild AD from normal aging, whether the delay is 10 or 30 minutes.

Other researchers have proposed that episodic memory tests that provide more cognitive support both at encoding (e.g., by inducing semantic categorization of the presented items) and retrieval (e.g., by giving categorical retrieval cues) are better predictors of dementia incidence than tasks involving less cognitive support (Buschke, Sliwinski, Kuslansky, & Lipton, 1997; Herlitz, Hill, Fratiglioni, & Bäckman, 1995; Small, Herlitz, et al., 1997). For example, Buschke et al. (1997) reported that measures of cued recall, especially when the cues at retrieval matched those available at encoding (the Category Cued Recall procedure), discriminated better between the normal elderly and individuals with mild AD than measures in which study-test compatibility was not maintained. In addition to the coordination between encoding and retrieval, an important advantage of this procedure is that it shows the existence of a memory impairment that is not caused by other cognitive deficits (i.e., attention and language deficits).

The Category Cued Recall (CCR) procedure used by Buschke et al. (1997) to coordinate encoding and retrieval cues involves the following steps:

1. A controlled encoding stage consisting in the presentation of four words on a screen, with each word belonging to a different semantic category. Appropriate category cues are shown, one at a time, in the center of the screen. The person is asked to find the corresponding word and name it aloud when its category cue is given (e.g., "cow" for "animal"). The same encoding task is administered for 64 words, belonging to 16 different, well-known categories (4 words in each category).
2. A cued recall stage. Cued recall is tested by asking the person to recall aloud the four target words from each category, in any order, when the category cue is read to the subject.

Buschke et al. (1997) showed that this CCR procedure has substantially higher sensitivity and specificity for diagnosis of mild AD (score of 0–10 on the Blessed Information, Memory and Concentration; Blessed, Tomlison, & Roth, 1968) than a memory procedure that does not coordinate encoding and retrieval (i.e., when semantic category cues are used only for retrieval and not for encoding) and the Wechsler Memory Scale-Revised (WMS-R; Wechsler, 1987) Logical Memory story recall, or the WMS-R Verbal Paired Associates immediate recall.

More recently, Brown and Storandt (2000) sought to extend Buschke et al.'s (1997) findings to patients with very mild AD (Clinical Dementia Rating, CDR, of 0.5). They replicated the sensitivity and specificity of the CCR procedure with respect to the differentiation of mild AD (CDR of 1) and healthy aging. However, the diagnostic accuracy of this test did not extend to the very mild stage of the disease. Indeed, there was substantial overlap in the distributions of the scores of the control and very mildly demented groups. In addition, the WMS Logical Memory subtest (Wechsler & Stone, 1973) showed discriminative accuracy comparable to Buschke et al.'s procedure. It should, however, be noted that Brown & Storandt (2000) used the WMS Logical Memory subtest, which requires rote memory of the stories, and Buschke et al. (1997) used the later WMS-R, which allows gist recall. Moreover, another recent study (Ivanoiu et al., 2000) using a 48-item version of Buschke et al.'s CCR procedure indicated that this task has a higher sensitivity and specificity than immediate and delayed free recall tasks for word lists (CERAD, Consortium to Establish a Registry for Alzheimer's Disease; Welsh et al., 1991, 1992) for discriminating, in a clinical setting, very mild AD patients (CDR of 0.5, with the AD diagnosis later confirmed by the evolution) from elderly people with subjective memory complaints.

Nevertheless, Grober et al. (2000) showed that a free recall measure also constitutes a good predictor of AD when learning was maximized by controlling attention and cognitive processes during encoding. They followed longitudinally 264 initially nondemented elderly subjects by using the Free and Cued Selective Reminding (FCSR) memory test (Grober & Bushke, 1987).

The Free and Cued Selective Reminding (FCSR) memory test is based on the same principle as the Buschke et al.'s (1997) CCR task; in fact, Buschke et al. elaborated the CCR task because the FCRS memory test proved to be limited by ceiling effects. The FCRS test also begins with a controlled encoding stage in which the participant is asked to name aloud an item (i.e., a line drawing of an easily recognized object) among four when its category cue is given. The same encoding procedure is administered for 16 words, belonging to 16 different categories.

The study phase is followed by three recall trials. For each trial, the person has first to recall freely as many items as possible. Then, category cues are provided for items not retrieved by free recall.

Dementia was defined by an algorithmic definition that required a Blessed Information, Memory, and Concentration score (Blessed et al., 1968) greater than 8 and clinical evidence of functional decline. Thirty-two incident cases of dementia developed during the follow-up. Analyses indicated that free recall impairment at baseline (measured by the total free recall performance on the three trials) was a powerful predictor of future dementia over the 5 years of follow-up, after adjusting for gender and education. More generally, these findings corroborate the existence of a preclinical phase of dementia characterized by memory impairments, which is present for at least 5 years before diagnosis.

Using a similar 16-item FCSR test (a version with words instead of drawings; Van der Linden et al., 2001), Tounsi et al. (1999) studied 131 patients (subdivided into four groups, according to their MMSE: > 25, 22–25, 18–21, < 18) and 20 normal elderly subjects. The authors showed that the free recall performance of the four subgroups was very poor and did not significantly differ, suggesting that severe memory disorders occur very early in AD, even in the subgroup of very mild patients who did not meet the criteria for dementia. On the other hand, the subgroups differed in terms of responsiveness to cuing by semantic categories: Sensitivity to semantic cues seemed relatively preserved in the early stages and decreased with the progression of the disease.

In conclusion, these different studies as a whole indicate that episodic memory tests are very useful in discriminating preclinical AD patients from normal elderly adults. However, there remain some uncertainties concerning the best discriminatory memory measure to use. Also, the view suggesting that the existence of executive deficits constitutes the best characterization of preclinical AD patients and that indicating the presence of episodic memory disorders remain to be reconciled. Both views are probably correct, but the challenge is to identify tasks that specifically assess each of these cognitive aspects: Indeed, executive processes contribute to performance on numerous episodic memory tasks, and, furthermore, several episodic memory tasks can be realized by using nonepisodic memory processes, such as semantic familiarity.

Interpretation of the Cognitive Deficits

The predictive aspect of episodic memory tasks is consistent with neuropathological and neuroimaging findings showing early changes in medial temporal structures in AD (Fox et al., 1996; Kaye et al., 1997; Kölher et al., 1998; Laakso et al., 1998). For example, in a longitudinal study, Fox et al. (1996) demonstrated that the presence of hippocampal atrophy does exist before AD patients experience memory problems. However, recent studies indicate that episodic memory is subserved by a large network of cerebral regions (including frontal areas, temporo-parietal association cortex, the cerebellum, and the anterior cingulate cortex; Nyberg & Cabeza, 2000; Van der Linden, Meulemans, Marczewski, & Collette, 2000). Consequently, besides atrophy of the hippocampal formation, the episodic memory deficit in early AD could be due not only to an impairment of the various regions involved in episodic memory tasks but also to defective connections between the different regions of the network. Moreover, from a more functional point of view, episodic memory implies the contribution of numerous (general and specific) processes (e.g., selective attention, inhibition abilities, working memory, semantic organization, contextual information processing, metamemory), which can be more or less affected by the disease.

In a recent study (Lekeu et al., 2002), we explored in AD patients the brain correlates of free versus cued recall performance using an adaptation (Van der Linden et al., 2001) of the FCSR procedure developed by Grober & Buschke (1987). This procedure, which ensures semantic processing and matches the cues used at encoding to those used at retrieval, is very sensitive to an early diagnosis of AD and also very useful in characterizing the memory deficits in AD patients (Grober et al., 2000; Tounsi et al., 1999). Statistical parametric mapping (SPM 99) was used to establish clinico-metabolic correlations between performance at free and cued verbal recall and resting brain metabolism in AD patients and normal elderly subjects. The results showed that the patient's performance on free recall was related to metabolic activity in right frontal regions (BA 10 and BA 45), suggesting that performance reflected a strategic retrieval attempt. Poor retrieval performance in AD was attributed to a loss of functional correlation between medial temporal and frontal regions. Indeed, interregional correlations between the right inferior frontal gyrus and whole brain metabolism showed greater correlations in elderly controls than in AD patients with the left middle frontal gyri, right inferior temporal gyrus, right inferior parietal lobule, and left parahippocampal gyrus. Scores of AD patients on the cued recall task were correlated to residual metabolic activity in bilateral parahippocampal regions (BA 36), suggesting that AD patients' performance reflected retrieval of semantic associations without recollection. In conclusion, it appears that memory deficits in early AD patients might be due to a dysfunction affecting the medial temporal structures, as well as to a lack of connectivity between these regions and frontal areas.

Consistently, with the existence of a disconnection problem in AD patients, neuropathological data in AD highlighted a relative isolation of the hippocampal formation from other parts of the brain (Van Hoesen, Hyman, & Damasio, 1991). More generally, the evidence from a number of neuropsychological and neuroimaging studies has suggested that AD can be characterized as a disconnection syndrome (Azari et al., 1992; Leuchter et al., 1992; for a review, see Delbeuck, Van der Linden, & Collette, 2002). For example, Leuchter et al. (1992) demonstrated a loss of connectivity by measuring the coherence of EEG activity and, more specifically, showed that there exists in AD patients a loss of coherence between the activity of anterior and posterior brain regions. In a similar way, PET studies also brought to light decreased interregional correlations in AD, especially between frontal and parietal regions (Azari et al., 1992).

Concerning the existence of early executive dysfunctions in AD patients, two different interpretations may also be proposed. The first one suggests that executive deficits are related to frontal lobe dysfunction (Shallice, 1988) and consequently that AD patients suffer from frontal damage. In this context, Waldemar et al. (1994) observed frontal hypometabolism in 19 out of 25 AD patients. Hypometabolism was found at least in one area of the superior, middle, and orbital regions for each patient. However, the presence of the frontal hypometabolism cannot be related to the disease severity or duration because AD patients with frontal damage are similar to those without on these two measures. The second interpretation considers that executive function requires the integration of information coming from different (anterior and posterior) cerebral areas (Collette & Van der Linden, 2002b; Fuster, 1993; Weinberger, 1993). In that perspective, the existence of a disconnection between different associative areas (see Azari et al., 1992; Leuchter et al., 1992) would lead to a deficient transfer of information, which could explain the difficulties of AD patients in executive tasks requiring rapid and simultaneous processing of different kinds of information (Morris, 1996). Other data supporting a disconnection hypothesis have been obtained by Collette, Van der Linden, Delrue, and Salmon (2002). They explored executive functions in two groups of AD patients: patients with hypometabolism restricted to the posterior (temporal and parietal) cerebral areas and patients with hypometabolism in both posterior and anterior (frontal) cerebral areas. The performance of the AD patients was inferior to control subjects on all executive tasks. However, both groups of patients did not differ from each other, suggesting that frontal lobe hypometabolism is not necessary to produce executive impairment in AD. Finally, a disconnection between cerebral areas could also explain the presence of attentional deficits relatively early in the disease. Indeed, some attentional tasks also require the rapid and simultaneous integration of multiple types of information. Consequently, a disconnection between the frontal and parietal lobes, which are both involved in attentional processes (Coull, Frith, Frackowiak, & Grasby, 1996; Pardo, Fox, & Raichle, 1991), might account for attentional disorders.

Considering the working memory (phonological loop and central executive) deficits observed in AD patients (Collette, Van der Linden, Bechet, et al., 1999), we have proposed a possible trajectory of cognitive impairment in AD, with an early stage being the consequence of disconnection mechanisms. Indeed, in our study, less-demented AD patients showed impairments affecting high-level executive processes as well as the contribution of long-term memory to span performance, whereas the more-demented patients showed deficits involving not only the central executive and the contribution of long-term memory to span performance but also the phonological loop. We suggested that the executive dysfunction observed in less-demented AD patients could be due to a breakdown in connections between the main cortical association areas. As the disease progresses, the neuropathological changes also affect specific cortical areas (and not only connections between them), which could explain the existence of deficits of automatic processes (e.g., of the phonological loop) in the more severely demented patients.

In conclusion, the predictive value of executive and episodic memory tasks in AD would come from an early and prevalent dysfunction of specific brain regions, such as the medial temporal regions which are involved in the realization of these tasks. However, it might also be the consequence of the multicomponent aspect of the tasks, which require the integration of information coming from different cerebral areas, the integration ability being disturbed in AD. Finally, the prevalence of some cognitive deficits in early AD is also consistent with the existence of a heterogeneity of other cognitive deficits, due to the heterogeneity of cortical pathology.

Prediction of AD: Combining Cognitive Factors and Other Factors

Converging evidence shows that AD can be better predicted by using specific executive and episodic memory measures in addition to global measures of cognitive functioning, such as the MMSE (Small, Rabbins, et al., 1997). But further studies are needed to compare the predictive potential of different measures of episodic memory and executive functions and to compare their efficiency both within prescreened or preselected, clinically based subject samples and nonselected, representative, community-dwelling populations.

Moreover, several studies have demonstrated the use of combining cognitive measures with biomedical risk factors of AD, such as APOE (Tierney et al., 1996) and structural (Juottonen et al., 1998; Kaye et al., 1997; Killiany et al., 2000) or functional (Bookheimer et al., 2000; Wagner, 2000) brain abnormalities. Other researchers also reported that the combination of the MMSE and the informant reports resulted in a more accurate prediction than either test alone (e.g., by using the Informant Questionnaire on Cognitive Decline in the Elderly, IQCODE; Mulligan, MacKinnon, Jorm, Giannakopoulos, & Michel, 1996). There also exists evidence that subjective memory complaints may announce dementia within an interval of 3 years (Schmand, Jonker, Hooijer, & Lindeboom, 1996). In addition, Barberger-Gateau, Dartigues, and Letenneur (1993) showed that difficulties in some everyday activities (e.g., ability to use the telephone, use transportation, take responsibility for one's own medication and finances) constitute a strong predictor of the risk of being diagnosed with dementia in the 3 subsequent years and that an increase in dependency between baseline and 3-year follow-up correlates with an increased risk of dementia at a 5-year follow-up.

These findings suggest it is possible to identify subjects with an increased risk of developing AD at very early stages of the disease process by evaluating risk factors in different domains (e.g., formal neuropsychological testing, subjective complaints, informant report, neuroimaging techniques, genetics).

Staging and Tracking AD: Differentiating AD From Non-AD Dementia

In addition to its diagnostic role, another important function of clinical neuropsychology in AD is to distinguish between the different levels of severity and track the disease's progression. A central problem is to determine whether the different patterns of change in cognitive test scores are due to changes in the respective cognitive functions they want to explore or dissimilarities in the tests' measurement properties (e.g., their level of difficulty; Venneri et al., 1996). Thus, it is particularly important to use unified scales across tests, which allow the clinician to identify levels of performance independently of the level of difficulty of each individual test (Capitani & Laiacona, 1988).

The clinical neuropsychologist is also confronted with the test-retest problem and the effect of practice. This effect may erroneously lead to show a flat trajectory of performance, although the patient has actually declined. To prevent the practice effect, it is necessary to have equivalent forms of cognitive tests. It is also important to adopt assessment tools with high test-retest reliability.

Locascio, Growdon, and Corkin (1995) confirmed that tests of episodic memory, including delayed recall, perform best at detecting mild or more severe AD but are less appropriate at staging the disease because of early floor effects. On the other hand, tests of confrontation naming, word fluency, and immediate recognition of geometric figures showed a steady linear decline across time. They are best suited to stage dementia severity. However, it appears that cognitive tests were not as efficient in differentiating stages of AD severity as they were in distinguishing patients from normal control subjects. The authors suggest that the tests that best characterize stages of dementia severity in AD are those that measure cognitive functions depending on higher order cortical areas (and not on the mediotemporal lobe, as episodic memory tests do). Although mediotemporal lobe structures are affected early in the majority of patients, the subsequent spread of AD-type lesions in higher order cortical areas is variable across cases, which explains the weak power of the cognitive tests for staging AD. From a clinical point of view, these findings imply that it is difficult to stratify AD patients according to dementia severity on the basis of specific cognitive tests. They also indirectly support the practice of staging dementia severity by global measures.

Even when dementia has been differentiated from normal cognitive aging, the clinical neuropsychologist is confronted with other diagnostic issues. In particular, AD has to be differentiated from non-AD dementia, especially frontotemporal dementia (FTD), subcortical dementias, and dementia with Lewy bodies. According to Knopman (1993), this differentiation process is possible mainly at the early stages of the disease. In the later stages, the deterioration might become too global to allow any differentiation. Indeed, some degree of overlap clearly exists between the cognitive deficits observed in AD and non-AD patients. However, some recent studies suggest that, by adopting cognitive tests designed to assess the integrity of specific cognitive systems and processes, it is possible to distinguish different types of dementia. For example, Pasquier, Grymonprez, Lebert, and Van der Linden (2001) found specific neuropsychological changes distinguishing AD from FTD patients, especially a higher rate of forgetting in AD patients, a significant improvement of memory performance in FTD patients when appropriate cues are provided at retrieval while free recall was similarly decreased in both groups (adaptation of FCSR; Van der Linden et al., 2001), and a better implicit memory (perceptual priming) performance in FTD patients than in AD patients.

Finally, developments in the rehabilitation of demented patients have confronted the clinical neuropsychologist with another challenge, beyond a strictly diagnostic function. The neuropsychological assessment must also help to understand the nature of the deficits and to identify preserved or residual abilities.

PRESERVED COGNITIVE ABILITIES AND OPTIMIZATION FACTORS

A number of studies have demonstrated the existence of preserved cognitive abilities in AD patients, as well as factors able to enhance their performance. These findings have given a new impulse to the rehabilitation of AD patients. This cognitive approach to rehabilitation would mainly consist in optimizing the patients' functioning by exploiting preserved abilities and factors susceptible to enhance their performance (see chap. 9 of this book).

For example, in the memory domain, converging evidence indicates that AD patients perform poorly on episodic (explicit) memory tests, such as recall or recognition, which require deliberate recollection of specific episodes. However, despite these episodic memory deficits, some studies have also demonstrated that AD patients may show preserved or partially preserved memory abilities in a variety of tasks. In particular, AD patients can exhibit preserved procedural learning, and they can perform normally in some implicit memory tasks, especially perceptual priming tasks (a characteristic of implicit memory tasks is that, contrary to explicit memory tasks, memory is assessed indirectly, without reference to a study episode).

Skill Learning Abilities

Procedural learning refers to the ability to acquire, through repetitive practice, new skills. In neuropsychology, three subclasses of procedural skills have been distinguished: sensorimotor skills, perceptual skills, and cognitive skills. Relatively few studies have investigated these procedural abilities in AD patients.

Sensorimotor Skills. Some studies have shown normal sensorimotor abilities in a group of AD patients with the pursuit-rotor task (Deweer et al., 1994; Heindel, Butters, & Salmon, 1988; Heindel, Salmon, Shults, Walicke, & Butters, 1989), in which the subject learns to maintain the point of a stylus on a target located on a rotating disk. Gabrieli, Corkin, Mickel, and Growdon (1993) have compared performance of a group of AD patients and normal controls in a mirror-tracing task, where subjects were asked to trace a pattern seen through a mirror. They showed that the patients learned the mirror-tracing skill as well as normal subjects did. Hirono et al. (1997) used a bimanual tracing task and showed that the tracing performance of AD patients improved as much as that of control subjects during training.

Other studies have investigated procedural learning with the serial reaction time (SRT) task. In this task, the subject has to respond, in a choice reaction-time situation, to a stimulus that may appear at one of four locations on the screen of a computer. The subject pushes one of four keys, corresponding to the position of the stimulus. Unknown to the subject, the sequence of stimuli within a block of trials corresponds either to a random condition (i.e., the stimuli appear in a pseudorandom order) or to a repeating-sequence condition, in which a sequence of stimuli is continuously repeated. Sequence-specific learning in this task is observed when reaction times for the stimuli belonging to the repeating-sequence blocks (even though the subjects are unaware of the presence of the repeating sequence) become faster than those of the stimuli belonging to the random blocks.

Knopman and Nissen (1987) compared the performance of 28 patients with probable AD to that of a group of normal elderly subjects. They found a similar difference between the reaction times for the repeating sequence and for random trials in the two groups. However, the mean reaction time of the patients was almost twice as slow as that of the normal subjects, an observation that makes the results' interpretation difficult. In another study, Knopman (1991) administered a SRT task to 11 AD patients in two sessions separated by a 1- or 2-week interval. With regard to the sequence learning, results showed better performance levels for normal subjects than for AD patients. For the retention measure, Knopman selected only the 8 patients and the 14 control subjects who showed a significant learning of the sequence during the first session; there was no difference between the two groups with regard to their knowledge of the repeating sequence from one session to the other. Grafman et al. (1990) also administered a SRT task to a group of 12 mild to moderately impaired AD patients. Although their patients showed a sequence learning effect, it was impossible to determine whether it was normal or not because of the absence of a control group (i.e., nondemented matched elderly subjects). Finally, Ferraro, Balota, and Connor (1993) compared elderly control subjects and AD patients with either mild or very mild dementia. Although no difference was observed between the control subjects and the very mildly demented patients, the patients with mild dementia showed virtually no sequence learning.

Perceptual Skills. The most classical task used to assess perceptual skills is the mirror-reading task, which consists of the subject reading words that are either seen in a mirror-reversed view or presented in geometrically transformed script. Deweer, Pillon, Michon, and Dubois (1993) have shown normal mirror-reading performance in AD patients. Likewise, Moscovitch, Winocur, and McLachlan (1986) showed that AD patients could learn to read sentences written in a geometrically transformed script at a similar rate as normal subjects. On the other hand, the AD patients of Grober, Ausubel, Sliwinski, and Gordon's study (1992) could not learn the procedural skill in a mirror-reading task. Heindel, Salmon, and Butters (1991) compared AD patients and elderly controls on an adaptation-level task involving the judgment of weights. In this task, subjects had to assess a standard set of weights following the presentation of either a set of lighter weights (light bias) or a set of heavier weights (heavy bias). Heindel et al. (1991) showed that the weight judgments of both AD patients and normal subjects were significantly influenced by prior exposure to heavier or lighter weights (i.e., they perceived the standard set of weight as heavier following the light bias trials and lighter following the heavy bias trials). And finally, Hirono et al. (1997) showed that AD patients' tactile reading speed of relief Japanese phonograms improved from one learning session to another as fast as that of normal subjects.

Cognitive Skills. Studies aimed at exploring cognitive skills in AD patients are very sparse and have led to contradictory results. Grafman et al. (1990) compared the performance of AD patients to that of depressed patients and normal controls in a task involving the repeated construction of a puzzle map of the United States; AD patients performed significantly worse than the two other groups in this task. On the other hand, Perani et al. (1993) found normal performance levels in AD patients with the same kind of task. In a more recent study, Hirono et al. (1997) compared 20 AD patients and 19 normal subjects in a computerized jigsaw puzzle in which the pieces could not be turned. The authors showed normal learning performance levels for 11 AD patients, whereas the 9 other AD patients failed to complete the task. Hirono et al. (1997) also showed that these nine patients were those who were the most impaired in the other cognitive functions.

It seems clear from these studies that skill learning is generally preserved during the first stages of AD. This suggests that although episodic memory is impaired early in AD, procedural memory is not or less affected by the disease. The procedural memory system makes possible the acquisition and retention of motor, perceptual, and cognitive skills; procedural knowledge is not accessible to conscious recollection and can only be demonstrated indirectly through some form of action.

Jacobs et al. (1999) recently confirmed that AD patients perform normally on the pursuit-rotor task and showed that these preserved procedural learning abilities are observed even in patients presenting an ideomotor apraxia. These data suggest that ideomotor apraxia and procedural learning can be dissociated: according to Jacobs et al., preserved skill learning could depend on frontostriatal systems that are less affected by the disease, whereas apraxic disorders would be the consequence of parietal damage.

In addition, Dick, Hsieh, Dick-Muehlke, Davis, and Cotman (2000) found that AD patients showed as much learning of a gross motor skill (viz., tossing) as healthy older adults when they received constant practice (i.e., when they performed all tosses at only one distance). However, contrary to healthy older adults, they failed to master the task under random practice (i.e., when they performed the tosses at four distances). These findings confirm that AD patients may acquire new skills, but they also indicate that retraining basic activities of everyday life in these patients should emphasize consistency.

In fact, many other questions remain to be investigated. Procedural memory tasks actually differ according to many aspects: They involve mechanisms that are either motor, perceptual, or both; other situations involve more complex cognitive skills, which may interact with other levels of the cognitive functioning, such as executive functions. To date, it is still unclear as to whether AD patients show preserved procedural learning abilities in all the aspects of procedural learning; it is probably more plausible to consider that some skill learning abilities (maybe the perceptual-motor ones) are preserved, whereas others would be impaired—particularly, in certain patients, those skills that also rely on working memory abilities or executive functions. Finally, the relationships between motor episodic memory and procedural memory would also deserve further investigations. In this context, it should be noted that motor episodic memory remains relatively intact in AD (see Dick, 1992).

Another way to explore procedural memory in AD patients is to ask whether some overlearned skills are maintained during the disease. Actually, several studies have documented the maintenance of specific abilities in areas where the patient had reached a high level of expertise before the disease. For example, Beatty, Brumback, and Vonsattel (1997) have described a number of AD patients with intact, complex cognitive skills performed throughout their lives (e.g., painting, trombone or piano playing, canasta or domino playing), in spite of being unable to perform simpler actions. Such observations suggest that extensive practice and the degree of expertise before the disease may render certain cognitive capacities less vulnerable to the dementia process (see also Greiner et al., 1997).

Repetition Priming

Priming refers to the facilitator or biasing effect that exposure to a stimulus has on subsequent processing of the same stimulus.

In a priming task, memory for an item is inferred from changes in the efficiency with which the item is processed when it is repeated or in the efficiency with which it is elicited by appropriate cues. More specifically, to measure repetition priming, stimuli are processed in a study phase, and subsequently the same or related stimuli are processed in a test phase along with unstudied, baseline stimuli. Priming is calculated as the difference in performance with studied and unstudied stimuli. On perceptual priming tests, a target item presented at study is cued at test by its fragmented or perceptually degraded form. On conceptual priming tests, the cue at test is conceptually related to the studied stimulus word, in the absence of any perceptual similarity between them.

The notion that perceptual priming is preserved in AD is generally accepted and is supported by studies on various tasks, including identification of words (e.g., Abbenthuis, Raaijmakers, Raaijmakers, & Van Woerden, 1990) and nonwords (e.g., Keane, Gabrieli, Growdon, & Corkin, 1994), naming of words (e.g., Moscovitch et al., 1986) and pictures (e.g., Gabrieli et al., 1999), lexical decisions (Balota & Ferraro, 1996), or novel pattern drawing (Postle, Corkin, & Growdon, 1996). Perceptual priming is considered dependent on the integrity of perceptual representation systems (PRS) that code information about the structure and form of objects and words and that are mediated by modality-specific cortices. For example, Badgayan (2000) showed that visual-perceptual priming is associated with reduced activation in the extrastriate cortex. The preservation of perceptual priming in AD patients has been interpreted as the consequence of the relative sparing of occipital cortices in AD (Arnold, Hyman, Flory, Damasio, & Van Hoesen, 1991).

More recently, Verfaellie, Keane, and Johnson (2000) revealed a preserved auditory priming in AD patients (in auditory perceptual identification of words), which would reflect the operation of a presemantic, phonological representation system, localized in posterior neocortical areas that are functionally less affected in AD than multimodal association cortices and limbic areas (Arnold et al., 1991). A similar PRS interpretation has also been applied to explain the existence, in AD patients, of a preserved mere exposure effect (referring to the increase of positive attitude that results from the repeated exposure to previously novel stimuli) for faces, despite a severe explicit recognition deficit (Willems, Adam, & Van der Linden, 2002; Winograd, Goldstein, Monarch, Peluso, & Goldman, 1999).

With regard to conceptual priming, several studies showed impaired conceptual priming in AD patients (see Fleischman & Gabrieli, 1998). This deficit has been attributed to damage affecting association cortices that underlie semantic memory. However, conceptual priming impairments are not pervasive in AD. For example, in Vaidya, Gabrieli, Monti, Tinklenberg, and Yesavage's (1999) study, AD patients showed impaired priming in a category-exemplar production task on which priming is measured as the production of more studied than nonstudied exemplars of semantic categories, and normal priming on a word-associate production task is measured as the production of more studied than nonstudied words as a free-association response to specified words. According to Vaidya et al. (1999), the vulnerability of conceptual priming to AD might depend on whether access into semantic memory is direct (such that the test cue guides the retrieval of the target word without any or with few competing response alternatives), or indirect.

Optimization of Memory Performance

Various studies suggest that it is possible to optimize episodic memory performance in AD patients by providing support at both encoding and retrieval—that is, by submitting patients to encoding conditions that give rise to richer, more elaborate, and more distinctive processing of the to-be-memorized material and by reinstating at retrieval the context prevailing during encoding (see Bäckman & Small, 1998; Herlitz, Lipinska, & Bäckman, 1992).

However, the effectiveness of retrieval cues seems particularly efficient when they are generated by the patients themselves during the encoding stage (Lipinska, Bäckman, Mäntylä, & Viitanen, 1994; see also Bird & Kinsella, 1996). Similarly, other studies have shown that motor memory can be improved by involving patients in the generation of the movements to be memorized (Dick, Kean, & Sands, 1989). Furthermore, Hutton, Sheppard, Rusted, and Ratner (1996) revealed that mild to moderate AD patients had a better memory performance for actions they realized themselves than for actions that were described to them. This effect is even stronger if a support is also given at retrieval and if the to-be-realized actions constitute a coherent and goal-oriented sequence (this way, patients can even maintain, for a short period, a complex action made of several goals and subgoals).

In a more recent study, Rusted, Gaskell, Watts, and Sheppard (2000) showed that moderate AD patients can use preestablished schemata (i.e., established knowledge associated with specific scenarios) to aid episodic memory. Finally, the extent to which support may improve memory performance in patients also appears to depend on the severity of dementia (Bäckman & Small, 1998; Herlitz, Adolfsson, Bäckman, & Nilsson, 1991).

Emotion seems to be another factor that could help enhance memory (and attention) performance in AD patients. Indeed, two studies found that emotional arousal is associated with enhanced memory in AD patients, to a similar or quasisimilar extent as in neurologically intact persons (Kazui et al., 2000; Moayeri, Cahill, Jin, & Potkin, 2000). However, Hamman, Monarch, and Goldstein (2000) showed that the memory effect was normal in early AD for positive events but abnormal for unpleasant stimuli. Finally, LaBar, Mesulam, Gitelman, and Weintraub (2000) revealed that in early AD patients as in young and aging controls, emotionally arousing scenes attracted more viewing time and also became the preferential target of the initial visual orientation.

CONCLUSIONS

The neuropsychological concept of AD has changed profoundly in the last 20 years. AD is no longer considered as an accumulation of deficits affecting all domains of cognition identically in each patient. On the contrary, heterogeneity of AD has been clearly demonstrated. However, beyond this heterogeneity, prevalence of some deficits (viz., episodic memory and executive function disorders) has also been shown.

This apparent paradox between the cooccurrence of an important heterogeneity of early AD patients' deficits and a prevalence of executive and episodic memory disorders in most AD patients may be resolved by considering both the nature of the memory and executive tasks and the neuropathological changes in AD. First, it is now clearly established that some brain areas (in particular, the hippocampal formation) are consistently affected in the early stages of AD, which can explain the frequency of episodic memory deficits. In addition, a main characteristic of the executive and episodic memory tasks is that they require a broad range of cognitive processes as well as the integration of information coming from different cerebral areas. Consequently, performance on these tasks can be affected by different types of cognitive deficits, by brain damage situated in different areas, and by a disconnection between these areas. Furthermore, it has also been shown that pathological cerebral changes (other than those affecting hippocampal structures) are heterogeneous, leading to cognitive deficits differing from one patient to another. A direct implication of this heterogeneity is that preserved cognitive abilities in AD patients, specific to each person, exist. In addition to these preserved cognitive processes or systems, several factors have also been identified that permit AD patients to optimize their cognitive performance.

From a clinical viewpoint, these modifications in the neuropsychological view of AD have considerably changed the neuropsychological assessment and rehabilitation practices. Indeed, by using executive and episodic memory tasks (along with other risk factors), it is now possible to identify who will be at risk to develop AD at the very early stages of the disease. Furthermore, it also seems possible to conceive early cognitive interventions in AD patients, which take into account the great heterogeneity of their cognitive deficits. This cognitive approach would mainly consist in optimizing the patients' functioning at each stage of the disease's progression by exploiting preserved abilities and susceptible factors to enhance their performance.

ACKNOWLEDGMENT

F. Collette is a postdoctoral researcher at the Belgian National Fund for Scientific Research.

REFERENCES

Abbenthuis, M. A., Raaijmakers, W. G. M., Raaijmakers, J. G. W., & Van Woerden, J. G. M. (1990). Episodic memory in dementia of the Alzheimer type and in normal aging: Similar impairment in automatic processing. *The Quarterly Journal of Experimental Psychology, 42A*, 569–583.

Adam, S., Van der Linden, M., & Juillerat, A. C. (1999). Exploration des processus contrôlés et automatiques chez des patients atteints de la maladie d'Alzheimer à un stade débutant par le biais de la procédure de dissociation des processus de Jacoby (Abstract). *Revue de Neuropsychologie, 9*, 273–274.

Agnew, S. K., & Morris, R. G. (1998). The heterogeneity of anosognosia for memory impairments in Alzheimer's disease: A review of the literature and a proposed model. *Aging & Mental Health*, 2(1), 7–19.

Albert, M. S. (1996). Cognitive and neurobiological markers of early Alzheimer disease. *Proceedings of the National Academy of Sciences, USA, 93*, 13457–13551.

Arnold, S. E., Hyman, B. T., Flory, J., Damasio, A. R., & Van Hoesen, G. W. (1991). The topographical and neuroanatomical distribution of neurofibrillary tangles and neuritic plaques in the cerebral cortex of patients with Alzheimer's disease. *Cerebral Cortex, 1*(1), 1–6.

Azari, N. P., Rapoport, S. I., Grady, C. L., Schapiro, M. B., Salerno, J. A., Gonzalez-Aviles, A., & Horwitz, B. (1992). Patterns of interregional correlations of cerebral glucose metabolism rates in patients with dementia of the Alzheimer type. *Neurodegeneration, 1*(1), 101–111.

Bäckman, L., & Small, B. J. (1998). Influences of cognitive support on episodic remembering: Tracing the process of loss from normal aging to Alzheimer's disease. *Psychology and Aging, 13*, 267–276.

Bäckman, L., Small, B. J., & Fratiglioni, L. (2001). Stability of the preclinical episodic memory deficit in Alzheimer's disease. *Brain, 124*(1), 96–102.

Baddeley, A. D. (1986). *Working memory*. Oxford, UK: Clarendon Press.

Baddeley, A. D., Bressi, S., Della Sala, S., Logie, R., & Spinnler, H. (1991). The decline of working memory in Alzheimer's disease. A longitudinal study. *Brain, 114*, 2521–2542.

Baddeley, A. D., Della Sala, S., Gray, C., Papagno, C., & Spinnler, H. (1997). Testing central executive functioning with a pencil-and-paper test. In P. Rabbitt (Ed.), *Methodology of frontal and executive function* (pp. 61–80). Hove, UK: Psychology Press.

Baddeley, A. D., Della Sala, S., & Spinnler, H. (1991). The two-component hypothesis of memory deficit in Alzheimer's disease. *Journal of Clinical and Experimental Neuropsychology, 13*, 372–380.

Baddeley, A. D., Logie, R., Bressi, S., Della Sala, S., & Spinnler, H. (1986). Dementia and working memory. *The Quarterly Journal of Experimental Psychology, 38A*, 603–618.

Badgayan, R. J. (2000). Neuroanatomical organization of perceptual memory: An fMRI study of picture priming. *Human Brain Mapping, 10*(4), 197–203.

Balota, D., & Ferraro, F. R. (1996). Lexical, sublexical, and implicit memory processes in healthy young and healthy older adults and in individuals with dementia of the Alzheimer type. *Neuropsychology, 10*(1), 82–95.

Barbeger-Gateau, P., Dartigues, J. F., & Letenneur, L. (1993). Four instrumental activities of daily living scores as a predictor of one-year incident dementia. *Age and Aging, 22*, 457–473.

Beatty, W. W., Brumback, R. A., & Vonsattel, J.-P. G. (1997). Autopsy-proven Alzheimer disease in a patient with dementia who retained musical skill in life. *Archives of Neurology, 54*, 1448–1450.

Belleville, S., Peretz, I., & Malenfant, D. (1996). Examination of the working memory components in normal aging and in dementia of the Alzheimer type. *Neuropsychologia, 34*, 195–207.

Belleville, S., Rouleau, N., & Caza, N. (1998). Effects of normal aging on the manipulation of information in working memory. *Memory and Cognition, 26*, 572–583.

Benson, D. F., & Zaias, B. W. (1991). Progressive aphasia: A case with postmortem correlation. *Neuropsychiatry, Neuropsychological and Behavioral Neurology, 4*, 215–223.

Benton, A. (1965). *Manuel pour l'application du test de retention visuelle. Applications cliniques et expérimentales* (2nd ed.). Paris: Centre de Psychologie Appliquée.

Berthier, M. L., Leiguarda, R., Stacksetin, S. E., Sevlever, G., & Taratuto, A. (1991). Alzheimer's disease in a patient with posterior cortical atrophy. *Journal of Neurology, Neurosurgery, and Psychiatry, 54*, 1110–1111.

Bhutani, G. E., Montaldi, D., Brooks, D. N., & McCulloch, J. (1992). A neuropsychological investigation into frontal lobe involvement in dementia of the Alzheimer type. *Neuropsychology, 6*, 211–224.

Binetti, G., Magni, E., Padovani, A., Cappa, S. F., Bianchetti, A., & Trabucchi, M. (1996). Executive dysfunction in early Alzheimer's disease. *Journal of Neurology, Neurosurgery and Psychiatry, 60*(1), 91–93.

Bird, M., & Kinsella, G. (1996). Long-term cued recall of tasks in senile dementia. *Psychology and Aging, 11*(1), 45–56.

Blessed, G., Tomlinson, B. E., & Roth, M. (1968). The association between quantitative measures of dementia and senile change in the cerebral grey matter of elderly subjects. *British Journal of Psychiatry, 114*, 797–811.

Boller, F., Forette, F., Khatchaturian, Z., Poncet, M., & Chrysten, Y. (1992). *Heterogeneity of Alzheimer's disease.* Berlin, DEU: Springer.

Bookheimer, S. Y., Strojwas, M. H., Cohen, M. S., Saunders, A. M., Pericak-Vance, M. A., Mazziotta, J. C., & Small, G. W. (2000). Patterns of brain activation in people at risk for Alzheimer's disease. *The New England Journal of Medicine, 343*, 450–456.

Braak, H., Braak, E., & Bohl, J. (1993). Staging of Alzheimer-related cortical destruction. *European Neurology, 33*, 403–408.

Brown, L. B., & Storandt, M. (2000). Sensitivity of category cued recall to very mild dementia of the Alzheimer type. *Archives of Clinical Neuropsychology, 15*, 529–534.

Bruyer, R., & Van der Linden, M. (1995). Face processing in Alzheimer's disease. *L'Année Gérontologique / Facts and Research in Gerontology, Supplement 1: Mood and Cognitive Disorders*, 105–118.

Burgess, P. W., & Shallice, T. (1996). Response suppression, initiation and strategy use following frontal lobe lesions. *Neuropsychologia, 34*, 263–273.

Buschke, H., Sliwinski, M. J., Kuslansky, G., & Lipton, R. B. (1997). Diagnosis of early dementia by the Double Memory Test: Encoding specificity improves diagnostic sensitivity and specificity. *Neurology, 48*, 989–997.

Camicioli, R., Howieson, D., Lehman, S., & Kaye, J. (1997). Talking while walking: The effect of a dual task in aging and Alzheimer's disease. *Neurology, 48*, 955–958.

Capitani, E., & Laiacona, M. (1988). Aging and psychometric diagnosis of cognitive impairment: Some considerations on test scores and their use. *Developmental Neuropsychology, 4*, 325–330.

Chapman, L. L., White, D. A., & Storandt, M. (1997). Prose recall in dementia. A comparison of delay intervals. *Archives of Neurology, 54*, 1501–1504.

Collette, F., & Van der Linden, M. (2002a). Attention disorders in degenerative disorders. In P. Zimmerman & M. Leclerq (Eds.), *Applied neuropsychology of attention* (pp. 305–338). Hove, UK: Psychology Press.

Collette, F., & Van der Linden, M. (2002b). Brain imaging of the central executive component of working memory. *Neuroscience & Biobehavioral Reviews, 26*, 105–126.

Collette, F., Van der Linden, M., Bechet, S., & Salmon, E. (1999). Phonological loop and central executive functioning in Alzheimer's disease. *Neuropsychologia, 37*, 905–918.

Collette, F., Van der Linden, M., Delrue, G., & Salmon, E. (2002). *Executive dysfunction in Alzheimer's disease: Frontal hypometabolism or dysconnection process?* Alzheimer Disease and Associated Disorders (in press).

Collette, F., Van der Linden, M., & Salmon, E. (1999). Executive dysfunction in Alzheimer's disease. *Cortex, 35*(1), 57–72.

Collie, A., & Maruff, P. (2000). The neuropsychology of preclinical Alzheimer's disease and mild cognitive impairment. *Neuroscience and Biobehavioral Reviews, 24*, 365–374.

Cosslett, H. B., & Safran, E. M. (1996). Visuospatial functioning. In R. G. Morris (Ed.), *The cognitive neuropsychology of Alzheimer-type dementia* (pp. 193–205). Oxford, UK: Oxford University Press.

Coull, J. T., Frith, C. D., Frackowiak, R. S. J., & Grasby, P. M. (1996). A fronto-parietal network for rapid visual information processing: A PET study of sustained attention and working memory. *Neuropsychologia, 34*, 1085–1095.

Danckert, J., Maruff, P., Crowe, S., & Currie, J. (1998). Inhibitory processes in covert orienting in patients with Alzheimer's disease. *Neuropsychology, 12*, 225–241.

Delbeuck, X., Van der Linden, M., & Collette, F. (2002). *Alzheimer's disease as a disconnection syndrome*. Manuscript submitted for publication.

Della Sala, S., Kinnear, P., Spinnler, H., & Stangalino, C. (2000). Color-to-figure matching in Alzheimer's disease. *Archives of Clinical Neuropsychology, 7*, 571–585.

Della Sala, S., Muggia, S., Spinnler, H., & Zuffi, M. (1995). Cognitive modelling of face processing: Evidence from Alzheimer patients. *Neuropsychologia, 33*, 675–687.

Deweer, B., Ergis, A. M., Fossati, P., Pillon, B., Boller, F., Agid, Y., & Dubois, B. (1994). Explicit memory, procedural learning and lexical priming in Alzheimer's disease. *Cortex, 30*(1), 113–126.

Deweer, B., Pillon, B., Michon, A., & Dubois, B. (1993). Mirror reading in Alzheimer's disease: Normal skill learning and acquisition of item-specific information. *Journal of Clinical and Experimental Neuropsychology, 15*, 789–804.

Dick, M. B. (1992). Motor and procedural memory in Alzheimer's disease. In L. Bäckman (Ed.), *Memory functioning in dementia* (pp. 135–150). Amsterdam: Elsevier.

Dick, M. B., Kean, M.-L., & Sands, D. (1989). Memory for action events in Alzheimer-type dementia. *Brain and Cognition, 9*(1), 71–87.

Dick, M. B., Hsieh, S., Dick-Muehlke, C., Davis, D. S., & Cotman, C. W. (2000). The variability of practice hypothesis in motor learning: Does it apply to Alzheimer's disease? *Brain and Cognition, 44*, 470–489.

Diesfeldt, H. F. A. (1992). Impaired and preserved semantic memory functions in dementia. In L. Bäckman (Ed.), *Memory functioning in dementia* (pp. 227–267). Amsterdam: Elsevier.

Duke, L. M., & Kaszniak, A. W. (2000). Executive control functions in degenerative dementias: A comparative review. *Neuropsychological Review, 10*(2), 75–99.

Elias, M. F., Beiser, A., Wolf, P. A., Rhoda, A., White, R. F., & D'Agostino, R. B. (2000). The preclinical phase of Alzheimer disease. A 22-year prospective study of the Framingham cohort. *Archives of Neurology, 57*, 808–813.

Emery, V. O. B. (1996). Language functioning. In R. G. Morris (Ed.), *The cognitive neuropsychology of Alzheimer-type dementia* (pp. 166–192). Oxford, UK: Oxford University Press.

Ergis, A. M., Van der Linden, M., Boller, F., Degos, J., & Deweer, B. (1995). Mémoire visuo-spatiale à court et à long terme dans la maladie d'Alzheimer. *Neuropsychologia Latina, 1*(1), 18–25.

Fabrigoule, C., Rouch, I., Taberly, A., Letenneur, L., Commenges, D., Mazaux, J. M., Orgogozo, J. M., & Dartigues, J. F. (1998). Cognitive process in preclinical phase of dementia. *Brain, 12*(1), 135–141.

Ferraro, F. R., Balota, D. A., & Connor, L. T. (1993). Implicit memory and the formation of new associations in nondemented Parkinson's disease individuals and individuals with senile dementia of the Alzheimer type: A serial reaction time (SRT) investigation. *Brain and Cognition, 21*(2), 163–180.

Filoteo, J. V., Delis, D. C., Massman, P. J., Demadura, T., Butters, N., & Salmon, D. P. (1992). Directed and divided attention in Alzheimer's disease: Impairments in shifting of attention to global and local stimuli. *Journal of Clinical and Experimental Neuropsychology, 14*, 871–883.

Fisher, N. J., Rourke, B. P., Bieliauskas, L. A., Giordani, B., Berent, S., & Foster, N. L. (1996). Neuropsychological subgroups of patients with Alzheimer's disease. *Journal of Clinical and Experimental Neuropsychology, 18*, 349–370.

Folstein, M. F., Folstein, S. E., & McHugh, P. R. (1975). Mini-mental state. A practical method for grading the cognitive state of patients for the clinician. *Journal of Psychiatric Research, 12*(3), 189–198.

Foster, J. K., Berhmann, M., & Stuss, D. T. (1999). Visual attention in Alzheimer's disease: Simple versus conjoined feature search. *Neuropsychology, 13*, 223–245.

Fox, N. C., Warrington, E. K., Freeborough, P. A., Hartikainen, P., Kennedy, A. M., Stevens, J. M., & Rossor, M. N. (1996). Presymptomatic hippocampal atrophy in Alzheimer's disease. A longitudinal MRI study. *Brain, 119*, 2001–2007.

Franconie, C., Gely-Nargeot, M. C., Van der Linden, M., & Touchon, J. (1998). Hétérogénéité des troubles visuo-perceptifs dans la maladie d'Alzheimer. In M. C. Gely-Nargeot, K. Ritchie, & J. Touchon (Eds.), *Actualités sur la maladie d'Alzheimer et les syndromes apparentés* (pp. 263–272). Marseille, France: Solal.

Fuster, J. M. (1993). Frontal lobes. *Current Opinion in Neurobiology, 3*(2), 160–165.

Gabrieli, J. D. E., Corkin, S., Mickel, S. F., Growdon, J. H. (1993). Intact acquisition and long-term retention of mirror-tracing skill in Alzheimer's disease and in global amnesia. *Behavioral Neuroscience, 107*, 899–910.

Gabrieli, J. D. E., Vaidya, C. J., Stone, M. V., Francis, W. S., Thompson-Shill, S. L., Fleischman, D. A., Tinklenberg, J. R., Yesavage, J. A., & Wilson, R. S. (1999). Convergent behavioral and neuropsychological evidence for a distinction between identification and production forms of repetition priming. *Journal of Experimental Psychology: General, 128*, 479–498.

Gainotti, G., Marra, C., & Villa, G. (2001). A double dissociation between accuracy and time of execution on attentional tasks in Alzheimer's disease and multi-infarct dementia. *Brain, 124,* 731–738.

Galton, C. J., Patterson, K., Xuereb, J. H., & Hodges, J. R. (2000). Atypical and typical presentations of Alzheimer's disease: A clinical, neuropsychological, neuroimaging and pathological study of 13 cases. *Brain, 123,* 484–498.

Grafman, J., Weingartner, H., Newhouse, P. A., Thompson, K., Lalonde, F., Litvan, I., Molchan, S., & Sunderland, T. (1990). Implicit learning in patients with Alzheimer's disease. *Pharmacopsychiatry, 23*(2), 94–101.

Green, J., Morris, J. C., Sandson, J., McKeel, D. W., Jr., & Miller, J. W. (1990). Progressive aphasia: A precursor of global dementia? *Neurology, 40,* 423–429.

Greene, J. D., Hodges, J. R., & Baddeley, A. D. (1995). Autobiographical memory and executive functions in early dementia of Alzheimer type. *Neuropsychologia, 33,* 1647–1670.

Grégoire, J., & Van der Linden, M. (1997). The effect of age on forward and backward digit spans. *Aging, Neuropsychology and Cognition, 4*(2), 140–149.

Greiner, F., English, S., Dean, K., Olson, K. A., Winn, P., & Beatty, W. W. (1997). Expression of game-related and generic knowledge by dementia patients who retain skill at playing dominoes. *Neurology, 49,* 518–523.

Grober, E., Ausubel, R., Sliwinski, L., & Gordon, B. (1992). Skill learning and repetition priming in Alzheimer's disease. *Neuropsychologia, 30,* 849–858.

Grober, E., & Buschke, H. (1987). Genuine memory deficits in dementia. *Developmental Neuropsychology, 3*(1), 13–36.

Grober, E., Lipton, R. B., Hall, C., & Crystal, H. (2000). Memory impairment on free and cued selective reminding predicts dementia. *Neurology, 54,* 827–832.

Hamann, S. B., Monarch, E. S., & Goldstein, F. C. (2000). Memory enhancement for emotional stimuli is impaired in early Alzheimer's disease. *Neuropsychology, 14*(1), 82–92.

Haxby, J. V., Parasuraman, R., Gillette, J., & Raffaele, K. (1991). Selective and divided attention to visual features are impaired in patients with early dementia of the Alzheimer type (Abstract). *Society for Neurosciences Abstracts, 17,* 696.

Heindel, W. C., Butters, N., & Salmon, D. P. (1988). Impaired learning of a motor skill in patients with Huntington's disease. *Behavioral Neuroscience, 102,* 141–147.

Heindel, W. C., Salmon, D. P., & Butters, N. (1991). The biasing of weight judgments in Alzheimer's and Huntington's disease: A priming of programming phenomenon? *Journal of Clinical and Experimental Neuropsychology, 13*(2), 189–203.

Heindel, W. C., Salmon, D. P., Shults, C. W., Walicke, P. A., & Butters, N. (1989). Neuropsychological evidence for multiple implicit memory systems: A comparison of Alzheimer's, Huntington's, and Parkinson's disease patients. *The Journal of Neuroscience, 9*(2), 582–587.

Herlitz, A., Adolfsson, R., Bäckman, L., & Nilsson, L. G. (1991). Cue utilization following different forms of encoding in mildly, moderately and severely demented patients with Alzheimer's disease. *Brain and Cognition, 15*(1), 119–130.

Herlitz, A., Hill, R. D., Fratiglioni, L., & Bäckman, L. (1995). Episodic memory and visuospatial ability in detecting and staging dementia in a community-based sample of very old adults. *Journal of Gerontology: Medical Sciences, 50A,* 107–113.

Herlitz, A., Lipinska, B., & Bäckman, L. (1992). Utilization of cognitive support for episodic remembering in Alzheimer's disease. In L. Bäckman (Ed.), *Memory functioning in dementia* (pp. 73–96). Amsterdam: Elsevier.

Hirono, N., Mori, E., Ikejiri, Y., Imamura, T., Shimomura, T., Ikeda, M., Yamashita, H., Takatsuki, Y., Tokimasa, A., & Yamadori, A. (1997). Procedural memory in patients with mild Alzheimer's disease. *Dementia and Geriatric Cognitive Disorders, 8*, 210–216.

Hodges, J. (1998). The amnestic prodrome of Alzheimer's disease (editorial). *Brain, 121*, 1601–1602.

Hulme, C., Lee, G., & Brown, G. D. A. (1993). Short-term memory impairment in Alzheimer-type dementia: Evidence for separable impairments of articulatory rehearsal and long-term memory. *Neuropsychologia, 34*(2), 161–172.

Hutton, S., Sheppard, L., Rusted, J. M., & Ratner, H. H. (1996). Structuring the acquisition and retrieval environment to facilitate learning in individuals with dementia of the Alzheimer type. *Memory, 4*(2), 113–130.

Isaacs, B., & Kennie, A. T. (1973). The Set Test as an aid to the detection of dementia in old people. *British Journal of Psychiatry, 123*, 467–470.

Ivanoiu, A., Adam, S., Van der Linden, M., Juillerat, A. C., Jacquemin, A., Godfrind, G., Prairial, C., Mulligan, R., George, M., Bechet, S., Salmon, E., & Seron, X. (2000). *Looking for cognitive markers of early Alzheimer's disease.* Paper presented at the meeting of the World Federation of Neurology—Aphasia and Cognitive Disorders Research Group, Praia do Forte, Brazil.

Jacobs, D. H., Adair, J. C., Williamson, D. J. G., Na, D. L., Gold, M., Foundas, A. L., Shuren, J. E., Cibula, J. E., & Heilman, K. M. (1999). Apraxia and motor-skill acquisition in Alzheimer's disease are dissociable. *Neuropsychologia, 37*, 875–880.

Jacoby, L. L. (1991). A process dissociation framework: Separating automatic from intentional uses of memory. *Journal of Memory and Language, 30*, 513–541.

Joanette, Y., Belleville, S., Gely-Nargeot, M.-C., Ska, B., & Valdois, S. (2000). Pluralité des patrons d'atteinte cognitive accompagnant le vieillissement normal et la démence de type Alzheimer. *Revue Neurologique, 156*, 759–766.

Joanette, Y., Ska, B., Poissant, A., & Bélant, R. (1992). Neuropsychological aspects of Alzheimer's disease: Evidence for inter- and intra-function heterogeneity. In F. Boller (Ed.), *Heterogeneity of Alzheimer's disease* (pp. 33–42). Berlin, DEU: Springer-Verlag.

Johnson, J. K., Head, E., Kim, R., Starr, A., & Cotman, C. W. (1999). Clinical and pathological evidence for a frontal variant of Alzheimer disease. *Archives of Neurology, 56*, 1233–1239.

Jorm, A. F. (1986). Controlled and automatic information processing in senile dementia: A review. *Psychological Medicine, 16*(1), 77–88.

Juottonen, K., Laakso, M., Insausti, R., Lehtovirta, M., Pitkanen, A., Partanen, K., & Soininen, H. (1998). Volumes of the entorhinal and perirhinal cortices in Alzheimer's disease. *Neurobiology of Aging, 19*(1), 15–22.

Kanne, S. M., Balota, D. A., Storandt, M., McKeel, D. W., & Morris, J. C. (1998). Relating anatomy to function in Alzheimer's disease: Neuropsychological profiles predict neuropathology 5 years later. *Neurology, 50*, 979–985.

Kaye, J. A., Swihart, T., Howieson, D., Dame, A., Moore, M. M., Karnos, T., Camicioli, R., Ball, M., Oken, B., & Sexton, G. (1997). Volume loss of the hippocampus and temporal lobe in healthy elderly persons destined to develop dementia. *Neurology, 48*, 1297–1304.

Kazui, H., Mori, E., Hashimoto, M., Hirono, N., Imamura, T., Tanimukai, S., Hanihara, T., & Cahill, L. (2000). *British Journal of Psychiatry, 177*, 343–347.

Keane, M. M., Gabrieli, J. D. E., Growdon, J. H., & Corkin, S. (1994). Priming in perceptual identification of pseudowords is normal in Alzheimer's disease. *Neuropsychologia, 32*, 343–356.

Killiany, R. J., Gomez-Isela, T., Moss, M. B., Kikinis, R., Jolesz, F. A., Sandor, T., Tanzi, R., Jones, K., Hyman, B. T., & Albert, M. S. (2000). The use of structural MRI to predict who will get Alzheimer's disease. *Annals of Neurology, 47*, 430–439.

Knight, R. G. (1998). Controlled and automatic memory process in Alzheimer's disease. *Cortex, 34*, 427–435.

Knopman, D. (1991). Long-term retention of implicitly acquired learning in patients with Alzheimer's disease. *Journal of Clinical and Experimental Neuropsychology, 13*, 880–894.

Knopman, D. (1993). The non-Alzheimer degenerative dementias. In F. Boller & J. Grafman, (Eds.), *Handbook of neuropsychology, Vol. 8* (pp. 295–313). Amsterdam: Elsevier.

Knopman, D. S., & Nissen, M. J. (1987). Implicit learning in patients with probable Alzheimer's disease. *Neurology, 37*, 784–788.

Kobayashi, S., Hirota, N., Saito, K., & Utsuyama, M. (1987). Aluminum accumulation in tangle-bearing neurons of Alzheimer's disease with Balint's syndrome in a long-term aluminum refiner. *Acta Neuropathologica, 74*, 47–52.

Köhler, S., Black, S. E., Sinden, M., Szekely, C., Kidron, D., Parker, J. L., Foster, J. K., Moscovitch, M., Winocur, G., Szalai, J. P., & Bronskill, M. J. (1998). Memory impairments associated with hippocampal versus parahippocampal-gyrus atrophy: An MR volumetry study in Alzheimer's disease. *Neuropsychologia, 36*, 901–914.

Koivisto, M., Portin, R., Seinela, A., & Rinne, J. (1998). Automatic influences of memory in Alzheimer's disease. *Cortex, 34*, 209–219.

Laakso, M. P., Soininen, H., Partanen, K., Lehtovirta, M., Hallikainen, M., Hänninen, T., Helkala, E.-L., Vainio, P., & Riekkinen, P. J. (1998). MRI of the hippocampus in Alzheimer's disease: Sensitivity, specificity and analysis of the incorrectly classified subjects. *Neurobiology of Aging, 19*(1), 23–31.

Labar, K. S., Mesulam, M.-M., Gitelman, D. R., & Weintraub, S. (2000). Emotional curiosity: Modulation of visuospatial attention by arousal is preserved in aging and early-stage Alzheimer's disease. *Neuropsychologia, 38*, 1734–1740.

Lafleche, G., & Albert, M. S. (1995). Executive function deficits in mild Alzheimer's disease. *Neuropsychology, 9*, 313–320.

Langley, L. K., Overmier, J. B., Knopman, D. S., & Prod'Homme, M. S. (1998). Inhibition and habituation: Preserved mechanisms of attentional selection in aging and Alzheimer's disease. *Neuropsychology, 12*, 353–366.

Lekeu, F., Van der Linden, M., Chicherio, C., Collette, F., Degueldre, C., Moonen, G., & Salmon, E. (2002). *Brain correlates of performance in a free/cued recall task with semantic encoding in Alzheimer's disease.* Manuscript submitted for publication

Leuchter, A. F., Newton, T. F., Cook, I. A., Walter, D. O., Rosenberg-Thompson, S., & Lachenbruch, P. A. (1992). Changes in brain functional connectivity in Alzheimer-type dementia and multi-infarct dementia. *Brain, 115*, 1543–1561.

Lindsay, D. S., & Jacoby, L. L. (1994). Stroop process dissociation: The relationship between facilitation and interference. *Journal of Experimental Psychology: Human Perception and Performance, 20*, 219–234.

Lines, C. R., Dawson, C., Preston, G. C., Reich, S., Foster, C., & Traub, M. (1991). Memory and attention in patients with senile dementia of the Alzheimer type and in normal elderly subjects. *Journal of Clinical and Experimental Neuropsychology, 13*, 691–702.

Lipinska, B., Bäckman, L., Mäntylä, T., & Viitanen, M. (1994). Effectiveness of self-generated cues in early Alzheimer's disease. *Journal of Clinical and Experimental Neuropsychology, 16*, 809–819.

Locascio, J. J., Growdon, J. H., & Corkin, S. (1995). Cognitive test performance in detecting, staging, and tracking Alzheimer's disease. *Archives of Neurology, 52*, 1087–1099.

Martin, A., Brouwers, P., Lalonde, F., Cox, C., Teleska, P., & Fedio, P. (1986). Towards a behavioral typology of Alzheimer's patients. *Journal of Clinical and Experimental Neuropsychology, 8*, 594–610.

Massman, P. J., Delis, D. C., Filoteo, J. V., Butters, N., Salmon, D. P., & Demadura, T. L. (1993). Mechanisms of spatial impairment in Alzheimer's disease subgroups: Differential breakdown of directed attention to global-local stimuli. *Neuropsychology, 7*(2), 172–181.

Mattis, S. (1976). Mental status examination for organic mental syndrome in the elderly patients. In L. Bellack & T. B. Karasu (Eds.), *Geriatric Psychiatry*. New York: Grune and Stratton.

Miyake, A., Friedman, N. P., Emerson, M. J., Witzki, A. H., & Howerter, A. (2000). The unity and diversity of executive functions and their contributions to complex "frontal lobe" tasks: A latent variable analysis. *Cognitive Psychology, 41*(1), 49–100.

Moayeri, S. E., Cahill, L., Jin, Y., & Potkin, S. G. (2000). Relative sparing of emotionally influenced memory in Alzheimer's disease. *Neuroreport, 11*, 653–655.

Money, E. A., Kirk, R. C., & McNaughton, N. (1992). Alzheimer's dementia produces a loss of discrimination but not increase in rate of memory decay in delayed matching to sample. *Neuropsychologia, 30*(2), 133–143.

Morris, R. G. (1984). Dementia and the functioning of the articulatory loop system. *Cognitive Neuropsychology, 7*(2), 143–157.

Morris, R. G. (1987a). The effect of concurrent articulation on memory span in Alzheimer type dementia. *British Journal of Clinical Psychology, 26*, 233–234.

Morris, R. G. (1987b). Articulatory rehearsal in Alzheimer type dementia. *Brain and Language, 30*, 351–362.

Morris, R. G. (1996). Neurobiological correlates of cognitive dysfunction. In R. G. Morris (Ed.), *The cognitive neuropsychology of Alzheimer-type dementia* (pp. 223–254). Oxford, UK: Oxford University Press.

Moscovitch, M., Winocur, G., & McLachlan, D. (1986). Memory as assessed by recognition and reading time in normal and memory impaired people with Alzheimer's disease and other neurological disorders. *Journal of Experimental Psychology: General, 115*, 331–347.

Mulligan, R., MacKinnon, A., Jorm, A. F., Giannakopoulos, P., & Michel, J. P. (1996). A comparison of alternative methods of screening for dementia in clinical settings. *Archives of Neurology, 53*, 532–536.

Neary, D., Snowden, J. S., Bowen, D. M., Sims, N. R., Mann, D. M. A., Benton, J. S., Northen, B., Yates, P. O., & Davison, A. N. (1986). Neuropsychological syndromes in presenile dementia due to cerebral atrophy. *Journal of Neurology, 49*(2), 163–174.

Nebes, R. D., & Brady, C. B. (1993). Phasic and tonic alertness in Alzheimer's disease. *Cortex, 29*(1), 77–90.

Nestor, P. G., Parasuraman, R., Haxby, J. V., & Grady, C. L. (1991). Divided attention and metabolic brain dysfunction in mild dementia of the Alzheimer's type. *Neuropsychologia, 29*, 379–387.

Nyberg, L., & Cabeza, R. (2000). Brain imaging of memory. In E. Tulving & F. I. M. Craik (Eds.), *The Oxford handbook of memory* (pp. 501–519). Oxford, UK: Oxford University Press.

Oken, B. S., Kishiyama, S. S., Kaye, J. A., & Howieson, D. B. (1994). Attention deficit in Alzheimer's disease is not simulated by an anticholinergic/antihistaminergic drug and is distinct from deficits in healthy aging. *Neurology, 44*, 657–662.

Orgogozo, J.-M., Fabrigoule, C., Rouch, I., Amieva, H., & Dartigues, J.-F. (2000). Prediction and early diagnosis of Alzheimer's disease with simple neuropsychological tests. *International Journal of Geriatric Psychopharmacology, 2*(1), 60–67.

Parasuraman, R., Greenwood, P. M., Haxby, J. V., & Grady, C. L. (1992). Visuospatial attention in dementia of the Alzheimer's type. *Brain, 115*, 711–733.

Pardo, J. V., Fox, P. T., & Raichle, M. E. (1991). Localization of a human system for sustained attention by positron emission tomography. *Nature, 374*(6304), 61–64.

Pasquier, F., Grymonprez, L., Lebert, F., & Van der Linden, M. (2001). Memory impairment differs in frontotemporal dementia and Alzheimer's disease. *Neurocase, 7*(2), 161–171.

Pate, D. S., Margolin, D. I., Friedrich, F. J., & Bentley, E. E. (1994). Decision-making and attentional processes in ageing and in dementia of the Alzheimer's type. *Cognitive Neuropsychology, 11*, 321–329.

Perani, D., Bressi, S., Cappa, S. F., Vallar, G., Alberoni, M., Grassi, F., Caltagirone, C., Cipolotti, L., Franceschi, M., & Lenzi, G. L. (1993). Evidence of multiple memory systems in the human brain: A [18F]FDG PET metabolic study. *Brain, 116*, 903–919.

Perry, R. J., & Hodges, J. R. (2000). Fate of patients with questionable (very mild) Alzheimer's disease: Longitudinal profiles of individual subjects' decline. *Dementia and Geriatric Cognitive Disorders, 11*, 342–349.

Perry, R. J., Watson, P., & Hodges, J. R. (2000). The nature and staging of attentional dysfunction in early (minimal and mild) Alzheimer's disease: Relationships to episodic and semantic memory impairment. *Neuropsychologia, 38*, 252–271.

Petrides, M., & Milner, B. (1982). Deficits in subject-ordered tasks after frontal and temporal lobe lesions in man. *Neuropsychologia, 20*, 249–262.

Postle, B. R., Corkin, S., & Growdon, J. H. (1996). Intact implicit memory for novel patterns in Alzheimer's disease. *Learning & Memory, 3*, 305–312.

Price, B. H., Gurvit, H., Weintraub, S., Geula, C., Leimkhuler, E., & Mesulam, M. (1993). Neuropsychological patterns and language deficits in 20 consecutive cases of autopsy-confirmed Alzheimer's disease. *Archives of Neurology, 50*, 931–937.

Reitan, R. M. (1979). *Manual for administration of neuropsychological test batteries for adults and children*. Tucson, AZ: Reitan Neuropsychological Laboratories.

Rizzo, M., Anderson, S. W., Dawson, J., Myers, R., & Ball, K. (2000). Visual attention impairments in Alzheimer's disease. *Neurology, 54*, 1954–1959.

Robinson-Whelen, S., & Storandt, M. (1992). Immediate and delayed prose recall among normal and demented adults. *Archives of Neurology, 49*(1), 32–34.

Rouleau, N., Belleville, S., & Van der Linden, M. (2001). *Exploration of multiple inhibitory systems and interference in dementia of the Alzheimer type*. Manuscript submitted for publication.

Rusted, J., Gaskell, M., Watts, S., & Sheppard, L. (2000). People with dementia use schemata to support episodic memory. *Dementia and Geriatric Cognitive Disorders, 11*, 350–356.

Salthouse, T. A., & Becker, J. T. (1998). Independent effects of Alzheimer's disease on neuropsychological functioning. *Neuropsychology, 12*, 242–252.

Schmand, B., Jonker, C., Hooijer, C., & Lindeboom, J. (1996). Subjective memory complaints may announce dementia. *Neurology, 46*(1), 121–125.

Scinto, L. F. M., Daffner, K. R., Castro, L., Weintraub, S., Vavrik, M., & Mesulam, M. (1994). Impairment of spatially directed attention in patients with probable Alzheimer's disease as measured by eye movements. *Archives of Neurology, 51*, 682–688.

Shallice, T. (1982). Specific impairments of planning. *Philosophical Transactions of the Royal Society of London B, 298*, 199–209.

Shallice, T. (1988). *From neuropsychology to mental structures.* Cambridge, UK: Cambridge University Press.

Shallice, T., & Burgess, P. (1993). Supervisory control of action and thought selection. In A. D. Baddeley & L. Weiskrantz (Eds.), *Attention: Selection, awareness and control. A tribute to Donald Broadbent* (pp. 171–187). Oxford, UK: Oxford University Press.

Simone, P. M., & Baylis, G. C. (1997). Selective attention in a reaching task: Effects of normal aging and Alzheimer's disease. *Journal of Experimental Psychology: Human Perception and Performance, 23,* 595–608.

Ska, B., Joannette, Y., Poissant, A., Béland, R., & Lecours, A. R. (1990, October). *Language disorders in dementia of the Alzheimer type: Contrastive patterns from a multiple case study.* Abstract of the Academy of Aphasia, 28th Annual Meeting, Baltimore.

Small, B. J., Fratiglioni, L., Vittanen, M., Winblad, B., Bäckman, L. (2000). The course of cognitive impairment in preclinical Alzheimer's disease. Three- and 6-year follow-up of a population-based sample. *Archives of Neurology, 57,* 839–844.

Small, B. J., Herlitz, A., Fratiglioni, L., Almkvist, O., & Bäckman, L. (1997). Cognitive predictors of incident Alzheimer's disease: A prospective longitudinal study. *Neuropsychology, 11,* 413–420.

Small, G. W., Rabbins, P. V., Barry, P. P., Buckholtz, N. S., DeKosky, S. T., & Ferris, S. H. (1997). Diagnosis and treatment of Alzheimer disease and related disorders. *Journal of American and Medical Association, 278,* 1363–1371.

Spieler, D. H., Balota, D. A., & Faust, M. E. (1996). Stroop performance in healthy younger and older adults and in individuals with dementia of the Alzheimer's type. *Journal of Experimental Psychology, 22,* 461–479.

Tierney, M. C., Szalai, J. P., Snow, W. G., Fisher, R. H., Nores, A., Nadon, G., Dunn, E., & St. George-Hyslop, P. H. (1996). Prediction of probable Alzheimer's disease in memory-impaired patients: A prospective longitudinal study. *Neurology, 46,* 661–665.

Tounsi, H., Deweer, B., Ergis, A.-M., Van der Linden, M., Pillon, B., Michon, A., & Dubois, B. (1999). Sensitivity to semantic cuing: An index of episodic memory dysfunction in early Alzheimer disease. *Alzheimer Disease and Associated Disorders, 13*(1), 38–46.

Tulving, E. (1983). *Elements of episodic memory.* Oxford, UK: Oxford University Press

Vaidya, C. J., Gabrieli, J. D. E., Monti, L. A., Tinklenberg, J. R., & Yesavage, J. A. (1999). Dissociation between two forms of conceptual priming in Alzheimer's disease. *Neuropsychology, 13,* 516–524.

Van der Linden, M. (1989). *Les troubles de la mémoire.* Bruxelles, BE: Mardaga.

Van der Linden, M. (1994). Neuropsychologie des syndromes démentiels. In X. Seron & M. Jeannerod (Eds.), *Neuropsychologie humaine* (pp. 558–573). Bruxelles, BE: Mardaga.

Van der Linden, M., Coyette, F., Wijns, C., & les membres du sous-groupe "Mémoire" du GRECO (2001). Elaboration d'une version verbale de la procédure de rappel libre/rappel indicé de Grober et Buschke. In M. Van der Linden, B. Deweer, S. Adam, F. Coyette, & J. Poitrenaud (Eds.), *L'évaluation de la mémoire épisodique: Mise au point et étalonnage de quatre épreuves.* Marseille, France: Solal.

Van der Linden, M., Meulemans, T., Marczewski, P., & Collette, F. (2000). The relationships between episodic memory, working memory, and executive functions: The contribution of the prefrontal cortex. *Psychologica Belgica, 40,* 275–297.

Van Hoesen, G. W. (1997). Ventromedial temporal lobe anatomy, with comments on Alzheimer's disease and temporal injury. *Journal of Neuropsychiatry and Clinical Neuroscience, 9,* 331–341.

Van Hoesen, G. W., Hyman, B. T., & Damasio A. R. (1991). Entorhinal cortex pathology in Alzheimer's disease. *Hippocampus, 1*(1), 1–8.

Venneri, A., Turnbull, O. H., & Della Sala, S. (1996). The taxonomic perspective: The neuropsychological diagnosis of dementia. *Revue Européenne de Psychologie Appliquée, 46,* 179–190.

Verfaellie, M., Keane, M. M., & Johnson, G. (2000). Preserved priming in auditory perceptual identification in Alzheimer's disease. *Neuropsychologia, 38,* 1581–1592.

Wagner, A. D. (2000). Early detection of Alzheimer's disease: An fMRI marker for people at risk. *Nature Neuroscience, 3,* 973–974.

Waldemar, G., Bruhn, P., Kristensen, M., Johnsen, A., Paulson, O. B., & Lassen, N. A. (1994). Heterogeneity of neocortical cerebral blood flow deficits in dementia of the Alzheimer type: A [Tc]-*d,l*-HMPAO SPECT study. *Journal of Neurology, Neurosurgery and Psychiatry, 57,* 285–295.

Wechsler, D. A. (1981). *WAIS-R manual.* New York: Psychological Corporation.

Wechsler, D. A. (1987). *Manual: Wechsler Memory Scale-Revised.* New York: Psychological Corporation.

Wechsler, D. A., & Stone, C. P. (1973). *Manual: Wechsler Memory Scale.* New York: Psychological Corporation.

Weinberger, D. R. (1993). A connectionist approach to the prefrontal cortex. *The Journal of Neuropsychiatry and Clinical Neurosciences, 5,* 241–253.

Welsh, K., Butters, N., Hughes, J., Mohs, R., & Heyman, A. (1991). Detection of abnormal memory decline in mild cases of Alzheimer's disease using CERAD neuropsychological measures. *Archives of Neurology, 48,* 278–281.

Welsh, K., Butters, N., Hughes, J., Mohs, R., & Heyman, A. (1992). Detection and staging of dementia in Alzheimer's disease: Use of the neuropsychological measures developed for the Consortium to Establish a Registry for Alzheimer's Disease. *Archives of Neurology, 49,* 448–452.

Willems, S., Adam, S., & Van der Linden, M. (2002). Normal mere exposure effect with impaired recognition in Alzheimer's disease. *Cortex, 38*(1), 77–86.

Winograd, E., Goldstein, F. C., Monarch, E. S., Peluso, J. P., & Goldman, W. P. (1999). The mere exposure effect in patients with Alzheimer's disease. *Neuropsychology, 13*(1), 41–46.

Zazzo, R. (1974). *Test des deux barrages. Actualités pédagogiques et psychologiques.* Neuchâtel, Switzerland: Delachaux et Nestlé.

4

Assessment: The Multidisciplinary Approach

Reinhild Mulligan
University Hospitals of Geneva

Early detection of dementia and in particular of Alzheimer's Disease (AD) is becoming more important with the development of efficient therapeutic strategies. A precise diagnosis at an early stage may give the patient time to come to terms with the disease, to plan the future, and to start treatment when global functioning can still be maintained over a period of time. Assessment of early dementia in clinical practice is complex and usually requires the following steps:

1. Establishing that dementia is present and excluding other possible explanations for symptoms and behavior
2. Determining the type or cause of dementia and the likely prognosis
3. Determining the patient's current level of disablement in daily living, including the effects of co-morbidity
4. Assessing all the resources available
5. Establishing a management plan adapted to the specific needs of patient and family

In the absence of a biological marker for degenerative dementias, diagnosis must be based on elicited information and analysis of a combination of factors, such as clinical presentation, cognitive profile, complaints and informant reports, neuroimaging techniques, and risk factors. This chapter deals with some important issues in the detection of early dementia, such as memory complaints, changes of cognition in normal cerebral aging, a critical appraisal of the concept of mild cognitive impairment (MCI), possible predictive factors in different types of dementia, the contribution of specialists, and ancillary tests in the overall assessment of these problems.

FROM NORMAL TO PATHOLOGICAL AGING

Memory Complaints: A Predictor of Dementia?

Complaints about everyday memory problems increase with age, with prevalence being 25% to 50%. The validity of such complaints and their relationship with cognitive decline has been a matter of much controversy (for a review, see Jonker, Geerlings, & Schmand, 2000). In the younger old memory complaints are often associated with psychosocial factors, such as depression, anxiety states, personality traits, social isolation, and disabling physical illness (Derouesné, Lacomblez, Thilbault, & Leponcin, 1999; Jorm, Christensen, & Korten, 1997). Memory complaints are also generally associated with the female gender and a low level of education. However, longitudinal studies indicate that memory complaints are a predictor of dementia, with odds ratios varying between 2.6 and 4.1 after a follow-up of at least 2 years. The risk of developing dementia is increased in the highly educated elderly with memory complaints (Jonker et al., 2000) and persons who, in addition to memory complaints, also show objective signs of cognitive impairment (mild cognitive impairment is discussed later in this chapter).

Patients with dementia frequently seem to have no awareness of their problems. The terms *unawareness, lack of insight,* and *anosognosia* are used interchangeably to describe this state, which is defined as a lack of knowledge of the disease, its degree, and its implications (Foley, 1992). The causative mechanism of anosognosia in dementia is still a matter of debate, and biological as well as psychodynamic explanations have been put forward. Studies suggest that anosognosia is not a unitary entity but consists of various subtypes involving deficits in different cognitive domains. Lack of insight also seems to be strongly associated with the degree of cognitive impairment (Zanetti et al., 1999).

Jorm, Christensen, Hendersen, Jacomb, and Mackinnon (1996) found a strong correlation between informant report and severity of cognitive impairment in the patient. Thus, informant report is a useful tool in the assessment of dementia.

Changes in Normal Cerebral Aging

The boundary between normal and pathological aging is difficult to define because cognition is not homogenous in the elderly. Moreover, there is also a large heterogeneity in the performance within different domains of cognition and even within the subsystems of one specific domain, for example, memory. However, some general factors have been identified in normal cerebral aging, which might be important mediators between age and cognition. There is a decrease in the capacity of working memory and information-processing speed as well as problems in the inhibition of nonrelevant information (Van der Linden et al., 1999). Some of the age-related differences in cognition in the elderly may also result from factors such as visual and auditory loss (Baltes & Lindenberger, 1997). Thus, most elderly persons will exhibit mild difficulties in acquiring new information that do not have any repercussions on everyday activities (Petersen, 1995).

Questionable Dementia: The Concepts of Age Associated Memory Impairment, Age Related Cognitive Decline, and Mild Cognitive Impairment

Cognitive impairment without dementia was thought to be a normal consequence of cerebral aging, and various terms, such as *benign senescent forgetfulness* (Kral, 1962), *age-associated memory impairment* (Crook et al., 1986), and *age-related cognitive decline* (American Psychiatric Association, 1994) have been proposed to describe this spectrum of normal cerebral aging. More recently, it was shown, however, that subjects falling into these categories are at an increased risk for developing dementia, with a conversion rate of 10% to 15%. They also show quantitative and qualitative differences in cerebral imaging in comparison to the normal elderly, and they share common biological risk factors with normal elderly people (Ritchie, Artero, & Touchon, 2001). Linking these changes to a pathological process, the concept of mild cognitive impairment (MCI) (Flicker, Ferris, & Reisberg, 1991) was proposed to describe the transitional state between normal aging and dementia. The diagnostic criteria for MCI include (1) memory complaints, (2) normal activities of daily living, (3) normal general cognitive function, (4) abnormal memory for age, (5) absence of dementia. Attempts have also been made to identify predictors for those MCI subjects who will convert to dementia, such as specific difficulties in episodic memory tests, the presence of the allele apolipoprotein E-ε4 and temporal lobe/hippocampal atrophy demonstrated by magnetic resonance imaging volumetric measurements (Petersen et al., 1999; Visser et al., 1999). MCI has become the focus of considerable interest in the United States during the last decade, especially in the context of pharmacological treatment designed to prevent or retard the development of dementia.

However, the clinical usefulness of MCI has been criticized, mainly because of its absence of standardized diagnostic criteria, its lack of conceptual consensus, and the absence of agreement on cognitive testing. Issues such as whether MCI is a prodromal state of AD or whether it encompasses a clinically heterogeneous group, with some subjects at increased risk of dementia due to any cause, are still controversial (Dubois, 2000; Ritchie & Touchon, 2000). The results of two longitudinal studies of MCI are somewhat contradictory (Morris et al., 2001; Petersen et al., 1999). Whereas Petersen and colleagues reported that memory deficits and rate of decline distinguished MCI from control subjects and mild AD and therefore constitutes a distinct clinical entity, Morris and co-workers concluded that MCI represents in fact early stage AD with the typical neuropathological features of AD. These findings underline the necessity to define and clarify preclinical stages of dementia and the importance of early diagnosis.

DEMENTIA

Dementia is a syndrome caused by a disease of the brain, which leads to disturbances in cognition, behavior, personality, and global functioning in everyday activities. Diagnostic criteria for dementia have been promulgated by the World Health Organization (1993) in the *International Classification of Disorders* (ICD-10) and the American Psychiatric Association (1994) within the *Diagnostic and Statistical Manual* (DSM-IV). The latter classification system has been more widely adopted in research and clinical settings. The DSM-IV criteria for dementia of the Alzheimer's type—the most frequent dementia—are shown in Table 2.1 in chapter 2.

Dementia ranks high in current and projected burden of disease estimates in both developed and undeveloping countries (Murray & Lopez, 1997). Although prevalence rates for dementia vary considerably between studies, all indicate that prevalence increases exponentially with age. In a meta-analysis of 22 studies conducted throughout the world, Jorm, Korten, and Henderson (1987) found that, from the age of 60 years, prevalence rates approximately double every 5.1. years and that about 25% of the population older than 85 years is affected.

Dementia has dramatic effects on the lives of those suffering from the disease and on their families. The disorder is also responsible for enormous health care costs, which will increase dramatically in industrialized nations as these societies age (see also chap. 1 of this book).

Classification of Dementia

Table 4.1 shows that dementia may be classified into a variety of subtypes and that numerous diseases can cause dementia.

Degenerative dementia, which represents more than 80% of all dementias, can be grouped into two categories:

- those with predominantly cortical features and without prominent motor signs, such as AD and frontotemporal dementia, and
- those with predominantly subcortical features with prominent motor features, such as dementia due do Parkinson's disease and Huntington's disease.

TABLE 4.1
Classification of Dementias

Vascular dementia	
Mixed dementia	
Degenerative dementias	
With predominantly cortical features:	*With predominantly subcortical features:*
AD	Dementia due to Parkinson's disease
Frontotemporal dementia syndromes	Dementia due to Huntington's disease
Pick's disease	Progressive supranuclear palsy
	With both cortical and subcortical features:
	Lewy body syndromes
	Cortico-basal ganglionic degeneration
Dementia due to general medical conditions	
Traumatic brain injury	
Brain tumors	
Normal-pressure hydrocephalus	
Anoxia	
Infectious disorders	
Endocrine conditions	
Vitamin deficiencies	
Immune disorders	
Substance abuse	
Neurological conditions, such as multiple sclerosis	
Prion diseases (Creutzfeldt-Jakob disease)	
Dementia due to depression → Pseudodementia	

The five most important causes for dementia are AD, vascular dementia, mixed (vascular and degenerative) dementia, dementia with Lewy bodies, and frontotemporal dementia.

Alzheimer's Disease. AD is the major cause of progressive, irreversible dementia in the elderly and accounts for about 60% of all dementias. Its etiology is heterogeneous, and its cause is still unknown. The diagnosis of AD can only made with certainty by autopsy on the basis of evidence of brain atrophy and characteristic histopathological features, including the formation of neurofibrillary tangles in neocortical associative areas, extracellular amyloid deposits (the main constituent of senile plaques), and substantial neuronal loss within the cerebral cortex. These changes affect primarily limbic, paralimibic, and neocortical structures.

The genesis of neuropathological alterations in AD is still a matter of some controversy, in particular the relationship between amyloid aggregation and neurofibrillary degeneration and the role of these substances in the clinical presentation of the disease (Naslund et al., 2000).

Multiple neurochemical deficits have also been found in AD and, in particular, impaired activity of enzymes associated with the synthesis (choline acetyltransferase) and degradation (acetylcholinesterase) of acetylcholine. Treatment strategies based on these deficits and new therapeutic approaches targeting the neuropathological processes are discussed in chapter 6.

The clinical features of AD—age at onset, pattern of neuropsychological and psychiatric symptoms, and progression—are highly variable. This may account for the high rate of diagnostic error in general practice in western European countries (Gifford & Cummings, 1999). Although the diagnostic criteria established by the American Psychiatric Association (1994) and the World Health Organization (1993) have helped to standardize disease classification, they are of limited use for the early diagnosis of AD. The development of the NINCDS-ADRDA criteria (McKhann et al., 1984; see Table 2.2 in chap. 2) has improved diagnosis. However, clinico-neuropathological correlations have shown that case identification on the basis of these criteria has an overall clinical accuracy of only 75%, with sensitivity ranging from 71% to 87% (Lim et al., 1999). Other diagnostic challenges are the differentiation between AD and other types of degenerative dementia and the distinction between AD and vascular dementia, which will be discussed later.

The vast majority of AD cases are sporadic with a late onset; only 5% are familial with autosomal dominant inheritance due to defective function in genes. Three genes have been identified: the amyloid precusor protein gene on chromosome 21, the presinilin gene 1 on chromosome 14, and the presenilin gene 2 on chromosome 1. The onset of the familial forms of AD is often early (between ages 40 and 55), and their course seems to be more rapid (Lovestone, 1999; Selkoe, 2000).

The course of sporadic AD is characterized by an insidious onset and a slow progression, passing through mild, moderate, and severe stages. The Clinical Dementia Rating Scale (Hughes, Berg, Danziger, Coben, & Martin, 1982) and the Global Deterioration Scale (Reisberg, Ferris, De Leon, & Crook, 1982; see Table 2.3 in chap. 2) are widely used to stage dementia. Although memory deficits are typical at onset, other deficits of higher cortical functions may vary considerably from one patient to another, particularly in the early stages of the disease. Psychiatric syndromes, such as anxiety, depression, psychosis, personality changes and behavior problems, are very frequent (Cummings, 2000). Patients may finally develop gait and motor disturbances and eventually become mute and bedridden. The average duration of the illness from onset of symptoms to death is 8 to 10 years.

Several risk factors for AD have been confirmed. These include age, a family history of AD, Down syndrome, and the genotype for apolipoprotein E (apoE; Plassman & Breitner, 1996; Strittmatter, 2000). This gene has three different forms, or alleles, apoE-ε2, apoE-ε3, apoE-ε4, which are encoded on chromosome 19. Each person has two of each allele. Individuals with one ε4 allele have an increased risk of developing AD and those with two (4 alleles have an even greater risk. The ε4 allele is present in approximately 50% of patients with late onset AD, compared with 16% in controls. ApoE genotyping is now commercially available. However, because the positive predictive value of genotyping as a test for dementia is only 13%, it cannot be regarded as a useful method to screen asymptomatic individuals, and its use should be restricted to supporting the clinical diagnosis (Kukull & Ganguli, 2000; Post et al., 1997).

At present, there are no definite known factors that provide protection against AD. However, the following variables are reported to have an inverse association with AD or cognitive impairment over time: a high level of education; presence of the ApoE-ε2 allele; antioxidant substances, such as vitamins E and C, beta-carotene, zinc, and selenium; and the use of nonsteroidal anti-inflammatory drugs (for a review, see Kukull & Ganguli, 2000). The possible neuroprotective effect of estrogen replacement therapy in postmenopausal women and the role of vitamin E in slowing the progress of the disease is under investigation (Sano et al., 1997).

Vascular Dementia. Dementia secondary to cerebrovascular disease is the second most frequent cause of dementia after AD. The current concept of vascular dementia (VaD) includes multiple physiopathological mechanisms related to deficiencies in cerebral blood supply, such as hemorrhage, multiple infarcts, a single strategic infarct, small vessel disease, and chronic hypoperfusion.

In an attempt to standardize diagnosis for vascular dementia, several classification systems have been proposed. The following criteria are the most widely used in clinic and research: the State of California Alzheimer's Disease Diagnostic and Treatment Centers—ADDTC (Chui et al., 1992; see Table 2.9 in chap. 2 of this book); the National Institute of Neurological Disorders and Stroke, with support from the Association Internationale pour la Recherche et l'Enseignement en Neurosciences—NINDS-AIREN (Roman et al., 1993); the DSM-IV (American Psychiatric Association, 1994); and the ICD-10 (World Health Organization, 1993). The diagnostic criteria of these sets differ somewhat, but the main requirements are presence of dementia, evidence of cerebrovascular disease by brain imaging, neurological signs, or all three, and, in the case of

NINDS-AIREN, a clear relationship between the dementia and cerebrovascular disease.

These criteria seem to have a satisfactory specificity: however, their sensitivity has been found to be low (Gold et al., 1997). Moreover, studies have shown that these criteria identify different patient populations and are therefore not interchangeable. Depending on the criteria selected, the prevalence of VaD will thus vary significantly (Chui et al., 2000).

The difficulty in diagnosing VaD is not surprising, considering its different underlying pathogenetic mechanisms. The clinical presentation and the cognitive deficits in particular will depend on factors such as underlying risk factors, the type of cerebrovascular disease, and the size, type, and localization of the cerebral lesion (Gold, Giannakopoulos, & Bouras, 2001). There is also some controversy about the temporal relationship between stroke and cognitive decline, the role of focal neurological signs, and the significance of deep, white matter lesions in vascular dementia (Chui, 2000). Further studies with clinical-pathological correlation are needed to explore the validity of current classification categories for emerging clinical subgroups of vascular dementia. Advances in neuroimaging techniques may also improve the performance of current clinical criteria.

A number of risk factors have been identified for vascular dementia, such as hypertension, stroke, diabetes mellitus, hyperlipidemia, age, male gender, race, heredity, smoking, and cardiac diseases (Skoog, 1994). These factors determine the type of cerebrovascular disease and thus the neuropathology and localization of the brain injury. The treatment or control of modifiable risk factors such as hypertension or hyperlipidemia, or both treatment and control, are effective measures to prevent vascular dementia associated with cerebrovascular disease (Chui, 2000). The issue whether the presence of an ApoE-ε4 allele represents a risk factor for VaD as well as for AD is currently unresolved (Slooter et al., 1997).

Mixed Dementia. This category refers to conditions where both neurodegenerative changes and vascular lesions are present. Although the DSM-IV diagnostic classification for AD excludes cerebrovascular disease, there is now evidence that vascular lesions are found in 10% to 18% of AD patients, and neuropathological modifications typical for AD are found in 55% of patients with vascular dementia (Victoroff, Mack, Lyness, & Chui, 1995). Other studies showed that patients with AD without cardiovascular risk factors have a high incidence of strokes and that a stroke often accelerates the course of early AD (Pasquier & Leys, 1997). It is therefore not surprising that mixed dementia has a significant impact on the accuracy of clinical criteria of AD as well as VaD. Arguments for an association of AD and cerebrovascular disease are the morphological changes of blood vessels in AD and the probable acetylcholine deficiency in both disorders. These findings raise important questions about the concept of mixed dementia. Rather than considering the condition as a simple coexistent of vascular and AD-type lesions, models in which the dynamic interaction between the two processes is recognized are more likely to reflect the actual nature of this disorder (Gold, Giannakopoulos, & Bouras, 1998).

Dementia With Lewy Bodies (DLB). In recent years, DLB has emerged as the second largest subgroup of degenerative dementias after pure AD. It has been estimated to account for about 20% of dementia syndromes in old age.

Lewy bodies are neuronal inclusion bodies that probably do not occur in normal aging. The clinical presentation of Lewy body disease depends on the localization of Lewy body formation, which can affect cortical and subcortical structures and associated neuronal loss. Thus, three clinical Lewy body syndromes have been described: Parkinson's disease, primary autonomic failure, and DLB (see Table 4.2).

International consensus criteria for the diagnosis of DLB have recently been established (McKeith et al., 1996; see Table 2.7 in chap. 2 of this book) and seem to show satisfactory specificity but rather low sensitivity.

The core diagnostic features of DLB are a progressive course of dementia, Parkinsonism, cognitive fluctuations, and recurrent visual hallucinations. The periodicity and amplitude of fluctuations are variable, both between subjects and within the same individual. Visual hallucinations, typically of people or animals intruding into the patient's home, seem to be a reliable feature for discriminating between DLB and AD or vascular dementia. Symptoms of Parkinsonism occur in 50% of the patients. The symptoms are usually mild, with rigidity and bradykinesia followed by hypo- phonic speech, stooped posture, and a slow and shuffling gait. Dementia occurs within 12 month of the onset of extrapyramidal motor symptoms. Early cognitive deficits are characterized by impairment of at-

TABLE 4.2

Clinical Lewy Body Syndromes

Syndrome	*Core Features*	*Pathologic Changes*
Parkinson's disease	Extrapyramidal movement disorder	Degeneration of subcortical neurons (substantia nigra)
Dementia with Lewy bodies	Dementia with Parkinsonism, fluctuations, visual hallucinations	Degeneration of cortical neurons (entorhinal anterior cingulate, insular, temporal, and frontal regions)
Primary autonomic failure	Syncope, orthostatic hypotension	Degeneration of neurons in spinal cord and autonomic ganglia

Note: Adapted from McKeith (2000). Clinical Lewy body syndromes. *Annals of New York Academy of Sciences, 920,* 1–18. Copyright 2001 by ANN Enterprises, Inc. Reprinted with permission.

tention and problem-solving and visuospatial function. Supportive features of DLB are repeated falls, syncope, transient loss of consciousness, and neuroleptic sensitivity. The onset of the disease is early (around 55 years of age). Men seem to be more affected than women, and the survival is significantly shorter than for AD (for a review, see McKeith, 2000; McKeith, Fairbairn, Perry, & Thompson, 1994).

Frontotemporal Dementias. The term frontotemporal dementias covers a heterogeneous group of disorders with variable clinical and histopathological features caused by selective degeneration of the frontal and anterior temporal lobes (Rossor, 2001). The clinical presentation of the disorder depends on the localization of pathological changes. Three main clinical syndromes have been identified: frontotemporal dementia (FTD), progressive nonfluent aphasia (PA), and semantic dementia (SD; see Table 4.3; for a review, see Hodges, 2001). Other rare primary degenerative disorders producing frontal lobe syndrome include Pick's disease, FTD with Parkinsonism, and FTD with motor neuron disease.

FTD is characterized by prominent behavior and personality changes, lack of insight, impaired reasoning, and stereotypical and utilization behavior, reflecting the bilateral involvement of the frontal lobes (see also Table 2.8 in chap. 2 of this book). The cognitive profile is dominated by a frontal dysexecutive syndrome, with deficits in attention, abstraction, planning, and problem solving. Patients are not amnesic, but memory performance is affected by frontal regulatory disturbances (e.g., inattention,

TABLE 4.3

Clinical Frontotemporal Dementia Syndromes

Syndrome	*Core Features*	*Pathologic Changes*
Frontotemporal dementia	Alteration of personality and social behavior, dysexecutive syndrome	Atrophy of the orbitobasal frontal lobe, bilateral and symmetric
Progressive nonfluent dementia	Disorder of expressive language (reduction and perserverations)	Left peri-Sylvian atrophy
Semantic dementia	Loss of meaning of verbal and nonverbal concepts:	Anteriolateral temporal atrophy, asymmetric
	disorder of naming and word comprehension;	left
	difficulty recognizing and naming faces	right

Note: Adapted from Hodges (2001). Frontotemporal dementia (Pick's disease). Clinical features and assessment. *Neurology, 56* (Suppl. 4), 6–10. Copyright 2001 by Lippincott, Williams, and Wilkins. Reprinted with permission.

lack of recall strategies). In contrast, orientation and visuospatial functions are relatively preserved. Patients with PA present with nonfluent spontaneous speech with distortion or word-finding difficulties and phonological errors. Writing and reading difficulties may be associated. Comprehension and other cognitive domains are well preserved in the early stages. Atrophy is asymmetric, involving mainly the left frontotemporal lobes. The main clinical features of SD are a severe naming and word comprehension impairment in the context of fluent, effortless, and grammatical speech and perceptual deficits (prosopagnosia, associative agnosia, or both). Symmetrical bilateral atrophy is most marked in the anterior temporal neocortex. An update and extension of previously published diagnostic criteria for FTD consensus statement (Lund and Manchester Group, 1994) has been proposed recently (Neary et al., 1998).

FTD is thought to be the third most common cause of cortical dementia after AD and DLB. FTD patients are frequently misdiagnosed with AD. The disorder most commonly manifests itself before the age of 65 years; however, sporadic cases with late onset have been described. A positive family history in a first-degree relative has been reported in as many as 50% of patients. Mutations in the tau gene on chromosome 17 and linkage to chromosome 3 have been identified in a few families.

Other Causes of Dementia. A variety of medical conditions can cause dementia (see Table 4.1). Dementia due do treatable etiologies, such as vitamin deficiencies, were thought to be reversible. However, research findings suggest that specific treatment may reduce cognitive impairment in these patients and, in particular, in those with early and mild deficits but that the dementia itself is rarely reversible (Eastley, Wilcock, & Bucks, 2000; Piccini, Bracco, & Amaducci, 1998).

Less common causes of degenerative dementia include dementia in Parkinson's disease, severe alcohol abuse, Creutzfeld-Jakob disease, Huntington's disease, and dementia due to AIDS.

How to Detect and Assess Early Dementia

A two-step procedure has been suggested for the diagnostic procedure of early dementia (Staehelin, Monsch, & Spiegel, 1997). According to this schedule, the primary care physician establishes provisionally the presence of dementia by taking a medical history, gathering information from relatives or friends of the patient, administering cognitive screening tests, and doing a basic laboratory workup. In the second step, specialists examine these patients to confirm the diagnosis of dementia and, after a thorough differential diagnostic process, provide the family physician with recommendations for management. To facilitate this multidisciplinary approach to diagnosis and management of dementia, memory clinics are now widely established. Their role is discussed in chapter 5 of this book.

Investigation at the Primary Health Care Level. The general practitioner (GP) plays a central role in the care of the elderly and the long-term management of those suffering from dementia. Essentially, the GP's contributions include early recognition, cognitive screening, exclusion of possibly reversible and secondary dementia, referral for further assessment, liaison with local resources, development and coordination of a plan of management, follow-up, and consideration of legal issues.

The GP should be aware that normal healthy aging does not mean a loss of intellectual capacities. As mentioned previously, memory complaints are frequent in the elderly and should be evaluated carefully. Informant reports contribute significantly to the prediction of AD (Tierney, Szalai, Snow, & Fisher, 1996) and correlate highly with the stage of the disease (Jorm, Christensen, et al., 1996). A detailed and systematic history should therefore be obtained from the patient and informants about changes in behavior and performance at work (if applicable), in complex hobbies, in activities of daily living (ADL), and instrumental activities of daily living (IADL). Problems in some IADLs, such as handling money, using the telephone, using public transport, and taking medication correctly were reported to be highly predictive for dementia (Barberger-Gateau, Dartigues, & Letenneur, 1993). The onset, duration, and evolution of the problems should also be noted systematically. Information should be obtained about a possible family history of dementia, neurological diseases of the patient, and past and current medication. Drugs known to have important side effects on cognitive capacities, such as tranquilizers, hypnotics, tricyclic antidepressants, and anti-Parkinsonian medication are frequently prescribed in the elderly and should be taken into account.

The physical examination should assess cardiovascular risk factors and other medical and psychiatric conditions—some of them listed in Table 4.1—which could present as dementia. Delirium caused by drugs, dehydration, cerebral hypoperfusion, and infection is frequent in the elderly. As patients with dementia are especially vulnerable to this condition, the detection of chronic confusional states can be difficult because of the overlapping cognitive symptoms in dementia and delirium.

A minimal laboratory workup recommended in AD to exclude possible reversible or secondary dementia is shown in Table 2.4 in chapter 2 of this book.

Failure to identify dementia may result in patients not receiving optimal medical treatment and care. Cognitive screening is therefore a crucial step in the detection of dementia. Although its importance is generally acknowledged by primary care physicians, only about one third of GPs carry out routine cognitive screening in the elderly (Bush, Kozak, & Elsmie, 1997). An ideal cognitive screening test should be quick to administer, easy to score, well tolerated, and acceptable to patients. It should tap early cognitive symptoms of dementia; should be relatively independent of culture, language, and education; and should have a high sensitivity in clinical settings. The Mini-Mental State Examination (MMSE; Folstein, Folstein, & McHugh, 1975) is the most widely used cognitive test in screening for dementia. Its psychometric properties have been found to be satisfactory for moderate to severe dementia, but it has limited use as a screen for early dementia. The MMSE is also affected by education and age, and its administration depends on intact language and sensorimotor abilities (Tombaugh & McIntyre, 1992). Moreover, it does not explore important cognitive domains that may be important in early dementia, such as executive functioning. An alternative or complementary approach to screening is the use of an informant report. The Informant Questionnaire on Cognitive Decline in the Elderly (IQCODE; Jorm, 1994) is the most widely used and studied informant questionnaire. It evaluates the impact of cognitive changes on everyday activities. It is a self-administered instrument that asks an informant about changes in an elderly patient's cognitive performance over the previous years. (For the short version of the IQCODE, see appendix AI). Unlike the MMSE, it is uncontaminated by education, premorbid intelligence, and physical incapacity, and it can be applied in situations where the patient refuses to undergo cognitive testing. It is, however, influenced by noncognitive factors, such as the affective state of the patient and the informant, the quality of their relationship, and the personality of the patient (Jorm, Broe, & Creasey, 1996). Because both instruments perform equally well as screens (Mulligan, Mackinnon, Jorm, Giannakopoulos, & Michel, 1996), the choice of the appropriate instrument will depend on the specific requirements of the case. An MMSE score less than 27 (maximum score, 30 points) and an IQCODE score greater than 3.31 (maximum score, 0) can indicate possible dementia, and further investigations should be carried out.

In a recent study, a combination of both the MMSE and the IQCODE resulted in more accurate prediction of dementia than either test alone (Mackinnon & Mulligan, 1998) and, as objective information is important in the assessment of dementia, both instruments are recommended together for screening.

Screening for depression might also be useful to identify this frequent condition in the elderly. The short version of the Geriatric Depression Scale (Yesavage, Brink, Rose, & Lum, 1983) demonstrated good validity and can be easily administered.

However, it is important to keep in mind that these tests should only be used as screening instruments; none of them can, in themselves, provide a diagnosis or differential diagnosis of dementia. If, for example, the MMSE were applied to a population of 65- to 74-year-old people, the risk of falsely identifying a person as demented would be 93% (Brodaty et al., 1998). Thus, cognitive screening alone can never replace a comprehensive clinical assessment.

Investigation at the Specialist Level. The complexity of detecting and diagnosing early dementia has been mentioned previously. Evaluation at the specialist level usually consists of neuropsychological testing, neurological and psychiatric examination, and neuroimaging and other ancillary tests.

The Contribution of Neuropsychology. A neuropsychological evaluation assesses the following capacities: orientation, the different memory systems, speech and language, visual perception, construction and motor abilities, and executive functions and reasoning. There is evidence that neuropsychological testing can provide higher sensitivity and specificity than any other diagnostic method, in particular for AD (Becker, Boller, Lopez, Saxton, & Mconigle, 1994). Longitudinal studies of normal subjects manifesting subclinical deficits have been particularly useful in identifying neuropsychological tests sensitive to early AD (Masur, Sliwinski, Lipton, Blau, & Crystal, 1994). Despite the heterogeneity of cognitive impairment in AD patients, early deficits have been identified in episodic memory and executive functioning (Small, Herlitz, Fratiglioni, Almkvist, & Backman, 1997). Episodic memory tests under controlled learning conditions with free, cued recall and recognition are particularly sensitive to early AD (Buschke, Sliwinski, Kulansky, & Lipton, 1997). These patients usually show poor free recall, intrusions at cued recall, false recognition, and, in contrast to normal elderly, they are not helped by semantic cues. The predictive aspect of episodic memory deficits is consistent with neuropathological and neuroimaging data showing early changes in the hippocampal volume in AD (Kaye et al., 1997). Other discriminating tasks for AD are those that involve the coordination of dual tasks or simultaneous mental activities, shifting abilities, and self-control activities (Baddeley, Bressis, Della Sala, Logie, & Spinnler, 1991). There is a marked decrease in the performance of AD patients under these conditions in comparison to controls, and the deficits are correlated with disease progression. These tests can therefore be considered as cognitive predictors for AD. The contribution of neuropsychology to the diagnosis of early AD is described in detail in chapter 3 of this book.

The Contribution of Neurology. The neurological examination should search for evidence of focal deficits, such as asymmetric and primitive reflexes and extrapyramidal symptoms. Rigidity, slowness, gait impairment, and difficulties in equilibrium and limb coordination accompany AD at various stages of the disease (Franssen, Souren, Torossian, & Reisberg, 1999). The presence of extrapyramidal features in AD has been reported to predict disease severity and outcome, but the clinical phenomenology and neurobiology of these symptoms in different types of degenerative dementia need clarification (Cummings, 2000; Kurlan, Richard, Papka, & Marshall, 2000). Camicioli, Howieson, Lehman, and Kaye (1997) found that AD patients have a greater risk of falls and injuries than normal elderly subjects and that dual task conditions, such as talking while walking, might contribute to this risk. Cognitive functions of these patients correlated with their performance on baseline motor tasks, suggesting that cognitive and motor performance might be impaired by the same pathological process.

The Contribution of Psychiatry. Psychiatric symptoms and behavioral disturbances are frequent in AD. Prevalence rates for these problems vary considerably because of a lack of consensus for assessment and selection bias in clinical samples. (For a review, see Borson & Raskind, 1997; Cummings, 2000).

There seems to be little correlation between neuropsychiatric symptoms and cognitive deficits. Behavior disturbances usually worsen in the course of the illness and show a fluctuating course. However, the well-established heterogeneity of cognitive deficits can also be observed in the presentation of behavior problems.

Psychosis and psychotic features, such as delusions, hallucinations, and misidentification are reported in 15% to 50% of AD patients. There is some evidence from neuropathological, neurochemical, and functional imaging studies that these patients have more pathological changes in the frontal and temporal regions than those without these symptoms.

Reports of depression rates in AD vary widely, between 2% and 85%. Major depression is reported in about 10%, dysthymia in about 25% and depressive symptoms in approximately 50% of AD patients at some stage of the disease (Borson & Fletcher, 1996). Depression may occasionally be a sentinel manifestation of AD (Visser, Verhey, Ponds, Kester, & Jolles, 2000). Depressed elderly persons may also be more vulnerable to dementia than healthy persons, especially if cognitive deficits do not improve after adequate treatment (Butters et al., 2000). In general, the clinical features of depression in patients with AD are similar to those observed in nondemented depressed elderly individuals. However, major depression in dementia patients seems to be associated with a greater impairment of executive functioning and a higher level of functional disability (Hargrave, Reed, & Mungas, 2000). A slowing in both cognitive and motor processes may distinguish AD from the solely psychomotor retardation in geriatric depression (Nebes, Halligan, Rosen, & Reynolds, 1998). Depressive symptoms have been reported to decrease as the illness advances, either because clinical assessment is no longer possible or because of the inability of the patient to experience integrated emotions. The neurobiological basis in AD depression is not well elucidated yet. Reduced metabolism in temporal-parietal regions, cell loss in the locus ceruleus, and reduction in norepinephrine and serotonin have been described.

An estimated 40% to 50% of patients with dementia experience anxiety, with a higher prevalence among nursing home residents. Anxiety might manifest itself in dementia patients as wandering, anticipatory concern about forthcoming events, screaming, or aggression.

Agitation and aggression are more frequent in moderate to severe dementia. These symptoms represent the most important burden for caregivers and are the main cause for institutionalization. Aggression seems to be significantly associated with psychosis but may also accompany agitation and anxiety (Rapoport et al., 2001). Other clinical correlates for agitation and aggressive behavior have been established, such as pain, acute medical illness, and unskillful care. Functional neuroimaging suggests that agitation and disinhibition correlate with frontal and temporal hypometabolism (Sultzer et al., 1995), but further studies are needed to investigate the neurobiology of these symptoms.

Apathy has emerged as another major behavior problem in AD. Its neuropathological and neurochemical correlates still remain to be defined.

The frequent coexistence of several noncognitive problems in the same patient presents an enormous challenge in the assessment and treatment of these disturbances. The Neuropsychiatric Inventory (Cummings et al., 1994) is a well-validated and widely used instrument for the assessment of behavior problems in dementia. Treatment possibilities of these disorders are discussed in chapters 6, 7, 8 and 9 of this book.

The Contribution of Neuroimaging Techniques. Structural brain imaging using computer tomography (CT) and magnetic resonance imaging (MRI) are required to rule out certain cases of dementia, such as normal pressure hydrocephalus, subdural hematoma, tumor, and cerebrovascular disease (see Table 2.5 in chap. 2 of this book). For the initial assessment of patients with dementia, structural neuroimaging with either a noncontrast CT or MRI scan is now recommended (Knopman et al., 2001). Volumetric measures of the medial temporal lobe, the amygdalo-hippocampal system, or both, in MRI discriminate AD from normal controls. Atrophy in these regions is highly associated with AD, correlates with neuropsychological performance, and seems to have some predictive power for the development of AD in individuals at genetic and cognitive risk for AD. However, hippocampal atrophy is also a feature of other dementias, such as VaD and FTD, and thus not specific to AD.

Functional imaging techniques include single photon emission tomography (SPECT) and positron emission tomography (PET), both of which depend on the administration of radio-isotope-labelled tracers, indicating cerebral blood flow (SPECT) or both blood flow and brain metabolism (PET). PET and SPECT studies have largely confirmed temporal and parietal hypometabolism, hypoperfusion, or both, in patients with AD. Although PET is more precise than SPECT, the latter is more widely used because it is cheaper and easier to perform. Bilateral parietotemporal hypoperfusion is highly indicative of early AD and might even precede clinical symptoms, but hypoperfusion of other areas of the brain does not exclude a diagnosis of AD (Johnson et al., 1998). Because of the lack of standardization in methods of image interpretation, these techniques should be used only for clinical purposes to improve diagnostic accuracy. Currently, they might be particularly useful in differentiating patients with AD from those with FTD, who show frontal and anterior temporal hypofunction.

Activation paradigms using both PET and functional MRI and magnetic resonance spectroscopy are currently indicated for research purposes only (for a review, see Jagust, 2000).

The Contribution of Electroencephalogram (EEG). Carrying out an EEG might be necessary to exclude a number of acute and subacute cerebral conditions and, in particular, seizures. Epidemiological studies have found that the incidence of unprovoked seizures in dementia was 6 to 10 times more than in a reference population, and AD represents 12% of the etiology of epilepsy in the elderly (Sirven, 1998). It is postulated that the alteration of neurons and glia in hippocampal and neocortical areas in AD may promote epileptogenesis. Seizures are difficult to diagnose in AD patients because they might be mistaken for other problems frequently associated with the disease or aging, such as confusional states, syncope, transient ischemic attacks, transient global amnesia, or even vertigo. EEG interpretation in AD patients might be difficult because sharp and spike waves can also be found in demented patients without seizures. Thus, other than recording a seizure, EEG interpretation in these patients remains quantitative and should be used to complement a clinical assessment.

Different EEG patterns distinguish normal aging from AD, with a particularly marked increase in slow-wave activity (both theta and delta) in the latter. These findings have been associated with cholinergic dysfunction, specific cognitive deficits and localized pathophysiological changes (Claus et al., 1998). Discriminating variables in EEG patterns predicting conversion to AD in MCI subjects have also been described (Jelic et al., 2000). However, these findings are not precise enough yet to be of diagnostic value. Quantified sleep EEG may prove to be a more sensitive indicator of cholinergic dysfunctioning in AD—in particular, paradoxical sleep. Changes in paradoxical sleep appear early in AD with an increase of delta and theta activity and a decrease of alpha and beta activity, again most marked in the parietotemporal regions. Moreover, is was found that the degree of slowing in paradoxical sleep is correlated with the degree of cognitive impairment (Hassaina et al., 1997). Thus, the study of paradoxical sleep by EEG might in the future prove to be a sensitive diagnostic marker for early AD.

Other complementary investigations, such as carotide doppler studies, lumbar puncture, and evoked potentials, should be reserved for special cases. As mentioned before, no diagnostic markers, such as presenilin genotyping, cerebrospinal fluid levels, of tau or beta-amyloid protein, have yet demonstrated their usefulness in complementing the clinical assessment in early AD. Although apoE genotyping can be a diagnostic aid in patients with cognitive deficits and in identifying possible responders to drug treatment, it is not recommended in asymptomatic individuals (National Institute on Aging/Alzheimer's Association Working Group, 1996).

CONCLUSION

With recent and promising developments in the treatment and management of dementia, consensus about clinical assessment procedures has increased, and the role of primary care physicians and specialists has become more clearly defined. The most important clinical target in degenerative dementia is the detection and diagnosis of the disorder before the onset of irreversible and progressive cerebral changes. Only an early and accurate diagnosis can ensure the implementation of efficient treatment and management programs. Unfortunately, most of the established diagnostic criteria for dementia are not sensitive enough to identify cases of early dementia. A multidisciplinary approach to dementia is therefore needed to gather all relevant information and results necessary to identify and follow up on at risk individuals and to diagnose those with early dementia. This assessment procedure can be regarded as a puzzle, in which clinical and neuropsychological evaluation, in combination with ancillary tests and the analysis of predictors (risk factors, cognitive factors, genetic constellation, neuroimaging, subjective complaints, informant report, and performance in specific IADL), represent the pieces necessary for the completion of the whole clinical picture.

REFERENCES

American Psychiatric Association. (1994). *Diagnostic and statistical manual of mental disorders* (4th ed.). Washington, DC: Author.

Baddeley, A. D., Bressi, S., Della Sala, S., Logie, R., & Spinnler, H. (1991). The decline of working memory in Alzheimer's disease. A longitudinal study. *Brain, 114*, 2521–2542.

Baltes, P. B., & Lindenberger, K. (1997). Emergence of a powerful connection between sensory and cognitive functions across the adult life span: A new window to the study of cognitive aging. *Psychology and Aging, 12*(1), 12–21.

Barberger-Gateau, P., Dartigues, J. F., & Letenneur, L. (1993). Four instrumental activities of daily living score as a predictor of one-year incident dementia. *Age and Ageing, 22*, 457–463.

Becker, J. T., Boller, F., Lopez, O. L., Saxton, J., & Mconigle, K. L. (1994). The natural history of Alzheimer's disease: Description of study cohort and accuracy of diagnosis. *Archives of Neurology, 51*, 585–594.

Borson, S., & Fletcher, P. M. (1996). Mood disorders. In W. E. Reichman & P. R. Katz (Eds.), *Psychiatric care in the nursing home* (pp. 67–93). New York: Oxford University Press.

Borson, S., & Raskind, M. A. (1997). Clinical features and pharmacologic treatment of behavioral symptoms of Alzheimer's disease. *Neurology, 48*(5, Suppl. 6), 17–24.

Brodaty, H., Clarke, J., Ganguli, M., Grek, A., Jorm, A. F., Khachaturian, Z., & Scherr, P. (1998). Screening for cognitive impairment in general practice: Towards a consensus. *Alzheimer Disease and Associated Disorders, 12*(1), 1–13.

Buschke, H., Sliwinski, M. J., Kulansky, G., & Lipton, R. B. (1997). Diagnosis of early dementia by the Double Memory Test: Encoding specifity improves diagnostic sensitivity and specificity. *Neurology, 48*, 989–997.

Bush, C., Kozak, J., & Elmslie, T. (1997). Screening for cognitive impairment in the elderly. *Canadian Family Physician, 43*, 1763–1768.

Butters, M. A., Becker, J. T., Zmuda, M. D., Mulsant, B. H., Pollock, B. G., & Reynolds, C. F. (2000). Changes in cognitive functioning following treatment of late-life depression. *American Journal of Psychiatry, 157*, 1949–1954.

Camicioli, R., Howieson, D., Lehman, S., & Kaye, J. (1997). Talking while walking. The effect of a dual task in aging and Alzheimer's disease. *Neurology, 48*, 955–958.

Chui, H. (2000). Vascular dementia, a new beginning. Shifting focus from clinical phenotype to ischemic brain injury. *Neurologic Clinics, 18*, 951–977.

Chui, H., Mack, W., Jackson, J. E., Mungas, D., Reed, B. R., Tinklenberg, J., Chang, F. L., Skinner, K., Tasaki, C., & Jagust, W. J. (2000). Clinical criteria for the diagnosis of vascular dementia: A multicenter study of comparability and interrater reliability. *Archives of Neurology, 57*, 191–196.

Chui, H., Victoroff, J. I., Margolin, D., Jagust, W., Shankle, R., & Katzman, R. (1992). Criteria for the diagnosis of ischemic vascular dementia proposed by the State of California Alzheimer's Disease Diagnostic and Treatment Centers. *Neurology, 42*, 473–480.

Claus, J. J., Kwa, V. I., Teunisse, S., Walstra, G. J., van Gool, W. A., & Koelman, L. O. (1998). Slowing on quantitative spectral EEG is a marker for rate of subsequent cognitive and functional decline in early Alzheimer disease. *Alzheimer's Disease and Associated Disorders, 12*, 167–174.

Crook, T., Bartus, R. T., Ferris, S. H., Whitehouse, P., Cohen, G. D., & Gershon, S. (1986). Age-associated memory impairment: Proposed diagnostic criteria and measures of clinical change—Report of a National Institute of Mental Health Work Group. *Developmental Neuropsychology, 2*, 261–276.

Cummings, J. L. (2000). Cognitive and behavioral heterogeneity in Alzheimer's disease: Seeking the neurobiological basis. *Neurobiology of Aging, 21*, 845–861.

Cummings, J. L., Mega, M., Gray, K., Rosenberg-Thompson, S., Carusi, D. A., & Gornbein, J. (1994). The neuropsychiatric inventory. Comprehensive assessment of psychopathology in dementia. *Neurology, 44*, 2308–2314.

Derouesné, C., Lacomblez, L., Thilbault, S., & Leponcin, M. (1999). Memory complaints in young and elderly subjects. *International Journal of Geriatric Psychiatry, 14*, 291–301.

Dubois, B. (2000). Prodromal Alzheimer's disease: A more useful concept than mild cognitive impairment? *Current Opinion in Neurology, 13*, 367–369.

Eastley, R., Wilcock, G. K., & Bucks, R. S. (2000). Vitamin B 12 deficiency in dementia and cognitive impairment: The effects of treatment on neuropsychological function. *International Journal of Geriatric Psychiatry, 15,* 226–233.

Flicker, C., Ferris, S. H., & Reisberg, B. (1991). Mild cognitive impairment in the elderly: Predictors of dementia. *Neurology, 41,* 1006–1009.

Foley, J. M.4 (1992). The experience of being demented. In R. H. Binstrick, S. G. Post, & P. J. Whitehouse (Eds.), *Dementia and aging: Ethics, values, and policy choices* (pp. 30–43). Baltimore: John Hopkins University Press.

Folstein, M. F., Folstein, S. E., & McHugh, P. R. (1975). Mini Mental State: A practical method for grading the cognitive state of patients for the clinician. *Journal of Psychiatric Research, 12,* 189–198.

Franssen, E. H., Souren, L. E. M., Torossian, C. L., & Reisberg, B. (1999). Equilibrium and limb coordination in mild cognitive impairment and mild Alzheimer's disease. *Journal of the American Geriatrics Society, 47,* 463–469.

Gifford, D. R., & Cummings, J. L. (1999). Evaluating dementia screening tests: Methodologic standard to rate their performance. *Neurology, 52,* 224–227.

Gold, G., Giannakopoulos, P., & Bouras, C. (1998). Re-evaluating the role of vascular changes in the differential diagnosis of Alzheimer's disease and vascular dementia. *European Neurology, 40*(11), 121–129.

Gold, G., Giannakopoulos, P., & Bouras, C. (2001). Vascular dementia. In P. Hof & C. Mobbs (Eds.), *Functional neurobiology of aging* (pp. 131–143). San Diego: Academic Press.

Gold, G., Giannakopoulos, P., Montes-Paixao, C., Herrmann, F. R., Mulligan, R., Michel, J. P., & Bouras, C. (1997). The sensitivity and specificity of newly proposed clinical criteria for possible vascular dementia. *Neurology, 49*(3), 690–694.

Hargrave, R., Reed, B., & Mungas, D. (2000). Depressive syndromes and functional disability in dementia. *Journal of Geriatric Psychiatry and Neurology, 13*(2), 72–77.

Hassainia, F., Petit, D., Nielsen, T., Gauthier, S., & Montplaisir, J. (1997). Quantitative EEG and statistical mapping of wakefulness and REM sleep in the evaluation of mild to moderate Alzheimer's disease. *European Neurologist, 37,* 219–224.

Hodges, J. R. (2001). Frontotemporal dementia (Pick's disease). Clinical features and assessment. *Neurology, 56*(Suppl. 4), 6–10.

Hughes, C. P., Berg, L., Danziger, W. L., Coben, L. A., & Martin, R. L. (1982). New clinical scale for staging of dementia. *British Journal of Psychiatry, 140,* 566–572.

Jagust, W. J. (2000). Neuroimaging in dementia. *Neurologic Clinics, 18,* 885–1001.

Jelic, V., Johansson, S. E., Almkvist, O., Shigeta, M., Julin, P., Nordberg, A., Winblad, B., & Wahlund, L. O. (2000). Quantitative electroencephalography in mild cognitive impairment: Longitudinal changes and possible prediction of Alzheimer's disease. *Neurobiology of Aging, 21,* 533–540.

Johnson, K., Jones, K., Holman, B. L., Becker, J. A., Spiers, P. A., Satlin, A., & Albert, M. S. (1998). Preclinical prediction of Alzheimer's disease using SPECT. *Neurology, 50,* 1563–1571.

Jonker, C., Geerlings, M. I., & Schmand, B. (2000). Are memory complaints predictive for dementia? A review of clinical and population-based studies. *International Journal of Geriatric Psychiatry, 15,* 983–991.

Jorm, A. F. (1994). A short form of the Informant Questionnaire on Cognitive Decline in the Elderly (IQCODE): Development and cross-validation. *Psychological Medicine, 24*(1), 145–153.

Jorm, A. F., Broe, G. A., & Creasey, H. (1996). Further data on the validity of the Informant Questionnaire on Cognitive Decline in the Elderly (IQCODE). *International Journal of Geriatric Psychiatry, 11*(2), 131–139.

Jorm, A. F., Christensen, H., Henderson, A. S., Jacomb, P. A., & Mackinnon, A. (1996). Informant ratings of cognitive decline of elderly people: Relationship to longitudinal change on cognitive tests. *Age Ageing, 25*(2), 125–129.

Jorm, A. F., Christensen, H., & Korten, A. E. (1997). Do cognitive complaints either predict future cognitive decline or reflect past cognitive decline? A longitudinal study of an elderly community sample. *Psychological Medicine, 27*(1), 91–98.

Jorm, A. F., Korten, A. E., & Henderson, A. S. (1987). The prevalence of dementia: A quantitative integration of the literature. *Acta Psychiatrica Scandinavica, 76*, 465–479.

Kaye, M. D., Swihart, T., Howieson, D., Dame, A., Moore, M. M., Karnos, T., Camicioli, R., Ball, M., Oken, B., & Sexton, G. (1997). Volume loss of the hippocampus and temporal lobe in healthy elderly persons destined to develop dementia. *Neurology, 48*, 1297–1304.

Knopman, D. S., Dekosy, S. T., Cummings, J. L., Chui, H., Corey-Bloom, J., Relkin, N., Small, G. W., Miller, B., & Stevens, J. S. (2001). Practice parameter: Diagnosis of dementia (an evidence-based review): Report of the Quality Standards Subcommittee of the American Academy of Neurology. *Neurology, 56*, 1143–1153.

Kral, V. A. (1962). Senescent forgetfulness, benign and malignant. *Canadian Medical Association Journal, 86*, 257–260.

Kukull, W. A., & Ganguli, M. (2000). Epidemiology of dementia. Concepts and overview. *Neurologic Clinics, 18*, 923–949.

Kurlan, R., Richard, I. H., Papka, M., & Marshall, F. (2000). Movement disorders in Alzheimer's disease: More rigidity of definition is needed. *Movement Disorders, 15*(1), 24–29.

Lim, A., Tsuang, D., Kukull, W., Nochlin, D., Leverenz, J., McCormick, W., Bowen J., Teri, L., Thompson, J., Peskind, E. R., Raskind, M., & Larson, E. B. (1999). Cliniconeuropathological correlation of Alzheimer's disease in a community-based series. *Journal of the American Geriatrics Society, 47*, 564–569.

Lovestone, S. (1999). Early diagnosis and the clinical genetics of Alzheimer's disease. *Journal of Neurology, 246*(2), 69–72.

Lund & Manchester Groups (1994). Clinical and neuropathological criteria for frontotemporal dementia. *Journal of Neurology, Neurosurgery and Psychiatry, 57*, 416–418.

Mackinnon, A., & Mulligan, R. (1998). Combining cognitive testing and informant report to increase accuracy in screening for dementia. *American Journal of Psychiatry, 155*, 1529–1535.

Masur, D. M., Sliwinski, M., Lipton, R. B., Blau, A. D., & Crystal, H. A. (1994). Neuropsychological prediction of dementia and the absence of dementia in healthy elderly persons. *Neurology, 44*, 1427–1432.

McKhann, G., Drachman, D., Folstein, M., Katyman, R., Price, C., & Stadlan, E. M. (1984). Clinical diagnosis of Alzheimer's disease: Report of the NINCDS/ADRDA Work/Group under the auspices of the Department of Health and Human Services Task Force on Alzheimer's Disease. *Neurology, 34*, 939–944.

McKeith, I. G. (2000). Clinical Lewy body syndromes. *Annals of New York Academy of Sciences, 920*, 1–8.

McKeith, I. G., Fairbairn, A. F., Perry, R. H., & Thompson, P. (1994). The clinical diagnosis and misdiagnosis of senile dementia of Lewy body type (SDLT). *British Journal of Psychiatry, 165*, 324–332.

McKeith, I. G., Galasko, D., Kosaka, K., Perry, E. K., Dickson, D. W., Hansen, L. A., Salmon, D. P., Lowe, J., Mirra, S. S., Byrne, E. J., Lennox, G., Quinn, N. P., Edwardson, J. A., Ince, P. G., Bergeron, C., Burns, A., Miller, B. L., Lovestone, S., Collerton, D., Jansen, E. N., Ballard, C., de Vos, R. A., Wilcock, G. K., Jellinger, K.

A., & Perry, R. H. (1996). Consensus guidelines for the clinical and pathologic diagnosis of dementia with Lewy bodies (DLB): Report of the consortium on DLB international workshop. *Neurology, 47,* 1113–1124.

Morris, J. C., Storandt, M., Miller, J. P., McKeel, D. W., Price, J. L., Rubin, E. H., & Berg, L. (2001). Mild cognitive impairment represents early-stage Alzheimer Disease. *Archives of Neurology, 58,* 397–405.

Mulligan, R., Mackinnon, A., Jorm, A. F., Giannokopoulos, P., & Michel, J. P. (1996). A comparison of alternative methods of screening for dementia in clinical settings. *Archives of Neurology, 53,* 532–536.

Murray, C. J., & Lopez, A. D. (1997). *The global burden of disease.* Cambridge, MA: Harvard University Press.

Naslund, J., Haroutunian, V., Mohs, R., Davis, K. L., Davies, P., Greengard, P., & Buxbaum, J. D. (2000). Correlation between elevated levels of amyloid beta-peptide in the brain and cognitive decline. *Journal of the American Medical Association, 283,* 1571–1577.

National Institute on Aging/Alzheimer's Association Working Group. (1996). Apolipoprotein E genotyping in Alzheimer's disease. *Lancet, 347,* 1091–1095.

Neary, D., Snowden, J. S., Gustafson, L., Passant, U., Stuss, D., Black, S., Freedman, M., Kertersz, A., Robert, P. H., Albert, M., Boone, K., Miller, B. L., Cummings, J., & Benson, D. F. (1998). Frontotemporal lobar degeneration. A consensus on clinical diagnostic criteria. *Neurology, 51,* 1546–1554.

Nebes, R. D., Halligan, E. M., Rosen, J., & Reynolds, C. F. (1998). Cognitive and motor slowing in Alzheimer's disease and geriatric depression. *Journal of the International Neuropsychological Society, 4,* 426–434.

Pasquier, F., & Leys, D. (1997). Why are stroke patients prone to develop dementia? *Journal of Neurology, 244,* 135–142.

Petersen, R. C. (1995). Normal aging, mild cognitive impairment, and early Alzheimer's disease. *The Neurologist, 1,* 326–344.

Petersen, R. C., Smith, G. E., Waring, S. C., Ivnik, R. J., Tangalos, E. G., & Kokmen, E. (1999). Mild cognitive impairment. Clinical characterization and outcome. *Archives of Neurology, 56,* 303–308.

Piccini, C., Bracco, L., & Amaducci, L. (1998). Treatable and reversible dementias: An update. *Journal of Neurological Sciences, 153*(2), 172–181.

Plassman, B. L., & Breitner, J. C. S. (1996). Recent advances in the genetics of Alzheimer's disease and vascular dementia with an emphasis on gene-environment interactions. *Journal of American Geriatrics Society, 44,* 1242–1250.

Post, S. G., Whitehouse, P. J., Binstock, R. H., Bird, T. D., Eckert, S. K., Farrer, L. A., Fleck, L. M., Gaines, A. D., Juengst, E. T., Karlinsky, H., Miles, S., Murray, T. H., Quaid, K. A., Relkin, N. R., Roses, A. D., St George-Hyslop, P. H., Sachs, G. A., Steinbock, B., Truschke, E. F., & Zinn, A. B. (1997). The clinical introduction of genetic testing for Alzheimer disease. An ethical perspective. *Journal of the American Medical Association, 277,* 832–836.

Rapoport, M. V., van Reekum, R., Freedman, M., Streiner, D., Simard, M., Clarke, D., Cohen, T., & Conn, D. (2001). Relationship of psychosis to aggression, apathy and function in dementia. *International Journal of Geriatric Psychiatry, 16*(2), 123–130.

Reisberg, B., Ferris, S. H., De Leon, M. J., & Crook, T. (1982). The Global Deterioration Scale for assessment of primary degenerative dementia. *American Journal of Psychiatry, 139,* 1136–1139.

Ritchie, K., Artero, S., & Touchon, J. (2001). Classification criteria for mild cognitive impairment. A population-based validation study. *Neurology, 56,* 37–42.

Ritchie, K., & Touchon, J. (2000). Mild cognitive impairment: Conceptual basis and current nosological status. *Lancet, 355,* 225–228.

Roman, G. C., Tatemichi, T. K., Erkinjuntti, T., Cummings, J. L., Masdeu, J. C., Garcia, J. H., Amaducci, L., Orgogozo, J. M., Brun, A., Hofman, A., Moody, D. M., O'Brien, M. D., Yamaguchi, T., Grafman, J., Drayer, B. P., Bennett, D. A., Fisher, M., Ogata, J., Kokmen, E., Bermejo, F., Wolf, P. A., Gorelick, P. B., Bick, K. L., Pajeau, A. K., Bell, M. A., De Carli, C., Culebras, A., Korczyn, A. D., Bogousslavsky, J., Hartmann, A., & Scheinberg, P. (1993). Vascular dementia: Diagnostic criteria for research studies. Report of the NINDS-AIREN International Workshop. *Neurology, 43,* 250–260.

Rossor, M. S. (2001). Pick's disease: A clinical overview. *Neurology, 56*(Suppl. 4), 3–5.

Sano, M., Ernesto, C., Thomas, R. G., Klauber, M. R., Schafer, K., Grundman, M., Woodbury, P., Growdon, J., Cotman, C. W., Pfeiffer, E., Schneider, L. S., & Thal, L. J. (1997). A controlled trial of selegiline, alpha-tocopherol, or both as treatment for Alzheimer's disease. The Alzheimer's Disease Cooperative Study. *New England Journal of Medicine, 336,* 1216–1222.

Selkoe, D. J. (2000). The genetics and molecular pathology of Alzheimer's disease: Roles of amyloid and the presenilins. *Neurologic Clinics, 18,* 903–922.

Sirven, J. I. (1998). Epilepsy in older adults: Causes consequences and treatment. *Journal of the American Geriatrics Society, 46,* 1291–1301.

Skoog, I. (1994). Risk factors for vascular dementia. A review. *Dementia, 5,* 137–144.

Slooter, A. J., Tang, M. X., van Duijn, C. M., Stern, Y., Ott, A., Bell, K., Breteler, M. M., Van Broeckhoven, C., & Tatemichi, T. K. (1997). Apolipoproteine E (4 and the risk of dementia with stroke. *Journal of the American Medical Association, 277,* 818–821.

Small, B. J., Herlitz, A., Fratiglioni, L., Almkvist, O., & Backman, L. (1997). Cognitive predictors of incident Alzheimer's disease: A prospective longitudinal study. *Neuropsychology, 11,* 413–420.

Staehelin, H. B., Monsch, A. U., & Spiegel, R. (1997). Early diagnosis of dementia via a two-step screening and diagnostic procedure. *International Psychogeriatrics, 9* (Suppl. 1), 123–130.

Strittmatter, W. J. (2000). Apolipoprotein E and Alzheimer's disease. *Annals of the New York Academy of Sciences, 924,* 91–92.

Sultzer, D. L., Mahler, M. E., Mandelkern, M. A., Cummings, J. L., Van Gorp, W. G., Hinkin, C. H., & Berisford, M. A. (1995). The relationship between psychiatric symptoms and regional cortical metabolism in Alzheimer's disease. *Neuropsychiatry and Clinical Neurosciences, 7,* 476–484.

Tierney, M. C., Szalai, J. P., Snow, G., & Fisher, R. H. (1996). The prediction of Alzheimer disease. The role of patient and informant perceptions of cognitive deficits. *Archives of Neurology, 53,* 423–427.

Tombaugh, T. N., & McIntyre, N. J. (1992). The Mini-Mental State Examination: A comprehensive review. *Journal of the American Geriatric Society, 40,* 922–935.

Van der Linden, M., Hupet, M., Feyereisen, P., Schelstraete, M. A., Bestgen, Y., Bruyer, R., Lories, G., Abdessadek, E. A., & Seron, X. (1999). Cognitive mediators of age-related differences in language comprehension and memory performance. *Aging, Neuropsychology and Cognition, 6*(1), 32–55.

Victoroff, J., Mack, W. J., Lyness, S. A., & Chui, H. C. (1995). Multicenter clinicopathological correlation in dementia. *American Journal of Psychiatry, 152,* 1476–1484.

Visser, P. J., Scheltens, P., Verhey, F. R., Schmand, B., Launer, L. J., Jolles, J., & Jonker, C. J. (1999). Medial temporal lobe atrophy and memory dysfunction as predictors for dementia in subjects with mild cognitive impairment. *Neurology, 246,* 477–485.

Visser, P. J., Verhey, F. R. J., Ponds, R. W., Kester, A., & Jolles, J. (2000). Distinction between preclinical Alzheimer's disease and depression. *Journal of the American Geriatric Society, 48*, 479–484.

World Health Organization. (1993). *The ICD-10 Classification of Mental and Behavioural Disorders. Clinical descriptions and diagnostic guidelines*. Paris: Masson.

Yesavage, J. A., Brink, T. L., Rose, T. L., & Lum, O. (1983). Development and validation of a geriatric depression screening scale: A preliminary report. *Journal of Psychiatric Research, 17*(1), 37–49.

Zanetti, O., Vallotti, B., Frisconi, G. B., Geroldi, C., Bianchetti, A., Pasqualetti, P., & Trabucchi, M. (1999). Insight in dementia: When does it occur? Evidence for a nonlinear relationship between insight and cognitive status. *Journal of Gerontology: Psychological Sciences, 54B*, 100–106.

APPENDIX

Short Form of the Informant Questionnaire on Cognitive Decline in the Elderly (Short IQCODE)

Now we want you to remember what your friend or relative was like 10 years ago and to compare it with what he/she is like now. Below are situations where this person has to use his/her memory or intelligence and we want you to indicate whether this has improved, stayed the same or got worse in that situation over the past 10 years. Note the importance of comparing his/her present performance *with 10 years ago*. So if 10 years ago this person always forgot where he/she had left things, and he/she still does, then this would be considered "Hasn't changed much." Please indicate the changes you have observed by *circling the appropriate answer.*

Compared with 10 years ago how is this person at:

	1	*2*	*3*	*4*	*5*
1. Remembering things about family and friends e.g. occupations, birthdays, addresses	Much improved	A bit improved	Not much change	A bit worse	Much worse
2. Remembering things that have happened recently	Much improved	A bit improved	Not much change	A bit worse	Much worse
3. Recalling conversations a few days later	Much improved	A bit improved	Not much change	A bit worse	Much worse
4. Remembering his/her address and telephone number	Much improved	A bit improved	Not much change	A bit worse	Much worse
5. Remembering what day and month it is	Much improved	A bit improved	Not much change	A bit worse	Much worse
6. Remembering where things are usually kept	Much improved	A bit improved	Not much change	A bit worse	Much worse
7. Remembering where to find things which have been put in a different place from usual	Much improved	A bit improved	Not much change	A bit worse	Much worse
8. Knowing how to work familiar machines around the house	Much improved	A bit improved	Not much change	A bit worse	Much worse

	1	2	3	4	5
9. Learning to use a new gadget or machine around the house	Much improved	A bit improved	Not much change	A bit worse	Much worse
10. Learning new things in general	Much improved	A bit improved	Not much change	A bit worse	Much worse
11. Following a story in a book or on TV	Much improved	A bit improved	Not much change	A bit worse	Much worse
12. Making decisions on everyday matters	Much improved	A bit improved	Not much change	A bit worse	Much worse
13. Handling money for shopping	Much improved	A bit improved	Not much change	A bit worse	Much worse
14. Handling financial matters e.g. the pension, dealing with the bank	Much improved	A bit improved	Not much change	A bit worse	Much worse
15. Handling other everyday arithmetic problems e.g. knowing how much food to buy, knowing how long between visits from family or friends	Much improved	A bit improved	Not much change	A bit worse	Much worse
16. Using his/her intelligence to understand what's going on and to reason things through	Much improved	A bit improved	Not much change	A bit worse	Much worse

Scoring the IQCODE :

To score the IQCODE, add up the score for each question and divide by the number of questions (that is by 16). The result is a score that ranges from 1 to 5. A score of 3 means the the subject is rated on average as "no change." A score of 4 means an average of "a bit worse." A score of 5 means an average of "much worse." A cutting point of 3.31/3.38 achieves a balance of sensitivity and specificity. (For further information on scoring and cutoff points for screening, see Jorm, 1994.)

Note: From "A Short Form of the Informant Questionnaire on Cognitive Decline in the Elderly (IQCODE): Development and Cross-Validation," by A. F. Jorm, 1994, *Psychological Medicine, 24*, pp. 145–153. Copyright 1994 by Cambridge University Press. Reprinted with permission.

5

The Role of Memory Clinics in Diagnosis and Management

Eli J. Jaldow
Juliana Onwumere
Michael D. Kopelman
King's College, University of London
St. Thomas' Hospital, London

THE HISTORY OF MEMORY CLINICS

The first memory clinic was developed in the United States in the mid-1970s. In the United Kingdom, a memory clinic was established at University College Hospital, London, the St. Pancras Clinic, in 1983. The Maudsley Hospital followed in 1984. Currently there are at least 23 memory clinics in the United Kingdom, with clinics in Europe, Australia, and the United States (Sutton et al., 1998; Wright & Lindesay, 1995). Statistics suggest that the number of memory clinics may be on the increase. In a 1995 survey of UK memory clinics, it was found that 60% of memory clinics had been set up in the previous 3 years (Lindesay, 1995).

It is of interest to note that the term *memory clinic* may be somewhat of a misnomer because the majority of clinics are in fact dementia clinics. However, as a term, memory clinic was felt to be more acceptable and less stigmatizing than dementia clinic. There is one notable exception where the term memory clinic may be fully appropriate and that is the Guy's and St. Thomas' memory clinic. A whole range of organic and psychogenic memory difficulties are seen within this clinic, with a diagnosis of dementia found in only approximately 13% of patients (Kopelman & Crawford, 1996).

RATIONALE

Memory clinics in geriatric and psychogeriatric settings were set up with a number of primary aims:

1. To assist in the early diagnosis of dementia.
2. To develop more sensitive measures in detecting dementia.
3. To determine the exact level of impairment.
4. To provide treatment of underlying reversible disease, where applicable.
5. To provide advice to the patients and their caregivers.
6. To provide an accessible pool of participants for research programs.
7. To provide trials of potential therapeutic agents.
8. To educate other health care professionals.

REFERRAL SOURCE AND TYPE OF PATIENTS REFERRED

The majority of referrals to memory clinics come from general practitioners (GPs) and health professionals, with a minority of memory clinics also accepting self-referrals. In a recent survey of British memory clinics, 100% of memory clinics accepted referrals from GPs, with only 17% accepting self-referrals. Further, 70% of the memory clinics surveyed accepted any adult referral, whearas 9% accepted only people over the age of 65. However, the majority of memory clinics reviewed (87%) reported that most of their clients were over 65 years of age (Sutton et al., 1998).

Demographic data suggest that approximately two thirds of the patients seen in memory clinics are female, with a mean age of 72 years (Hill, O'Brien, Morat, & Levy, 1995; Philpot, 1996).

ASSESSMENTS USED AND THEIR PROCEDURES

Most memory clinics assess patients by taking a detailed history and carrying out a physical examination, routine blood tests, and a cognitive assessment. Most memory clinics also carry out neuroimaging studies (e.g., magnetic resonance imaging, computer tomography) and electroencephalography (EEG; Lindesay, 1995; Wright & Lindesay, 1995).

The most frequently used psychometric test within memory clinics is the Mini Mental State Exam (MMSE; Folstein, Folstein, & McHugh, 1975), although some clinics also use the CAMCOG (Cambridge Cognitive Examination; Roth et al., 1986). Overall, the most commonly used diagnostic instruments in British memory clinics are (Sutton et al., 1998) the NART (National Adult Reading Test; Nelson & Willison, 1991), which is used in 52% of cases, and the WAIS-R (Wechsler Adult Intelligence Scale-Revised; Wechsler, 1981), which is used in 48% of cases. The MMSE (Folstein et al., 1975) is used in 52% of these clinics as a screening instrument.

At the St. Thomas's memory clinic, we most often use the following tests, which experience has shown, offer a good first screening of cognitive functioning and can be carried out within about 2 hours:

- **NART,** used to establish premorbid levels of intellectual function;
- **WAIS-R,** used to assess current intellectual function. We tend to use an abbreviated form and prorate overall intelligence scores from that (see Crawford, Mychalkiw, Johnson, & Moore, 1996);
- **Logical Memory** (from the Wechsler Memory Scale-Revised; Wechsler, 1987), which is a measure of verbal recall;
- **Kendrick Object Learning Test** (KOLT), which is a measure of visual recall (Gibson & Kendrick, 1979);
- **Warrington Recognition Memory Test** (Warrington, 1984), used for both verbal and visual recognition memory;
- **Verbal Fluency** (see Spreen & Strauss, 1991), which is a measure of executive function; and
- **Cognitive Estimates** (Shallice & Evans, 1978), which is another measure of executive function.

In addition we routinely ask patients to complete the Beck Depression Inventory (BDI; Beck & Steer, 1993), as a measure of current mood. Where appropriate we offer fuller assessment, to include the complete Wechsler Adult Intelligence Scale-Revised, Wechsler Memory Scale-Revised, Doors and People memory battery (Baddeley, Emslie, & Nimmo-Smith, 1994), Wisconsin Card Sorting (Heaton, Chelune, Talley, Kay, & Curtiss, 1993) and measures of reading and naming (McKenna & Warrington, 1983).

STAFFING AND STAFF PROCEDURES

All memory clinics are multidisciplinary in nature. The core professionals within memory clinics are clinical psychologists, psychiatrists, and physicians/geriatricians. Some clinics also have input from occupational therapists, nurses, speech therapists, and social workers.

All new patients attending a memory clinic are normally encouraged to attend with a caregiver or family member. Patients and their caregivers are normally first seen by a doctor and a psychologist who will carry out a cognitive assessment. The duration of the overall first assessment can range from 1 to 6 hours (Lindesay, 1995; Wright & Lindesay, 1995). Normally, the team will reconvene after the assessment has been completed to discuss their findings and the need for further assessment, or both. This information is then fed back as appropriate to the patient and his or her family or caregivers. Where applicable, a follow-up appointment is scheduled and an appropriate care package is devised.

Memory clinics aim to provide the following:

- Sharing of the diagnosis;
- Practical help on dealing with memory problems;
- Counseling and emotional support to caregivers;
- Referral to appropriate local services; and
- Domicilliary visits by occupational therapists and care staff (Burningham, 1991; Robinson, 1992).

In our clinic at St. Thomas's, patients normally spend about 3 to 4 hours on their first visit. A detailed history is taken first, which is then fed back to the memory team. In our case the team consists of two permanent staff members, a consultant neuropsychiatrist, and clinical psychologist/neuropsychologist. The rest of the team usually consists of a specialist registrar, medical and psychology students, and researchers. Eminent clinicians and scientists from the fields of psychology and medicine have visited the clinic and may often be present with the consent of the patient. Such visits are encouraged because they serve to disseminate knowledge uniquely gained from the memory clinic, as well as publicizing its work.

After feedback and discussion with the memory team, blood tests and brain imaging studies are arranged as appropriate. Cognitive assessment is then carried out, which on average, as noted previously, will take about 2 hours. Preliminary brief feedback of testing is then given to the patient, his or her family or partner, and the care worker. Sometimes further cognitive assessment may have to be scheduled. Patients are normally given a follow-up appointment, 4 to 6 weeks after their first visit, at which time they are given definitive feedback. Because attendees at the memory clinic may often have depression as a primary or secondary diagnosis (see the following section), the memory team will, when necessary, initiate a course of cognitive behavior therapy (CBT), medication, or both. Patients and their caregivers will also be seen for one or two additional sessions, as appropriate, and instructed in ways to manage their memory difficulties.

OUTCOME

The majority of attendees to memory clinics are likely to receive a diagnosis of dementia, with, as noted, the exception of the attendees of the St. Thomas's memory clinic, where dementia was diagnosed in only 13% of patients (Kopelman & Crawford, 1996; see Fig. 5.1). Wright and Lindesay (1995) showed that on average 75% of all memory clinic attendees were diagnosed with dementia, of which the majority, (47%) had Alzheimer's Disease (AD).

Hill et al. (1995) reported that for most patients who attended memory clinics and their families, diagnosis expectations were generally met. However, some people came with expectations of being prescribed drug treatment to alleviate their memory difficulties and halt decline in intellec-

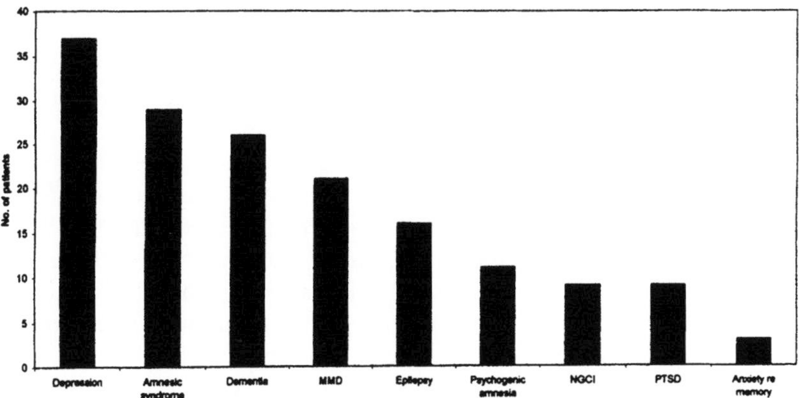

FIG. 5.1. The most common primary diagnoses in the St. Thomas's neuropsychiatry and memory disorders clinic. MMD = moderate memory disorder. NGCI = nonprogressive generalized cognitive impairment. PTSD = post-traumatic stress disorder (adapted from Kopelman & Crawford, 1996).

tual functioning, but these expectations were unlikely to be met. Requests for drug treatment, though, tended to be made by caregivers of the more impaired patients.

FUTURE DEVELOPMENTS

One of the major areas for the future development of memory clinics is the expansion of long-term follow-up of patients and their caregivers. Memory clinics are ideally suited for the setting up and coordination of multidisciplinary outreach teams from both the statutory and voluntary sectors (Lindesay, 1995). These teams consist of community psychiatric nurses, occupational therapists, and social workers, and are trained to work with patients and their caregivers in their homes. The multidisciplinary teams also are in an ideal position to provide continuing psychological support to patients, their caregivers and their families (see Moniz-Cook & Woods, 1997).

There might be a need for pretest counseling because it only occurs in 5% of memory clinics in the British Isles (Lindesay, 1995; Sutton et al., 1998). An explanation of what attendance at the memory clinic would entail (Hill et al., 1995) might also be needed. Particular points that may be raised in such brief sessions are the nature, need, and, particularly, the length of cognitive investigations and how much feedback, if any, patients wish to receive from their assessment.

Reducing waiting times whenever possible and making psychometric testing shorter and more user friendly without impairing accuracy, would alleviate some anxieties voiced by memory clinic attendees. Being faced with tests that directly confront patients' cognitive difficulties can be very stressful and upsetting for patients. Generally, providing more information on the nature and management of dementia, where appropriate, would be welcome by most caregivers and clients (Hill et al., 1995).

Finally, as pointed out by Dukes (1999), the planners and purchasers of mental health services would be well advised to allocate increasing resources to the development of memory clinics because such clinics, by pooling professionals with a range of expertise, will be in an ideal position to offer the best care and management for dementia sufferers and their families in the future. Memory clinics also facilitate the early diagnosis of dementia, thus enabling families to plan care well in advance of serious difficulties. Further, as witnessed by the St. Thomas's memory clinic, memory clinics in the future may need to expand their range to include the treatment and management of memory disorders in general, alongside that of dementia.

SUMMARY

Memory clinics have been shown to be in an ideal position to offer the following:

1. The early diagnosis of memory difficulties;
2. Treatment of reversible causes of memory problems;
3. Initiation and provision of care packages for patients and caregivers;
4. Provision of psychological support to patients and families;
5. Education of mental health professionals; and
6. Research, including trials of antidementia drugs.

With the predicted growth in the number of older adults and the concomitant increase in dementia sufferers, the significance of memory clinics in provision of appropriate diagnoses, care, and management will undoubtedly increase. In the final analysis, however, memory clinics exist to foster a humane and caring approach to the devastating effects of memory disorders of whatever cause—organic or psychogenic, static or progressive—which can have lasting repercussions on sufferers and their loved ones.

REFERENCES

Baddeley, A., Emslie, H., & Nimmo-Smith, I. (1994). *Doors and people.* Bury St. Edmunds, UK: Thames Valley Test Company.

Beck, A. T., & Steer, R. A. (1993). *Beck Depression Inventory.* San Antonio, TX: The Psychological Corporation, Harcourt Brace and Company.

Burningham, S. (1991). Good practice: Cardiff community memory project. *Alzheimer's Disease Society Newsletter,* 8.

Crawford, J. R., Mychalkiw, B., Johnson, D. A., & Moore, J. W. (1996). WAIS-R short-forms: Criterion validity in healthy and clinical samples. *British Journal of Clinical Psychology, 35,* 638–640.

Dukes, C. (1999). Thanks for the memory. *Medical Interface,* 17–19.

Folstein, M. F., Folstein, S. E., & McHugh, P. R. (1975). Mini-mental state. *Journal of Psychiatric Research, 12,* 189–198.

Gibson, A. J., & Kendrick, D. C. (1979). *The Kendrick battery for the detection of dementia in the elderly.* Windsor, UK: NFER Publishing Company Ltd.

Heaton, R. K., Chelune, G. J., Talley, J. L., Kay, G. G., & Curtiss, G. (1993). *Wisconsin Card Sorting Test.* Odessa, FL: Psychological Assessment Resources, Inc.

Hill, K., O'Brien, J., Morat, N. J., & Levy, R. (1995). User expectations of a memory clinic. Clinical Psychology Forum. *The British Psychological Society, 83,* 9–11.

Kopelman, M., & Crawford, S. (1996). Not all memory clinics are dementia clinics. *Neuropsychological Rehabilitation, 6(3),* 187–202.

Lindesay, J. (1995). Memory clinics: Past, present and future. *Alzheimer's Review, 5,* 97–100.

McKenna, P., & Warrington, E. K. (1983). *Graded Naming Test.* Windsor, UK: NFER-NELSON Publishing Company Ltd.

Moniz-Cook, E., & Woods, R. T. (1997). The role of memory clinics and psychosocial intervention in the early stages of dementia. *International Journal of Geriatric Psychiatry, 12,* 1143–1145.

Nelson, H. E., & Willison J. R. (1991). *National Adult Reading Test (NART).* Berkshire, UK: NFER-NELSON Publishing Company Ltd.

Philpot, M. (1996). The Maudsley hospital memory clinic. *International Journal of Geriatric Psychiatry, 11,* 305–308.

Robinson, S. (1992). Occupational therapy in a memory clinic. *British Journal of Occupational Therapy, 55,* 394–396.

Roth, M., Tym, C., Mountjoy, L. Q., Huppert, F. A., Hendrie, M., Verma, S., & Goddard, R. (1986). CAMDEX—a standardised instrument for the diagnosis of mental disorders in the elderly. *British Journal of Psychiatry, 149,* 698–709.

Shallice, T., & Evans, M. E. (1978). The involvement of the frontal lobes in cognitive estimation. *Cortex, 14,* 294–303.

Spreen, O., & Strauss, E. (1991). *A compendium of neuropsychological tests.* Oxford, UK: Oxford University Press.

Sutton, L., Bucks, R., Moniz-Cook, E., Lamers, C., Royan, L., & Woods, B. (1998). Newsletter, Psychologist's Special Interest Group in Elderly People. *The British Psychological Society, 63,* 2–38.

Warrington, E. K. (1984). *Recognition Memory Test.* Windsor, UK: NFER-NELSON Publishing Company Ltd.

Wechsler, D. (1981). *Wechsler Adult Intelligence Scale-Revised.* San Antonio, TX: The Psychological Corporation. Harcourt Brace Jovanovich, Inc.

Wechsler, D. (1987). *Wechsler Memory Scale-Revised.* San Antonio, TX: The Psychological Corporation. Harcourt Brace Jovanovich, Inc.

Wright, N., & Lindesay, J. (1995). A survey of memory clinics in the British Isles. *International Journal of Geriatric Psychiatry, 10,* 379–385.

6

Pharmacological Treatment: Recent Developments

Ezio Giacobini
University Hospitals of Geneva

DEVELOPMENT OF CHOLINESTERASE INHIBITORS IN ALZHEIMER'S THERAPY

Currently, cholinesterase inhibitors (ChEI) represent the treatment of choice for Alzheimer's Disease (AD) (Fig. 6.1). Following the 1980s introduction of a first generation of drugs such as physostigmine and tacrine, a second generation of more suitable compounds was developed in the 1990s. These drugs are clinically more efficacious and produce less severe side effects at effective doses.

Contrary to the discovery of other neurotransmitter-based CNS drugs such as neuroleptics, tricyclic antidepressants, and anxiolytics, the clinical application of ChEI in the treatment of cognitive deficits in AD was neither accidental nor serendipitous. Its rationale was solidly founded on data derived from experimental physiology and behavioral pharmacology of the cholinergic system in animals and humans. Clinical results on the effect of these drugs on cognition (memory, attention, and concentration) and more recently on behavioral symptoms in AD (apathy, hallucinations, and motor agitation) confirmed predictions of potential clinical efficacy based on laboratory data.

The first ChEI to be used against AD was physostigmine, administered under various modes (Davis & Mohs, 1979) and followed by oral tacrine (Summer, Viesselman, Marsh, & Candelora, 1981). Subsequently, metrifonate (Becker & Giacobini, 1988) and galantamine (Rainer, Mark, & Haushofer, 1989) were also tested orally.

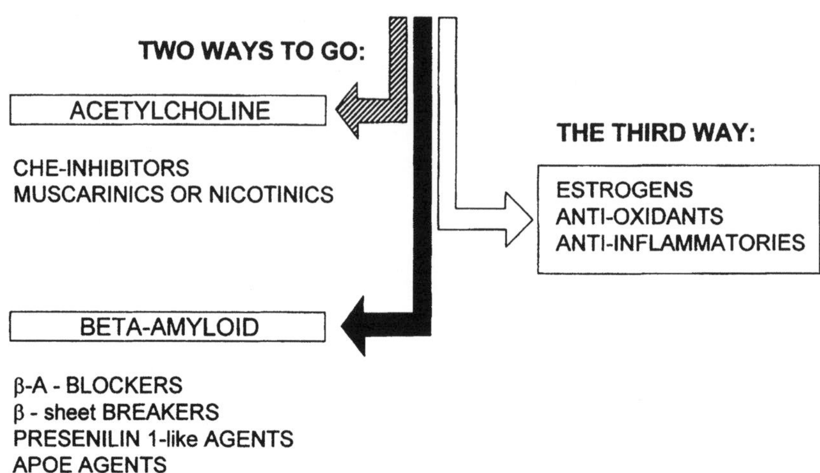

FIG. 6.1. Treatment of Alzheimer Disease. Which Way to Go?

CHANGES IN CHOLINESTERASE ACTIVITY RELATED TO AD

Table 6.1 shows the changes in cholinesterase activity in the cortex of AD patients. Acetylcholinesterase (AChE) activity decreases progressively in certain brain regions from mild to severe stages of the disease to reach 10 to 15% of normal values, whereas butyrylcholinesterase (BuChE) activity is unchanged or even increased by 20% (Atack, Perry, Bonham, Candy, & Perry, 1987; Giacobini, DeSarno, Clark, & McIlhany, 1989; Perry, Perry, Blessed, & Tomlinson, 1978).

In spite of the general reduction in brain AChE activity, the enzyme appears to be increased within and around neuritic plaques. In the plaques, AChE is closely associated with β-amyloid. As examples of regional differ-

TABLE 6.1

Percent Variation in Cholinergic Enzyme Activity Determined in Human Cortex of AD Patients (Late Stages) Compared to Normal Controls

Enzyme	*Localization*	*Activity (% of Normal)*	*Molecular Form*
AChE	Neuronal	10–15	50%–70% decrease, mainly G4
BuChE[a]	Glia-plaques	120	20% decrease, mainly G1
ChAT[b]	Neuronal	10–15	

[a]BuCHE = butyrylcholinesterase. [b]ChAT = Choline acetyltransferase.

ence in changes, BuChE/AChE ratio increases from 0,6 to 0,9 in the frontal cortex but from 0,6 to 11 in the enthorinal cortex (Geula & Mesulam, 1994). This change may reflect a combination of reactive gliosis following severe neuronal damage (glial cells having preponderantly BuChE) and an accumulation of BuChE in neuritic plaques, which contain both enzymes (Wright, Geula, & Mesulam, 1993). As the disease progresses and the concentration of synaptic AChE (in particular the membrane-anchored G4 form) decreases (Ogane, Giacobini, & Struble, 1992), ChEI probably increases ACh concentrations to levels that may be inhibitory for AChE activity. This increase in substrate concentration may trigger glial BuChE to hydrolyze ACh (acetylcholine) and could thus represent a compensatory mechanism to the loss of neuronal AChE activity. Given the close spatial relationship between glial cell protoplasm and the synaptic gap, it is likely that extracellularly diffusing acetylcholine may come into contact with glial BuChE and be effectively hydrolyzed, as demonstrated in our experiments in the rat with intracerebral microdialysis (Cuadra, Summers, & Giacobini, 1994).

ACETYLCHOLINESTERASE MOLECULAR FORMS IN THE HUMAN BRAIN: ARE THERE SELECTIVE INHIBITORS?

Human brain AChE exists in multiple molecular forms as defined by their different sedimentation coefficient. Based on their shapes, collagen-tailed asymmetric forms and globular forms can be separated. Studies on whole brain fractions suggest that 60% to 90% of the tetrameric (G4) form is extracellular and membrane located whereas the monomeric (G1) form is 90% intracellular and cytoplasmic (Enz & Florsheim, 1996; Ogane et al., 1992). The different effect of certain inhibitors may be primarily related to the localization of the enzyme and the penetration of the inhibitor, rather than to pharmacological or tissue selectivity. Selective loss of the membrane-bound G4 form has been reported in AD, suggesting a presynaptic localization. In patients with severe AD, the membrane bound G4 form is decreased in the frontal (–71 %), the parietal cortex (–45 %), and the caudate putamen (–47%) in comparison to control levels. The exact function of the G1 form, which is not significantly decreased in AD, has not been elucidated yet. The most effective inhibitor ideally would be one that selectively inhibits brain AChE forms without having any effect on peripheral tissues, such as skeletal or cardiac muscle. Rivastigmine, a carbamate compound, inhibits preferentially the G1 form (Enz & Florsheim, 1996), whereas tacrine and metrifonate inhibit G4 and G1 forms with similar potency (Ogane et al., 1992).

DECLINE IN CHOLINERGIC FUNCTION WITH AD PROGRESSION: PREMISES FOR A CHOLINERGIC THERAPY

During a course of 15 to 20 years of AD, a continuous loss of cholinergic neurons (50% to 87%) in the nucleus basalis Meynert (nbM) and the cortical cholinergic synapses is observed (Giacobini, 1994). From a total average of 350,000 neurons in young adult controls, a number as low as 72,000 is found in the nbM of AD patients. This profound loss in subcortical nuclei results in a progressive cortical cholinergic denervation (Geula & Mesulam, 1994). It is still controversial whether or not early decline in cognition in AD is associated with a decrease in cortical choline-acetyltransferase (ChAt) activity or with other changes in cholinergic function, such as selective choline uptake, ACh vesicular storage, and release or ACh synthesis.

A cholinomimetic strategy should therefore improve brain cholinergic function and consequently improve cognitive capacities of AD patients. The most efficacious intervention so far has been the use of drugs such as ChEI. Research data suggest that doses of ChEI capable of doubling ACh levels in the cortex of mild to moderately severe AD patients could reestablish normal levels of the neurotransmitter. Preclinical experimental results in animals and clinical data in humans demonstrate that such a goal can be achieved with most of the second-generation ChEI without causing severe or irreversible side effects (Giacobini & Cuadra, 1994).

THE EFFECT OF CHOLINESTERASE INHIBITORS IN THERAPY

Cholinesterase Inhibitors and Cognition

Cholinesterase inhibitors tested in clinical trials or in current use in Japan, the United States and Europe include less than 10 drugs. Most of these compounds have advanced to clinical phase III and IV, and three (tacrine, rivastigmine, donepezil) were registered in the United States and Europe. Tacrine, a first-generation ChEI, has been withdrawn from the market. Galantamine (galantamine hydrobromide), the latest reversible inhibitor of AChE, already available in some European countries and awaiting approval in the United States, is also an allosteric modulator of nicotinic acetylcholine receptors (Bores et al., 1996). Because galantamine binds to a site on nicotine acetylcholine receptors that is different than the acetylcholine binding site, it has been suggested that galantamine is provided with an additional mechanism of action, which may activate noncholinergic pathways impaired in AD (Francis, Palmer, Snape, & Wilcock, 1999). Further clinical development of two other compounds, eptastigmine and metrifonate, were stopped because of severe side effects (bone marrow suppression for eptastagmine and muscular weakness for metrifonate). To replace tacrine, the second-generation ChEI (i.e., donepezil, rivastigmine, galantamine) had to fulfill specific requirements, such as lower toxicity (hepatic) and easier administration besides demonstrable clinical efficacy (Giacobini & Cuadra, 1994).

There are differences between the tested compounds with regard to efficacy, percentage of treatable patients and responders, dropouts, and severity and incidence of side effects. Table 6.2 compares the effect of seven ChEI using

TABLE 6.2

Effects of Seven Cholinesterase Inhibitors on ADAS-cog Test[a] (ITT)[b]

Drug	*Dose (mg/day)*	*Duration of Study (weeks)*	*Treatment Difference (from placebo[c] / Baseline[d])*	*Improved Patients (percent)*	*Drop out (percent)*	*Side Effects (percent)*
Tacrine	120–160	30	4.0–5.3 / 0.8–2.8	30–50	55–73	40–58
Eptastigmine	45	25	4.7 / 1.830	12	35	
Donepezil	5–10	24	2.8–4.6 / 0.7–1	40–58	5–13	6–13
Rivastigmine	6–12	24	1.9–4.9 / 0.7–1.2	25–37	15–36	15–28
Metrifonate	25–75–80	12–26	2.8–3.1–3.2 / 0.75–0.5	35–40	2–21–8	2–12
	60–80	26	3.9 / 2.240	15	7	
Galanthamine	24	20–24	3.1–3.9 / 1.733	10–23	10–13	
	32	24	3.8–3.9 / 1.6	34	32	13–16

[a]ADAS-cog = AD Assessment Scale-cognitive subscale, [b]ITT= Intention to treat, [c]Study end point versus placebo, [d]Study end point vs baseline.
Note: Adapted from Giacobini (1998). Cholinergic foundations of Alzheimer's Disease therapy. *Journal de physiologie (Paris), 92,* pp. 283–287.

intention to treat criteria (ITT; Becker et al., 1996; Giacobini, 1998; Imbimbo & Lucchelli, 1994; Knapp et al., 1994; Morris et al., 1998; Raskind, Peskind, Wessel, Yuan, & the Galantamine USA-1 Study Group, 2000; Rogers, Farlow, Doody, Mohs, & Friedhoff, 1998; Rosler et al., 1999; Tariot et al., 2000).

Pharmacologically, these drugs represent either reversible (tacrine, eptastigmine, donepezil and galanthamine) or pseudoirreversible or irreversible (rivastigmine, metrifonate) ChEI. The duration of these phase III clinical trials varied from 24 to 30 weeks, included more than 10,000 patients, and took place in 26 different countries. The six most extensively clinically tested ChEI (tacrine, eptastigmine, donepezil, rivastigmine, metrifonate, and galantamine) all produced statistically significant improvement in multiple clinical trials using similar standardized and internationally validated measures of both cognitive and noncognitive functions. The most frequently used instrument for the evaluation of cognition, the ADAS-Cog, measures memory, orientation, language, and praxis, with a total score of 70 points. The mean annual change in ADAS-Cog scores in untreated AD patients was estimated to be approximately 9 points per year in longitudinal studies. Obviously, there are large variations among patients because the level of change seems to be dependent on the stage of the illness. The magnitude of cognitive effects measured with the ADAS-Cog scale for all six drugs—either expressed as the difference between drug- and placebo-treated patients or as the difference between drug-treated patients and baseline—is similar under present treatment conditions. This similarity after 26–30 weeks of treatment suggests a ceiling effect of approximately 5 ADAS-Cog points on average for approximately one third of patients in mild to moderate stages of the disease. It should be pointed out that this gain becomes more substantial, both clinically and economically, when evaluated after 1 year (8–9 points or more). Differences in effect between the drugs may be partly related to the rate of deterioration of the placebo group, which can vary from trial to trial. The results obtained with some irreversible compounds suggest that the maximal clinical effect has not been reached yet. On the other hand, cholinergic toxicity related to maximal tolerated doses indicates a limit in safe achievable levels of ChE inhibition. Analyses of results also imply that both very mild and more severe cases need to be studied. Furthermore, the data showed wide variations of effect among patients; in some patients, the gain was twice as large as the average. Cholinergic side effects were transient, reversible, and similar for all drugs. The percentage of improved patients varied from 25% to 50%, with an average of 34%. This indicates that more than one third of treated patients showed a significant clinical response to ChEI. This effect can be maintained for five drugs (tacrine, donepezil, rivastigmine, galantamine, and metrifonate) for at least 1 year, representing a high impact value for patients and caregivers. A smaller percentage (about 10% to 15%) of patients did not improve on the

ADAS-Cog with any of the used drugs, whereas a second group of patients (5% or more) showed a response significantly higher than 5 points. The similarity in clinical efficacy of the tested drugs is underlined by a practically identical effect on global scales such as the Clinicians Interview-Based Impression of Change-plus (CIBIC-plus).

An even more important result of the 6-month data is the observation that patients treated with the active compound changed little cognitively and behaviorally from the beginning of the study to the end (Fig. 6.2). This suggests a stabilization effect of disease-related deterioration, which is clinically more significant than expected symptomatic improvement. Placebo-controlled studies also indicate that this effect can be prolonged for at least 1 year (Fig. 6.3). Four drugs (donepezil, galantamine, metrifonate, and rivastigmine) have shown a long-term effect, extending from 1 to 4.5 years (Giacobini, 2000). Differences between responders (i.e., stable or improved patients) and nonresponders may reflect the level of cholinergic damage present in the brain, genetic factors (such as the presence of APOE-ε4 alleles), gender, or too low levels of ChE inhibition in the brain (Farlow et al., 1999; Giacobini, 1998; MacGowan, Wilcock, & Scott, 1998).

The question whether rivastigmine has a protective effect on subjects suffering from mild cognitive impairment is presently evaluated in ongoing trials. Evidence of such an effect would modify the present definition of ChEI as drugs with symptomatic effects only.

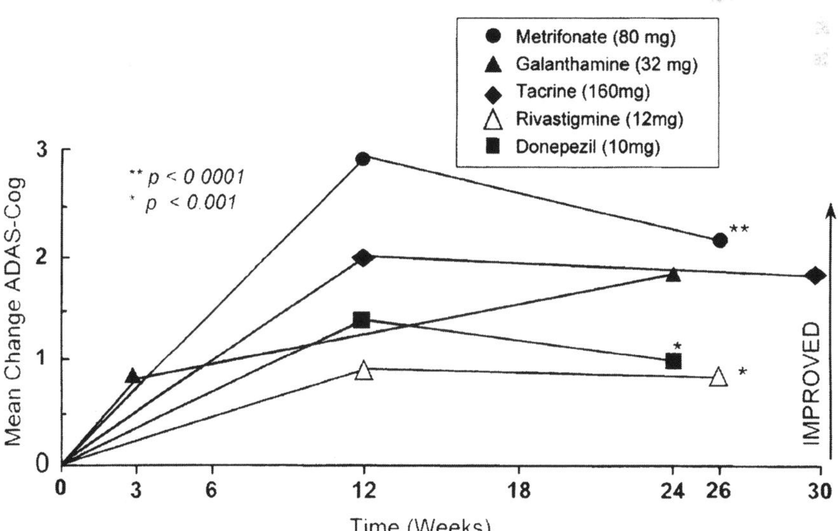

FIG. 6.2. Stabilization effect of 6-month treatment with ChE inhibitors tested with ADAS-Cog.

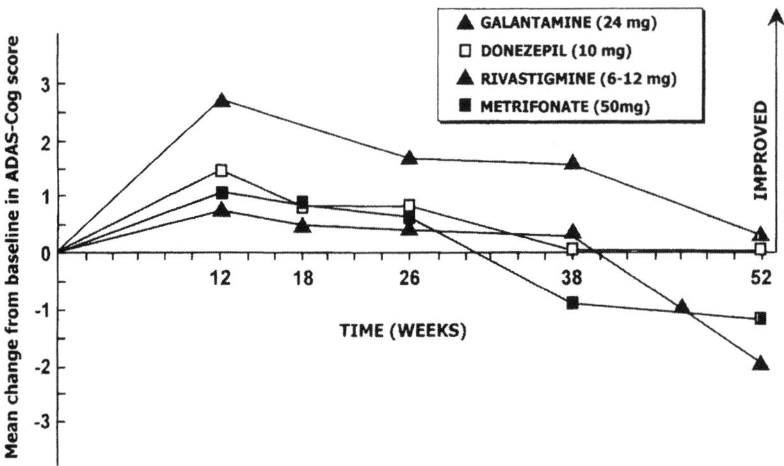

FIG. 6.3. Stabilization effect of 12-month treatment with ChE inhibitors tested with ADAS-Cog.

Cholinesterase Inhibitors and Behavior

Neuropsychiatric symptoms occur in almost 90% of AD patients and are the most important factor of stress for caregivers (see also chap. 7 of this book). Biochemical and pharmacological considerations suggest the involvement of cholinergic deficiency in the mechanism of psychotic symptoms in AD. Ameliorating cholinergic function with ChEI should therefore decrease these problems.

Several studies have confirmed the beneficial effects of ChEI on neuropsychiatric symptoms in AD patients, as measured by changes in the Neuropsychiatric Inventory (NPI) scores (Cummings & Masterman, 1998; Levy, Cummings, & Kahn-Rose, 1999; Morris et al., 1998; Tariot et al., 2000). Significant improvement was seen for four drugs (tacrine, donepezil, galantamine, and metrifonate) in delusions, hallucinations, apathy, motor agitation, depression, and anxiety. Thus, these studies support the hypothesis of a cholinergic link between cognitive and behavioral deficits in AD. They also demonstrated that the attenuation of such symptoms reduces caregiver burden, delays nursing home placement, and in consequence could decrease the costs of patient care.

DIFFERENCES IN CHOLINERGIC EFFECTS AMONG CHOLINESTERASE INHIBITORS

As mentioned previously, cholinomimetic therapy is based on the principle that brain ChE inhibition increases synaptic ACh levels, which may lead to cognitive improvement. Ideally, the correlation between cognitive effects and level of AChE inhibition would be best observed in the brain or in the cerebrospinal fluid (CSF; Giacobini, 1998). However, as CSF monitoring is difficult to achieve, peripheral inhibition of AChE in red blood cells (RBC) or plasma BuChE has been studied as an indirect measure of the drug effect. Inhibition varies between 30% and 80%, depending on dose and pharmacokinetic characteristics of the compound. For some drugs (donepezil and metrifonate) the mean level of peripheral ChE inhibition is 65% to 70% and could be safely brought to as high as 90%. For other drugs, such as tacrine, the practical limit of inhibition can be as low as 30% and may be increased only with increased risk for severe side effects. There is little correlation between central AChE inhibition and side effects; the severity of side effects is mainly due to peripheral inhibition (Becker & Giacobini, 1988; Imbimbo & Lucchelli, 1994).

A direct clinical implication of this relationship is that drugs producing high levels of central AChE inhibition at a low dose with a short half-life (see the following section) will produce only mild peripheral cholinergic side effects. A high increase of brain ACh may be achieved within a full range of therapeutic potency. As an example, rivastigmine at doses of 6 mg (corresponding to 62% AChE inhibition in CSF) produces a significantly greater improvement in cognitive function than at doses between 1mg to 4 mg (Giacobini, 1998).

PHARMACOKINETIC DIFFERENCES

A summary of pharmacokinetic properties of six ChEI is presented in Table 6.3 (Anand, Hartman, & Hayes, 1996; Bores et al., 1996; Giacobini, 1998; Lilienfels & Parys, 2000; Pettigrew et al., 1998; Rogers et al., 1998). Several important differences are apparent with regard to metabolism as well as other characteristics. Whereas tacrine, galanthamine, and donepezil are metabolized through the hepatic route (P-450), rivastigmine and metrifonate are not. This difference is clinically important because elderly patients show decreased hepatic metabolism, and therefore drugs not hepatically metabolized should be preferred.

Another important characteristic is the difference in drug elimination with a half-life (T½) between 2 to 73 hours. Such differences are important because a short T½ reduces the time of exposure of the peripheral pool of ChE to the inhibitor, decreasing side effects. Galantamine and metrifonate have maximal bioavailability (100% and 90%, respectively) and the lowest plasma protein binding (10 and 20%, respectively). With 96%, plasma protein binding is highest for donezepil. Because elderly patients are generally treated with several drugs simultaneously, this factor is of particular interest in relation to drug interactions.

Pharmacokinetic properties may also cause important differences in efficacy and severity of side effects. To maximize therapeutic central effects

TABLE 6.3

Comparison of Pharmacokinetic Properties of Five Cholinesterase Inhibitors after Oral Dosage in Humans

Drug	*Plasma Conc. (ug/L) C-Max*	*Time to Peak (h) T-Max*	*Elimin. Half-Life (h) T ½*	*Metabolism*
Tacrine	—	1–2	2–4	Hepatic(P450)
Donepezil	30–60	3–4	73	Hepatic (P450)
Rivastigmine	114	1.7–1	5	Nonhepatic
Metrifonate	500	0.5	2	Nonhepatic
Galanthamine	543	0.5	4.4–5–7	Hepatic (P450)

Note: Adapted from Giacobini (1998). Cholinergic Foundations of Alzheimer's Disease Therapy. *Journal de Physiologie (Paris), 92,* pp. 283–287.

and to minimize peripheral (bronchial, muscular, gastrointestinal, and cardiac) side effects, elimination half-life should be short (around 1–2 hours). The effective dose should be low but able to produce a substantial CNS enzyme inhibition (60% to 80%) and a steady (small diurnal/nocturnal variations) and long-lasting (several days) level of inhibition. Irreversible ChEI, such as metrifonate, satisfy such criteria more closely than reversible ones.

LONG-TERM EFFECTS OF CHOLINESTERASE INHIBITORS

Prolonged clinical efficacy of ChEI is deduced from the two observations. First, if drug treatment is interrupted, the cognitive effect may continue for 3 to 4 weeks, even in the absence of ChE inhibition. Second, as mentioned previously, treatment benefits can be maintained in a number of patients for at least 1 year. This suggests that ChEI effect may not be related exclusively to an elevation in brain acetylcholine levels but also to a modification of the amyloid-linked pathology in AD (see also section "Immunization in AD" later in this chapter).

NEW INDICATIONS FOR CHOLINESTERASE INHIBITOR THERAPY

A logical challenge to the findings of a prolonged effect of ChEI is to investigate whether or not early treatment can alter the course of the disease by delaying its clinical onset. This approach could be of interest in at-risk subjects, such as asymptomatic members of familial AD pedigrees or in persons with mild cognitive impairment (Fox, Warrington, Seiffer, Agnew, & Rossor, 1998; Sunderland, 1998).

Dementia with Lewy bodies (DLB) is thought to be the second most common cause of dementia after AD. Studies have shown that neocortical cholinergic activity is more severely depleted in DLB than in AD and that this deficit also affects the caudate nucleus, the thalamus, and the brain stem (Perry, McKeith, & Perry, 1998). It is likely that this pattern is related to the occurrence of hallucinations characteristic for the disease. Because typical neuroleptic treatment is contraindicated in DLB, cholinergic therapy has been investigated in a multicenter, with statistically and clinically significant effects on behavior (McKeith et al., 2000).

One attempt to treat vascular dementia with a ChEI (rivastigmine) has been published with encouraging results (Kumar, Anand, Messina, Hartman, & Veach, 2000), and, more recently, positive preliminary findings have been reported in the treatment of vascular and mixed dementia with galantamine (Kurz & Lilienfeld, 2001). However, clinical evaluation of these cases remains difficult in the absence of consensus on valid criteria for the diagnosis of vascular dementia.

Finally, ChEI treatment might also be indicated in Down syndrome (Kishnai et al., 1999).

FUTURE APPLICATIONS OF CHOLINESTERASE INHIBITOR THERAPY

The introduction of ChEI represents a milestone in AD with the availability of drugs tested for the first time in randomized, placebo-control studies in vast populations of patients. The effect of these drugs is reflected not only in an amelioration of cognition but also in activities of daily living, global functioning, and behavioral disturbances.

Attempts have been made to develop alternatives to ChEI, such as nicotinic and muscarinic agonists, but receptor nonselectivity and severe side effects (mainly cardiovascular and gastrointestinal) have so far prevented therapeutic applications of these compounds in AD. A combination of these agents with ChEI could possibly enhance treatment efficacy. The mechanisms of allosteric modulation of nictonic acetylcholine receptors of galantamine may be a first step in this direction.

Ongoing clinical trials are also investigating the effects of nonsteroid anti-inflammatory drugs (NSAID), antioxidants, and estrogen replacement therapy on AD.

The NSAID approach is based on the observation that inflammatory processes play an important role in the neuropathology of AD and that a suppression of these mechanisms may therefore slow down the course of the disease. Studies have shown that NSAID may protect against the disease and decrease the rate of its progression. However, the important side effects of these drugs are preventing their use in long-term applications (Stewart, Kawas, Corrada, & Metter, 1997). The therapeutic effect of a combination of ChEI and cyclooxygenase inhibitors, a new NSAID with fewer side effects (McGeer, 2000), is under investigation.

Because extensive oxidative damage is seen in the brain of AD patients, studies have sought to establish whether antioxidants can prevent, delay, or alter the course of the disease (Sano et al., 1997). Additional information is needed to demonstrate whether substances such as vitamin E, selegiline, or gingko biloba are effective either alone or in combination with ChEI.

Although estrogen replacement therapy has not shown benefits in the treatment of AD, it may have a neuroprotective effect by delaying the onset of the disease (Mulnard et al., 2000). If this is the case, it will be necessary to develop selective estrogen agonists for brain receptors that are devoid of cancerogenic activity.

IMMUNIZATION IN AD: β-AMYLOID AS A TARGET

An entirely new therapeutic approach, based on the development of an experimental vaccine that can reverse Alzheimer-like pathology in animal models, is now being tested in humans.

It is well established that the brain of AD patients is characterized by a diffuse loss of neurons, mainly in the neocortex and hippocampus, accompanied by an accumulation of intracellular protein deposits (neurofibrillary tangles) and the aggregation of an extracellular protein (β-amyloid, A-β), the main constituent of senile plaques. Aβ amyloid is generated from the proteolytic cleavage of a transmembrane protein, the Aβ precursor protein (APP). APP may be processed by a nonpathogenic α-secretase or by an amyloidogenic pathway involving β- and γ-secretase. The latter involves a first cleavage by β-secretase and a second by γ-secretase to generate a A β-γ-amyloid fragment, which is subsequently secreted (Sisodia, 2000). Evidence for the critical enzymatic steps involved in amyloid processing was provided by genetic research. Mutations in either the presenilin PS 1 (chromosome 14) or the preseniline PS 2 (chromosome 2) gene in the rare early onset form of familiar AD (FAD; Emilen, Maloteaux, Beyreuther, & Masters, 2000) induce a shift in the secretase cleavage site in APP which results in a generation of A-β fragments of 42, rather than 40, amino-acids (Fig. 6.4). This longer peptide has a strong tendency to aggregate to form protein deposits and to be toxic to neurons.

Brain levels of Aβ 40, and particularly of Aβ 42, were found to increase early in AD, and the latter fragment seems to be correlated particularly with cognitive decline (Naslund et al., 2000). These results support the role of Aβ deposition in the initial pathogenic events of AD and form a logical basis for treatment strategies targeting formation, accumulation, and cytotoxic effects of Aβ. Such interventions should result in a reduction of the amyloid burden thought to be responsible for the clinical presentation of the disease.

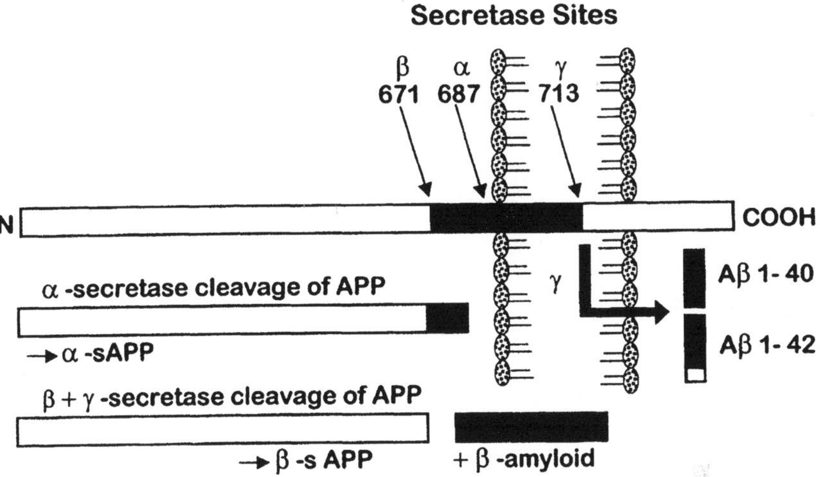

FIG. 6.4. Cleavage sites of secretases.

DEVELOPMENT OF ANIMAL MODELS OF AD

To generate animal models of Aβ amyloidogenesis and AD-related lesions, different laboratories have created transgenic mice that overexpress wild-type APP or FAD-linked APP variants.

Overexpression of A-beta in different mouse lines has produced a variety of phenotypes that are remarkably similar to the human neuropathological condition of AD and in particular in a rodent strain encoding the FAD-linked APP V717 mutation (Schenk et al., 1999).

At ages 6 to 9 months, these animals begin to exhibit diffuse deposits of Aβ and plaques in the hippocampus, corpus callosum, and cortex. As in human AD, the density of plaques, together with dystrophic neuritic components and loss of synaptic density with typical regional specificity increases with age. These mice also show some behavioral and cognitive changes at later stages of their lives. However, neurofibrillary tangles are not present in the brain of these animals. Thus, the similarities in onset, localization, and progression of neuropathological changes demonstrate the usefulness of this animal model for human AD, despite a fully transgenic mouse not yet being available.

IMMUNIZATION OF TRANSGENIC ANIMALS

The immunization of transgenic mice with the peptide Aβ 42 before the onset of AD-type neuropathology prevented the development of Aβ formation, neuritic dystrophy, and astrogliosis. Treatment of older animals with established neuropathology also markedly reduced extent and progression of these AD-like changes (Schenk et al., 1999) (Table 6.4). These results suggests that immunization with Aβ may be effective in preventing the development of plaque formation at several stages of the disease. The underlying mechanism of immunization has been explained as follows: Aβ 42 immunization results in the generation of anti-Aβ antibodies, which trigger the appearance of microglial cells supposed to reduce plaque burden (Bard et al., 2000).

Moreover, several researchers (Arendash et al., 2001; Morgan et al., 2000) showed that Aβ vaccination preserved learning ability in transgenic mice, confirming the results using tests of learning, working memory, and other cognitive tasks.

VACCINATION: FROM MOUSE TO HUMAN

The results obtained with the transgenic mice raises the possibility that immunization with Aβ peptides may be effective for more than AD in at-risk subjects, such as asymptomatic members of families with genetic linked forms of AD (FAD), persons with mild cognitive impairment (MCI), or APOEε-4 allele carriers; it might also be effective in treating patients with a diagnosis of AD.

TABLE 6.4

Summary of Data From Transgenic Mice Vaccination Experiments

Effects on pathology
Beta-amyloid deposition is prevented.
Beta-amyloid is destroyed, but APP is not altered by immunization.
Neuritic dystrophy is prevented.
Astrocytosis is decreased.
Number of microglial cells is increased.
Behavioral effects
Memory and learning ability is preserved.
Morris water maze is used (two independent studies).
Other effects
Immunized mice develop antibodies against beta-A, which are found in the circulation.
Antibodies enter the mouse brain.
Endogenous Ig-G is not altered.

Note: Adapted from Schenck et al. (1999). Immunization with Amyloid-β Attenuates Alzheimer-Disease-like Pathology in the PDAPP Mouse. *Nature, 400,* pp. 173–177.

So far, human studies with healthy volunteers who received the vaccine every 2 months for 1 year showed the following results: (1) Antibodies against Aβ were found in the blood, (2) there was no autoimmune reaction, and (3) no side effects were observed.

Because of these encouraging results, the clinical Phase I of these studies was rapidly completed, and Phase II initiated. Unfortunately, this was arrested because of severe side effects (encephalitis).

The immunologic approach will be crucial in confirming the validity of the Aβ-amyloid cascade dogma. If reduction of cerebral amyloid burden influences the clinical manifestations of AD, this will not only be clinically relevant but would also support the hypothesis that amyloid deposition is critical in causing the disease. If, on the other hand, prevention or reduction of amyloid deposition, or both, has no effects on clinical symptoms, the relevance of cerebral amyloid accumulation is confuted. In fact, many elderly persons showing extensive postmortem Aβ deposits in the brain had normal cognition through the later stages of their lives. APP and its metabolism may therefore be a part of a normal physiological process, during which Aβ is produced in response to neural injury in various diseases. Thus, APP changes may be part of the defense mechanisms of the aging brain rather than being detrimental. Finally, neurofibrillary degeneration (tangles) may be a more important factor in the cause of AD symptoms than Aβ accumulation. The effect of amlyoid plaque depletion on cognitive and behavior deficits in AD is therefore not clear, and the question "Will immunization be able to save neurons and cure the disease at the same time?" has yet to be answered (Giacobini, 2001).

ALTERNATIVE EXPERIMENTAL THERAPIES TARGETING β-AMYLOID

Alternative strategies to diminish amyloid burden in the AD brain are being investigated. The first is based on selective inhibition of one or both of the enzymes β- and γ-secretase responsible for the cleavage of the transmembrane APP protein (see Fig. 6.1). This approach should block Aβ production and thus ameliorate AD symptoms. Inhibitors of both secretases are being developed by several drug companies and will soon be tested in humans.

The second approach is based on the development of a synthetic peptide that disrupts the formation and deposition of Aβ (Soto, 1999). This β-sheet breaker mimics the region of the amyloid protein that regulates the aggregation of Aβ, a process essential to plaque formation, and thus prevents aggregation. Clinical trials with these peptides started in 2002.

The third approach is based on the observation that copper and zinc allow secretases to cleave the amyloid protein. On the other hand, compounds that bind copper and zinc can dissolve plaques in the postmortem brain tissue of AD patients. Searching for a drug with such properties, Cherny et al. (2000) discovered an antibiotic called clioquinol, which proved to be most potent in dissolving amyloid in brain tissue in vitro. The drug also appears to be able to inhibit plaque formation in transgenic AD mice. Clioquinol was used widely in the past but has been discontinued because it may cause acute vitamin B12 deficiency. It has not yet been tested in AD patients.

As mentioned previously, ChEI also modify APP metabolism and secretion, thus reducing Aβ formation (Svensohn & Giacobini, 2000). They may also exert a neuroprotective effect by activating normal APP processing (Inestrosa et al., 1996; Lahiri, Farlow, Hintz, Utsuki, & Greig, 2000; Pakaski, Rakonczay, Fakla, Papp, & Kasa, 2000). This noncholinergic effect may explain the long-term efficacy of these drugs as cognitive stabilizers. The understanding of the molecular mechanisms of this antiamyloidogenic effect could help in developing a new generation of ChEI.

In conclusion, only ChEI are presently available to stabilize temporarily the natural course of AD. However, other strategies targeting the pathogenesis of AD are being explored, and new compounds that could one day delay or prevent the onset of, slow the progression of, or even cure AD are in the pipeline.

REFERENCES

Anand, R., Hartman, R. D., Hayes, P. E. (1996). An overview of the development of SDZ ENA 713, a brain selective cholinesterase inhibitor disease. In R. Becker & E. Giacobini (Eds.), *Alzheimer disease: From molecular biology to therapy* (pp. 239–243). Boston: Birkhäuser.

Arendash, G. W., King, D. L., Gordon, M. N., Morgan, D., Hatcher, J. M., Hope, C. E., & Diamond, D. M. (2001). Progressive, age-related behavioral impairments in transgenic mice carrying both mutant amyloid precursor protein and presenilin-1 transgenes. *Brain Research, 891*(11), 42–53.

Atack, J. R., Perry, E. K., Bonham, J. R., Candy, J. M., & Perry, R. H. (1987). Molecular forms of butyrylcholinesterase in the human neocortex during development and degeneration of the cortical cholinergic system. *Journal of Neurochemistry, 48,* 1687–1692.

Bard, F., Cannon, C., Barbour, R., Burke, R. L., Games, D., Grajeda, H., Guido, T., Hu, K., Huang, J., Johnson-Wood, K., Khan, K., Kholodenko, D., Lee, M., Lieberburg, I., Motter, R., Nguyen, M., Soriano, F., Vasquez, N., Weiss, K., Welch, B., Seubert, P., Schenk, D., & Yednock, T. (2000). Peripherally administered antibodies against amyloid beta-peptide enter the central nervous system and reduce pathology in a mouse model of Alzheimer disease. *Nature Medicine, 6,* 916–919.

Becker, R. E., Colliver, J. A., Markwell, S. J., Moriearty, P. L., Unni, L. K., & Vicari, S. (1996). Double-blind, placebo-controlled study of metrifonate, an acetylcholinesterase inhibitor for Alzheimer disease. *Alzheimer Disease and Associated Disorders, 1*(7), 124–131.

Becker, E., & Giacobini, E. (1988). Mechanisms of cholinesterase inhibition in senile dementia of the Alzheimer type. *Drug Development Research, 12,* 163–195.

Bores, G. M., Huger, F. P., Petko, W., Mutlib, A. E., Camacho, F., Rush, D. K., Selk, D. E., Wolf, V., Kosley, R. W., Davis, L., & Vargas, H. M. (1996). Pharmacological evaluation of novel Alzheimer's disease therapeutics: Achetylcholinesterase inhibitors related to galanthamine. *The Journal of Pharmacology and Experimental Therapeutics, 277*, 728–738.

Cherny, R. A., Atwood, C. S., Xililnas, M. E., Gray, D. N., Jones, W. D., McLean, C. A., Barnham, K. J., Volitakis, I., Fraser, F. W., Kim, Y., Huang, X., Goldstein, L. E., Moir, R. D., Lim, J. T., Beyreuther, K., Zheng, H., Tanzi, R. E., Masters, C. L., & Bush, A. I. (2001). Treatment with a copper-zinc chelator markedly and rapidly inhibits beta-amyloid accumulation in Alzheimer's disease transgenic mice. *Neuron, 30*, 665–676.

Cuadra, G., Summers, K., & Giacobini, E. (1994). Cholinesterase inhibitor effects on neurotransmitters in rat cortex in vivo. *The Journal of Pharmacology and Experimental Therapeutics, 270*, 277–284.

Cummings, J. L., & Masterman, D. K., (1998). Assessment of treatment-associated changes in behavior and cholinergic therapy of neuropsychiatric symptoms in Alzheimer's disease. *Journal of Clinical Psychiatry, 59*, (Suppl. 13), 23–30.

Davis, K. L., & Mohs, R. C. (1979). Enhancement of memory by physostigmine. *The New England Journal of Medicine, 301*, 946–956.

Emilen, G., Maloteaux, J.-M., Beyreuther, K., & Masters, C. (2000). Alzheimer disease. Mouse models pave the way for therapeutic opportunities. *Archives of Neurology, 57*(6), 176–181.

Enz, A., & Florsheim, P. (1996). Cholinesterase inhibitors: An overview of their mechanism of action. In E. Giacobini & R. Becker (Eds.), *Alzheimer's Disease: From Molecular Biology to Therapy* (pp. 211–215). Boston: Birkhäuser.

Farlow, M. R., Cyrus, P. A., Nadel, A., Lahiri, D. K., Brashear, A., & Gulanski, B. (1999). Metrifonate treatment of AD: Influence of APOE genotype. *Neurology, 53*, 2010–2016.

Fox, N. C., Warrington, E. K., Seiffer, A. L., Agnew, S. K., & Rossor, M. N. (1998). Presymptomatic cognitive deficits in individuals at risk of familial Alzheimer's disease. A longitudinal prospective study. *Brain, 121*, 1631–1639.

Francis, P. T., Palmer, A. M., Snape, M., & Wilcock, G. K. (1999). The cholinergic hypothesis of Alzheimer's disease: A review of progress. *Neurology, Neurosurgery and Psychiatry, 66*(6), 137–147.

Geula, C., & Mesulam, M. M. (1994). Cholinergic systems and related neuropathological predilection patterns in Alzheimer disease. In R. D. Terry, R. Katzman, & K. L. Bick (Eds.), *Alzheimer disease* (pp. 263–291). New York: Raven Press.

Giacobini, E. (1994). Cholinomimetic therapy of Alzheimer disease: Does it slow down deterioration? In G. Racagni, N. Brunello, & S. Z. Langer (Eds.), *Recent advances in the treatment of neurodegenerative disorders and cognitive dysfunctions* (pp. 51–57). New York: Karger.

Giacobini, E. (1998). Cholinergic foundations of Alzheimer' disease therapy. *Journal de Physiologie (Paris), 92*, 283–287.

Giacobini, E. (2000). Cholinesterase inhibitors stabilize Alzheimer's disease. *Annals of the New York Academy of Sciences, 920*, 321–327.

Giacobini, E. (2001). Do cholinesterase inhibitors have disease-modifying effects in Alzheimer's disease? *CNS Drugs, 15*(3), 85–91.

Giacobini, E., & Cuadra, G. (1994). Second and third generation cholinesterase inhibitors: From preclinical studies to clinical efficacy. In E. Giacobini & R. Becker (Eds.), *Alzheimer disease: Therapeutic strategies* (pp. 155–171). Boston: Birkhäuser.

Giacobini, E., DeSarno, P., Clark, B., & McIlhany, M. (1989). The cholinergic receptor system of the human brain—Neurochemical and pharmacological aspects in aging and Alzheimer. In A. Nordberg, K. Fuxe, & B. Holmstedt (Eds.), *Progress in brain research* (pp. 335–343). Amsterdam: Elsevier.

Imbimbo, B. P., & Lucchelli, P. E. (1994). A pharmacodynamic strategy to optimize the clinical response to eptastigmine. In R. Becker & E. Giacobini (Eds.), *Alzheimer disease: Therapeutic strategies* (pp. 223–230). Boston: Birkhäuser.

Inestrosa, N. C., Alvarez, A., Perez, C. A., Moreno, R. D., Vicente, M., Linker, C., Casanueva, O. I., Soto, C., & Garrido, J. (1996). Acetylcholinesterase accelerates assembly of amyloid-beta-peptides into Alzheimer' s fibrils: Possible role of the peripheral site of the enzyme. *Neuron, 16,* 881–891.

Kishnani, P. S., Sullivan, J. A., Walter, B. K., Spiridigliozzi, G. A., Doraiswamy, P. M., & Krishnan, K. R. (1999). Cholinergic therapy for Down's syndrome. *Lancet, 353,* 1064–1065.

Knapp, M. J., Knopman, D. S., Solomon, P. R., Pendlebury, W. W., Davis, C. S., & Gracon, S. I. (1994). A 30 week randomized controlled trial of high-dose tacrine in patients with Alzheimer's disease. *The Journal of the American Medical Association, 271,* 985–991.

Kumar, V., Anand, R., Messina, J., Hartman, R., & Veach, J. (2000). An efficacy and safety analysis of Exelon in Alzheimer's disease patients with concurrent vascular risk factors. *European Journal of Neurology, 7,* 159–169.

Kurz, A., & Lilienfeld, S. (2001, May). *Galantamine improves cognitive and global abilities in Alzheimer's disease with cerebrovascular components and vascular dementia (preliminary results).* Poster session presented at the 53rd annual meeting of the American Academy of Neurology, Philadelphia.

Lahiri, D. K., Farlow, M. R., Hintz, N., Utsuki, T., & Greig, N. H. (2000). Cholinesterase inhibitors, beta-amyloid precursor protein and amyloid beta-peptides in Alzheimer's disease. *Acta Neurologica Scandinavica Supplementum, 176*(6), 60–67.

Levy, M. L., Cummings, J. L., & Kahn-Rose, R. (1999). Neuropsychiatric Symptoms and cholinergic therapy for Alzheimer's Disease. *Gerontology, 45,* 15–22.

Lilienfels, S., & Parys, W. (2000). Galantamine: Additional benefits to patients with Alzheimer's disease. *Dementia and Geriatric Cognitive Disorders, 11*(Suppl. 1), 19–27.

MacGowan, S. H., Wilcock, G., & Scott, M. (1998). Effect of gender and apolipoprotein E genotype on response to anticholinesterase therapy in Alzheimer's disease. *International Journal of Geriatric Psychiatry, 13,* 625–630.

McGeer, P. L. (2000). Cyclo-oxygenase-2 inhibitors: Rationale and therapeutic potential for Alzheimer's disease. *Drugs & Aging, 17,* 1–11.

Morgan, D., Diamond, D. M., Gottschall, P. E., Ugen, K. E., Dickey, C., Hardy, J., Duff, K., Jantzen, P., DiCarlo, G., Wilcock, D., Connor, K., Hatcher, J., Hope, C., & Gordon, M. (2000). A beta peptide vaccination prevents memory loss in an animal model of Alzheimer's disease. *Nature, 408,* 982–985.

Morris, J. C., Cyrus, P. A., Orazem, J., Mas, J., Bieber, F., Ruzicka, B. B., & Gulanski, B. (1998). Metrifonate benefits cognitive, behavioral, and global function in patients with Alzheimer's disease. *Neurology, 50,* 1222–1230.

Mulnard, R. A., Cotman, C. W., Kawas, C., van Dyck, C. H., Sano, M., Doody, R., Koss, E., Pfeiffer, E., Jin, S., Gamst, A., Grundman, M., Thomas, R., & Thal, L. J. (2000). Estrogen replacement therapy for treatment of mild to moderate Alzheimer disease: A randomized controlled trial. Alzheimer's Disease Cooperative Study. *The Journal of the American Medical Association, 283,* 1007–1015.

Naslund, J., Haroutunian, V., Mohs, R., Davis, K. L., Davies, P., Greengard, P., & Buxbaum, J. D. (2000). Correlation between elevated levels of amyloid beta-peptide in the brain and cognitive decline. *The Journal of the American Medical Association, 283*, 1571–1577.

Ogane, N., Giacobini, E., & Struble, R. (1992). Differential inhibition of acetylcholinesterase molecular forms in normal and Alzheimer disease brain. *Brain Research, 589*, 307–331.

Pakaski, M., Rakonczay, Z., Fakla, I., Papp, H., & Kasa, P. (2000). In vitro effects of metrifonate on neuronal amyloid precursor protein processing and protein kinase C level. *Brain Research, 863*, 266–270.

Perry, E. K., McKeith, I. G., & Perry, R. H. (1998). Dementia with Lewy bodies: A common cause of dementia with therapeutic potential. *Internal Journal of Geriatric Pharmacology, 1*, 120–125.

Perry, E. K., Perry, R. H., Blessed, G., & Tomlinson, B. E. (1978). Changes in brain cholinesterases in senile dementia of Alzheimer type. *Neuropathology and Applied Neurobiology, 4*, 273–277.

Rainer, M., Mark, T. H., & Haushofer, A. (1989). Galanthamine hydrobromide in the treatment of senile dementia of Alzheimer's type. In T. Kewitz, L. Thomsen, & A. Bickel (Eds.), *Pharmacological interventions on central mechanisms in senile dementia* (pp. 53–71). Munchen: Zuckschwerd.

Raskind, M. A., Peskind, E. R., Wessel, T., Yuan, W., & the Galantamine USA-1 Study Group. (2000). Galantamine in AD. A 6-month randomized, placebo-controlled trial with a 6-month extension. *Neurology, 54*, 2261–2268.

Rogers, S. L., Farlow, M. R., Doody, R. S., Mohs, R., & Friedhoff, L. T. (1998). A 24 week, double blind placebo controlled trial of donepezil in patients with AD. *Neurology, 50*(6), 136–145

Rosler, M., Anand, R., Cicin-Sain, A., Gauthier, S., Agid, Y., Dal-Bianco, P., Stahelin, H. B., Hartman, R., & Gharabawi, M. (1999). Efficacy and safety of rivastigmine in patients with Alzheimer's disease: International randomized controlled trial. *British Medical Journal, 318*, 633–658.

Sano, M., Ernesto, C., Thomas, R. G., Klauber, M. R., Schafer, K., Grundman, M., Woodbury, P., Growdon, J., Cotman, C. W., Pfeiffer, E., Schneider, L. S., & Thal, L. J. (1997). A controlled trial of selegiline, alpha-tocopherol, or both as treatment for Alzheimer's disease: The Alzheimer's Disease Cooperative Study. *The New England Journal of Medicine, 336*, 1216–1222.

Schenk, D., Barbour, R., Dunn, W., Gordon, G., Grajeda, H., Guido, T., Hu, K., Huang, J., Johnson-Wood, K., Khan, K., Kholodenko, D., Lee, M., Liao, Z., Lieberburg, I., Motter, R., Mutter, L., Soiano, F., Shopp, G., Vasquez, N., Vandevert, C., Walter, S., Wogulis, M., Yednock, T., Games, D., & Seubert, P. (1999). Immunization with amyloid-beta attenuates Alzheimer-disease-like pathology in the PDAPP mouse. *Nature, 400*, 173–177.

Sisodia, S. (2000). An accomplice for gamma-secretase brought into focus. *Science, 289*, 2296–2297.

Soto, C. (1999). Plaque busters: Strategies to inhibit amyloid formation in Alzheimer's disease. *Molecular Medicine Today, 5*, 343–350.

Stewart, W. F., Kawas, C., Corrada, M., & Metter, E. J. (1997). Risk of Alzheimer's disease and duration of NSAID use. *Neurology, 48*, 626–632.

Summer, W. K., Viesselman, J. O., Marsh, G. M., & Candelora, K. (1981). Use of THA in treatment of Alzheimer-like dementia: Pilot study in twelve patients. *Biological Psychiatry, 16*(12), 145–153.

Sunderland, T. (1998). Cholinergic therapy. *The American Journal of Geriatric Psychiatry, 6*(Suppl. 1), 57–63.

Svensson, A.-L., & Giacobini, E. (2000). Cholinesterase inhibitors do more than inhibit cholinesterase. In E. Giacobini (Ed.), *Cholinesterases and cholinesterase inhibitors* (pp. 227–235). London: Martin Dunitz.

Tariot, P. N., Solomon, P. R., Morris, J. C., Kershaw, P., Lilienfeld, F. C. P., Ding, C., & the Galantamine USA-10 Study Group. (2000). A 5-month, randomized, placebo-controlled trial of galantamine in AD. *Neurology, 54*, 2269–2276.

Wright, C. I., Geula, C., & Mesulam, M. M. (1993). Neuroglial cholinesterases in the normal brain and in Alzheimer's disease: Relationship to plaques, tangles and patterns of selective vulnerability. *Annals of Neurology, 34*, 373–384.

7

Psychiatric and Behavioral Problems: Pharmacological Approaches

Philippe H. Robert
Memory Center,
Federation of Neuroscience's Clinics,
CHU—Nice

Alzheimer's Disease (AD) is characterized by neuropsychological and neurological deficits associated with behavior problems. The latter have received much less attention than cognitive symptoms in studies of dementia in the past. However, these disturbances are important manifestations of AD and other forms of dementia because they are associated with caregiver distress, increase the likelihood of institutionalization, and may be associated with more rapid cognitive decline (Mortimer & Ebbitt, 1992; Teri, Hughes, & Larson, 1990). Several terms, such as behavioral disturbances and noncognitive symptoms, have been used to describe these manifestations, and they are only briefly mentioned in major manuals for the classification and diagnosis of mental disorders. For example, the criteria for dementia of the *ICD-10 Classification of Mental and Behavioural Disorders* (ICD 10; World Health Organization, 1993) include certain behavioral symptoms such as deteriorating emotional control, social behavior, and motivation. In the fourth edition of the *Diagnostic and Statistical Manual of Mental Disorders* (DSM IV; American Psychiatric Association, 1994), the diagnostic criteria of AD specifies subtypes based on either age at onset or clinical features such as delirium, delusions, and depressed mood. Furthermore, the specifier "with behavioral disturbances," which cannot be coded, is used to indicate clinically significant behavioral disturbances, such as wandering. Given the need for a better understanding and description of the origin, diagnosis, and treatment of behavioral disturbances in dementia, the International Psychogeriatric Association (IPA) recently organized a consensus conference on this topic. The consensus statement (Finkel, Costa e Silva, Cohen, Miller, & Sartoruis, 1996) indicated that the chief characteristics of dementia include multiple cognitive deficits and a deteriorating course. In addition to the cognitive symptoms, people with dementia have other symptoms that have been largely neglected until recently. These other symptoms commonly have been called behavioral disturbances of dementia. The participants of the conference thought that the term *disturbances* is too general, has many meanings, and is difficult to define. They recommended that the term *behavioral disturbances* be replaced by the term *behavioral and psychological symptoms of dementia* (BPSD), defined as follows: Signs and symptoms of disturbed perception, thought content, mood, or behavior that frequently occur in patients with dementia.

The present chapter is divided into two sections. The first emphasizes the need to evaluate and analyze behavioral problems before the initiation of pharmacological treatment.

The second proposes general guidelines for the prescription of pharmacological treatment in elderly subjects with AD and also reviews some main studies of potentially useful pharmacological agents in the treatment of BPSD in AD.

THE NEED FOR A MULTIDIMENSIONAL ASSESSMENT OF BPSD

BPSD in AD have several characteristics. First, they are often caused by multiple factors that could act in combination (i.e., medical causes, such as dehydration; environmental problems, such as difficulties with a caregiver; misunderstanding of a specific context as a consequence of cognitive deficits; or direct expression of dysfunction in specific brain regions; Benoit et al., 1999; Sultzer, Mahler, Mandelkern, Cummings, & Van Gorp, 1995). Second, because of their impaired judgment, patients find it more difficult to evaluate their behavior and correct it, if inappropriate (Bertogliati et al., 2002). Third, BPSD presents with a great variety of symptoms (see Table 7.1), progressing in a variable manner and with chronological inconstancy (Cummings, 1997; Cummings, Diaz, & Levy, 1996). Some symptoms, such as agitation and aberrant motor behavior, increase with the severity of dementia, but others do not.

Behavioral Evaluation

Several rating tools have been developed over the years on the basis of a variety of data sources. Certain tools are derived from clinical psychiatric practice and are either used unmodified (e.g., the Hamilton Depression Scale and the Brief Psychiatric Rating Scale) or adapted to dementia (e.g., the Cornell Scale for Depression in Dementia). Other instruments have

TABLE 7.1

Percentage of AD Patients With Different Mini-Mental State Examination (MMSE) Score Ranges Presenting Behavioral Disturbances as Identified by the Neuropsychiatric Inventory (NPI) for patients with a score different from 0 in a given NPI score.

NPI Domains	*MMSE 30–21 n = 33 (%)*	*MMSE 20–11 n = 30 (%)*	*MMSE 11 – 30 n = 63 (%)*	*NPI Scores of Symptomatic Patients Mean (SD)*
Anxiety	20 (61.6)	21 (70)	41 (65.1)	4.3 (3.6)
Apathy	19 (58.6)	18 (60)	37 (58.7)	4.8 (3)
Dysphoria	19 (58.6)	18 (60)	37 (58.7)	3.7 (2.6)
Irritability	15 (45.4)	15 (50)	30 (47.6)	3.8 (2.6)
Agitation	17 (52.6)	12 (40)	29 (46.3)	4 (2.2)
Motor behavior	10 (30.3)	9 (30)	19 (30.2)	3.4 (2.3)
Eating	11 (43.3)	8 (26.7)	19 (30.2)	3.9 (2.9)
Delusions	6 (17.3)	8 (26.4)	14 (22)	4.7 (3.4)
Sleep	7 (21.2)	3 (10)	10 (15.9)	3.7 (2.4)
Disinhibition	5 (15.2)	4 (13.3)	9 (14.3)	2.5 (1.1)
Euphoria	5 (15.2)	2 (6.7)	7 (11.1)	2.8 (1.5)
Hallucinations	1 (3)	3 (10)	4 (6.3)	1.5 (0.5)

Note: Adapted from "Behavioral and Psychological Symptoms in Alzheimer's Disease," by M. Benoit et al., 1999, *Dementia and Geriatric Cognitive Disorders, 10.*

been specifically developed for use with patients with dementia, such as the BEHAVE-AD (Reisberg, Borenstein, Salob, Ferris, & Franssen, 1987), the Cohen-Mansfield Agitation Inventory (Cohen-Mansfield, 1989), and the Neuropsychiatric Inventory (Cummings, Mega, Gray, Rosemberg-Thompson, & Gornbein, 1994). These tools are based on a variety of approaches, each having its specific advantages and drawbacks (see Table 7.2).

A comprehensive evaluation of behavior should cover the following points:

- Elucidate the presence of all possible behavioral problems, even if one is prominent
- Consider the report and point of view of both the patient and his or her family or caregiver
- Identify psychosocial or environmental triggers
- Determine if BPSD is acute or chronic

TABLE 7.2

Different Techniques Used for the Assessment of BPSD

Assessment	*Advantages*	*Disadvantages*
Patient self-evaluation	Direct observation	Subjective Limited awareness of the problem
Family (caregiver) interview	More objective Knowledge of the patient's daily life	Nonprofessional. Biased by the caregivers' relationship with the patient
Professional observation (physician, psychologist)	Expertise in behavioral disturbances	Observation limited in time Limited knowledge of the patient's daily life

Medical and Cognitive Evaluation

Medical evaluation particularly should take into account all the changes in the physical and therapeutical condition of the patient (e.g., pain, fecal retention, fever, introduction or withdrawal of a pharmacological agent).

The cognitive evaluation should not only assess global functioning but also include a detailed exam of the patients' cognitive abilities (see chap. 3 of this book). Before deciding whether to treat BPSD with a pharmacological agent, the clinician must consider the following questions: Is the symptom drug responsive? Which class of drug is the most suitable for the symptom? What are the predictable side effects of a given medication for this particular patient? Finally, the decision to treat also depends on the impact of the BPSD on the caregiver's distress and on the patient's adaptability to activities of daily living.

GENERAL PRINCIPLES FOR PHARMACOLOGICAL TREATMENT

The current published guidelines for the treatment of BPSD (American Psychiatric Association, 1997; International Psychogeriatric Association, 1998) propose the following general principles:

- Select an agent whose most typical side effects are least likely to cause problems for a given patient.
- Use a low starting dose and maintain treatment on the lowest effective dose.
- If BPSD decreases, consider periodical attempts to reduce or withdraw pharmacological medication.
- Reevaluate symptoms frequently because fluctuations are characteristic of BPSD. Thus, a single evaluation measure for each patient (e.g., be-

ginning, end of the treatment) could underestimate behavior problems and usually does not provide a correct picture of treatment efficacy.

- If possible, make only one treatment change at a time, if multiple agents or approaches are being used without efficacy.

The use of different pharmacological agents is summarized in Table 7.3.

ANTIPSYCHOTICS

Neuroleptics

Neuroleptics are also called conventional or typical antipsychotics. Most of these drugs act by blocking dopamine receptors located in the brain's mesolimbic striatal mesocortical systems. D2 or D3 receptors blockade is needed to obtain antipsychotic activity.

Neuroleptics were extensively studied, but most of the studies were uncontrolled. In a review of the literature, Schneider, Pollock, and Lyness (1990) and Schneider (1996) identified 33 studies of elderly patients, in which neuroleptics were compared with placebos or other drugs. They found only seven double blind, placebo-controlled, parallel-group trials with patients suffering from primary dementia. Global reanalysis of the data suggested an improvement in 59% of the subjects taking neuroleptics and in 41% of the subjects taking the placebo. Moreover, there were no differences between the different neuroleptics evaluated.

It is also important to point out that the magnitude of the treatment effect varies considerably; some patients improve substantially and others minimally. The dosage for elderly demented patients is usually lower than the dosage used in adults (see Table 7.4).

Side effects associated with neuroleptics can be divided into three main categories: neurological, cardiovascular, and anticholinergic (see Table 7.5). Advanced age substantially increases both the risk of develop-

TABLE 7.3
Pharmacological Treatment and BPSD

Drug Category	*Target Symptom*
Antipsychotics	Psychosis, agitation, hostility, aggression
Neuroleptics	
Newer antipsychotics	
Benzodiazepines	Anxiety, agitation, tension, sleep disturbances
Anticonvulsants	Agitation, manic-type behavior
Antidepressants	Depressive symptoms, apathy, irritability, emotionality, sleep disturbances
Cholinergic agents	Apathy and visual hallucinations

TABLE 7.4

Clinical Recommendations for Doses of Neuroleptics and Newer 'Atypical' Antipsychotics[a]

Drug Name	*Starting Dose (mg/day)*	*Approximate Dose (mg/day)*
Thioridazine	10	10–75
Haloperidol	0.5	0.25–2
Loxapine	10	10–50
Thiothixene	1	1–10
Tiapride	20	50–300
Clozapine	6.25	10–100
Risperidone	0.5	0.5–2
Olanzapine	5	5–10

[a]These values are recommendations; treatment must be adapted to the specific needs of each patient.

TABLE 7.5

Side-Effect Profile of Neuroleptics

Neurological	Extrapyramidal symptoms, seizures, catatonia, neuroleptic malignant syndrome
Cardiovascular	Orthostatic hypotension, tachycardia, electrical conduction abnormalities
Anticholinergic	Peripheral: dry mouth, constipation, urinary retention, blurred vision, glaucoma
	Central: confusion, delirium, cognitive impairment

ing tardive dyskinesia and its severity (Jeste et al., 1995). The best prevention against these effects would be to minimize exposure to these drugs. Long-term use of neuroleptics seems to be correlated with a more rapid decline in functional abilities and cognition (McShane et al., 1997). However, these findings did not take into account the different types of neuroleptics and in particular those from the benzamide family, which tend to have less cholinergic and cognitive side effects (Allain et al., 2000; Robert & Allain, 2001).

It is important to mention the case of dementia with Lewy bodies (DLB) in this context. DLB is a relatively common clinical syndrome characterized by prominent visual hallucinations and psychotic symptoms. Although neuroleptics should be avoided because of the severe and sometimes fatal sensitivity to these drug, they are in fact often prescribed in clinical practice (McKeith, Galasko, & Kosaka, 1996).

Newer or Atypical Antipsychotics

Some newer drugs have a higher or equal binding affinity to serotonin receptors than for dopamine receptors in comparison to the classical neuroleptics (see Table 7.6). Newer antipsychotics are already being studied in dementia. However, results of several of these studies are not available yet or are rather limited (e.g., for quetiapine or ziprasidone).

Clozapine. There are no placebo-controlled randomized studies and only one retrospective study on elderly demented patients for this drug (Schneider, 1999). Side effects (e.g., anticholinergic effects, sedation, confusion) are common and require cautious use.

Risperidone. Risperidone is the most widely studied newer antipsychotic. Available data include several case reports and the results of a large multicenter placebo-controlled nursing home trial (Katz, Jeste, & Mintzer, 1999). This study included 625 patients (73% of them suffering from AD) at the most severe stages of dementia. Treatment response, defined as a reduction higher than 50% in the BEHAVE-AD total score, was seen in significantly more patients receiving Risperidone than the placebo. The same effect was seen on the BEHAVE-AD psychosis and aggressiveness subscale. Significant behavior improvement was observed after 2 weeks. Despite a significant number of side effects, such as sedation, dizziness, orthostasic hypotension, constipation, insomnia, and confusion, in treated patients, medication had to be discontinued only for a few. Extrapyramidal symptoms were reported in up to 21 patients.

Olanzapine. The efficacy of Olanzapine in BPSD has been investigated in a double blind placebo-controlled study of patients with dementia in nursing homes (Street et al., 2000). Patients receiving 5 and 10 mg of Olanzapine had a significantly higher response rate than those receiving the placebo, although the latter also showed a high response. No extrapyramidal symptoms were reported. Significant side effects included somnolence and abnormal gait, both of which were dose related. In an-

TABLE 7.6

Binding Affinities for Serotonin, Dopamine, and Muscarinic Receptors

	D1	*D2*	*5-HT2A*	*Muscarinic*
Haloperidol	++	++	+	
Clozapine	+	+	++	++
Risperidone	+	++	++	0
Olanzapine	++	++	++	++
Quetiapine	+	++	++	++

other study comparing haloperidol, olanzapine, and risperidone, Edell and Tunis (2001) found olanzapine superior on measures of aggression and delusions/hallucinations in comparison to the two other drugs.

ANTIDEPRESSANTS

The bulk of our knowledge on the treatment of depression in AD comes from case reports and extrapolations from studies of cognitively intact elderly depressed subjects. Carrier and Brodaty (1996) indicated that "the choice of the most appropriate pharmacological agent will be based on a previous personal or familial history of a positive response to a specific agent, the pharmacokinetics, the adverse effects profile and the drug interactions of the various antidepressants." Selective serotonin reuptake inhibitors (SSRI), such as sertraline, citalopram, paroxetine, fluvoxamine, and fluoxetine, are interesting choices because of their tolerability, safety in overdose, and absence of anticholinergic effects.

Moreover, it is now clearly established that neurons that synthesize and release 5-HT participate in the control of many central functions and that alterations of serotoninergic transmission are associated with various neuropsychiatric conditions, such as depression, anxiety, and impulsiveness (Robert, Aubin-Brunet, & Darcourt, 1999).

Clinical trials have demonstrated the efficacy of serotoninergic agents in AD (Burke, Folks, Roccaforte, & Wengel, 1995; Nyth & Gottfries, 1990). In addition, the preservation of postsynaptic 5-HT 1A receptors in AD patients suggests that subjects with depressive symptoms could benefit from SSRI or even 5-HT 1A agonists. Similarly, the selective preservation of 5-HT 2A receptors in the orbitofrontal and temporal neocortex of anxious AD patients (Chen et al., 1994) implies that agents acting on 5-HT 2A receptors could be useful for treatment.

Literature on apathy in AD suggests a link between these symptoms, reduced dopaminergic and noradrenergic activity, and cingulate metabolism (Migneco et al., 2001; Volkow et al., 2000). However, the clinical efficacy of dopaminergic or noradrenergic antidepressants for this indication has yet to be demonstrated in clinical trials. Currently, the best choice seems to be the use of antidepressants acting on multineurotransmitters (e.g., venlafaxine, mirtazapine).

Whichever antidepressant is used, overall tolerability must be evaluated. Tricyclic antidepressants are associated with frequent side effects, such as postural hypotension, blurred vision, and urinary and cardiac conduction disorders and must therefore be used with caution. SSRI tend to have a more favorable side effect profile.

Finally, the use of serotoninergic agents at low doses might also be useful for other behavior symptoms in AD, such as disinhibition or irritability (Robert et al., 1999). Open trials and some controlled trials (Lawlor, Radcliffe, &

Molchan, 1994; Lebert, Pasquier, & Petit, 1994; Sultzer, Gray, & Gunay, 1997) support the use of trazodone for agitation. Postural hypotension, sedation, and dry mouth are the principal side effects of this drug.

BENZODIAZEPINES AND ANTICONVULSANTS

Benzodiazepines seem to be effective in the treatment of AD-related anxiety but have not been studied extensively in terms of risk-benefit ratio (Stern, Duffelmeyer, Zemishlani, & Davidson, 1991). There is little evidence to support the use of a benzodiazepine as a first-choice treatment for any of the behavioral symptoms in AD, including anxiety and sleep disturbances (Borson & Raskind, 1997). Benzodiazepines seem to perform better than the placebo in agitation but not as well as antipsychotics. More studies are needed before use of anticonvulsivants for the treatment of agitation in demented patients can be recommended (Tariot, 1999). Table 7.7 summarizes the characteristics of benzodiazepines and anticonvulsants used for the treatment of BPSD in AD.

CHOLINERGIC THERAPY

Acetylcholinesterase inhibitors (AChEI) have been introduced as cognition-enhancing agents in the treatment of patients with mild to moderate AD. These agents exert their effect by blocking acetylcholinesterase and increasing cholinergic function (see chap. 6 of this book). Research has shown that AChEI also ameliorate behavioral disturbances in AD

TABLE 7.7

Benzodiazepines and Anticonvulsants in AD

Benzodiazepines

Efficacy: Controlled studies have shown that benzodiazepines perform better than the placebo but not as well as antipsychotics in reducing BPSD.

Side-effect profile: The most common are sedation, ataxia, amnesia, confusion.

Practice guidelines:

Short-acting benzodiazepines are preferred to avoid accumulative effect.

Benzodiazepines are most effective if used for short periods.

If the treatment has been maintained for over 4–6 weeks, the drug has to be discontinued gradually and slowly.

Anticonvulsants (Carbamazepine and Valproic acid)

Efficacy: Little data available on the treatment of agitation.

Side-effect profile:

Carbamazepine: ataxia, sedation and confusion

Valproic acid: gastrointestinal disturbances and ataxia

TABLE 7.8

Studies of Cholinesterase Inhibitors That Used Structured Assessments of Behavioral Effects

Agent	*Assessment*	*Behavioral Response*
Tacrine	ADAS noncognitive scale	Improved cooperation, reduction of delusions and pacing
	NPI	Diminished apathy, anxiety, disinhibition, and aberrant motor activity
Velnacrine	Relative's assessment of global symptomatology	No increase in behavioral symptoms (versus increasing symptoms in placebo group)
Donepezil	NPI	Improved total score
Metrifonate	NPI	Improved total score, reduction of visual hallucinations, apathy, depression, anxiety, and aberrant motor behavior
Rivastigmine	NPI	Significant behavioral improvement, reduced psychosis
Galantamine	NPI	Improved total score

Note: ADAS = Alzheimer's Disease Assessment Scale. NPI = Neuropsychiatric Inventory. Adapted from "Cholinesterase inhibitors: A new class of psychotropic compounds," by J. L. Cummings, 2000, *American Journal of Psychiatry, 157*(1), 4–15.

(Cummings, 2000; Levy, Cummings, & Kahn-Rose, 1999; Tariot et al., 2000) and, in particular, visual hallucinations and apathy (see Table 7.8). The variability of behavioral symptoms and the responsiveness to cholinergic therapy may reflect dynamic interactions between cholinergic changes and other transmitter systems involved in AD. Cholinergic agents may have a particularly strong effect on the attentional or executive system, with a secondary modulating influence on memory, language, and visuospatial skills (Lawrence & Sahakian, 1995). Improvement in attention may be responsible for the reduction in apathy, which is commonly associated with AChEI treatment. This could explain why apathy is one of the most responsive neuropsychiatric symptoms to cholinergic therapy and why it correlates highly with cognitive improvement.

In summary, the use of pharmacological treatment is indicated if clinicians are confronted with major behavioral disturbances in AD. However, the importance of nonpharmacological interventions must be emphasized. As stated by the American Psychiatric Association and the International Psychogeriatric Association, nonpharmacological interventions are the first choice of approach to BPSD. Pharmacological treatment of these problems is only indicated when symptoms become moderate to severe, have an impact on the patient's everyday functioning and on his or her caregivers' quality of life, or both. If this is the case, drug treatment should be combined with nonpharmacological interventions whenever possible.

In conclusion, a comprehensive treatment plan must include at least the following steps:

1. An accurate evaluation of the severity and origin of BPSD
2. A definition of treatment goals, including decreasing problematic behavior, improving function, reducing emotional distress, decreasing caregiver stress, and preventing complications
3. The choice of appropriate nonpharmacological interventions, pharmacological treatment, or both
4. An evaluation of the treatment effects

REFERENCES

Allain, H., Dautzenberg, P. H. J., Maurer, K., Schuck, S., Bonhomme, D., & Gerard, D. (2000). Double blind study of tiapride versus haloperidol and placebo in agitation and aggressiveness in elderly patients with cognitive impairment. *Psychopharmacology, 148*(4), 361–366.

American Psychiatric Association. (1994). *Diagnostic and Statistical Manual of Mental Disorders* (4th ed.). Washington, DC: Author.

American Psychiatric Association. (1997). Practice guideline for the treatment of patients with Alzheimer's disease and other dementia of late life. *American Journal of Psychiatry, 154*(Suppl. 5), 1–39.

Benoit, M., Dygai, I., Migneco, O., Robert, P. H., Bertogliati, C., Darcourt, J., Benoliel, J., Aubin-Brunet, V., & Pringuey, D. (1999). Behavioral and psychological symptoms in Alzheimer's disease. *Dementia and Geriatric Cognitive Disorders, 10*, 511–517.

Bertogliati, C., Robert, P. H., Lafont, V. Bedoucha, P., Benoît, M., & Salame, P. (2002). Metacognition et maladie d' Alzheimer. *Annėe Gerontologique*, 27–31.

Borson S., & Raskind, M. A. (1997). Clinical features and pharmacologic treatment of behavioral symptoms of Alzheimer's disease. *Neurology, 48*(Suppl. 6), 17–24.

Burke, W. J., Folks, D. G., Roccaforte, W. H., & Wengel, S. P. (1995). Serotonin reuptake inhibitors for the treatment of coexisting depression and psychosis in dementia of Alzheimer type. *American Journal Geriatry Psychiatry, 2*, 352–354.

Carrier, L., & Brodaty, H. (1996). Mood and behaviour management. In S. Gauthier (Ed.), *Clinical diagnosis and management of Alzheimer's disease* (pp. 205–218). London: Martin Dowitz.

Chen, C. P. L. H., Hope, R. A., Adler, J. T., Keene, J., McDonald, B., Francis, P. T., Esiri, M. M., & Bowen, D. M. (1994). Loss of 5HT2A receptors in Alzheimer's disease neocortex is associated with disease severity while preservation of 5HT2A receptors is associated with anxiety [Abstract]. *Annals of Neurology, 36*, 308–309.

Cohen-Mansfield, J. (1989). Agitation in the ederly. In N. Bilig & P. Rabins (Eds.), *Advances in psychosomatic medicine: Geriatric psychiatry* (pp. 101–113). Basel: S. Karger AG.

Cummings, J. L. (1997). The Neuropsychiatric Inventory: Assessing psychopathology in dementia patients. *Neurology, 48 (Suppl. 6), 10–16.*

Cummings, J. L. (2000). Cholinesterase inhibitors: A new class of psychotropic compounds. *American Journal of Psychiatry, 157*(1), 4–15.

Cummings, J. L., Diaz, C., & Levy, M. (1996). Behavioral syndromes in neurodegenerative diseases: Frequency and significance. *Seminar in Neuropsychiatry, 1*, 241–247.

Cummings, J. L., Mega, M. S., Gray, K., Rosemberg-Thompson, S., & Gornbein, T. (1994). The Neuropsychiatric Inventory: Comprehensive assessment of psychopathology in dementia. *Neurology, 44*, 2308–2314.

Edell, W. S., & Tunis, S. L. (2001). Antipsychotic treatment of behavioral and psychological symptoms of dementia in geropsychiatric inpatients. *American Journal of Geriatric Psychiatry, 9*, 289–297.

Finkel, S. I., Costa e Silva, J., Cohen, G., Miller, S., & Sartorius, N. (1996). Behavioral and psychological signs and symptoms of dementia: A consensus statement on current knowledge and implications for research and treatment. *International Psychogeriatrics, 8*, 497–500.

International Psychogeriatric Association. (1998). *Behavioral and psychological symptoms of dementia. Educational pack*. Macclesfield, UK: Gardiner-Caldwell.

Jeste, D. V., Caliguiri, M. P., Paulsen, J. S., Heaton, R. K., Lacro, J. P., Harris, M., & Bailey, A. (1995). Risk of tardive dyskinesia in older patients: A prospective longitudinal study of 266 outpatients. *Archives of General Psychiatry, 52*, 756–765.

Katz, I. R., Jeste, D. V., & Mintzer J. E. (1999). Comparison of risperidone and placebo for psychosis and behavioral disturbances associated with dementia: A randomized, double-blind trial. *Journal of Clinical Psychiatry, 60*(2), 107–115.

Lawlor, B. A., Radcliffe, J., & Molchan, S. E. (1994). A pilot placebo-controlled study of tradozone and buspirone in Alzheimer's disease. *International Journal of Geriatric Psychiatry, 9*, 55–59.

Lawrence, A. D., & Sahakian, B. J. (1995). Alzheimer disease, attention, and the cholinergic system. *Alzheimer Disease and Associated Disorders, 9*(Suppl. 2), 43–49.

Lebert, F., Pasquier, F., & Petit, H. (1994). Behavioral effects of trazodone in Alzheimer's disease. *Journal of Clinical Psychiatry, 55*, 536–538.

Levy, M. L., Cummings, J. L., & Kahn-Rose, R. (1999). Neuropsychiatric symptoms and cholinergic therapy for Alzheimer's disease. *Gerontology, 45*(Suppl. 1), 15–22.

McKeith, L. G., Galasko, D., & Kosaka, K. (1996). Consensus guidelines for the clinical and pathologic diagnosis of dementia with Lewy bodies (DLB): Report of the consortium on DLB international workshop. *Neurology, 47*, 1113–1124.

McShane, R., Keene, J., Gedling, K., Fairburn, C., Jacoby, R., & Hope, T. (1997). Do neuroleptic drugs hasten cognitive decline in dementia? Prospective study with necropsy follow up. *British Medical Journal, 70*, 266–314.

Migneco, O., Benoit, M., Koulibaly, P. M., Dygai, I., Bertogliati, C., Desvignes, P., Robert, P. H., Malandain, C., Bussiere, F., & Darcourt, J. (2001). Perfusion brain SPECT and statistical parametric mapping analysis indicate that apathy is a cingulate syndrome: A study in Alzheimer's disease and nondemented patients. *Neuroimage, 13*, 896–902.

Mortimer, J. A., & Ebbitt, B. (1992). Predictors of cognitive and functional progression in patients with probable Alzheimer's disease. *Neurology, 42*, 1689–1696.

Nyth, A. L., & Gottfries, C. G. (1990). The clinical efficacy of citalopram in treatment of emotional disturbances in dementia disorders. *British Journal of Psychiatry, 157*, 894–901.

Reisberg, B., Borenstein, J., Salob, S. P., Ferris, S. H., & Franssen, E. (1987). Behavioral symptoms in Alzheimer's disease: Phenomenology and treatment. *Journal of Clinical Psychiatry, 48*(Suppl. 9), 9–15.

Robert, P. H., & Allain, H. (2001). Clinical management of agitation in the elderly with tiapride. *European Psychiatry, 16*(Suppl. 1), 42–47.

Robert, P. H., Aubin-Brunet, V., & Darcourt, G. (1999). Serotonin and the frontal lobes. In J. L. Cummings & B. L. Miller (Eds.), *The frontal lobes* (pp. 125–138). New York: Guilford Press.

Robert, P. H., Migneco, O., Koulibaly, M., Bertogliati, C., Dygai, C., Benoît, M., Salame, P., Darcourt, J., & Danion, J. M. (2001). Cingulate and attentional correlates of apathy in Alzheimer's disease. *Brain and Cognition, 47,* 300–303.

Schneider, L. S. (1996). Meta-analysis of controlled pharmacologic trials. *International Psychogeriatrics, 8,* 375–379.

Schneider, L. S. (1999). Pharmacologic management of psychosis in dementia. *Journal of Clinical Psychiatry, 60*(Suppl. 8), 54–60.

Schneider, L. S., Pollock, V. E., & Lyness, S. A. (1990). A meta-analysis of controlled trials of neuroleptic treatment in dementia. *Journal of the American Geriatric Society, 38,* 553–563.

Stern, R. G., Duffelmeyer, M. E., Zemishlani, Z., & Davidson, M. (1991). The use of benzodiazepines in the management of behavioral symptoms in demented patients. *Psychiatry Clinical North America, 14,* 375–384.

Street, J. S., Clark, W. S., Gannon, K. S., Cummings, J. L., Bymaster, F. P., Tamura, R. N., Mitan, S. J., Kadam, D. L., Sanger, T. M., Feldman, P. D., Tollefson, G. D., & Breier, A. (2000). Olanzapine treatment of psychotic and behavioral symptoms in patients with Alzheimer disease in nursing care facilities: A double-blind, randomized, placebo-controlled trial. The HGEU Study Group. *Archives of General Psychiatry, 57,* 968–976.

Sultzer, D., Gray, K. F., & Gunay, I. (1997). A double-blind comparison of trazodone and haloperidol for treatment of agitation in patients with dementia. *American Journal Geriatry Psychiatry, 5,* 60–69.

Sultzer, D. L., Mahler, M. E., Mandelkern, M. A., Cummings, J. L., & Van Gorp, W. G. (1995). The relationship between psychiatric symptoms and regional cortical metabolism in Alzheimer's disease. *The Journal of Neuropsychiatry and Clinical Neurosciences, 7,* 476–484.

Tariot, P. N. (1999). Treatment of agitation in dementia. *Journal of Clinical Psychiatry, 60*(Suppl. 8), 11–20.

Tariot, P. N., Solomon, P. R., Morris, J. C., Kershaw, P., Lilienfeld, S., Ding, C., & the Galantamine USA-10 Study Group. (2000). A 5-month randomized, placebo-controlled trial of galantamine in AD. *Neurology, 54,* 2269–2276.

Teri, L., Hughes, J. P., & Larson, E. B. (1990). Cognitive deterioration in Alzheimer's disease: Behavioral and health factors. *Journal of Gerontology, 45,* 58–63.

Volkow, N. D., Logan, J., Fowler, J. S., Wang, G. J., Gur, R. C., Wong, C., Felder, C., Gatley, S. J., Ding, Y. S., Hitzemann, R., & Pappas, N. (2000). Association between age-related decline in brain dopamine activity and impairment in frontal and cingulate metabolism. *American Journal of Psychiatry, 157*(1), 75–80.

World Health Organization. (1993). *The ICD-10-classification of mental and behavioural disorders. Clinical descriptions and diagnostic guidelines.* Geneva: Author.

8

Psychiatric and Behavioral Problems: Psychosocial Approaches

Michael Bird
Australian National University

> The light of lights,
> Looks always on the motive, not the deed,
> The shadow of shadows on the deed alone.
> —W. B. Yeats, *The Countess Cathleen*

Though Alzheimer's classic case was referred for challenging behavior (Alzheimer, 1907), many reviews have noted that, more than 90 years later, treatment remains limited and somewhat primitive. That is, predominantly attempting to reduce behavior pharmacologically, most commonly with antipsychotics, a practice whose dangers and limited efficacy have been well documented (Aisen, Deluca, & Lawler, 1992; Elmståhl, Stenberg, Annerstedt, & Ingvad, 1998; Nygaard et al., 1994; Schneider, Pollock, & Lyness, 1990). Unfortunately, those advocating more focus on psychosocial techniques tend to be very vague about what those techniques might be and silent on evidence for their relative efficacy.

One reason for this vagueness is the impossibility of encapsulating psychosocial methods into discrete therapies analogous to classes of medication, to be prescribed perhaps once a day, although many authors attempt to do this. Some approaches are even given proprietary labels, exacerbating a fundamental misconception. As this chapter shows, a psychosocial approach to challenging behavior is extraordinarily diffuse and cannot be reduced to a neat, shorthand label. It has almost nothing in common with pharmacological approaches, though both should form part of the toolkit. They are complementary, not opposed approaches.

Another reason for vagueness may be that the psychosocial literature is inferior to its pharmacological equivalent—itself extremely poor (Devanand & Levy, 1995; Peisah & Brodaty, 1994). Though there are excellent studies describing these phenomena, until recently the intervention literature was largely the land of the unsupported assertion. Fortunately, there is now movement away from the enthusiastically anecdotal towards empirical science, and this chapter seeks to use recent literature, together with case examples, to present the essence of a psychosocial approach. Conceptual issues are first addressed, followed by a long section on assessment and selection of management options. The issue of those exposed to the behavior is then addressed, a fourth section comments on recent research on standard intervention techniques, and finally four case studies are presented to reinforce critical points made throughout the chapter.

THE NATURE OF CHALLENGING BEHAVIOR

Though there is still no formal consensus on conceptualization, there is abundant evidence in the psychogeriatric literature of the prevailing clinical paradigm. This paradigm is to see the person with dementia as the identified patient and the behavior as the sole focus of interest—the disease to be treated. Evidence for this conclusion derives, firstly, from the rapidly growing list of classification instruments where disparate behaviors are clustered into syndromes (e.g., Cummings et al., 1994). Secondly, there are the many journal articles appearing each year advocating a standard treatment for a mysterious syndrome called agitation (Finkel et al., 1995). Though agitation does have a meaning in psychiatry, it is used indiscriminately in dementia for just about any behavior that causes problems and is therefore debased.

What may be called the syndrome-standard cure model probably makes sense to the clinician whose strategy is suppression of behavior with antipsychotics. For those with a more sophisticated pharmacological or psychosocial repertoire it is grossly deficient on two grounds.

First, these problems are far from homogeneous; however much the manifested behavior might resemble behavior in other cases. The nature of the behavior is actually relatively insignificant in comparison with the diverse idiosyncratic factors that produce the behavior and, equally, those that determine treatment choice. Etiology is the obvious example. The same behavior in different cases will have different causes. For example, management of patients who are screaming because of pain (Cohen-Mansfield, & Werner, 1997) will be different from cases in which social overstimulation is implicated (Meares & Draper, 1999) and different again if the cause is loneliness or despair (Hallberg, Edberg, Nordmark, & Johnsson, 1993). Moreover, many other idiosyncratic case-specific variables influence choice of treatment, ranging from the residual capacity of the patient to whether a given care regime has a flexible view of dementia care (see p. 149).

The second objection to using manifested behavior to define the syndrome is that the behavior is not the determining factor in whether a case requires intervention. Identical behaviors can be challenging in one setting, for example, wandering in one facility, not in another with a safe perimeter fence. (See also cases A and C in the last section of this chapter.) Behavior can be challenging before career education, not after it (Hagen & Sayers, 1995), or intolerable before prescription of medication to depressed careers, but no problem thereafter (Hinchliffe, Hyman, Blizard, & Livingston, 1995). Bird, Llewellyn-Jones, Smithers, and Korten (2002) found very low intraclass correlations between senior nursing home staff regarding which of their residents displayed challenging behavior and, equally, between hands-on care staff on the degree of stress caused them by specific disturbed patients.

That is, challenging behavior is usually abnormal, but abnormal behavior is not necessarily challenging. It is the effects not the nature of the behavior that determine whether it is a problem, and these effects are highly subjective and idiosyncratic. The syndrome-standard cure model, with the nature of the behavior defining the syndrome, does not fit this situation, nor that both etiology and treatment options in any given case are highly idiosyncratic. There is no standard syndrome and no standard cure.

Accordingly, the definition of challenging behavior in dementia adopted for this chapter is as follows: "Any behavior associated with the dementing illness which causes distress or danger to the patient and/or others" (Bird et al., 1998).

The purpose of treatment, accordingly, is the amelioration of the effects of the behavior, most commonly career distress, given that cases usually come to the attention of health services because caregivers or residential staff can no longer cope. Treatment may involve addressing the behavior, but in a significant minority of cases it will not (see pp. 150, 151).

ASSESSMENT AND SELECTION OF INTERVENTION STRATEGIES

If challenging behavior is the end product of an interaction between many case-specific variables, and if what can be done in any given case is dependent on similar variables, the key is multidimensional assessment. It is essential to go in with questions rather than answers. If sufficient information is gathered to provide a reasonable understanding of what is going on, the answers mostly present themselves, with implementation the only major remaining problem. A 70% to 75% clinical success rate in reducing behavior, or career stress, or both, in a community sample by Hinchliffe et al. (1995), and a combined community and residential care sample by Bird et al. (2002), was achieved by understanding multiple parameters of the case profile. This is only possible through holistic assessment.

Multiple sources of information are required, in particular from the people who know the patient best. In nursing homes it is essential to include hands-on care staff as well as more senior staff and family (see Case A, in the last section of this chapter). Another main source, equally often ignored, is the person with dementia, using direct discussion where possible, empathic and focused listening, and behavioral observation (see Cases A, C, and D). Though assessment cannot be covered adequately here, the primary questions may be encapsulated under the following headings. Other useful texts are Hope and Patel (1993) and Zandi (1994).

Is the Behavior Causing Distress or Danger to the Patient or Others?

If the behavior is not causing distress or danger, then it is not challenging and not a legitimate target for clinicians other than allaying, if necessary, the concerns of those exposed to it. The most obvious example is benign hallucinations or delusions (Peisah & Brodaty, 1994). However, many other bizarre phenomena in dementia often classified as aberrant or agitated, such as pacing or endlessly sorting clothing, also require assessment as to whether it is a problem for anybody (Cummings et al., 1994). Treating behaviors simply because they challenge the clinician's perception of what is normal risks producing nonbenign outcomes, especially with psychotropic medication.

Even if there is distress among caregivers, it is important to discover who is distressed and the source and severity of that distress to determine whether home caregiver or nursing staff concerns are a more appropriate target than the behavior (see pp. 150, 151).

What Is the Patient Actually Doing and What Is the Context?

Labels such as *agitation* carry no information. It is essential to find out what the patient is actually doing and the context in which it occurs. The term *aggression* may be used as an example. It can range from occasional verbal abuse or innocuous pushing away, in which case dealing with career concerns is likely to figure prominently, to severe violence (Bridges-Parlet, Knopman, & Thompson, 1994). The context can range from its very common occurrence during intimate personal care because of misperceptions about the caregiver's intentions, deficient caregiver skills, or both (Bird et al., 2002; Bridges-Parlet et al., 1994), to a response to hallucinations (Tsai, Hwang, Yang, & Liu, 1996). These completely different phenomena require completely different interventions.

Etiology: What Is Causing or Exacerbating the Behavior?

Though brain impairment is a necessary condition, it is only one of many variables with the potential to produce challenging behavior or exacerbate it beyond comfortably manageable levels. Important within-patient variables include past history and character, pattern of cognitive and sensory impairment, physical health and comfort, mood state, and presence of hallucinations. External variables are the vast complex of physical and social phenomena that form the patient's immediate world (Haryadi, 1989). The role of assessment here is to develop evidence-based hypotheses about the factors that produce the behavior or that are realistically adjustable, or both.

The following sections provide only a flavor of the critical importance of this information.

Within-Patient Variables. The most common adjustable patient characteristics relate to physical discomfort and include pain and depression. Other physical phenomena, such as constipation, drug interactions, and infections, are also frequent causal factors in behavioral disturbance (Meagher, O'Hanlon, O'Mahony, & Casey, 1996; Peisah & Brodaty, 1994). Though interventions for these phenomena will be primarily medical (see Beck & Heacock, 1988), psychosocial methods can be used as adjuncts (Bird et al., 2002). In any case, the high frequency with which they go unassessed or untreated in dementia (Elmståhl et al., 1998) means that no psychosocial practitioner can afford to ignore them.

Beyond this, even nonadjustable factors in etiology, such as past history can provide vital information when planning an intervention. For example, when staff learned that a woman who screamed and was violent during bathing was probably manifesting panic based on known premorbid trauma the staff changed their approach and largely eliminated the behavior (Bird, 2000).

External Variables. Many texts concentrate on the physical environment in dementia care (e.g., Weisman, Calkins, & Sloane, 1994), and it can be an important causal and, by adjustment, ameliorating factor in challenging behavior. This applies to either the presence or absence of stimuli. For example, incontinence has been reduced by visual, auditory, or situational cues (Bird, 1998; Bird, Alexopoulos, & Adamowicz, 1995; Hanley, 1986); screaming by room relocation (Meares & Draper, 1999); wandering by visual barriers (Hussian & Brown, 1987); and self-harm by removal of cues precipitating it (Bird et al., 1998). The patient who screamed in the bathroom because of panic could have her hair washed without incident in a local salon (Bird, 2000).

It is, however, more often the social and in particular the care environment that is critical in assessment. The association between violence and care interactions has already been noted. In other examples, Cohen-Mansfield, Marx, Werner, and Freedman (1992) found a relationship between disturbed behavior and staff schedules. Edberg, Nordmark, Sandgren, and Hallberg (1995) showed that the nature of nurse–patient interactions during care has an association with screaming, and Baltes, Neumann, and Zank (1994) found that career practices increase patient dependence.

These data are unsurprising. Most patients with dementia live, by necessity, in dependent and dynamic relationships, either at home or in institutions. What the patient does and feels affects caregivers, whose actions and emotions in turn affect the patient. Assessment must therefore include the way care is carried out. Even if caregiver practices are not causing the behavior, it is often easier to change what they are doing than patient behavior. Working with home or institutional caregivers to adapt their attitudes and approaches predominated a large intervention study by Bird et al. (2000; see Appendix to this chapter).

What Can Be Done in This Particular Case, and How?

Realism is essential. Though rarely discussed, it is an aspect of the psychosocial approach that is as critical as etiology and, equally, because of its idiosyncrasy, gives it absolutely no concordance with the syndrome-standard cure model. It requires assessment of what is possible, both with the patient and the environment in which the intervention must take place.

Patient Possibilities. Entirely dependent on assessment of individual characteristics and capability, a planned intervention might range from highly structured counseling in very early dementia (e.g., Teri, 1994; Woods & Bird, 1998) to acceptance that nothing direct is possible because the patient is too impaired or too difficult. For example, another female resident with advanced dementia who screamed and hit during bathing and toileting had suffered all her life from cleanliness-related obsessive compulsive disorder. A change in behavior was therefore unlikely, and the objective, successfully realized, became to empower and assist all nursing staff to develop the confidence and skills to undertake what was always going to be a difficult task (Bird, 2000).

Formal neuropsychological assessment can provide guidance, but a more direct method is behavioral experiment. For example, in a case of habitual physical sexual assault during showering (Bird et al., 1998) operant conditioning was tried, even though it is often ineffective in dementia. Assessment showed some insight and a capacity to learn simple associations. The experiment of having a novel no-nonsense nurse shower the patient showed that the behavior was under the patient's partial control and the reinforcer for abstaining from assault (reading the newspaper with a caregiver) genuinely pleasurable.

At an apparently more mundane but equally important level, the number of barely legible cues one sees in nursing homes underlines that assessing the patient's capacity to respond to an intervention is rarely considered before it is put in place. Cues are useless in dementia unless the patient can learn to attend to them and, having done so, remember what they mean and, having done that, act on them (Bird, 1998; Hanley, McGuire, & Boyd, 1981).

Environmental Possibilities. Assessment to become familiar with the physical and care environment is equally critical. Case A (see the final section of this chapter) is a good illustration of this assessment. It was necessary to engage a volunteer to take the patient out because there was no outside access for patients and insufficient motivated staff to perform this task. In Case D, the provision of care at timed intervals was only implemented because assessment showed flexible organization and because the empathy of staff guaranteed that the patient would not be ignored altogether. This would not have been possible in a nursing home with a rigid structure, nor in one where caregivers were burned out, nor in one where management regarded psychotropic medication as the universal panacea.

As this implies, part of the assessment must include determining whether there is capacity for change within a given care setting. There is no research data, and clinicians must rely on clinical judgment. The author's rough rule of thumb with home caregivers is that if distress—for example, depression or anger—inhibits them from looking at the behavior objectively—even if only minimally—an intervention requiring a change in caregiver behavior is not possible until that distress is addressed. In residential facilities, the closer the institution approximates to the acute hospital medical model, the more difficult it will be to implement a nonmedical intervention. In certain facilities only a masochist would attempt complex psychosocial interventions, though sometimes even a small core of committed staff is sufficient to start the ball rolling. The clinician must look for flexibility of approach and the presence of, or potential to develop, some kind of dementia literacy, with an understanding of and empathy for how the patient experiences the world. This is more important than a theoretical knowledge of brain–behavior relationships.

Despite the near invisibility of this critical issue in the literature, there is some movement. Schnelle, Cruise, Rahman, and Ouslander (1998) have discussed the problem of compliance by staff with psychosocial interventions in nursing homes. Some authors are beginning to tackle the problem of quantifying the characteristics of aged residential facilities, including culture and quality of care practices (e.g., Ooi, Morris, Brandeis, Hossain, & Lipsitz, 1999). Hallberg and Norberg (1995) have developed a scale measuring attitudes of nurses to difficult patients with dementia, which has proved sensitive to change in both Sweden and, in a modified form, Australia (Bird et al., 2002).

CAREGIVER DISTRESS AS A CLINICAL TARGET

As already discussed, the response of those exposed to a behavior is the main factor that determines whether it is defined as a problem. Restricting treatment to the behavior alone, accordingly, is an absurd limitation of options. In a significant minority of cases, addressing caregiver concerns is sufficient. Beyond this, even if patient behavior change is necessary, the most common method will probably involve working with home caregivers or nursing staff to change their attitude or approach (see Appendix). Interventions aimed at caregiver attitudes or behavior require the same rapport as normal psychotherapy, though, in institutions, multiple staff of varying levels of skill, insight, flexibility, and motivation make the task more complex. If caregiver concerns are not at least listened to, there can be little rapport and little chance of compliance.

At least two intervention studies with a strong psychosocial component, and which have included career measures (Bird et al., 2002; Hinchliffe et al., 1995), have shown a relationship between reduced problem behavior and alleviation of career distress; however, causal direction is impossible to attribute. In some situations caregiver distress was alleviated such that, though the behavior remained, it ceased to be seen as a significant problem. (See also Case B in the final section of this chapter) Another large intervention study has shown that the initial visit alone, when the case is first discussed, can produce a reduction in behavior and distress (Opie, Doyle, & O'Connor, 2002).

Often it is necessary to reduce career distress before attempting an intervention requiring their input (e.g., Bird et al., 1998, 2002). For example, it was necessary to work first on the anger of a home caregiver whose confrontational response to her husband's obsessive toileting was exacerbating the problem. Emotional support, education on dementia, and learning that her husband was genuinely anxious enabled her to begin to respond with empathy, physical comfort, and gentle assertion, reducing the behavior to more manageable proportions and improving her own mental health (Bird et al., 1998).

Factors that lead caregivers to be distressed by patient behavior are complex. Known examples include appraisal—not necessarily the reality—of physical threat (Rodney, 2000); nursing home organizational factors (Baillon, Scothern, Neville, & Boyle, 1996); interpretation of the behavior (Harvath, 1994); depression in caregivers (Hinchliffe et al., 1995; Teri, 1997); low dementia literacy (Hagen & Sayers, 1995); and morale and attitude to care (Jenkins & Allen, 1998).

These are variables that can be addressed directly with the caregiver. Though controlled clinical intervention studies are astonishingly rare within the vast home caregiver burden literature, a few structured support and education programs have demonstrated clear benefits, including managing behavior problems and concomitant delayed entry into residential care (see Teri, 1999, for review). In institutions, programs that have addressed attitude and care practices have produced not only improved staff morale (Berg, Hansson, & Hallberg, 1994) but also reduced problem behavior (Hagen & Sayers, 1995; Rovner, Steele, & Folstein, 1996), reduced patient dependence (Baltes et al., 1994), reduced patient anxiety and depression (Bråne, Karlsson, Kihlgren, & Norberg, 1989), improved staff–patient cooperation and therefore reduced problems in personal care (Edberg, Hallberg, & Gustafson, 1996), and reduced use of physical restraint and antipsychotic drugs (Levine, Marchello, & Totolos, 1995; Ray et al., 1993).

That is, abundant evidence shows that the clinician called to treat a case of challenging behavior who ignores caregiver distress about that behavior as the primary clinical target, or as a critical ancillary to dealing with the behavior, is working with a grossly circumscribed repertoire. Twenty percent of cases reported by Bird et al. (2002) were ameliorated without changing patient behavior.

RESEARCH ON STANDARD APPROACHES

Though the syndrome-standard cure model rarely fits the individual case, the search for standard approaches has been the predominant paradigm in psychosocial intervention research to date. This section attempts merely to present a flavor of recent work.

Special Care Units

The most holistic standard approach is the movement toward units that use physical design, a dementia-dedicated care culture, or both, to produce a minimally challenging environment for the patient and, thus, fewer problems and a more informed approach when problems do arise (Leon, 1994). There is currently a strong research effort attempting to resolve the formidable methodological problems involved in evaluating their efficacy (Weisman et al., 1994), including defining what a special care unit (SCU) actually is. For example, though Australia contains excellent units, some nursing homes dedicate a wing to residents with dementia but pay no attention to design or care culture. This is warehousing, not special care.

There is at least one study where Group Living Units, the Swedish equivalent, produced worse outcomes than traditional care (Wimo et al., 1993). However, a strong theme of this chapter, that the physical and care environment strongly impinges on challenging behavior, potentially makes SCUs an important development. Readers are directed to an entire supplement of *Alzheimer Disease and Associated Disorders* (Holmes, Ory, & Teresi, 1994).

Standard Methods for Specific Behaviors

This section contains two examples of methods. For a more thorough review, see an entire supplement to *International Psychogeriatrics* (Radebaugh, Buckholz, & Khachaturian, 1996).

Disruptive noisemaking has been much studied, though, like much of the literature, intervention research is rare. However, in a careful study, Burgio, Scilley, Hardin, Hsu, and Yancey (1996) tried waterscape sounds with 13 severely impaired noisy dementia unit residents. Despite 50% noncompliance by nursing staff or patients throwing off the headphones, there was a 23% decrease in noise among the patients who responded. Helmes and Wiancko (1997) found that playing quiet baroque music significantly reduced noisemaking in some individuals. Other authors have found that music played, regardless of individual taste, has no effect, but Gerdner and Swanson (1993) showed that music based on known preference produced a short-term effect. See Cohen-Mansfield and Werner (1997) for a recent review on disruptive vocalizations.

Incontinence in dementia is a major stressor for caregivers and a predictor of institutionalization (Hope, Keene, Gedling, Fairburn, & Jacoby, 1998), where it also stresses staff and nursing home budgets (Colling, Ouslander, Hadley, Eisch, & Campbell, 1992). There is now expanding scientific literature on psychosocial methods, in particular prompted voiding, and enough evidence to disprove the common nihilistic view of incontinence and dementia. For example, Colling et al. (1992) trained staff in management programs that, despite 30% noncompliance, produced a significant reduction in incontinence with physically and cognitively impaired residents. See Skelly and Flint (1995) for a review of the dementia literature.

Generic Methods for Diverse Behaviors

Camp, Bird, and Cherry (2000) and Bird and Kinsella (1996) have shown repeatedly that patients with mild to moderate dementia can be trained to associate specific cues with behavior. The method capitalizes on retrieval assisting in laying down an accessible memory trace. Cases described in Alexopoulos (1994), Bird et al. (1995), and Bird (1998) describe its adaptation to ameliorate behaviors as diverse as sexual assault, incontinence, and repetitive questions. Failures are also reported; like all attempts to produce standard therapeutic methods, it is far from a panacea.

Cue-behavior learning was based on solid experimental research. The same cannot be said about the ability of patients with dementia to associate behavior with reinforcers, despite many authors advocating reinforcement principles in dementia (e.g., McGovern & Koss, 1994; Peisah & Brodaty, 1994). Clearly, many behaviors are performed because the patient finds them reinforcing, but it is important for clinicians to know that there are almost no cases reported in the literature of the last 30 years where adjustment of reinforcers has alleviated challenging behavior in dementia. Studies often cited in support (Vaccaro, 1988) did not involve residents with dementia.

This is not to say that differential reinforcement cannot be used—for example the sexual assault case described on page 148, though even here it was only partially successful (Bird et al., 2002). However, the research remains to be done. At present, clinicians who try reinforcement as a stand-alone method, and without substantial input into caregiver education and compliance, are not likely to find it very rewarding.

Comment: Limitations of Standard Approaches

The recent entry of scientific investigation into the psychosocial intervention literature, where techniques are described and outcomes—including failure—objectively measured and reported, is already showing promise. However the body of work is still small, and it is tempting to speculate that a much-cited study by Hussian and Brown (1987), who limited wandering using a grid pattern on the floor, is much cited because of its rarity. It failed on replication (Chafetz, 1990).

In addition, most studies are frank about nonresponders and thus, either explicitly or implicitly, the limitations of the standard cure model. These are simply techniques to add to the toolkit that will work with some patients in some situations some of the time—probably the best that can be hoped for. At the individual case level, thorough assessment is still required. If a patient is verbally disruptive because of chronic pain, analgesics will be more effective than baroque music. If disturbed sleep/wake cycles are caused by night nurses waking patients, which is commonly the case (Schnelle, Ouslander, Simmons, Alessi, & Gravel, 1993), training staff to exhibit common sense is likely to be more relevant than bright-light therapy, which recent studies suggest has some promise (e.g., Lovell, Ancoli, & Gervitz, 1995).

As the Appendix to this chapter clearly shows, psychosocial interventions rarely require high-tech methods or specific expertise, such as training in cued recall. Most of the interventions involved sensitively changing the attitude, the care approach, or both of those around the person with dementia. This depends entirely on holistic assessment and rapport building, not the rote application of standard solutions

CASE STUDIES

Four cases are presented here to illustrate and reiterate key points made in the text. Outcomes are presented in Table 8.1 for the target behavior and, apart from Case C, for caregivers. Cases A, B, and D formed part of a large intervention study (Bird et al., 2002) where a predominantly psychosocial approach took no longer than a predominantly pharmacological (mainly antipsychotic) approach and was at least as effective and produced far fewer drug side effects. Cognitive decline over the measurement period was controlled for.

Behavior frequency in Table 8.1 was monitored at baseline and two postintervention points using time-limited observation periods and mechanical counters for high frequency behaviors C and D) or forms tailored to the problem for the low-frequency behaviors in A and B. The relevant caregiver measures are as follows: Caregiver stress related to the referred behavior was assessed on a 7-point scale (7 = *extreme stress*, 1 = *very relaxed*) at all three time points. Perceived change in ability to cope with the patient was assessed on a 7-point scale (4 = *no change*) at follow-up, with a maximum possible change therefore of +3 (improvement) or –3. In institutions, multiple staff closely involved with the patient completed these measures; the scores in Table 8.1 represent the mean. A senior nurse, usually the director of nursing, rated the severity of the referred behavior for its overall impact on the facility on a 5-point scale (5 = *extreme problem*) at baseline and final follow-up. These measures have adequate concurrent validity and test-retest reliability (Bird et al., 2002). Home caregivers also completed the General Health Questionnaire 28 (Goldberg & Hillier, 1979).

Case A. 'Terry,' age 63, had AD and scored 9 on the Mini Mental State Exam (Folstein, Folstein, & McHugh, 1975). He fell in the moderate range on the Clinical Dementia Rating (Morris, 1993). He was cared for by some excellent staff in a badly designed nursing home that was dark and had no outside access. He was referred for almost daily violent verbal outbursts that, because of his size and fitness, were extremely threatening. He was assessed, first by a psychiatric nurse, where he scored 0 on a depression scale, and then by a psychiatric registrar, who prescribed 5 mg Serenace twice daily. This had no effect other than making him sleep more during the day.

On assessment by a clinical team with dementia expertise, 'Terry' soon began crying in response to sensitive questions and, despite some aphasia, spoke frankly of his despair at lack of access to his young sons and at living in "this prison." Nursing notes described frequent crying, particularly at night when, unable to sleep, he spoke of hopelessness and suicide. Night staff were clear about the depth of his depression and angry that no one had sought their views. 'Terry' was prescribed 10 mg of Tolvon twice daily and, at the same time, a male volunteer engaged to befriend him and take him out of "prison" for regular exercise. His affect quickly improved, and his outbursts all but ceased. Staff stress related to this patient dropped significantly, and their ability to cope increased (see Table 8.1).

Problems later resurfaced, directly connected to family nonvisits. Some senior staff wanted sedation. However, 'Terry' was eventually transferred to a dementia-specific unit with a garden. Occasional outbursts still oc-

TABLE 8.1

Clinical outcomes of four cases: Patient behaviour and caregiver response

Case	Variable measured	Pre-intervention	2 month follow-up	5 month follow-up
A	Mean severe outbursts daily	0.8	0.2	0
	Mean staff stress related to the behaviour	5	3	2
	Mean change in staff's ability to cope		+2.5	+2
	Overall severity of problem for the facility	*severe*		*moderate*
B	Mean weekly contacts with brothels	2.7	2.5	3.7
	Spouse's stress related to the behaviour	7	7	1
	Spouse's GHQ28 Score (Chronic scoring)	14	9	9
	Change in spouse's ability to cope		+2	+2
C	Mean repetitive questions per hour	44.2	26.1[1]	16.5
	Caregiver measures not taken for Case C			
D	Mean repetitive questions per hour	85.7	23.3	18.9
	Mean staff stress related to the behaviour	5	4	5
	Mean change in staff's ability to cope		+2	+2.5
	Overall severity of problem for facility	*severe*		*moderate*

[1]first follow-up taken at 1 month

curred because his wife remained recalcitrant about access, but staff allowed him to stride about the garden shouting and then comforted him when he started to quieten. He was not seen as a management problem.

Case B. 'Barry,' age 75, had mild impairment, then of unknown cause but since identified as Picks disease (MMSE = 23; Clinical Dementia Rating level mild). He lived at home and was referred because, after a long and relatively happy marriage, he had taken to openly visiting brothels. His medical practitioner had prescribed Androcur with 'Barry's' notional agreement, but 'Barry' spat the tablets out. In any case, initial assessment showed no evidence of increased libido; the case was seen more as loss of inhibition and insight into consequences. Though ethically shaky, a decision was made to intervene because his wife was in severe distress, with antidepressants only minimally effective. In addition, the habit was eating away their savings.

When the money supply was restricted with his agreement, 'Barry' began telephoning brothels from local pay phones for "quotes" (his terminology), until his pocket money was exhausted. The frequency count in Table 8.1 is based on known occasions when he did this and is certainly an underestimate. His wife found this practice equally impossible to accept. She was questioning the validity of her whole married life and was unsure whether she would continue to look after him. Assessment showed, however, that she had coped well with severe adversity earlier in life using a strong rational intelligence. Accordingly, the intervention took the form of emotionally supporting her and helping her to see the behavior in the context of the onset of dementia in contrast to 'Barry's' responsible premorbid behavior. Though her husband continued to contact brothels, she came, over time, to see the behavior as sad rather than culpable and ceased to find it stressful. There was a marked and sustained improvement in her mental health.

Case C. 'Pauline,' age 81 years, had probable AD (MMSE = 9; CDR level-severe), and lived in an excellent dementia-specific unit. She was referred because she would attach herself like a limpet to staff and ask the same questions up to 150 times an hour (mean = 45), and refuse to be left. Answers produced only short-term calm. She was dangerously sensitive to psychotropics. Only someone who has never experienced repetitive questions in dementia could regard it as a minor problem.

Observation showed two types of questions: anxiety about her mother and helpless questions to which she knew the answer or were frank demands for reassurance. Information from her only surviving contact revealed a life of appalling insecurity and abuse from childhood on. Focused further questions confirmed a long-term tendency by 'Pauline' to seek reassurance, despite high premorbid competence. It was hypothesized that the behavior was the residue of this habitual method of allaying anxiety, restricted by dementia to a small and unsubtle repertoire, and endlessly repeated because of impaired memory.

Behavioral experiment showed that if the questions were ignored but her hand was held and stroked, the questions would become frantic but then die away after a few minutes, with 'Pauline' often calm enough to leave. This became the intervention, backed by staff discussion to deal with guilt about not replying and a video showing that the technique worked. Career measures were not gathered for this patient.

Subsequently, 'Pauline' was transferred to a much larger dementia unit. Here she sought reassurance in the old way, but her behavior was not a problem because there were several male residents to whom she could attach herself and who seemed to enjoy her chattering company and physical closeness.

Case D. 'Marie,' 77 years old, was a nursing home resident who had sustained hypoxic brain damage during a knee reconstruction 4 years previous (MMSE = 17; CDR level-severe). She was referred for violence at night and wandering around in the day making repetitive demands. The violence related entirely to being woken up when wet, and the intervention consisted of persuading night nurses, not without difficulty, that modern absorbent pads can usually keep the patient dry until morning. There were no more incidents.

The demands were more serious. They occurred up to 120 times an hour and were more clearly perseverative, for example, shouting without pause for a cup of tea while holding one. However, there was some environmental influence, with the behavior particularly bad at mealtimes. Many medications had been unsuccessfully tried; most had a short-term effect that evaporated.

Multiple parameters of assessment were vital in this case. Possibly because 'Marie' often demanded and received drinks, there was an assumption that she was drinking them. In fact, she was sometimes dehydrated and notorious for offensive urine and proneness to urinary tract infections. She was on analgesics as required, but could sometimes be seen grimacing and rubbing her knees. Behavioral experiment, undertaken with enthusiastic cooperation by excellent staff in this facility, showed that ignoring the demands had little effect on the behavior or on 'Marie's' apparent distress and arousal, possibly even reducing it.

The intervention consisted first of 100 mg of Tegretol twice daily and more systematic administration of analgesics to see whether 'Marie's' arousal could be reduced pharmacologically. Improvement lasted only 10 days. Thereafter, the full intervention was implemented: (a) aggressive monitoring of fluid intake and urinary tract infections; (b) meals alone in her room with activity outside her visual field; and (c) empowering nurses not to respond to her questions but, instead, to provide warm personal care at regular intervals. Key staff were given timers to ensure that she was not ignored. The behavior was reduced by roughly 75%. Staff stress measures did not register this change, but the coping measure did (see Table 8.1).

Comments

The initial approach to Terry epitomizes much that is currently wrong with the treatment of challenging behavior in dementia, in particular inadequate assessment. This includes not only failure to look beyond the manifested behavior but also belief that a depression scale score is a better representation of the world than clinical evidence plentifully and freely available from the patient, nursing records, and the caregivers who knew the patient best. Self-report is inherently unreliable in dementia (Elmståhl et al., 1998; Feher, Larrabee, & Crook, 1992), and alternative or supplementary means are often required, also evident with the pain in Case D.

The sequel to this case and that of Pauline illustrate a major theme of this chapter. It is not the nature of the behavior that defines it as challenging. In different nursing homes, the same behavior by the same patients was no longer a problem.

The intervention with Barry illustrates the main issue aired in the section on "caregiver distress on a clinical target"; the absolute necessity of considering caregiver distress as a clinical target, either wholly or in part. Staff distress was also a component with Marie. The purpose of the ostentatious behavioral experiment where the questions were ignored was to give nurses permission to do the same, by demonstrating that it made no difference.

The interventions with Pauline and Marie were included together to reiterate another underlying theme. The nature of the behavior provides no information about etiology, nor about optimum treatment. Both were repetitive questions cases and, on the face of it, even similar in part of the intervention—ignoring the questions. However, with Pauline, there was a relatively well-supported hypothesis that this was an anxiety-reduction problem, and it proved possible to find a nonverbal means of providing it. With Marie, ignoring the behavior was only one component in a multimodal intervention and, in itself, aimed at staff distress. The overall aim was to undercut factors that exacerbated the behavior—almost certainly directly related to brain lesions—beyond tolerable levels.

CONCLUSIONS

Finally, these four cases and others described illustrate the primary underlying theme of this chapter. A complex constellation of biopsychosocial factors produces challenging behavior in dementia, and, accordingly, there can be few if any standard treatments. The four case examples alone show variously the influence of past and recent history, physical environment, physical and psychiatric problems, specific brain lesions, and caregiver issues and practices. Cases A and D illustrate a consequent point, made at the outset. Psychosocial and pharmacological approaches are not in opposition. They are complementary, and the approach outlined in this chapter makes no distinction. Though the holistic assessment described may seem unrealistically time-consuming, Bird et al. (2002) have demonstrated that this problem is more apparent than real. Taking the trouble to work out at the start what is going on may be no more time-consuming than the apparent quick fix of psychotropics, given the frequency with which medical practitioners have to repeatedly return, often in a kind of scatter-gun approach, to adjust the dosage of expensive medications, experiment with others, control for side effects, or arrange admission to a hospital for treatment. The problem, epitomized by Case A, is not pharmacology, however. It is that lack of knowledge, lack of skills, or adherence to a model where surface symptoms are treated without thought of causality leads to a strong and limiting overemphasis on pharmacology.

Other authors have written about the multifactorial and therefore idiosyncratic nature of challenging behavior in dementia, in both etiology and treatment options (e.g., Haryadi, 1989; Zandi, 1994). Until more pharmacological and psychosocial intervention research comes to grips with this messy reality, instead of trying to fit it into traditional and methodologically convenient but invalid models, clinicians will continue to work with a grossly inadequate repertoire. At an absolute minimum, to paraphrase Yeats, the longer they remain fixated on the deed—the behavior—instead of the motive— causality—the longer we will remain in shadow.

ACKNOWLEDGMENTS

The author gratefully acknowledges, firstly, the support of the Commonwealth Government Office for Older Australians, who funded some of the research reported in this chapter. Secondly, profound thanks are due to all the people with dementia, their families, and residential aged-care nursing staff who participated in the clinical interventions described and so generously assisted in providing research data. The Appendix is reproduced from Bird et al. (2002) by the kind permission of the Australian Commonwealth Government, Department of Health and Ageing, Office for Older Australians.

REFERENCES

Aisen, P. S., Deluca, T., & Lawler, B. A. (1992). Falls among geropsychiatry inpatients are associated with PRN medications for agitation. *International Journal of Geriatric Psychiatry, 7*, 709–712.

Alexopoulos, P. (1994). Management of sexually disinhibited behavior by a demented patient. *Australian Journal on Ageing, 13*, 119.

Alzheimer, A. (1907). A characteristic disease of the cerebral cortex. In E. Schultze & O. Snell (Eds.), *Allgemeine zeitschrift für psychiatrie und psychisch-gerichtliche medizin* (Vol. LXIV, pp. 146–148). Berlin: Georg Relmer.

Baillon, S., Scothern, G., Neville, P. G., & Boyle, A. (1996). Factors that contribute to stress in care staff in residential homes for the elderly. *International Journal of Geriatric Psychiatry, 11*, 219–226.

Baltes, M. M., Neumann, E.-M., & Zank, S. (1994). Maintenance and rehabilitation of independence in old age: An intervention program for staff. *Psychology and Aging, 9*(2), 179–188.

Beck, C. & Heacock, P. (1988). Nursing interventions for patients with Alzheimer's disease. *Nursing Clinics of North America, 23*(1), 95–124.

Berg, A., Hansson, U. W., & Hallberg, I. R. (1994). Nurses' creativity, tedium and burnout during one year of clinical supervision and implementation of individually planned nursing care: Comparisons between a ward for severely demented patients and a similar control ward. *Journal of Advanced Nursing, 20*, 742–749.

Bird, M. (1998). Clinical use of preserved learning capacity in dementia. *Australasian Journal on Ageing, 17*(4), 161–166.

Bird, M. (2000). Psychosocial rehabilitation for problems arising from cognitive deficits in dementia. In R. Hill, L. Bäckman, & A. Stigsdotter-Neely (Eds.), *Cognitive rehabilitation in old age*. Oxford, UK: Oxford University Press.

Bird, M., Alexopoulos, P., & Adamowicz, J. (1995). Success and failure in five case studies: Use of cued recall to ameliorate behavior problems in senile dementia. *International Journal of Geriatric Psychiatry, 10*(4), 5–11.

Bird, M., & Kinsella, G. (1996). Long-term cued recall of tasks in senile dementia. *Psychology and Ageing, 11*(1), 45–56.

Bird, M., Llewellyn-Jones, R., Smithers, H., Andrews, C., Cameron, I., Cottee, A., Hutson, C., Jenneke, B., & Kurrle, S. (1998). Challenging behaviors in dementia: A project at Hornsby/Ku-ring-gai Hospital. *Australian Journal on Ageing, 17*(1), 10–15.

Bird, M., Llewellyn-Jones, R., Smithers, H., & Korten, A. (2002). *Psychosocial approaches to challenging behaviour in dementia: A controlled trial*. Report to the Commonwealth Department of Health and Ageing, Office for Older Australians: Commonwealth Department of Health and Ageing, Canberra.

Bråne, G., Karlsson, I., Kihlgren, M., & Norberg, A. (1989). Integrity-promoting care of demented nursing home patients: Psychological and biochemical changes. *International Journal of Geriatric Psychiatry, 4*(3), 165–172.

Bridges-Parlet, S., Knopman, D., & Thompson, T. (1994). A descriptive study of physically aggressive behavior in dementia by direct observation. *Journal of the American Geriatrics Society, 42*, 192–197.

Burgio, L., Scilley, K., Hardin, J., Hsu, C., & Yancey, J. (1996). Environmental "white noise": An intervention for verbally agitated nursing home residents. *Journal of Gerontology: Psychological Sciences, 51B*, P364–P373.

Camp, C., Bird, M., & Cherry, K. (2000). Retrieval strategies as a rehabilitation aid for cognitive loss in pathological aging. In R. Hill, L. Bäckman, & A. Stiggsdotter-Neely (Eds.), *Cognitive Rehabilitation in old age*. Oxford, UK: Oxford University Press.

Chafetz, P. K. (1990). Two-dimensional grid is ineffective against demented patients exiting through glass doors. *Psychology and Aging, 5*(1), 146–147.

Cohen-Mansfield, J., Marx, M., Werner, P., & Freedman, L. (1992). Temporal patterns of agitated nursing home residents. *International Psychogeriatrics, 4*, 197–206.

Cohen-Mansfield, J., & Werner, P. (1997). Typology of disruptive vocalizations in older persons suffering from dementia. *International Journal of Geriatric Psychiatry, 12*, 1079–1091.

Colling, J., Ouslander, J., Hadley, B.-J., Eisch, J., & Campbell, E. (1992). The effects of patterned urge-response toileting (PURT) on urinary incontinence among nursing home residents. *Journal of the American Geriatrics Society, 40*(2), 135–141.

Cummings, J., Mega, M., Gray, K., Rosenberg-Thompson, S., Carusi, D., & Gornbein, J. (1994). The Neuropsychiatric Inventory: Comprehensive assessment of psychopathology in dementia. *Neurology, 44*, 2308–2314.

Devanand, D. P., & Levy, S. R. (1995). Neuroleptic treatment of agitation and psychosis in dementia. *Journal of Geriatric Psychiatry and Neurology, 8*, S18–S27.

Edberg, A.-K., Hallberg, I. R., & Gustafson, L. (1996). Effects of clinical supervision on nurse-patient cooperation quality. *Clinical Nursing Research, 5*(2), 127–149.

Edberg, A.-K., Nordmark, Å., Sandgren, Å., & Hallberg, I. R. (1995). Initiating and terminating verbal interaction between nurses and severely demented patients regarded as vocally disruptive. *Journal of Psychiatric and Mental Health Nursing, 2*(3), 159–167.

Elmståhl, S., Stenberg, I., Annerstedt, L., & Ingvad, B. (1998). Behavioral disturbances and pharmacological treatment of patients with dementia in family caregiving: A 2-year follow-up. *International Psychogeriatrics, 10*, 239–252.

Feher, E., Larrabee, G., & Crook, T. (1992). Factors attenuating the validity of the Geriatric Depression Scale in a dementia population. *Journal of the American Geriatrics Society, 40*, 906–906.

Finkel, S. I., Lyons, J. S., Anderson, R. L., Sherrell, K., Davis, J., Cohen-Mansfield, J., Schwartz, A., Gandy, J., & Schneider, L. (1995). A randomized, placebo-controlled trial of thiothixene in agitated, demented nursing home patients. *International Journal of Geriatric Psychiatry, 10*(2), 129–136.

Folstein, M. F., Folstein, S. E., & McHugh, P. R. (1975). Mini-mental state: A practical method for grading the cognitive state of patients for the clinician. *Journal of Psychiatric Research, 12*, 189–198.

Gerdner, L., & Swanson, E. (1993). Effects of individualized music on confused and agitated elderly patients. *Archives of Psychiatric Nursing, 7*, 284–291.

Goldberg, D., & Hillier, V. (1979). A scaled version of the General Health Questionnaire. *Psychological Medicine, 9*(1), 139–145.

Hagen, B., & Sayers, D. (1995). When caring leaves bruises: The effects of staff education on resident aggression. *Journal of Gerontological Nursing, 21*(11), 7–16.

Hallberg, I. R., Edberg, A.-K., Nordmark, Å., & Johnsson, K. (1993). Daytime vocal activity in institutionalized severely demented patients identified as vocally disruptive by nurses. *International Journal of Geriatric Psychiatry, 8*(2), 155–164.

Hallberg, I. R., & Norberg, A. (1995). Nurses' experiences of strain and their reactions in the care of severely demented patients. *International Journal of Geriatric Psychiatry, 10*, 757–766.

Hanley, I. (1986). Reality orientation in the care of the elderly patient with dementia: Three case studies. In I. Hanley & M. Gilhooly (Eds.), *Psychological therapies for the elderly* (pp. 65–79). London: Croom Helm.

Hanley, I., McGuire, R., & Boyd, W. (1981). Reality orientation and dementia: A controlled trial of two approaches. *British Journal of Psychiatry, 138*(Jan), 10–14.

Harvath, T. (1994). Interpretation and management of dementia-related behavior problems. *Clinical Nursing Research, 3*(1), 7–26.

Haryadi, T. (1989). The confused patient: A multi-dimensional approach. In P. R. Katz & E. Calkins (Eds.), *Principles of nursing home care* (pp. 180–207). New York: Springer.

Helmes, E., & Wiancko, D. (1997). *Effects of music in reducing disruptive behavior in a general hospital.* Paper presented at the 16th Congress of the International Association of Gerontology, Adelaide, Australia.

Hinchliffe, A. C., Hyman, I. L., Blizard, B., & Livingston, G. (1995). Behavioral complications of dementia—Can they be treated? *International Journal of Geriatric Psychiatry, 10*, 839–847.

Holmes, D., Ory, M., & Teresi, J. (Eds). (1994). Special dementia care: Research, policy, and practice issues. *Alzheimer Disease and Associated Disorders, 8*(Suppl. 1).

Hope, T., Keene, J., Gedling, K., Fairburn, C., & Jacoby, R. (1998). Predictors of institutionalization for people living at home with a career. *International Journal of Geriatric Psychiatry, 13*, 682–690.

Hope, T., & Patel, V. (1993). Assessment of behavioral phenomena in dementia. In A. Burns (Ed.), *Ageing and dementia: A methodological approach* (pp. 221–236). London: Edward Arnold.

Hussian, R. A., & Brown, D. C. (1987). Use of a two dimensional grid pattern to limit hazardous ambulation in demented patients. *Journal of Gerontology, 5*, 558–560.

Jenkins, H., & Allen, C. (1998). The relationship between staff burnout/distress and interactions with residents in two residential homes for older people. *International Journal of Geriatric Psychiatry, 13*, 466–472.

Leon, J. (1994). The 1990/1991 National Survey of special care units in nursing homes. *Alzheimer Disease and Associated Disorders, 8*(Suppl. 1), 72–85.

Levine, J. M., Marchello, V., & Totolos, E. (1995). Progress toward a restraint-free environment in a large academic nursing facility. *Journal of the American Geriatrics Society, 43*, 914–918.

Lovell, B., Ancoli, I., & Gervitz, R. (1995). Effect of bright light treatment on agitated behavior in institutionalized elderly subjects. *Psychiatry Research, 57*(1), 7–12.

McGovern, R. J., & Koss, E. (1994). The use of behavior modification with Alzheimer patients: values and limitations. *Alzheimer Disease and Associated Disorders, 8*(Suppl. 3), 82–91.

Meagher, D. J., O'Hanlon, D., O'Mahony, E., & Casey, P. R. (1996). The use of environment strategies and psychotropic medication in the management of delirium. *British Journal of Psychiatry, 168*, 512–515.

Meares, S., & Draper, B. (1999). Treatment of vocally disruptive behavior of multi-factorial etiology. *International Journal of Geriatric Psychiatry, 14*(4), 285–290.

Morris, J. C. (1993). The Clinical Dementia Rating (CDR): Current version and scoring rules. *Neurology, 43*, 2412–2414.

Nygaard, H. A., Brudvik, E., Juvik, O. B., Pedersen, W. E., Rotevatn, T. S., & Vollset, Å. (1994). Consumption of psychotropic drugs in nursing home residents: A prospective study in patients permanently admitted to a nursing home. *International Journal of Geriatric Psychiatry, 9*, 387–391.

Ooi, W., Morris, J., Brandeis, G., Hossain, M., & Lipsitz, L. (1999). Nursing home characteristics and the development of pressure sores and disruptive behavior. *Age and Ageing, 28*(1), 45–52.

Opie, J., Doyle, C., & O'Connor, D. (2002). Challenging behaviours in nursing home residents with dementia: A randomized controlled trial of multidisciplinary interventions. *International Journal of Geriatric Psychiatry, 17*(1), 6–13.

Peisah, C., & Brodaty, H. (1994). Practical guidelines for the treatment of behavioral complications of dementia. *The Medical Journal of Australia, 161*, 558–564.

Radebaugh, T., Buckholz, N., & Khachaturian, Z. (1996). Behavioral approaches to the treatment of Alzheimer's disease: Research strategies. *International Psychogeriatrics, 8* (Suppl. 1), S7–S12.

Ray, W., Taylor, J., Meador, K., Lichtenstein, M., Griffin, M., Fought, R., Adams, M., & Blazer, D. (1993). Reducing antipsychotic drug use in nursing homes: A controlled trial of provider education. *Archives of Intern Medicine, 22*, 713–721.

Rodney, V. (2000). Nurse stress associated with aggression in people with dementia: Its relationship to hardiness, cognitive appraisal and coping. *Journal of Advanced Nursing, 31*(1), 172–180.

Rovner, B., Steele, C., & Folstein, M. (1996). A randomized trial of dementia care in nursing homes. *Journal of the American Geriatrics Society, 44*(1), 7–13.

Schneider, L., Pollock, V., & Lyness, S. (1990). A meta-analysis of controlled trials of neuroleptic treatment in dementia. *Journal of the American Geriatrics Society, 38,* 553–563.

Schnelle, J., Cruise, P., Rahman, A., & Ouslander, J. (1998). Developing rehabilitative behavioral interventions for long-term care: Technology transfer, acceptance, and maintenance issues. *Journal of the American Geriatrics Society, 46,* 771–777.

Schnelle, J., Ouslander, J., Simmons, S., Alessi, C., & Gravel, M. (1993). The nighttime environment, incontinence care, and sleep disruption in nursing homes. *Journal of The American Geriatrics Society, 41,* 910–914.

Skelly, J., & Flint, A. J. (1995). Urinary incontinence associated with dementia. *Journal of the American Geriatrics Society, 43,* 286–294.

Teri, L. (1994). Behavioral treatment of depression in patients with dementia. *Alzheimer Disease and Associated Disorders, 8* (Suppl. 3), 66–74.

Teri, L. (1997). Behavior and caregiver burden: Behavioral problems in patients with Alzheimer disease and its association with caregiver distress. *Alzheimer Disease and Associated Disorders, 11* (Suppl. 4), 35–38.

Teri, L. (1999). Training families to provide care: Effects on people with dementia. *International Journal of Geriatric Psychiatry, 14,* 110–119.

Tsai, H., Hwang, J., Yang, C., & Liu, K. (1996). Physical aggression and associated factors in probable Alzheimer disease. *Alzheimer Disease and Associated Disorders, 10*(2), 82–85.

Vaccaro, F. J. (1988). Application of operant procedures in a group of institutionalized aggressive geriatric patients. *Psychology and Aging, 3*(1), 22–28.

Weisman, G. D., Calkins, M., & Sloane, P. (1994). The environmental context of special care. *Alzheimer Disease and Associated Disorders, 8* (Suppl. 1), 308–320.

Wimo, A., Nelvig, A., Nelvig, J., Adolphsson, R., Mattesson, B., & Sandman, P. O. (1993). Can changes in ward routines affect the severity of dementia? *International Psychogeriatrics, 5*(2), 169–180.

Woods, B., & Bird, M. (1998). Non-pharmacological approaches to treatment. In G. Wilcock, R. Bucks, & K. Rockwood (Eds.), *Diagnosis and management of dementia: A manual for memory disorders teams* . Oxford, UK: Oxford University Press.

Zandi, T. (1994). Understanding difficult behaviors of nursing home residents: A prerequisite for sensitive clinical assessment and care. *Alzheimer Disease and Associated Disorders, 8* (Suppl. 1), 345–354.

APPENDIX

Psychosocial techniques used by Bird et al. (2002) in their case series ($n = 44$) in the 90% of cases where nondrug methods were the sole, main, or a significant component. Most cases involved several techniques in combination.

Working Primarily With the Patient Direct	*Cases*
*Dealing with physiological precipitants of behavior**	
• Managing physical discomfort (especially pain) more systematically	5
• Reducing frequency of, and ensuring prompt attention to, urinary tract infections	1
• Reducing alcohol intake	1
**Note*: These are not strictly psychosocial but are included here because of the frequency with which these very basic causes are ignored	
Using spared memory	
• Using spaced retrieval and the method of fading cues to teach patient to associate a tangible cue with a behavior	4
• Augmenting effect of changed caregiver responses by using spaced retrieval to teach patient the reason	2
Direct discussion with patient	
On grounds for stopping behavior and backed up by simple letter to be repeatedly read by caregiver and patient together (only possible with mild impairment)	3

*Working Primarily With Caregivers**	*Cases*
* *Note*: The term caregivers is used for both home caregivers and residential care staff	
Education in basic dementia skills	
• Avoiding confrontation and replacing it with empathy or going with the flow	7
• Listening to and taking account of what the person with dementia is saying (or at least feeling), instead of blithely assuming that what they say or do has no meaning	6
• Not being abrupt, impulsive, or noisy in presence of patient	3
• Learning about dementia (especially Lewy body dementia)	2
• Planning excursions ahead of time	2
• Allowing time to deal with the patient	2

• Approaching gradually into the patient's visual field	1
Support/Attitude change	
• Presentation of the patient as a person as well as a problem; often involves education on patient's past and achievements, who they were, and the difference between now and then	13
• Education in causes of the behavior	13
• Emotional support of the caregivers	12
• Validation of what caregivers are already doing	6
• Change in caregiver perception of the behavior by reframing it in the context of the disease	4
• Caregiver empowerment to set limits—"caregivers have rights."	4
• Emphasis on difference between bizarre and challenging behavior, assistance in perception of nondangerous behavior so that it is not seen as in need of treatment	3
• Assistance to accept realities of situation (e.g., dementia diagnosis) and the parameters of what is and what is not possible	3
Residential care/family interaction	
• Working with family of nursing home resident to reduce demands on staff	2
• Working with distressed family to increase visits (lack of them causing the behavior)	1
Changing nursing care practices	
• Structuring patient-specific exercise/activity (as opposed to ad hoc) at strategic times	8
• Letting patient sleep till natural waking time	5
• Not waking patient at night, even if wet	5
• Going away and trying later. Leaving a distressed or resistant resident (if safe to do so) to avoid confrontation and returning when he or she (or the caregiver) is calmer	4
• Empowering staff to use physical touch at strategic times, such as hugs, stroking, holding hands (after first checking that the patient is not offended by this method of providing comfort or calm)	3
• Increasing sensitivity in intimate personal care; asking permission or giving choices (including about when undertaken), rather than simply "doing" the patient	3
• Selecting a specialized team of staff within a facility to primarily deal with a particularly difficult resident; often involves negotiating roster change	3

• Attending promptly to physical needs and activities of daily living	2
• Reducing arousal at strategic times (e.g., by giving a bath, massage) before incidents for patients whose behavior shows a temporal pattern, or is clearly signaled in advance	2
• Providing diversion when episodes appear to be looming	2
• Increasing one-to-one interaction with staff	2
• Structuring rest periods	2
• Using empathy instead of stricture after incontinence episodes	1
• Gradually changing patient's sleep/wake cycle so patient sleeps through the night	1
• Developing nonfrightening lifting methods	1
• Providing culture-specific food	1
• Giving patient a placebo in a special pillbox: "Only to be taken when desperate"	1
Arranging support from external sources	
• Referral to Alzheimer's association	3
• Regular respite	2
• Arrangement of more support from family	1

*Changing the Physical, Social, or Sensory Environment**	*Cases*
* *Note*: These methods also obviously involve working with the caregivers for implementation	
• Decreasing social interaction at known trouble times (e.g., meals)	7
• Restricting means to undertake the behavior	3
• Removing patient to quiet environment (sometimes with music) when patient is distressed or likely to be	3
• Engaging a volunteer for regular visits and to take the patient out regularly	3
• Hiding physical cues that precipitate behavior	2
• Restricting access to physical cues that precipitate behavior	2
• Adding cues to assist orientation	2
• Using music/radio at strategic times	2
• Increasing social interaction	2
• Moving patient to a single room	2

Operant conditioning (not normally effective in dementia; these cases stroke related)	
• Caregiver ignoring (not reinforcing) the behavior	3
• Response prevention; caregiver stopping or preempting the behavior, in combination with reinforcement for abstention	2
• Reinforcement from caregiver for undertaking alternative behavior	2
• Caregiver shaping the desired behavior	2
Damage Control	*Cases*
• Patient-specific sensor to alert staff that a patient has wandered	2
• Contingency plans for immediate removal during an episode to limit effects on other residents	1

Note: Reproduced by kind permission of Australian Commonwealth Government.

9

Cognitive Intervention

Martial Van der Linden
University of Geneva

Anne-Claude Juillerat
University Hospitals of Geneva

Stéphane Adam
University of Liège

Because dementia, and more specifically Alzheimer's Disease (AD), represents such a problem in our society from both the psychological and the socioeconomic aspects, it seems essential that multidisciplinary and synergetic management be put into place. This should include not only psychological interventions and medication but also social and legal help, support to caregivers (dementia also affects the family), as well as home services.

Psychological interventions in AD have long been dominated by three approaches: reality orientation therapy (ROT; Powell-Proctor & Miller, 1982), reminiscence therapy (Thornton & Brotchie, 1987), and behavior therapy (Burgio & Burgio, 1986; Ylieff, 1989, 2000). ROT was developed to improve spatiotemporal disorientation and mental confusion in patients through mental stimulation, social interaction, and adjustment of behavioral contingencies. More specifically, staff are instructed to present basic orienting information during interactions with confused persons, to involve them in what is happening around them, and to reinforce the individual's interest in their environment. The primary goal of reminiscence therapy is to facilitate recall of past experiences (by using various themes, props, and triggers) to promote intrapersonal and interpersonal functioning and consequently improve well-being. This approach was originally developed for elderly people without dementia (Butler, 1963), but it has also been applied to demented individuals, focusing more on its socialization functions than on its interpersonal aspects (see Kasl-Godley & Gatz, 2000). Finally, behavior therapy aims to reinforce, maintain, or reduce the frequency of a behavior by modifying the existing relations between its antecedents and consequences. The domains in which behavioral interventions have been applied are numerous: therapy for troublesome behaviors, increase of verbal communication, maintenance of self-care skills (e.g., grooming, eating and toileting, spatial orientation).

The efficiency of these approaches has been discussed in several systematic reviews (see Miller & Morris, 1993; Spector, Davies, Woods, & Orrell, 2000; Spector, Orrell, Davies, & Woods, 1998a, 1998b). Even though these techniques have proved to be relatively beneficial to patients with dementia (see Spector et al., 2000, for a review of ROT efficiency from randomized controlled trials), their main limitation is that they prioritize a functional and phenomenological analysis of problematic behaviors, without a theoretical reference to the nature of the underlying deficits. Furthermore, they are based on the implicit principle that all demented patients suffer from similar cognitive deficits and will, therefore, respond similarly to the same rehabilitation programs (Van der Linden & Seron, 1989). Finally, they were generally applied to severely (and mainly institutionalized) demented individuals. Indeed, these intervention methods were particularly popular during the 1970s and 1980s, and their principles were very coherent within the theoretical framework of AD that was dominant at the time (see, however, Spector, Orrell, Davies, & Woods, 2001, who recently developed a revised ROT program, capitalizing on the most beneficial elements identified from previous studies). AD was characterized then as a generalized and homogeneous cognitive impairment. Furthermore, due to the absence of effective diagnostic tools, AD was identified only when patients showed relatively important cognitive disorders, behavioral disorders, or both. With this "defective" approach, it is easy to understand why such global approaches dominated and why specific cognitive rehabilitation programs were not developed.

The changes recently observed in the neuropsychological characterization of AD—especially the identification of preserved cognitive abilities and of factors able to enhance performance as well as the development of methods allowing one to discriminate early AD patients from nondemented persons (see chap. 3 of this book)—have given a new impulse to the rehabilitation of AD patients. It now seems possible to conceive early neuropsychological interventions in AD patients that take into account the extreme complexity of mental processes and the vast heterogeneity of their disorganization (Juillerat, Van der Linden, Seron, & Adam, 2000; Van der Linden et al., 1991). This approach should mainly consist in optimizing the patients' psychological and social functioning at each stage of the disease as it progresses, by exploiting preserved abilities and susceptible factors to improve their performance. More generally, the intervention will aim, by means of individual and fitted measures, to help the patients lead, as long as possible, an autonomous and pleasant existence and maintain their dignity as well as a sense of meaningfulness. Considering the existing possibilities of early diagnosis, the neuropsychologist will be more frequently confronted with the rehabilitation of very mild AD patients who are still relatively autonomous, professionally active, and aware of their disease and related deficits. In this context, the neuropsychologist will have to examine the impact of the disease not only on the personal, familial, and social adjustments of the patients but also on their professional integration. The patients may also be helped to understand the disease, learn how to deal with it, and turn themselves toward those goals in life that do not yet have to be given up (see Romero & Wenz, 2001). In addition, more general problems, such as the disease prognosis, the treatment perspectives, the financial and legal arrangements, or the biological testament, will also have to be addressed, if necessary by referring the patient to specialists according to his or her needs or problems. Thus, it clearly appears that, more than ever, intervention in AD should be developed by considering the patient as a responsible participant.

Nevertheless, the management of cognitive and behavioral problems in AD patients also implies the active participation of a caregiver, both during the assessment and the rehabilitation (see chap. 11 of this book). The caregiver should be trained to adapt the patient's physical environment (see Day, Carreon, & Stump, 2000; Teresi, Holmes, & Ory, 2000), help with the use of external aids, and favor the use of optimizing factors and preserved capacities. The caregiver should also be trained to choose the best conditions for interactions with the patient (e.g., not interacting in dual-task situations), to use differential reinforcement to change the maladaptive behaviors of the patient (see Bird, 2000), and to improve their competence in accompanying the patient in a way that should have a positive effect on the patient's self. However, caregivers also need to be helped by education programs and group support to stabilize their well-being and prevent decompensation resulting from the burden of caregiving. Because caregivers stress is an important factor leading to the institutionalization of the patient, interventions that provide support to both patients and caregivers are therefore essential (Brodaty, McGilchrist, Harris, & Peters, 1993; Brodaty, Roberts, & Peters, 1994; Mittelman, Ferris, Shulman, Steinberg, & Levin, 1996; see chap. 12 of this book). It should be noted that caregivers' appraisals of distress seem to be partly determined by their attributions about the causes of patients' behavior problems. In addition, attributions that contribute to subjective distress appear to be important determinants of caregiver depression (Schultz, Galagher-Thompson, Haley, & Czaja, 2000). Regarding this aspect, recent data (Wadley & Haley, 2001) indicate that the presence of an AD diagnosis (versus a depression label or no label) was associated by female undergraduates with primarily biological causes and was effective in evoking greater sympathy and less anger, judgments of less responsibility and lower personality contributions to inappropriate behavior, and a greater willingness to help. This suggests that diagnosis, coupled with education emphasizing the disease process and the link between the disease and problem behaviors (i.e., encouraging caregivers to attribute disruptive behavior to the disease, rather than to the patient) may help alleviate the distress that can give rise to caregiver depression.

Finally, such an approach requires adapted structures, both for assessment and management. A promising approach seems to be the creation of day-care centers, where a real-life environment can be reproduced, optimization strategies can be put into place, and satisfying leisure activities can be proposed.

In this chapter, we will successively consider the pre- and postrehabilitation neuropsychological assessment, the different rehabilitation strategies (by illustrating them in different cognitive and behavioral domains), and finally the use and functions of a day-care center.

PRE- AND POSTREHABILITATION NEUROPSYCHOLOGICAL ASSESSMENT

Before implementing a rehabilitation program, the neuropsychologists have to understand the nature of the cognitive, mood, and behavioral dysfunctions, to examine the impact of these deficits on daily life activities, and to identify the preserved abilities and optimization factors that could be exploited in the intervention. They also have to establish the optimal conditions that enable them to receive informed consent from the patient and family members and to analyze the factors that could contribute to acceptance or refusal of participation in the rehabilitation program as well as to regular attendance at the intervention sessions. Finally, they must evaluate the outcome of the rehabilitation.

Prerehabilitation Cognitive Assessment

In a cognitive rehabilitation perspective, the objective of neuropsychological assessment is not only to identify deficits but also to understand their nature and to find preserved abilities and optimization factors. A simple phenomenal identification of the defective behavior or a functional analysis of the relations between its antecedents and consequences does not provide information about the nature of the disorder.

For example, recent cognitive models suggest that memory has a complex structure, composed of several independent systems (see Schacter, Wagner, & Buckner, 2000). Furthermore, neuropsychological studies show that AD can selectively impair some systems or some particular process in a system, whereas others are spared (Fleischman & Gabrieli, 1999; Salmon, 2000; Van der Linden, 1994; see also chap. 3 of this book). In this theoretical context, the objective of assessment is to detect the impaired memory systems and processes as well as those that remain intact. To do this, the clinician has to use various tests specifically designed to assess the integrity of each memory system and process (see Van der Linden, Meulemans, Belleville, & Collette, 2000). In particular, because some learning or relearning methods that can be useful in AD patients are considered to exploit preserved memory systems (especially procedural memory or perceptual representation systems), it is essential to examine whether these systems are intact or not. The assessment also aims to identify the cognitive supports that can facilitate memory performance in a particular patient. For example, it may be useful to explore whether a patient could benefit from enactment at encoding, namely by administering a Subject Performed Task paradigm, in which memory for action events is compared to verbal events (e.g., Bird & Kinsella, 1996; Hutton, Sheppard, Rusted, & Ratner, 1996; Lekeu, Van der Linden, Franck, Moonen, & Salmon, 2002) or whether he or she could take advantage of sensory retrieval cues (e.g., auditory or olfactory cues; Rusted, Marsh, Bledski, & Sheppard, 1997). More generally, the challenge that confronts the neuropsychologist is to find the best way to optimize memory in a given patient. It should be noted that traditional psychometric memory tests, such as the Benton Visual Retention Test (Benton, 1965), the Rey Auditory Verbal Learning Test (Rey, 1964), or the Wechsler Memory Scale-Revised (Wechsler, 1987) are not very useful in this prerehabilitation memory assessment context; indeed, they only provide extremely limited qualitative information and do not explore the complexity of memory systems and processes, nor the variety of possible memory disorders and facilitatory memory effects.

Assessment of Everyday Activities

In addition to the cognitive neuropsychological assessment, neuropsychologists also have to identify the consequences of cognitive disorders in everyday activities. Indeed, the purpose of rehabilitation is not to upgrade performance on cognitive tests but to improve the quality of life for the patient, family, and caregivers. A way to approach this question is to consider the distinction proposed by the World Health Organization (1980) between *impairment, disability,* and *handicap* (see Seron, 1997). Impairment refers to a dysfunctioning of a particular cognitive mechanism; for example, a deficit may specifically concern dual-task coordination, a function of the central executive component of working memory which is frequently and specifically affected in early AD (Baddeley, Baddeley, Bucks, & Wilcock, 2001; Collette, Van der Linden, Bechet, & Salmon, 1999). A disability concerns the consequence of this impairment on different cognitive activities; for example, a dual-task coordination impairment will make it difficult to talk and walk simultaneously (Camicioli, Howieson, Lehman, & Kaye, 1997), hold conversations with several persons (Alberoni, Baddeley, Della Sala, Logie, & Spinnler, 1992), drive (Rizzo, McGehee, Dawson, & Anderson, 2001), and so forth. A handicap identifies the impact of these disabilities on the social and personal adaptation of the patients to their environment; for example, the difficulty to hold conversations will affect differently patients with frequent or rare social activities.

The objective of the neuropsychologist is clearly to help the patients in their psychological and social adjustment, and therefore they will have to move from the identification of impairments to the selection of objectives in terms of disabilities and handicaps. However, it is not easy to predict the existence of cognitive difficulties in everyday life (or to control the effects of a therapy on psychological and social adaptation) on the basis of laboratory cognitive tests. Indeed, the conditions under which cognitive efficiency is usually tested are very different from real life. In the latter situation, noise, weariness, interruptions during tasks, and simultaneous involvement in several activities introduce additional difficulties. On the other hand, various factors such as task familiarity or level of premorbid expertise may have a facilitating influence. In other words, the demands placed on cognition by the environment and the patient's lifestyle will partly determine the occurrence of problems. This raises the question of the ecological relevance of the tests used in clinical settings (Van der Linden, 1989).

To tackle this ecological validity problem, some studies attempted to analyze relationships between scores in various psychometric tests and a patient's functioning in everyday situations (see, for example, Goldstein, McCue, Rogers, & Nussbaum, 1992). However, these correlation studies were generally conducted in the absence of preliminary hypotheses concerning the nature of relationships between psychometric testing and real-life situations. In other words, no precise analysis of the processes involved in the tests and in everyday situations was ever conducted. Consequently, it is very difficult to identify factors responsible for the existing correlations. Thus, neuropsychologists clearly need methods allowing them to understand more directly the consequences of cognitive problems in real-life situations. In addition, due to the progressive nature of AD, an immediate—or quasi-immediate—benefit should be the aim of the rehabilitation program. Consequently, the patient's evaluation should, as much as possible, be directly focused on everyday situations so that well-defined, limited goals could be set, aimed at increasing the patient's autonomy. This does not mean that a cognitive analysis of the deficits is no longer needed but that it should be put into a perspective of daily-life cognitive neuropsychology (i.e., trying to understand the nature of the deficits influencing specific real-life activities). In this respect, the simulation of everyday cognitive activities or even the direct assessment of activities in daily life is a particularly well-adapted approach (see chap. 10 of this book for a description of these methods). This simulation or direct approach to assessment should allow the examiner to discern the nature of the impairments affecting everyday activities. However, this can only be made if a precise cognitive analysis of the processes involved in each activity is conducted according to existing theoretical models. In other words, a neuropsychological analysis of the cognitive processes that impinge on the patient's everyday functioning is a critical adjunct to a phenomenal analysis of problem situations.

With this in mind, Marson, Sawrie, et al. (2000) have designed a battery (the Financial Capacity Instrument; FCI) devoted to the assessment of several financial capacity domains in AD patients (e.g., basic monetary skills, financial conceptual knowledge, cash transactions). Furthermore, Earnst et al. (2001) recently attempted to identify the core knowledge types (declarative, procedural) involved in the eight FCI tasks. They also showed that financial abilities of AD patients were closely related to the efficiency of the central executive component of working memory. Even if Earnst et al.'s (2001) cognitive analysis of financial capacity remains rather rudimentary and should be more articulated on recent cognitive models (e.g., models of numerical abilities; see Pesenti, Seron, & Noël, 2000), it constitutes an interesting and promising example of what might be a cognitive neuropsychological exploration of daily-life activities.

Assessment of Mood and Behavioral Disorders

Besides the cognitive and everyday life explorations, it is also important to assess the mood and behavioral disorders that are frequently observed in AD patients (Ballard, Cassidy, Bannister, & Mohan, 1993; Cummings, Ross, Absher, & Gornbein, 1995; Lyketsos et al., 1997; Patterson & Bolger, 1994). Chen, Ganguli, Mulsant, and DeKosky (1999) pointed out that depressive symptoms appeared to be an early manifestation of AD. However, they also found an association between depression and the self-awareness of memory loss, suggesting that depression in early AD could reflect a psychological reaction by subjects to awareness of their declining cognitive function and their loss of autonomy in everyday activities (see also Harwood, Sultzer, & Wheatley, 2000, for similar findings). Identifying and understanding mood and behavioral changes in AD patients, as well as establishing adequate behavioral, psychosocial, or pharmacological treatment, is important for several reasons (Jacobs, Strauss, Patterson, & Mack, 1998). In particular, the existence of mood disorders may exacerbate cognitive difficulties and impair functional abilities even further. In addition, the presence of mood and behavioral symptoms in AD is associated with increased burden and stress for caregivers (Coen, Swanwick, O'Boyle, & Coakley, 1997). In the same vein, Neundorfer et al. (2001) showed that AD patient depression was associated with more caregiver depression at baseline and that an increase in patient depressive symptoms (and an increase in patient dependency on instrumental activities of daily living) was related to an increase in caregiver depression. In other respects, if certain mood changes, such as depression or anxiety, constitute, even partly, a reaction to the existence of a cognitive and functional decline, it might be hypothesized that decreasing the impact of the cognitive and functional deficits would have a positive effect on the mood state (see Adam, Van der Linden, Juillerat, & Salmon, 2000). Therefore, it is essential to distinguish mood changes that are either the direct consequence of AD or the reaction to cognitive decline and loss of autonomy. It should be noted that AD patients appear capable of providing valid information about their mood state; indeed, Chemerinski, Petracca, Sabe, Kremer, and Starkstein (2001) found that only 3% of the AD patients with major depression (diagnosed on the basis of information from caregivers) denied being depressed. Nevertheless, they also observed that AD patients underrate the severity of their depressive symptoms compared with caregivers' reports, which emphasizes the importance of questioning both patients and caregivers for the presence of depressive symptoms. Moreover, depression must be distinguished from apathy. Indeed, Starkstein, Petracca, Chemerinski, and Kremer (2001) showed that apathy is a behavioral syndrome independent of depression and that it can be identified on the basis of specific clinical criteria. Interestingly, the authors also observed that apathetic AD patients (with or without depression) had significantly more severe impairments in everyday activities.

Finally, a relatively unexplored and poorly understood, although important domain, is pain experience in AD patients and its assessment. In a review of the rare studies devoted to this domain, Huffman and Kunik (2000) concluded that AD patients, and more generally cognitively impaired elderly persons, apparently made less pain complaints. However, the nature of this decrease is not clear due to the existence of several confounding factors, such as the use of verbal self-reports, which can be affected by memory loss and language disorders, the definition of a too narrow pain domain, and the possible decreased medical burden due to exclusion criteria necessary in the diagnosis of AD. It also appears that although cognitively impaired persons have fewer pain complaints, their complaints are as reliable and valid as those of cognitively intact elderly persons. However, many questions about pain in AD patients remain, and therefore future research is required, focusing especially on early AD, using more adequate pain assessment tools, and examining the relationships between pain, cognitive deficits, and affective functioning.

Consent to Treatment

Another important question to be addressed when considering a rehabilitation program in an AD patient is the ability of the patient to consent to treatment. Substantial progress has been recently made in the identification of the cognitive predictors of competency for decision making on medical treatment and research participation in AD patients as well as in the assessment methods of this faculty (see Moye, 1999). For example, Marson, Earnst, Jamil, Bartolucci, and Harrell (2000) found that experienced physicians demonstrated significant agreement assessing competency in AD patients when judgments were based on specific legal standards assessed by considering the patient's responses to clinical vignettes (i.e., a description of an imaginary situation in which the patient is asked to decide on a proposed treatment). In fact, personal competency judgments of physicians showed a substantially higher level of agreement than that found in a previous study (Marson, McInturff, Hawkins, Bartolucci, & Harrell, 1997), where specific legal standards were not used and in which physicians showed statistically insignificant agreement levels (even when shown a structured assessment). Finally, in a parallel study, Earnst, Marson, and Harrell (2000) observed that the decline in semantic knowledge, recent verbal memory, and simple reasoning ability predicted physicians' judgments on the most difficult legal standards as well as their personal competency judgments (see also Schmand, Gouwenberg, Smit, & Jonker, 1999, who showed that mental competency specifically measured by the vignette method was determined mainly by measures of recent memory, expressive language, and abstract thinking).

More concretely, in Marson, Earnst, et al.'s (2000) study, the AD patients were videotaped being administered the Capacity to Consent to Treatment Instrument (CCTI). The CCTI consists of two clinical vignettes presenting a hypothetical medical problem and associated symptoms along with two treatment alternatives, with associated risks and benefits. After reading and listening to each vignette, participants answer questions designed to assess competency under five well-established and increasingly stringent legal standards (LS): the capacity to evidence a treatment choice (LS1); the capacity to make the reasonable treatment choice (when the alternative is clearly unreasonable; LS2); the capacity to appreciate the consequences of a treatment choice (LS3); the capacity to provide rational reasons for a treatment choice (LS4); and the capacity to understand the treatment situation and choices (LS5). Each study physician viewed the videotaped vignette individually, made judgments under each of the legal standards, and then made his or her own personal competency judgment. It should be noted that physicians' personal competency judgments were most closely associated with comprehension and reasoning LS (LS4 and LS5). Finally, in Earnst et al.'s (2000) study, physicians' judgments on the three most difficult LS (LS3, LS4, LS5) were predicted by cognitive measures of semantic knowledge (Boston Naming Test; Kaplan, Goodglass, & Weintraub, 1983), simple reasoning ability (Dementia Rating Scale; DRS; Conceptualization subscale; Mattis, 1973) and verbal memory (DRS Memory subscale; WMS-R Logical Memory I; Wechsler; 1987).

A limitation of Marson and collaborators' studies (2000a) is that the different levels of competency—the legal standards—they used are not easily dissociable (see Schmand et al., 1999). Consequently, it is difficult to identify which cognitive functions are essential at each level and, therefore, to elaborate a more precise cognitive model of competency as well as to identify more specific cognitive predictors. However that may be, their findings globally suggest that the use of competency-sensitive cognitive measures coupled with specific competency measures and legal standards can increase the clinical reliability and accuracy of physicians' competency judgments. A similar approach might be developed to assess the patient's faculty to decide on a proposed psychological treatment, while bearing in mind that different contexts may require different levels of competency.

Finally, there exist some data indicating that persons with dementia do have a sufficient capacity to state specific preferences and make care-related decisions. For example, Feinberg and Whitlatch (2001) showed that when being interviewed twice within a week using a parallel interview, persons with mild to moderate cognitive impairments (i.e., Mini Mental State Examination from 13–26) were able to respond consistently to questions about preferences, choices, and their own involvement in decisions about daily life, and to provide accurate and reliable responses to questions about demographics.

Assessing the Outcome of Intervention

Another essential task of the neuropsychologist is to assess the effect of the rehabilitation program—that is, to establish that some improvements occurred and that they are due to the specific intervention. Different methods have been developed to establish the efficiency of neuropsychological therapy in patients with a focalized lesion (see Seron, 1997, 2000). However, assessing effects of treatment in AD and, more generally, in dementia is particularly complex because the neuropsychologist has to determine the specific effects of a therapy in a patient who continues to deteriorate because of the course of the disease. In addition, the speed of deterioration varies considerably from one patient to another and, in a particular patient, between the different cognitive functions and the different stages of the disease. Consequently, pre- and posttreatment baselines have to be designed according to this progressive characteristic of dementia and the variability of disease progression (see Faure, 1995).

The question of treatment efficiency cannot be solely limited to improvement of cognitive functions. Psychoaffective, social, and economic factors also have to be taken into account. In particular, the impact of rehabilitation on costs of care should be examined, whether indirect (mainly time spent by the caregiver with the patient) or direct (medical, hospitalization, and institutionalization costs; see Souêtre, Thwaites, & Yeardley, 1999, and chap. 1 of this book).

Caregiver burden and quality of life (of both the patient and the caregiver) also constitute important measures of treatment effects. Concerning quality of life, Selai, Trimble, Rossor, and Harvey (2001) recently showed that patients with mild to moderate dementia can rate their own quality of life (using the Quality of Life Assessment Schedule (QOLAS). Nevertheless, the caregivers rated the patients as having a poorer quality of life than did the patients themselves on all domains of the QOLAS, and this might be due to a lack of insight or anosognosia. This discrepancy raises a number of important technical and ethical issues concerning who is the best judge of quality of life in patients with dementia.

> It should be noted that assessment of quality of life may require other methods than questionnaires (e.g., on the form of skilled observation) to provide the perspective of the person with dementia (see Bond & Corner, 2001). So, an in-depth case study of the discourse of an AD patient (Sabat & Collins, 1999) revealed a variety of intact social and cognitive abilities as well as intact manifestations of selfhood, despite losses of cognitive functioning as measured by standard neuropsychological tests. These preserved abilities include those that typically have been found as indicators of well-being among the healthy (Kitwood & Bredin, 1992). Further studies should be conducted to better characterize the psychological and neurobiological substrates of these preserved functions. More generally, taking the perspective of the patient requires the ability to examine the impact of AD (and of rehabilitation) on the self system, which supports feeling of continuous identity and meaning of life, and also to explore how the patient's way of behaving may be influenced by the social context (see Sabat & Harré, 1992). In this matter, Sabat (1994) described an AD patient whose spouse reported that certain abilities were absent at home but which were readily observed at the day-care center, thus lending support to the idea that the patient's behavior was affected not only by the extant neuropathology but also by social relationships. These findings suggest that an important aspect of rehabilitation in AD patients is preventing the development of a malignant social psychology within the family system and more general social environment. (Kitwood, 1997)

Finally, treatment outcome also seems to be influenced by anosognosia. Indeed, Koltai, Welsh-Bohmer, and Schmechel (2001) showed that the gains in perceived memory functioning as a result of a nonpharmacological memory and coping intervention program were significantly greater in participants with insight than those without. In contrast, informants perceived greater gains among treated patients compared with waiting-list controls, irrespective of insight. However, the methodology of this study did not permit clarification of whether the gains were true or only perceived.

Acceptance of the Rehabilitation Program

When a rehabilitation program is proposed to the AD patient and family members, a refusal—or at least a reluctance—to participate sometimes may be observed. Furthermore, once the intervention is accepted, the patient's attendance to the therapy sessions may be irregular, which clearly contributes to disorganize both the rehabilitation unit and intervention methodology. In fact, the acceptance of a cognitive intervention and the patient's assiduity depends on several factors, namely, the existence of anosognosia or denial in the patient, the family members, or both; the socioeducational, anxiety, and depression level of the participants; the clarity of diagnostic announcement; the person who recommends the intervention (e.g., the general practitioner whom the patient and family generally trust or a specialist physician who examined the patient only on a single occasion); and so forth.

Anosognosia, especially, may considerably hinder rehabilitation because the patients who are unaware of their deficits will not see the reasons why they have to invest time and effort in a rehabilitation program. Moreover, because lack of insight has been associated (at least partly) to frontal dysfunction (McGlynn & Schacter, 1989), the patients with anosognosia may prove unable to benefit from the intervention technique because of executive dysfunction. Finally, they will put strain on the family members and caregivers by wanting to undertake activities they are not able to master. However, it should be noted that anosognosia in AD (especially in the early stages of the disease) is not so severe and generalized as previously postulated; in fact, there exists an important variability in the presentation and existence of anosognosia in AD patients (see Agnew & Morris, 1998) and a significant number of patients may be fully aware of their deficits or of some of them (anosognosia may only affect a particular domain of cognitive deficits; Schacter & Prigatano, 1991). In this perspective, Zanetti et al. (1999) showed that the association of disease insight with the cognitive level of disease severity follows a trilinear pattern: an initial period of stability before detectable decline (Mini Mental State Examination [MMSE] scores ≥ 24), a period of decline (MMSE scores between 23 and 13), and a final period of stability with uniformly low insight (MMSE scores ≤ 12). It should, however, be noted that although patients with MMSE scores between 24 and 12 are impaired, they preserve some degree of insight. Other data also suggest the existence of two domains of insight, one associated to behavioral problems and the other associated to cognitive impairments (e.g., Starkstein, Sabe, Chemerinsky, Jason, & Leiguarda, 1996), the former being relatively preserved compared with the latter (Kotler-Cope & Camp, 1995). In addition, patients may be aware of a deficit but unaware of its consequences (Feher, Mahurin, Imbody, Crook, & Pirozzolo, 1991). Finally, it should be possible to reduce anosognosia by confronting the patients with their difficulties. However, it is very important to weigh the benefits and the drawbacks of this confrontation; indeed, a better awareness may increase the involvement of the patient in the rehabilitation program, but it can also lead to depression or anxiety. Consequently, in addition to a detailed assessment of anosognosia, an evaluation of the patient's personality, frustration tolerance, and decompensation risks should also be conducted.

Different methods for measuring anosognosia may be used: the comparison of the patient's ratings to those obtained from the caregivers (McGlynn & Kaszniak, 1991) or to objective performance-based scores (Anderson & Tranel, 1989); physician or psychologist ratings of insight (Reed, Jagust, & Coulter, 1993); discourse prompt question about AD ("Tell me what you know about Alzheimer's disease?"); endorsement on several items of the Geriatric Depression Scale (Yesavage et al., 1983), or a sentence-completion task (see Arkin & Mahendra, 2001a, for information about these three last methods in a longitudinal study); the Guidelines for the Rating of Awareness Deficits, specifically targeted at memory impairments (GRAD; Vehey, Ponds, Rozendaal, & Jolles, 1995); and the Clinical Insight Rating Scales (CIR; Ott et al., 1996). The CIR and GRAD scales have a semistructured interview format, and insight scores are derived from the comparison of the patient's response and the clinical information provided by an interview with the patient's primary caregiver, during which the reason of the visit, duration of illness, rate of progression of cognitive deficits, functional impairments, and behavioral disturbances are examined (see Zanetti et al., 1999). The validity of each of these methods appears to be relatively limited (see Van der Linden, 1989): limited shared variance between subjective ratings and objective test performance, over- and underestimation errors made by informants, important variations in insight deficits and evolution according to the chosen method and absence of correlation between insight assessment methods (see Arkin & Mahendra, 2001a), and poor sensibility (CIR; Ott et al., 1996). Consequently, in the present state of affairs, the most prudent approach is probably to use a combination of methods (Koltai et al., 2001).

It is also necessary to distinguish the neurobiological and psychological aspects of anosognosia. In psychological anosognosia, the cognitive processes that contribute to awareness of the disorders are preserved, but for some reasons (self-esteem, social desirability, etc.), the patients may deny (consciously or not) their deficits. In this case, the neuropsychologist has to identify the secondary benefits of the situation and discuss with the patient and family members other means of restoring self-esteem. Moreover, the neuropsychologist must take all the opportunities to notify and reinforce the patient's preserved or residual abilities. Denial may also be found in the family members who cannot resign themselves to the loss of the spouse or a father or mother image.

The way the elderly are considered in our society and especially the negative beliefs associated with aging and AD (e.g., low self-efficiency, lack of control over the decline, limited potential for improvement; see Lachman, 2000) also constitute factors that may limit the involvement of the patient and the family members in the rehabilitation. So the neuropsychologist may be confronted with resigned comments such as "At my (his or her) age, it's not worth the trouble"; "Leave him alone, he is old, these exercises make him tired"; "I also have memory problems; his difficulties are normal at his age." A last factor concerns the motivation of the neuropsychologist who is engaged in the cognitive rehabilitation of AD patients. Because the objectives and benefits of this rehabilitation may be very modest (in most cases, they are far more limited than those related to the cognitive rehabilitation of patients with focal lesions), and because the disease progression is unavoidable and the intervention efficiency difficult to assess, the clinician might be led to doubt the use of cognitive interventions in AD and to consider that working with demented patients is rather unproductive. Unquestionably, the meaning and motivation the members of the rehabilitation unit give to their activity constitutes an important factor that can influence the involvement of the patient and family members in the intervention program. In this context, it is essential to bear in mind that very modest gains (such as being able to retrieve grandchildren's names, to prepare a simple soup, or to go alone to the supermarket) may have an enormous impact on the patient's dignity and on the image he or she transmits to others.

COGNITIVE REHABILITATION STRATEGIES

The clinical management of cognitive problems in early AD patients can follow three main directions (Butters, Soety, & Becker, 1997; Camp & Foss, 1997; Van der Linden, 1995; Van der Linden & Juillerat, 1998): using optimizing factors to improve or facilitate cognitive performance; teaching specific knowledge (i.e., facts or skills) to make the patients more independent in everyday life by using techniques, such as spaced retrieval, vanishing-cues, or errorless methods, that tap preserved memory systems; and structuring the patient's environment and providing external cognitive aids to compensate for defective cognitive functions.

We will illustrate the use of these strategies for different types of deficits and objectives.

Facilitating Cognitive Performance

The first rehabilitation strategy that can be adopted for AD patients aims to exploit optimization factors to facilitate cognitive performance. This strategy may be used for several types of cognitive deficits, including episodic memory, language skills, numerical skills, and so forth.

Facilitating Episodic Memory Performance. Episodic memory enables an individual to remember and to be aware of events experienced in a particular spatial and temporal context. It depends on numerous cognitive processes and on a large network of brain regions (see Van der Linden, Meulemans, Marczewski, & Collette, 2000). The impairment of episodic memory is one of the earliest and most important symptoms of AD, which has been shown to be present already at the preclinical phase of the disease (see chap. 3 of this book). Memory deficits in AD affect free recall, cued recall, as well as recognition and have been attributed to poor encoding, retrieval difficulties, or both. Given the importance of the episodic memory deficit in AD, numerous studies have tried to identify which form of cognitive support would improve the memory performance of AD patients (see Bäckman, Mäntilä, & Herlitz, 1990). When considering the different ways of facilitating memory, it is crucial to characterize the specific memory problem (see Morris, 1979).

> First, does the person have to remember to do something (a prospective memory task) or rather remember some facts or episodes? Remembering to carry out intended actions is an important everyday life activity (see Van der Linden, 1989). In addition, prospective memory failures seem to be very prevalent in early stages of dementia (Huppert, Johnson, & Nickson, 2000) and to have a greater impact than retrospective memory failures on the lives of AD patients' caregivers (Smith, Della Sala, Logie, & Maylor, 2000). The aids usually involved to help a person to remember to do things are external memory aids (diaries, alarms, etc.). In cases where the situation concerns memory for facts or episodes, determine whether the problem is situated at the encoding phase (how can one learn something to maximize later recall?) or at the retrieval phase (how can one retrieve an item of information believed to be in memory?). If the problem is to acquire new information, the encoding strategies will be different depending on whether the to-be-learned material is organized and meaningful. In the case of meaningful information (e.g., a text or a conference), the subject's task will be to increase comprehension of the material by relating the different items of information to each other and by relating them to preexisting knowledge (by using active learning, self-testing, etc.). For example, memory for texts may be facilitated by using a method aimed to organize material and to increase the subject's interactions with the text, such as the PQRST (Preview; Question; Read; State; Test) method (e.g., Glasgow, Zeiss, Barrera, & Lewinshon, 1977) or a technique leading the person to extract the different propositions from the text and reinsert them in a story schema (see Van der Linden & Van der Kaa, 1989). In contrast, if the to-be-encoded material is poorly structured or meaningless, the person will have to impose meaning and relationships. For this purpose, one may resort to mnemonic techniques that will make up for the lack of meaning and supply retrieval cues. Various mnemonic strategies, including visual imagery and verbal techniques, have been described and used successfully in nondemented, memory-impaired patients (see Van der Linden, Coyette, & Seron, 2000; Van der Linden & Van der Kaa, 1989). For example, the face-name visual imagery mnemonic (McCarthy, 1980) has been used to address a common memory complaint in brain-damaged patients, namely, remembering peoples' names (for a detailed illustration of its use, see Coyette & Van der Linden, 1999). Briefly, the technique consists of three steps: identifying a prominent facial feature, transforming the name into a concrete image, and forming an interactive visual image of these two elements. More generally, efficient encoding strategies aim to promote binding of target information with contextual (cognitive, environmental, emotional) information. This contextual information makes the target information more distinctive and, later, may serve as a retrieval cue. Finally, if the memory problem is located at the retrieval stage, relevant cues that elicit recall and whose relevance depends on the initial encoding situation will have to

> be found. In other words, the efficiency of a retrieval cue would be linked to the fact that information contained in this cue has been encoded and that this information is an integral part of the memory trace (the encoding specificity principle; Tulving, 1983). It should also be noted that if there is a sufficient matching between the information contained in the retrieval cue and that contained in the trace, the retrieval cue may automatically activate a memory trace (the associative retrieval processes). However, in some cases, an active research that allows reinstating a retrieval context from which retrieval cues will operate is required (strategic or controlled retrieval processes). Consequently, effective memory retrieval requires sufficient processing resources and adequate executive functioning.

Herrmann and Palmisano (1992) have established an important distinction between memory facilitation and memory improvement. A memory facilitation technique is aimed at providing temporary help for another person to learn specific new information or to retrieve something that presumably he or she already knows (e.g., to help a patient acquire the neuropsychologist's name by indicating a mnemonic strategy). In other words, facilitation constitutes a temporary adoption (on a particular occasion) of an effective memory process or strategy. On the other hand, memory improvement concerns the relatively permanent adoption of facilitation procedures or, put differently, the habitual use of a facilitating procedure every time it is necessary (e.g., using the face-name imagery technique every time the patient has to learn a new name). Although a memory facilitation technique is relatively easy to find and apply in most daily-life memory situations (even by nonprofessionals, such as the spouse or a volunteer), the adoption and habitual use of a facilitating technique by the patient is much more demanding; it requires extensive practice to automate the use of the facilitating strategy, the acquisition of an appropriate belief system (which supports the strategy and corrects deleterious memory attitudes), and finally the ability to identify the specific daily-life situations in which the strategy is useful, to remember to use the strategy, and to maintain it in memory while it is applied (Camp & McKitrick, 1992). Consequently, because of a reduction of processing resources as well as planning and comprehension difficulties frequently associated with AD, learning the spontaneous use of a mnemonic strategy in everyday situations will be very difficult for most AD patients, and, therefore, intervention will only consist in temporarily facilitating encoding or retrieval of specific information. In this perspective, an important challenge will be to teach the caregivers how to facilitate the patient's memory in everyday life. In this teaching process, role playing might prove more beneficial than simple verbal instructions. However, memory improvement (i.e., the acquisition and habitual use of a facilitating method by the patients themselves) might be considered in very early AD patients.

A number of studies using list-learning paradigms have identified several contextual manipulations that can contribute to enhanced episodic memory performance in AD patients (see chap. 3 of this book, and Bird, 2001). In particular, at acquisition, it seems possible to facilitate memory encoding in AD patients by presenting the material in a way that gives rise to semantic, motor, or multimodal processing (e.g., Bäckman & Small, 1998; Bird & Luszcz, 1991; Hutton et al., 1996; Lekeu et al., 2002) and by associating the to-be-remembered information with positive emotional features (Hamman, Monarch, & Goldstein, 2000; Kazui et al., 2000; Moayeri, Cahill, Jin, & Potkin, 2000). More generally, the objective will be to force the subject to link the target information with potentially efficient contextual cues and to install more accessible memory traces. At retrieval, the assistance will consist of providing contextual cues reflecting features of the processes highlighted at acquisition (e.g., Bäckman & Small, 1998; Bird & Luszcz, 1993). It should be added that retrieval cues seem to be particularly efficient when they are generated by the patients themselves during the encoding stage (e.g., Bird & Kinsella, 1996); in other words, active assistance at both acquisition and retrieval is recommended, although the amount of assistance that is needed may vary according to the severity of dementia (e.g. Bäckman & Small, 1998). Until now, very few studies have described the use of these optimization factors (or others) in facilitating AD patients' memory functioning in everyday situations.

Several studies found that mild AD patients' text memory difficulties are due to a reduction of working memory resources and to patients' encoding of text information in an unsystematic way, independent of their thematic importance (e.g., Haut et al., 1998). These findings suggest that text memory may be facilitated in AD patients by presenting text information in a manner that is well organized, by omitting less important details, and by highlighting the salient elements. To compensate for the working memory impairments, the neuropsychologist might also consider refreshment techniques, which should permit continuous reactivation of information in working memory (e.g., dividing text material into several parts, where each part is summarized before the presentation of the next part). In this prospect, Stevens, King, and Camp (1993) administered a Question Asking Reading (QAR) method to increase the memory for the content of stories used in a reading group organized at an adult day-care center. This QAR intervention distributed the task of reading across group members and required the patients to follow a scripted procedure when reading. To facilitate the patients' interactions with the text and with each other, they were also given questions to ask about the text they read, as part of the script. Both story memorization and amount of verbal interactions among group members increased following the intervention. It also appeared that staff members of the day-care center could implement the intervention and maintain the levels of improvement initially achieved by the experimenter. In the same vein, it also seems possible to oppose the negative effects of working memory deficits on autobiographical knowledge retrieval by providing the AD patient with a guideline for cyclically searching through the hierarchical structure of autobiographical memory (identifying a life period, then a general life event, and finally the specific phenomenal episode; see Conway & Pleydell-Pearce, 2000).

Bird and Kinsella (1996) attempted to give more clinical relevance to list-learning findings. They trained patients with AD and vascular dementia to associate a tangible contextual cue, such as a beeper, with a motor action, such as opening a notebook. They hypothesized that, consistent with the encoding specificity principle, the cue that was encoded with the to-be-remembered action should prompt the later recall of the motor action. The acquisition process was organized according to the spaced-retrieval method, which contains a principle to prompt recall of information over increasingly longer retention intervals and with errorless learning which guarantees that only the correct information is acquired on most trials (see "Teaching Specific New Knowledge" on page 196). When, at a particular interval, the patients failed to respond to the primary cue (the beeper) or gave a wrong answer, they were provided supplementary elaborative cues, in a graded way, until they did remember the target action. For example, if a participant failed to open the notebook when the beeper sounded, the experimenter then raised a card reading *NOTEBOOK*. If the patient still failed, the experimenter said, "When you hear this beep you have to do something with a notebook." If the patient failed again, he or she was shown the notebook. It is only when the patient failed forced-choice recognition that the information was assumed to be lost, and, consequently, the patient was administered forced-choice recognition with the correct answer heavily highlighted. Results showed that 12 of 24 patients could recall the target action 1 day after the acquisition sessions requiring only the primary cue. The authors also indicated that an important learning parameter is to provide the patients with the opportunity to actually perform the action when the beeper sounded on each trial (whether the patients spontaneously recalled the action or not). This is consistent with the known sensitivity of AD patients to the positive mnemonic effect of enactment at encoding. However, even if motor performance significantly contributed to learning, a condition in which motor performance was associated with verbal recall on each trial (i.e., when the patient was required to consciously recall the action before performing it) proved to be the most effective learning method. This method was applied by Bird (see chap. 8 of this book; see also Bird, 2001; Bird, Alexopoulos, & Adamowicz, 1995) to address several clinically relevant difficulties, including delusions, obsessive toileting, incontinence, sexual assault, intrusive behavior, and violence. For example, a patient with mild AD who showed delusions related to a belief that the staff had stolen her belongings (because she had forgotten how she had disposed of them) was taught to consult a poster describing where her most cherished things were. As indicated by Bird (2001), when planning the use of the technique, it is essential to understand the patient's viewpoint. To illustrate this remark, he showed that training to associate a beeper with visits to the bathroom contributed to a reduction in obsessive toileting in one AD patient but not in another, although in both patients obsessive toileting was related to an inability to remember whether or not they had toileted. However, in the patient for whom the training did not work, the memory deficit interacted with anxiety due to a lifelong belief that negative consequences ensue without a daily bowel movement.

A less theoretically grounded optimizing factor has been evidenced by Foster and Valentine (2001). They demonstrated a facilitatory effect of background music on autobiographical recall in patients with mild-moderate and moderate dementia. In addition, they observed a superiority of music over noise, which suggests the importance of structured sound. These results are interpreted in terms of increased arousal or attention deployment (the auditory stimulus masking potentially distracting, extraneous stimuli or absorbing surplus attention that might otherwise divert attention from the primary task). However, they also hypothesized a possible subsidiary role for associative facilitation, although there was no significant difference between familiar and novel music. In this prospect, it should be interesting to explore the possible positive contribution of individually selected pieces of music, tailored for each patient. More generally, replications of these findings are clearly needed before considering a general rehabilitation application.

Two studies have also explored the usefulness of a visual imagery mnemonic for the enhancement of AD patients' memory performance. Both studies revealed very modest beneficial effects. However, Juillerat, (2001) recently observed that imagery mnemonics can be used to improve daily-life memory functioning in very early AD patients.

Hill, Evankovitch, Scheikh, and Yesavage (1987) attempted to train a patient with mild primary degenerative dementia to use the face-name mnemonic. They showed that training extended the amount of time for which two newly learned face-name combinations (the patient was unable to retain more than two face-name pairs at any given time) were retained. After training, the associations could be retained for 7 minutes whereas before training, the retention interval attained only 4 minutes. In addition, performance benefits persisted for 1 month. However, the patient showed considerable difficulty remembering all three steps of the mnemonic and especially the interactive component of the method.

Bäckman, Josephsson, Herlitz, Stigsdotter, and Viitanen (1991) found that the face-name imagery technique did not result in a better acquisition of face-name associations in 7 out of 8 demented patients (7 AD patients and 1 patient with multiinfarct dementia). However, in one AD patient, the method increased the time during which the face-name associations could be maintained in memory; he attained the maximum retention duration possible of 21 minutes, 30 seconds, with the improvement being maintained after a 1-month delay. All patients except this one were unable to master the three steps of the mnemonic. In particular, they had problems forming interactive images and reported interference from previous face-name combinations and from their spontaneous attempts to rehearse the names.

Globally, these results questioned the generalizability of the face-name method for increasing AD patients' memory. However, it is possible that more AD patients might benefit from a simplified face-name method and that very early AD patients might successfully adopt the standard method to improve their memory functioning in everyday life. In this prospect, Juillerat (2001) showed that a 58-year-old man with very early AD (MMSE of 26) had learned to spontaneously use the face-name method, as well as the peg method (which consists of an imagery association of items to be memorized with a previously learned ordered list of peg words) every time he needed to acquire new names and short lists of errands.

Finally, two recent studies explored the effect of a multicomponent memory training program on memory functioning (and more general cognitive and behavioral functioning) in mild to moderate AD patients (Davis, Massman, & Doody, 2001; Moore, Sandman, McGrady, & Kesslak, 2001).

Moore et al. (2001) administered to 25 patients with mild to moderate AD and their caregivers (who served as controls) a 5-week memory training program. More specifically, the participants were submitted to several interventions including face-name rehearsal, the Significant Event Technique (SET), and effortful recall of television sitcoms. The face-name rehearsal intervention was aimed at enhancing memory for the names of the group members. Photographs of the members were distributed to every participant, and the participants were asked to introduce themselves by name and to give a short autobiography. To facilitate deeper encoding, relevant details, such as hobbies, interests, and children were described to the group, and participants also chose a particular motor movement that matched their interest (e.g., flying an airplane). Repeating the person's name along with pantomiming personal motor movements was practiced routinely during each group session and at home with the caregiver. Verbal recognition tests were administered weekly, along with immediate feedback on the progress. In the SET, couples were asked to plan and stage a novel, unique, and unusual event (such as a picnic to an important place with food they had never eaten). Afterwards, participants were asked to discuss their activity, and a series of objective questions about the SET were asked, along with questions about a non-SET control day. In the effortful recall intervention, the participants were shown a video with four television sitcoms of 20 minutes each. They were asked to watch one sitcom per week and were tested weekly on details of the program (by means of free recall and recognition tests). On the 3rd week, they were asked to develop five questions about the video to pose to the other group members, and for the 4th and 5th weeks, they were requested to make up 10 questions about the video, similar to the recall and recognition test questions. Task specific tests regularly administered during the memory training program showed improved performance in memory for names and faces, significant events, and television sitcom information, even though controls consistently performed better that the AD group. Furthermore, the improvement remained at a 1-month follow-up. On general cognitive and behavioral measures, however, the effects of the intervention were modest and variable: AD patients' scores improved on the Kendrick Digit Copy Test (assessing psychomotor speed) and Geriatric Depression Scale but not on the Memory Functioning Questionnaire, the Blessed Dementia Scale, and the Relative Stress Scale. Finally, caregivers indicated that the AD patients had improved in their perceived functional ability as rated on the Memory Functioning Questionnaire. The authors concluded that the most significant improvements appear to be specific to the type of strategies and that the memory training program did not substantially extend to other cognitive functions. They also identified several factors that might be responsible for the memory performance improvements: binding relevant details to names and faces and providing immediate feedback, active learning of the television sitcoms, and the novelty and emotionality component of the SET.

In a randomized placebo-controlled study, Davis et al. (2001) tested the efficacy of a cognitive intervention consisting of training in face-name imagery associations, spaced retrieval (see "Teaching Specific New Knowledge" on page 196), and cognitive stimulation in a sample of 37 AD patients. The spaced-retrieval technique was applied to personal information items (among them, name, street address, city and state, zip code, age, date of birth, and telephone number) the patients had been unable to recall initially. In the face-name training task, patients attempted to learn and recall a minimum of three staff members' names when shown their photographs, by making visual images associating the face to an imageable transformation of the name (e.g., "knee" for "Naomi"). The cognitive stimulation intervention consisted of a series of home attention exercises. AD patients were randomly assigned to receive either the cognitive intervention or a placebo condition for 5 weeks. Patients in the intervention group showed enhanced recall of personal information and face-name recall during the 5-week intervention and had improved significantly on these tasks at the end of the study. In addition, the intervention group showed enhanced performance on an attention/concentration task, whereas the placebo group's performance remained constant. However, the intervention group did not improve significantly after treatment with regard to measures of dementia severity, verbal memory, visual memory, word generation, motor speed, depressive symptoms, and caregiver-rated patient quality of life. These results led the authors to conclude that although face-name training, spaced retrieval, and cognitive stimulation may produce small gains in learning personal information and on a measure of attention, improvement failed to extend to other psychometric tests and quality of life improvement.

Both Moore et al.'s (2001) and Davis et al.'s (2001) studies confirmed that when they are submitted to memory interventions that promote efficient encoding and retrieval processes, AD patients may acquire new, specific information and retain it for an extended period of time. However, the interventions revealed only modest generalized effects. In other words, the facilitating influence of the training program was mainly restricted to the targeted material and tasks and did not extend to other cognitive functions. Furthermore, the beneficial effects on the quality of life were very limited. In fact, these findings are not really surprising if we consider the specific objective of these studies, the principles of memory (cognitive) functioning, and also the distinction between facilitation and improvement established by Herrmann and Palmisano (1992). Indeed, in both studies, the intervention programs had not been designed from a detailed analysis of the particular problems (or handicaps) specific to each patient (and family caregivers). Consequently, it is only to be expected that the interventions did not affect the quality of life in a substantial manner. Moreover, efficient memory functioning in everyday life seems to depend on the flexible use of different strategies adjusted to different memory situations. Furthermore, memory cannot be considered as a muscle that can be trained by means of repeated memory exercises or stimulations. Indeed, several studies conducted in nondemented, memory-impaired patients clearly showed the absence of any beneficial effect of this stimulation approach (Berg, Koning-Haanstra, & Deelman, 1991; Godfrey & Knight, 1988; Middleton, Lambert, & Seggar, 1991; Prigatano et al., 1984). In fact, when memory benefits were observed following repeated memory exercises, they only concerned the material and tasks on which the exercises had focused and did not extend to other types of material and tasks (see Chase & Ericsson, 1981). This lack of generalization can be easily understood if one considers memory as a complex function made up of several specialized systems. It follows from this that intervention programs should promote the adoption of multiple facilitation strategies. In addition, considering the heterogeneity of the AD patients' cognitive impairments, these strategies should be adapted to the particular deficits of each patient (and also to his or her cognitive preferences), after having made a detailed pretherapeutical evaluation. Yet, because there is a considerable demand for treatment, and numerous and urgent problems need to be solved, it is tempting to systematically adopt ready-made programs. It seems to us that this pragmatic position does not constitute an adequate approach to AD patients' difficulties. We clearly privilege an approach in which made-to-measure facilitation interventions are designed to address some concrete and specific daily-life difficulties of the patient and which take into account both the nature of these difficulties and the existence of specific optimization factors identified in a preintervention assessment. Finally, as already mentioned earlier, because of a reduction of processing resources and planning or comprehension deficits, it will be difficult for most AD patients to spontaneously use a facilitation strategy in all situations in which it would be useful (i.e., to improve their memory functioning). For example, it is unlikely that practicing the face-name mnemonic to learn three staff members' names (as in the study conducted by Davis et al., 2001) will automatically extend to other face-name learning tasks. Put differently, in most cases, the intervention will mainly consist in temporary facilitating memory function (e.g., helping the patient to learn a few relevant names). However, a memory improvement may possibly be considered in some (mild or very mild) AD patients, but in any case this will require a long and demanding acquisition and generalization phase.

Most of the preceding comments may also be made about the cognitive stimulation intervention program developed by Quayhagen and Quayhagen (2001; Quayhagen, Quayhagen, Corbeil, Roth, & Rodgers, 1995) as well as about similar stimulation programs.

> Quayhagen and Quayhagen's (2001) cognitive stimulation program was designed for use in the home, with the family caregivers as the intervening persons. The spousal caregivers were asked to cognitively stimulate the patient through several types of exercises: memory exercises (activities such as picture recognition or a search-a-word puzzle, along with rehearsal, association, and elaboration of detail related to these activities; free recall and association of recent information, such as television news and book passages; cuing techniques for remembering dates and time), conversation fluency tasks (eliciting facts, opinions and rationale or justification of opinions), and problem-solving tasks (solving practical problems, such as a fire at home, with practice in generating alternative solutions and identifying possible causes of the problem and consequences of different solutions). The authors mentioned

that an important ingredient of the program was emphasis on positive feedback and encouragement. Quayhagen and Quayhagen (2001) reported the results of two studies that varied in the duration of the intervention (12 weeks vs. 8 weeks) and direction of weekly focus (in the first study, only one intervention component, either memory or conversation fluency or problem solving, was addressed each week, whereas in the second study, each weekly focus included the three components). Composite measures (elaborated from several neuropsychological tests and scales) were used to evaluate, initially and at 3-month follow-up, immediate and delayed memory, verbal fluency, and problem solving, along with the degree of marital satisfaction. In the first study, the cognitive stimulation group was compared to a placebo treatment (passive activities, such as watching television) group and a control (waiting list) group. The results showed that the stimulation group improved in immediate memory and verbal fluency tasks when compared with the control group, who exhibited a decrease in these abilities (the comparison between the stimulation group and the placebo group only revealed a trend interaction). In addition, the stimulation group maintained, but did not improve, their level of marital satisfaction, whereas in the control group it declined (yet a stability of marital satisfaction was also observed in the placebo group). Finally, no significant difference was observed for delayed memory and problem solving. In the second study, the stimulation group was compared with a control group. The results showed that the stimulation group demonstrated a significant increase over time in both fluency and problem solving, whereas the control group tended to decrease. No other difference was observed. On the whole, the beneficial effects of the cognitive stimulation intervention proved to be rather modest and varied between both studies. In addition, in the first study, the specific contribution of the stimulation program versus the placebo treatment was not clearly demonstrated. Furthermore, it might be argued that the limited beneficial effects of the program were not actually due to the cognitive stimulation but rather to the positive interactions that were established with the spousal caregiver. Finally, and more important, the impact of the improvement in one or another neuropsychological task, such as the fluency task, on everyday life functioning was not established.

It should be noted that memory performance can also be facilitated by affecting various nonmemory factors (see Hermann & Palmisano, 1992) and, in particular, the person's physical state (insufficient sleep, poor or unbalanced nutrition, and limited physical exercise may all contribute to a poor memory performance), the emotional state (memory performance may be impaired by stress and by the attitudes the patients hold about their memory abilities and, consequently, the removal of stress factors or the reduction of their influence on the patient, for example, through relaxation, and changing the attitudes about a task can be expected to facilitate memory performance; see Suhr, Anderson, & Tranel, 1999, for a presentation of a relaxation method adapted to AD patients), and environmental conditions (numerous neurochemical agents, such as alcohol, tranquilizers and antidepressants, impair memory performance).

Facilitation of Conversational Interaction. Several types of difficulty affecting conversational interactions have been demonstrated in AD (see Arkin & Mahendra, 2001a; Kempler, 1995). Consequently, facilitating the AD patients' conversational abilities is important in maintaining quality of communication and social involvement. Besides word-finding difficulties, use of generic or empty words, ideational perseveration, and intermittent repetitions of the same sentences, the analysis of the AD patients' discourse indicates that they produce fewer utterances per turn, use a higher proportion of pronouns without antecedents as well as more omission and referent errors, and show reduced cohesion and coherence. In addition, they are more dependent on the incitements of their partners, introduce less conversational themes, and present more difficulties to stay on topic. Finally, besides language production deficits, they also present difficulties understanding spoken language (whether at the single sentence or discourse level). Although language production and compre- hension impairment in AD is probably multifactorial in nature, a (great) part of these difficulties appears to be the consequence of a reduction of working memory (central executive) resources. With this in mind, several general recommendations may be given to those communicating with AD patients. For example, with regard to comprehension difficulties, the following indications may be proposed to the communication partner: using concrete and specific words; making short and simple sentences; in the case of long sentences, seeing that the first segment of the sentence contains the key information and that the complementary information is presented afterwards (indeed, when the following segments are necessary to understand information contained in the first segment, memory load and related comprehension difficulties increase). It should also be noted that the frequent use of pronouns increases working memory load, which can be avoided by repeating the referent (e.g., Almor, Kempler, MacDonald, Andersen, & Tyler, 1999). Similarly, the use of closed questions can prevent the patient from elaborating complex syntactical statements. The simultaneous use of verbal and nonverbal (gestual) modalities might have beneficial effects on statement understanding. Furthermore, working memory deficits and especially dual-task coordination difficulties (which are frequently observed in early AD; see Baddeley et al., 2001; Collette et al., 1999) may especially affect conversational abilities when several partners are involved. In this perspective, Alberoni et al. (1992) presented patients with recordings of conversations with two to five people engaged in the conversation. The patients were then asked to identify the person who made a particular statement. The results showed that the AD patients performed very poorly on this task when three or more people were conversing. Consequently, it appears that limiting the number of conversational partners may help facilitate conversation in AD patients. Finally, it appears that comprehension difficulties may be due (at least partly) to auditory deficits. In this matter, Palmer, Adams, Bourgeois, Durrant, and Rossi (1999) observed the beneficial effects of a hearing aid on communication abilities in AD patients.

Recently, Done and Thomas (2001) evaluated whether a short training workshop in communication techniques was more effective than an information booklet for improving communications skills in informal caregivers of people suffering from dementia. Thirty informal caregivers were allocated to the workshop sessions and 15 to the booklet. At a 6-week follow-up, the workshop group demonstrated a significantly greater awareness of communication strategies than the booklet group. However, ability to manage problems in communication at home improved significantly in both groups. In addition, a reduction in the level of emotional distress associated with communication breakdown was observed in both groups, whereas measures of general emotional stress were unaffected by either intervention.

In addition, the studies that focus on the analysis of conversation considered as a collaboration enterprise between several persons may also help indicate to caregivers how to properly interact with the patient, according to his or her particular conversational difficulties.

Watson, Chenery, and Carter (1999) explored the frequency and nature of trouble and repair in conversations between persons with senile dementia of the Alzheimer's type (SDTA) and their communication partners. When a communication rupture (or a situation of poor communication) is observed, it is useful to identify how and who indicates the communication rupture (i.e., the trouble indicating behavior or TBI) and which types of strategies are installed to restore communication continuity and who initiates them (i.e., the repairs). The authors analyzed spontaneous conversations according to type of TBI, pattern of repair trajectory, specific repair types, and whether or not the repair was successful. The results showed that SDTA patients used more noninteractive TBI, reflecting topic maintenance and elaboration difficulty that contributed to conversational dysfluency and discontinuity. The patients also produced more inappropriate repairs, which were sometimes accepted by the normal partner in an attempt to maintain the flow of conversation, to preserve the patients' self-esteem, or both. Considering these data, Watson et al. (1999) made some suggestions that may prove useful for familiar conversational partners, namely, using hypothesis formation rather than requests for specific information (especially requests for information from long-term memory, which are especially problematic) to indicate trouble to the dementia partner. Indeed, in hypothesis formation, the partner indicates the problem but also proposes a solution in the form of a paraphrase, whereas by requesting supplementary information, the partner leaves the patient to execute the repair, which he or she may not necessarily be able to do. Other studies are required to explore the applicability and efficacy of these general strategies in the individual rehabilitation of communication disorders as well as to examine the effect of partner familiarity, dementia severity, and communicative activity on trouble indication and repair. However that may be, it seems that only an individual analysis of conversation samples along with a detailed neuropsychological examination will constitute an efficient approach. Indeed, conversation ruptures and changes of theme may appear for different reasons, such as working memory deficit, lexico-semantic deficit, attention deficit, and so forth.

In a recent study, Arkin (2001) described a language intervention aimed at addressing discourse deficits (thinking, generating, and ordering ideas; understanding linguistic information; maintaining thematic structure) in mild to moderate AD patients. More specifically, the objective of this language intervention was to facilitate access to semantic memory by considering that blocks of ideas in semantic memory are related to each other and may be accessed via different routes. This language intervention is part of a more general program implemented by undergraduate students and also including physical fitness, memory training (aimed to reteach biographical information to AD patients), and partnered volunteering (volunteer service or other personally meaningful community activity, such as reading to preschool-age children or packaging bulk rice or beans at a food bank, plus a brisk walk with the student partner). More specifically, students supervised physical fitness training and volunteer work sessions for all participants (11 patients with mild to moderate AD) and administered specific memory and language training to 7 of them (experimental group).

With regard to the language intervention, Arkin (2001) proposed a variety of tasks to prime and revive semantic information and connections between different aspects of semantic memory: picture description; word association; category fluency; proverb interpretation; an adaptation of a children's game that requires thinking of a famous person's last name that goes with a proposed letter ("A, my name is ...; my husband's/wife's name is ... name beginning with A; and we come from ... place beginning with A"); and a car bingo administered in the students' car on the way from the participants' home to the fitness center. To broaden conversational opportunities and to increase self-esteem, the patients were also asked for their opinions on controversial topics, involving a moral issue.

To assess discourse intervention outcome, Arkin and Mahendra (2001b) developed a content-focused method of analyzing the discourse of AD patients. They demonstrated that it is an ecologically valid method of monitoring change after intervention, useable by clinicians not trained in linguistics. This discourse battery consisted of eight specific stimulus prompts or questions designed to elicit discourse, a picture description task, and a five-item proverb interpretation task. These tasks were chosen to represent five distinct discourse types: narrative discourse, procedural discourse (to tell how a task is accomplished), expository discourse (a less-structured discourse type that is present when a subject simply talks about a topic), conversational discourse, and descriptive discourse. Three classes of codes (positive, negative, and neutral utterances) are described and illustrated. The discourse-based outcome measures used were as follows: the ratio of topic comments to total utterances, the ratio of different nouns to total nouns, the ratio of vague nouns to total nouns, and information units produced on a picture description task. Finally, the patients were also administered a standardized language battery as well as several cognitive and mood tests and a functional status assessment.

Outcomes of this rehabilitation program implemented by students were evaluated by project-specific measures and more general cognitive and mood testing before and after two semesters of participation. The general results showed that after two semesters of physical exercise and cognitive, language, and social intervention, the 11 AD patients showed no significant decline on 13 of 14 cognitive and language measures. However, as there was no control group that underwent another type of intervention, it is difficult to draw clear conclusions, especially concerning the specificity of this program and the extent of its possible beneficial influence on cognition and language. Furthermore, the AD patients made significant fitness and mood gains. In addition, highly significant learning was achieved by the seven experimental subjects when compared with the four control subjects on the biographical knowledge test which confirms that AD patients may learn or relearn factual information (see "Teaching Specific New Knowledge" on page 196 for an interpretation of these benefits). On the other hand, the results related to the specific language intervention were particularly disappointing because the patients who underwent no specific language intervention did as well at posttest as experimental patients on all measures of the discourse battery (except on the ratio of different nouns to total nouns) and the standardized language battery. Even if definitive conclusions cannot be drawn because of the sample size of this study, it seems likely that the language intervention designed by Arkin (2001) was too global and did not take in account the heterogeneity of the language deficits observed in AD patients (see chap. 3 of this book). In other words, an efficient language intervention probably requires a detailed individual cognitive analysis to adjust a specific training program to the particular deficits of a patient.

Facilitation of Numerical Abilities. A number of recent group studies and single-case investigations have shown that the early stage of AD may selectively affect various numerical abilities: basic number skills, number transcoding, or calculation processes (Girelli & Delazer, 2001). Considering the social and daily importance of these faculties, the development of effective intervention should be urgently promoted. In fact, several studies have described rehabilitation programs (concerning the transcoding of numerals and the retrieval of arithmetical facts) in patients with focalized lesions (see Girelli & Seron, 2001). On the other hand, the studies concerning AD patients are very rare.

Jacquemin, Calicis, Van der Linden, Wijns, and Noël (1991) reported the intervention in an early demented patient presenting important deficits in the reading of Arabic numerals that resulted in an incorrect representation of the corresponding quantities: for example, if 371 was read as "three thousand seven hundred one," and 1208 was read correctly, then in a magnitude comparison task, the patient considered that 371 was bigger than 1208. These difficulties were particularly disturbing when the patient was doing her shopping. The reeducation consisted in using her preserved abilities to read verbal numerals to reconstruct her reading of the Arabic ones. First, she was asked to count the number of digits in numerals of various lengths (up to six). Then, she was trained to read numerals three to six digits long, with the aid of a written frame (see Fig. 9.1). For example, when she was given a three-digit Arabic numeral, she had to place it inside a three-position frame containing the word *hundred* in the right position. When she had to read a four-digit Arabic numeral, she was proposed a four-position frame containing the words *thousand* and *hundred* in the right positions. The written aid was progressively withdrawn (she was asked to read Arabic numerals with the help of limited cues, such as 5/c 61 or 3/m 2/c 48), until the patient could read the numerals without assistance. Then, she was trained to read and compare ticket prices. Thirteen sessions were necessary to obtain a level of 92% correct reading.

Teaching Specific New Knowledge

The various studies that have documented preserved (procedural and implicit) memory abilities in AD patients (see chap. 3 of this book) suggest that it is possible to teach AD patients specific knowledge by exploiting their intact learning capabilities to make them more autonomous in everyday life. Such an objective involves, on the one hand, identifying specific domains of knowledge that are important for the patient to acquire, retain, and use, and, on the other hand, developing techniques that mobilize patients' intact memory capacities.

We will describe three techniques considered to exploit spared implicit memory abilities in AD patients to facilitate new learning of several kinds of information: the spaced-retrieval technique, the vanishing-cues proce-

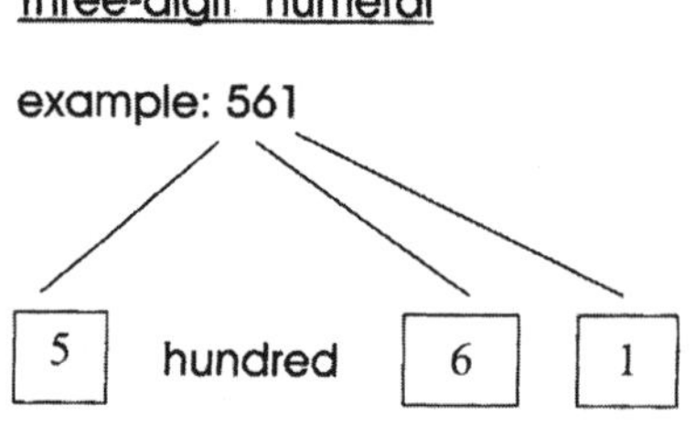

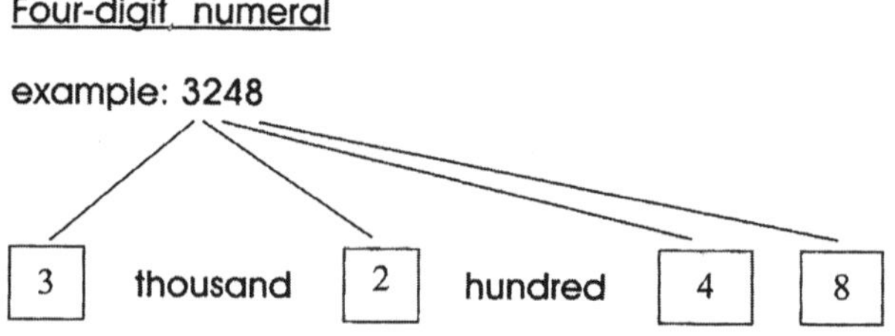

Fig. 9.1. Example of the written assistance frame used by Jacquemin et al. (1991).

dure, and the errorless learning method. Finally, the exploitation of preserved procedural memory to increase functional independence in AD patients will also be presented.

The Spaced-Retrieval Technique. The spaced-retrieval technique prompts recall of information over increasingly longer retention intervals (Bjork, 1988; Landauer & Bjork, 1978). It has been adapted by Camp and his associates for use in AD (see Camp, 1989; Camp, Bird, & Cherry, 2000; Camp, Foss, O'Hanlon, & Stevens, 1996; Camp & McKitrick, 1992). In Camp's spaced-retrieval procedure, patients are given specific information to remember, followed by immediate recall. If the retrieval attempt is successful, the next intertrial interval is increased systematically (e.g., 5 seconds, 10 seconds, 20 seconds, 40 seconds, 60 seconds, increasing in 30-second intervals thereafter). If a recall fails, the intertrial interval is decreased to that of the previous trial. Interestingly, it has been observed that if the patients were able to successfully recall information over a critical interval (6–8 minutes), the information seemed to be consolidated in long-term memory and could be retained for days (Camp, Foss, Stevens, & O'Hanlon, 1996; see, however, Bird & Kinsella, 1996, who reported that a longer retention interval, 15 minutes or 1 hour, is needed to predict long-term retention). These findings have important practical implications because the knowledge of a critical recall interval can be used to determine when to stop training sessions.

This method enabled AD patients to learn new face-name associations (Camp, 1989; Camp & Schaller, 1989; Camp et al., 1993; Vanhalle, Van der Linden, Belleville, & Gilbert, 1998), to remember object localization (Camp & Stevens, 1990), and to improve their ability to name objects (Abrahams & Camp, 1993; Jacquemin, Van der Linden, & Feyereisen, 1993; McKitrick & Camp, 1993; Moffat, 1992). It has also been successfully used to teach use of an external memory aid (e.g., a calendar; Camp, Foss, O'Hanlan, et al., 1996; Stevens, O'Hanlon, & Camp, 1993), to enhance prospective memory (Camp, Foss, Stevens, et al., 1996; Lekeu, Chicherio, Van der Linden, & Salmon, 2000; McKitrick, Camp, & Black, 1992), and to lessen behavior problems in dementia (Bird & Kinsella, 1996).

The spaced-retrieval effects appear to be robust. Indeed, Camp and collaborators successfully increased the duration of retention of associations for weeks after initial encoding in AD patients who could not retain new information for 60 s without training (see Camp & McKitrick, 1992; Cherry, Simmons, & Camp, 1999). These effects also generalized across settings, material, and procedures (Camp, 1989; Cherry et al., 1999). Finally, caregivers may learn to apply the spaced-retrieval technique (cited in Camp, Foss, O'Hanlan, et al., 1996; McKitrick, 1993; Riley, 1992), and some very early patients might also be trained to use this technique spontaneously (Riley, 1992; see also Schacter, Rich, & Stampp, 1985, for a demonstration of the spontaneous use of spaced-retrieval in nondemented patients). There is also evidence that simple timing devices, such as an interval chart and digital timer, can be developed for providing spaced-retrieval training (Camp, Foss, O'Hanlan, et al., 1996). It should also be noted that the intervals between different retrieval trials can be filled by conversation, playing games, looking over photo albums, and so forth which make the intervention very pleasant and flexible.

The efficacy of spaced retrieval in AD patients has been attributed to implicit memory processes that are thought to be spared in AD (Camp et al., 1993), and thus the spaced-retrieval technique has been described as effortless because learning seems to occur without full cognitive effort on the part of the patient. In this respect, Foss and Camp (1994; cited in Camp & Foss, 1997) have shown that spaced retrieval may be successfully used to teach face-name associations in AD patients and that face-name learning and retrieval was unaffected by the level of effort required by a secondary task. In addition, some authors reported that the patients were surprised when they gave correct answers because they did not consciously remember having been presented with this information in the past (Camp & McKitrick, 1992; Schacter, Rich, & Stampp, 1985). In other words, the correct response was given hesitantly, as if the patients were unsure why they were giving that particular answer. Similarly, it appears that when the patients are provided with the correct answer (after giving a wrong one), they often mention that they had considered this response at first, but, because they were not certain, they had looked for another one. More direct, though modest, evidence in favor of the implicit nature of spaced retrieval has been recently obtained by Cherry et al. (1999).

In Cherry et al.'s (1999) study, three training sessions were administered on alternate days during a week. On each training trial, patients were asked to select a designated object from an array of items at increasingly longer retention intervals. After each session, implicit memory (repetition priming) for the target object was assessed by using a category exemplar task, in which the patients were asked to produce items that belonged to the same taxonomic category as that of the trained object. Similarly, explicit memory was examined by soliciting recall and recognition of the target object. Despite poor explicit memory performance, all patients showed implicit memory effects for at least one trained object (in other words, they produced the name of the object in the category exemplar task).

Clearly, these findings have to be confirmed by using more sensitive methods of assessing implicit memory. In addition, the contribution of perceptual versus conceptual priming to spaced-retrieval performance should also be explored. Finally, other data suggest that conscious retrieval may contribute to the spaced-retrieval effects in some individuals with dementia but not in others and in the same person on some occasions but not on others (see Bird & Kinsella, 1996; Camp, Bird, & Cherry, 2000). Thus, it appears that no single factor can explain spaced-retrieval effects and that the exploration of these effects should benefit from memory procedures that permit dissociation of, in the same task, the automatic and controlled aspects of memory retrieval (such as the process dissociation procedure elaborated by Jacoby, 1991; see also Adam, Van der Linden, & Salmon, 2000; Ste-Marie, Jennings, & Finlayson, 1996). Finally, future research should examine what characterizes patients who can benefit from spaced retrieval and who maintained the acquired information over long periods, in comparison with those whose memory seems to fade quickly, or who cannot learn at all (Camp et al., 2000).

The Vanishing-Cues Technique. The vanishing-cues method involves giving subjects a cue in the form of a word stem; across learning trials, cue information is gradually withdrawn until responses are eventually given in the absence of partial cues.

This method has been frequently and successfully used in nondemented, amnesic patients (e.g., Glisky, Schacter, & Tulving, 1986; Leng, Copello, & Sayegh, 1991; Van der Linden & Coyette, 1995; Van der Linden, Meulemans, & Lorrain, 1994).

> For example, Glisky et al. (1986) found that amnesics were able to acquire a substantial amount of computer vocabulary by means of the vanishing-cues method, designed to allow patients to use their preserved priming (implicit memory) abilities to respond to fragment cues. A series of definitions was presented to the patient on a computer screen (e.g., "programs that the computer carries out" = *SOFTWARE*). When a definition appeared, the patients tried to complete the definition with the appropriate word. If they failed, they were prompted with the first letter of the word as a cue. The cue was extended as needed (i.e., *S*——, *SO*——, *SOF*——) until the patient successfully recalled the answer. On the next trial, the definition was presented along with a cue that was one letter shorter than the previous cue required for successful completion on the last trial. Thus, the cue was withdrawn gradually, one letter at a time, until the patient could complete the definition without a cue. The results demonstrated that even severely amnesic patients could learn the vocabulary, although they had little conscious recollection of the learning experience. Consistent learning was also observed with a standard anticipation learning method, but the vanishing-cues method yielded higher levels of learning. However, such learning was slow compared with controls. Moreover, it was tightly bound to stimulus context (the first letter of the word) and was not readily accessible to changed cues (even if the vanishing-cues method led to a more flexible knowledge than the anticipation method). Leng et al. (1991) also showed that a memory-disordered patient acquired more quickly vocabulary definitions with the vanishing-cues method, but, in addition, the patient did not remain dependent on the first letter.

A few studies showed that it may also be efficient in the acquisition of new facts in AD patients (Fontaine, 1995; Fontaine, Van der Linden, Guyot, & Châtelois, 1991; Moffat, 1992). For example, using the procedure developed by Glisky et al. (1986), Fontaine (1995) attempted to teach 2 AD patients name-face and name-profession associations. The results showed that both patients were progressively able to produce the names (and the professions) without a letter cue. In addition, retention of this newly acquired information remained stable for more than 12 months in one patient. Finally, both patients were able to transfer the new knowledge to other contexts.

Baddeley and Wilson (1994) criticized the vanishing-cues procedure initially developed by Glisky et al. (1986), suggesting that it promotes the production of errors. This was the case especially at the initial learning trial, where, for example, subjects were required to guess a target word in response to its definition without any letter cues. According to Baddeley and Wilson (1994), amnesic patients do not learn implicit memory tasks well when they are allowed to make errors during training because they cannot remember and eliminate errors during the learning process (due to their severe episodic memory deficit). In the same vein, Hayman, Macdonald, and Tulving (1993) clearly demonstrated that semantic learning in amnesia is better when the patients are administered errorless testing procedures that preclude interfering responses. They also showed that amnesic patients would be able to learn semantic information if it is meaningful (i.e., if it concerns a domain they already know or if it is consistent with already stored concepts). Glisky and Delaney (1996; see also Hunkin & Parkin, 1995) therefore modified the vanishing-cues procedure in such a way that the first trial of each training session began with the presentation of the complete target item (*DUPONT*), and then the cue was gradually withdrawn (*DUPON—*, *DUPO—*, *DUP—*, etc.). Nevertheless, contrary to Glisky et al. (1986) and Leng et al. (1991), Hunkin and Parkin (1995) did not find any advantage of the vanishing-cues method over the classical anticipation learning method in nondemented, memory-disordered patients (even when the procedure was adapted to prevent the production of errors). Several factors could explain these discordant results (see Van der Linden, Coyette, et al., 2000). In particular, it might be that the vanishing-cues method is not efficient when the patients are administered an explicit retrieval test or that only some amnesic patients can benefit from this technique (viz., patients with very severe amnesia, in which the exploitation of implicit memory is not contaminated by residual explicit memory abilities). Further research should be conducted to systematically explore the efficiency of the vanishing-cues method in amnesia depending on whether or not it permits the production of errors, whether or not the retrieval instructions induce conscious retrieval, the severity of memory disorders, and the compatibility of the to-be-remembered material with the preexisting knowledge. More fundamentally, it remains to be determined whether the method of vanishing cues is mediated by the same system that supports perceptual repetition priming (i.e., the perceptual representation system) or by the semantic memory system.

Errorless Learning. Another method that may be useful in AD is termed errorless learning. This technique limits the opportunity to commit an error by repeatedly exposing the patients to the correct answer, rather than asking them to guess or explicitly retrieve it. Several recent studies have shown that it is possible to teach amnesic patients new factual information by using this errorless learning method.

> Parkin, Hunkin, and Squires (1998) showed that an amnesic, nondemented patient was able to relearn the names of politicians he had been unable to produce before training. The patient was presented with items from the training set, one at a time. He was asked to look at each face and read the name underneath; the name was then covered up, and the patient was asked to write the name down on a piece of paper. This procedure was repeated six times in each session. After six learning sessions, he could name successfully six of the eight politicians he had been unable to name at the outset of the study. Surprisingly, however, it also emerged that he became unable to recall the names of other politicians that he had been able to produce before training. The authors interpreted this effect as the consequence of a retrieval inhibition mechanism (Anderson & Spellman, 1995) by which repeated use of a subset of facts might be facilitated if other parts of the set are inhibited. To prevent this inhibition effect, the authors proposed that the errorless learning phase should focus on both the to-be-learned and the surviving premorbid knowledge. Squires, Hunkin, and Parkin (1997) also observed a clear advantage of the errorless method on a errorful method in the acquisition of new associations in amnesic patients. Finally, the advantage of errorless learning was confirmed by single-case studies where nondemented, memory-impaired patients had to learn a variety of material, including the names of people and objects, orientation and general knowledge items, as well as the programming of an electronic memory aid (Wilson, Baddeley, & Evans, 1994). Furthermore, it has been argued that both the spaced-retrieval and vanishing-cues techniques may have succeeded because an indirect result of these methods was to limit the opportunity for subjects to commit errors (Baddeley & Wilson, 1994; Squires et al., 1997; Wilson, Baddeley, Evans, & Shiel, 1994).

In a recent multiple single-case study, Clare et al. (2000; see also Clare, Wilson, Breen, & Hodges, 1999) described several successful interventions in AD based on the errorless principle and targeted at a specific everyday memory problem.

> More specifically, four of the interventions in the Clare et al. (2000) study involved learning or relearning specific information (names of people or personal information), using a multiple baseline across item design and follow-up assessments scheduled at 1, 3, and 6 months after completion of the intervention. The authors adopted either a combination of several strategies (a verbal elaboration of the name based on a prominent facial feature, training the name by using vanishing cues, and practicing it by expanding rehearsal or only expanded rehearsal). Participants were requested not to guess and to give answers only if they were certain these were correct. The remaining two interventions involved training in the use of a memory aid (calendar or diary) so as to reduce repetitive questioning by the caregiver,

using an ABA design. The results show that early AD patients can display significant improvement on specific everyday memory tasks using training methods based on the errorless learning principle. These improvements are not due to changes in cognitive or behavioral functioning and indeed may be demonstrated in the context of global deterioration. It must be added that most of the patients were involved in daily practice following intervention, and this may have been an important factor contributing to the success of the interventions. More recently, in a single-case follow-up study, Clare, Wilson, Carter, Hodges, and Adams (2001) evaluated the long-term maintenance of the effects of cognitive rehabilitation intervention conducted with an AD patient (the patient, VJ, is described in detail in Clare et al., 1999). In the initial intervention, VJ had acquired the names of 11 members of his club, performing at ceiling when assessed 1, 3, 6, and 9 months after the end of the program. These benefits were supported by daily practice. The authors observed that once the daily practice was stopped, the name learning remained relatively stable during Year 1 and showed a modest decline during Year 2 (also affecting untrained previously known items), although at the end of Year 2, performance on trained items remained well above initial baseline levels. These results indicate that long-term maintenance of specific gains can be observed in AD patients as a result of a cognitive rehabilitation intervention. Nevertheless, as suggested by the authors, future research will need to address the question of the interaction between repeated testing and maintenance of gains. Indeed, even if no feedback on performance was provided during tests, it might be that test trials in themselves had a beneficial effect on performance. More generally, the contribution of continued input (in the form of regular recall trials, with or without feedback) to maintenance facilitation should be examined. If this regular testing appeared to be efficacious, it could be administered by a partner, friend, or volunteer or even self-help methods might be proposed in early AD patients.

A contribution of errorless learning has also been considered by Arkin (2001) to interpret the beneficial effect of a memory training program focusing on biographical information. The purpose of this program was to help the patients to relearn information they had forgotten about their lives. This objective is important because autobiographical memory gives the patients a feeling of continuity and is essential in maintaining their dignity. The technique was developed after the discovery that repeated presentation of a videotape in which AD patients observed themselves being quizzed about a recent event, with the correct answer supplied for each error, led to enhanced recall of the event. In this method, the patients were exposed to a customized tape-recorder exercise that consisted of a series of paragraphs containing factual statements about their life history, followed by questions about the statements, a pause for their response, and the correct answer. In a series of studies (see Arkin, 1992, 1998, 2000), the researcher administered this program to 14 AD patients and an amnesic patient (whose MMSE scores ranged from 10 to 27). Substantial learning occurred in 13 of the 15 patients, and 78% to 100% of questions answered correctly at a 1-h delay posttest were answered correctly at a 1- or 2-week follow-up. According to Arkin (2001), the success of the memory training was due to memory training facilitating memory formation through automatic (implicit) memory processes, providing practice in retrieving information (which increases the likelihood that the correct answer will be given on a subsequent presentation of the same question), and, finally, minimizing the production of errors.

Nevertheless, the nature of the processes that underlie errorless learning remains to be determined. Evans et al. (2000) found that errorless learning was superior to errorful learning in the acquisition of face-name associations, only in a recall condition in which the first letter of the names was presented to the patients. According to the authors, this suggests that implicit memory is involved in the facilitatory effect of errorless learning. However, as suggested by Squires et al. (1997), although the first letter of the names may serve to probe implicit memory, it may also constitute an explicit retrieval cue. If the implicit memory interpretation is correct, it could be argued that asking the patients not to guess but only to answer when they are sure (as Clare et al., 1999, 2000, 2001, did) does not represent the best way to recruit implicit memory processes.

Recently, Komatsu, Mimura, Kato, Wakamatsu, and Kashima (2000) demonstrated that errorless learning is beneficial to face-name learning but that the effortful component in the retrieval task does not constitute an important factor.

Komatsu et al. (2000) explored the learning of face-name associations in Korsakoff patients by using four study conditions that differed from one another in the error and effort required to fulfill the task demands. The patients were shown a photograph of a face and were asked to learn the corresponding surname under the following conditions: in the initial letter condition, participants were presented with the initial letter of a target surname and were required to generate it; in the vanishing-cues condition, the letter of a target surname was gradually withdrawn across training trials; in the target selection condition, subjects were asked to select the correct surname from a set of alternatives; in the paired associate condition, a target surname was presented in its intact form together with the corresponding face. The initial letter and vanishing-cues conditions were considered to involve effortful processes because patients were required to generate a target surname. The target selection and the paired associate conditions were assumed to be effortless because subjects were presented with a target surname with no requirement to generate. With regard to error production, the initial letter and target selection conditions were regarded to be errorful because guessing in response to an initial letter or selecting a target among five alternatives was more likely to induce errors. The vanishing-cues and paired associate conditions were considered as errorless because there was no opportunity for incorrect answers under the paired associate condition, and the gradual reduction of cue information ensured correct responses in the vanishing-cues condition. The results showed that the paired associate and the vanishing-cues methods led to superior recall in comparison with the two other procedures, indicating an advantage of errorless learning. In contrast, the effort factor was found to have little effect.

Finally, in a recent study conducted in very mild to moderate AD patients, Arkin, Rose, and Hopper (2000) showed that the repeated act of processing and retrieving visual and verbal information with immediate feedback not only results in enhanced learning of the exposed information but also stimulates the production of semantically related output. They interpreted these findings by suggesting that repeated exposure contributed to a conceptual priming effect, which applied not only to the exposed items but also to related but nonexposed items

More specifically, in the Arkin et al. (2000) study, the AD patients were administered an eight-session study task in which they were asked to identify picture cards and answer a related question for each item; this study task exposed them to a total of 33 words from the target category "things people wear." In the picture-naming task and related quiz, the examiner recorded the response and repeated the correct answer. The test phase consisted of eight trials of a category fluency test of the target category. The purpose of the category fluency test was to determine if exposure to the study task served as priming and resulted in the production of words encountered in the study task but never produced on baseline testing (priming refers to the facilitating or biasing effect that exposure to a stimulus has on subsequent processing of the same or related stimuli). The results showed that all patients increased the number of correct responses to confrontational naming and related quiz questions. In the category fluency task, they produced words to which they had been exposed on the study task but had never produced on baseline tests, and they produced a significantly higher percentage of baseline exposure words than baseline nonexposure words. Interestingly, the patients also produced novel words that were not exposure words and that had never been produced during baseline testing. In addition, the patients were frequently reported by their examiners to initiate relevant elaboration of factual statements and responses to related quiz questions that appeared on an interactive biographical memory exercise that they were administered every week. The authors suggested that repeated exposure to the target concept "things people wear" may have activated inaccessible items in the subjects' lexical repertoire and facilitated their retrieval. Altogether, these results may be accounted for by suggesting that repeated exposure contributed to a conceptual priming effect (see chap. 3 of this book) which applied not only to the target items but also to related but nonexposed items. In other words, exposition to target words in the naming and quiz study task was sufficient to activate corresponding and related memory traces in semantic memory that resulted in priming of the target and related items and the subsequent increased production of these items on the naming, quiz, and fluency tasks. More generally, similar interventions, supposedly based on conceptual priming (or implicit memory), could contribute to the activation of knowledge that might prove useful with regard to daily life, for example, in the framework of leisure activities. Further studies should be conducted to determine the conditions in which conceptual priming may be observed in AD patients. Indeed, evidence for conceptual priming in individuals with AD is mixed (see Fleischman & Gabrieli, 1998). According to Vaidya, Gabrieli, Monti, Tinklenberg, and Yesavage (1999), the preservation of conceptual priming in AD might depend on whether access to semantic memory is direct (such that the test cue guides the retrieval of the target word without any or with few competing response alternatives) or indirect. Finally, considering Baddeley & Wilson's (1994) findings, conditions that minimize error production during exposition at the study phase should be favored.

Procedural Learning. Considering the preservation of procedural memory in AD even long after the onset of the disease (Dick, 1992; see also chap. 3 of this book), it also seems possible to teach or reteach AD patients new skills that might increase their autonomy in everyday life. Effective learning or support of motor skills should contribute to the preservation of functional independence in basic daily tasks (e.g., dressing, toileting) as well as social and leisure activities.

Some progress has been recently made about how to promote acquisition, retention, and transfer of new skills in AD patients. In two recent studies, Dick et al. (2000) and Dick, Hsieh, Dick-Muehlke, Davis, and Cotman (2000) explored in AD patients the variability of practice hypothesis (Schmidt, 1975), according to which practicing variations of a movement in a random fashion leads to better retention and transfer than practicing the skill in a constant manner (e.g., in a tossing task, performing the tosses at four distances should lead to better acquisition than performing all tosses at only one distance). In fact, Dick and collaborators found that in moderately to severely affected AD patients, contrary to healthy older adults, acquisition, retention, and transfer of a gross motor skill (viz., tossing) did not benefit from variable forms of practice, suggesting that they may have difficulty accessing or forming motor schemas, or both. Furthermore, Dick et al. (2001) also showed that mild to moderate AD patients were relying more heavily on visual information for accurate performance on a motor skill learning task (rotary pursuit) than healthy control subjects; more specifically, AD patients showed a significantly larger drop in performance than normal controls when vision was restricted. Globally, these findings indicate that retraining basic activities of everyday life in these patients should emphasize consistency as well as efforts to enhance the visual information available (directions, cueing, and uninterrupted visual feedback). However, further studies should examine if these conclusions also apply to patients with very early AD.

Several findings also suggest that methods that prevent error production should be privileged in AD patients' skill learning. Indeed, it has been observed that procedural learning may or may not lead to normal performance in patients with severe episodic memory disorders. For example, Wilson, Baddeley, and Cockburn (1989) observed that two nondemented, amnesic patients had extreme difficulty in learning a procedural task that consisted of entering the date and time into an electronic memory aid, despite their having showed normal performance in the traditional procedural learning tests. This procedural task involves about six simple steps and was mastered by control subjects within two or three trials. Baddeley (1992) interprets this failure by suggesting that the number of steps to be mastered in this task exceeds the capacity of working memory, and, consequently, errors are produced on Trial 1 by both the amnesics and the controls. However, because of their defective episodic memory, the amnesic patients (contrary to the controls) fail to recall their error and how it was corrected and thus cannot avoid repeating it. These views can easily explain why amnesic patients whose episodic memory is severely defective do not necessarily show normal skill learning. In fact, normal skill acquisition should be observed in amnesia only when the task does not depend on episodic memory for its acquisition. However, as indicated by Wilson et al. (1989), the testing of this hypothesis is confronted with the problem of establishing in advance whether the acquisition of a given task will or will not depend on episodic memory. Nevertheless, at a practical level, this suggests that the technique of errorless learning should optimize procedural learning in patients suffering from serious episodic memory disorders, including AD patients.

At the present time, very few studies have explored how to capitalize on preserved procedural memory to increase the functional autonomy of AD patients in everyday life. For example, Zanetti et al. (2001; see also Zanetti et al., 1997) recently showed that training of activities of daily life (by exploiting preserved procedural memory and providing high support) constitutes a realistic goal for AD patients' rehabilitation (see also Josephsson et al., 1993, for a similar approach).

More specifically, Zanetti et al. (2001) explored the efficiency of a daily living activity training program in mild and mild-moderate AD patients. Patients were individually trained by an occupational therapist for 3 consecutive weeks (1 h/day; 5 days/week), in 13 basic activities, such as personal hygiene, using the telephone, dressing, using money, and so forth. When invited to execute a task, the patients were assisted by cues, reinforcement, verbal and nonverbal prompts, and modeling of the task. The effectiveness of the stimulation was evaluated by recording the total mean time required to perform all the activities, and this was assessed, for both the trainee and control patients, at baseline and 4 months later (follow-up). Results demonstrated a significant reduction in the time necessary to perform the activities in the trainee group but not in the control group. The authors indicated that this improvement was probably because of a set of converging variables, including procedural learning but also a greater motivation exhibited by the patients, possibly induced by the caregivers' growing awareness of the importance of giving the patients more independence in the execution of daily activities. In the absence of information concerning the nature of the difficulties shown by the patients, it is not easy to identify the factors that contributed to the progress. In fact, daily living activities may be affected by AD in very different ways (limb apraxia, reduction of attentional resources, etc.; see chap. 10 of this book). Further studies in this domain should benefit from a more detailed cognitive and functional analysis of performance (at baseline and follow-up), from a more standardized and theoretically grounded learning program, and also from the examination of individual differences in patients' performance and progress. A longitudinal follow-up exploring long-term effects of the intervention should also be particularly informative. Considering that AD patients presenting an ideomotor apraxia perform normally on a motor skill learning task (Jacobs et al., 1999), it might also be interesting to examine whether and how these patients can relearn gestures by using their preserved procedural memory.

An interesting therapy of activities of daily living has been conducted by Goldenberg and Hagmann (1998) in nondemented patients with apraxia (consecutive to left hemisphere stroke) and might inspire interventions in AD. The therapy concerned three activities of daily living (ADL; buttering a slice of bread, putting on a pullover or a T-shirt, and brushing teeth) and was administered to 15 patients who made fatal errors (i.e., errors that prevented successful completion of the activity) on at least two of the three activities. Each week the patients completed an ADL test; between tests, one of the three activities was trained, whereas maximal support but no therapeutic advice was given when the patients had to perform the other activities in their daily life. In the 2nd and 3rd weeks, respectively, the two other activities were trained. The cycle was repeated until no more fatal errors were observed. Basically, the therapy combined errorless completion of the whole activity and training the details. For achieving errorless completion, support was given at all critical stages and was reduced when the patients were able to succeed at these stages on their own. The successive supports consisted of taking the patient's hand to lead it through a difficult action, doing the same action simultaneously with the patient (by being sited beside the patient), and, finally, demonstrating the required action and asking the patient to copy it. Training the details was aimed to direct the patient's attention to the functional significance of single perceptual details (e.g., the bristles of a toothbrush) and to critical features of the actions associated with them; this was made for steps of actions that caused difficulties when executing the complete activity. Also, actions connected to perceptual details were practiced outside the context of the activity (e.g., looking for and preparing the sleeve hole without actually inserting the arm into it), and single-motor actions included in the activity were illustrated by similar actions in the context of other activities (e.g., the action of squeezing toothpaste onto the toothbrush was illustrated by squeezing colors from tubes onto paint brushes). The results showed that at the end of the training, 10 of the patients could perform all three activities without fatal errors, and 3 made only one fatal error. In addition, there was no simultaneous improvement in nontrained activities. A follow-up conducted 6 months later in seven patients showed that the training benefits were preserved only in those patients who had practiced the activities at home. However, it appears that the cause for abandoning independence in ADL might be due to the interaction between patients and relatives, rather than in the patients' own incapacities or refusal. This points to the necessity for extending intervention to the relative's attitude towards the patients' autonomy.

Another domain in which both preserved procedural memory and errorless learning could be applied is topographical memory. Indeed, it seems possible for AD patients to learn or relearn a specific route by using a backward chaining technique, designed to allow the patient to acquire the route in a gradually increasing succession of stages and, therefore, to promote errorless learning (see Brooks et al., 1999, for use of this technique in a nondemented, amnesic patient using virtual environment). As suggested by Brooks et al. (1999), the inability to correct errors may be one of the reasons why patients with severe episodic memory deficits do not learn to find their own way around a new environment they motorically explore regularly. The backward chaining technique involves the patient withdrawing backwards from the target location, and the distance the patient is instructed to withdraw is gradually increased until it eventually includes the whole route.

Structuring the Patient's Environment and Providing External Cognitive Aids

Another option in AD patients' rehabilitation is to provide them with physical support or external aids (such as a notebook, diaries, and alarms) or to structure their (physical or human) environment to reduce the impact cognitive deficits may have on everyday activities. It should be noted that a compensatory or external aid method will be efficient only if the patient is able to master it; in other words, the external aid has to be made-to-measure according to the patient's deficits, and in some cases a learning phase will have to be planned to teach the patient how to use the method.

> For example, to increase the patient's autonomy, it might be decided to teach the patient to use a compensatory memory book consisting of different sections in which the patient could record and refer to information concerning things to do, names of new people, information concerning transportation, and so forth. However, as AD patients frequently show working memory, planning, and inhibition deficits, this memory book must be as simple as possible and avoid irrelevant information. In some cases, single index cards that for example, describe step-by-step how to prepare a meal or how to go to the shopping center, could be used if the patients have difficulties dealing with the complexity of a diary or memory book. The regular and correct use of the memory book (or index card) can be trained by using a spaced-retrieval technique. According to Sohlberg and Mateer (1989), the training program has to contain three phases: an acquisition stage, in which the patient has to become familiar with the purpose and use of each different section in the memory book; an application stage, in which the patient has to learn when and where to use the notebook; and, finally, an adaptation stage, in which the patient has to demonstrate appropriate notebook use in natural settings.

The structuration of the patient environment and the use of external aids will be illustrated in three domains: improving conversations, reducing apathy, and enhancing topographical orientation.

Improving Conversations. Bourgeois (1990, 1991, 1993), Bourgeois and Masson (1996), and Hoerster, Hickey, and Bourgeois (2001) demonstrated that persons with moderate to severe dementia are able to use a prosthetic memory aid (memory wallets) to improve the quality and quantity of their conversations. Memory wallets contain information (simple sentences and corresponding pictures) about relevant personal facts (concerning family, friends, daily activities, and life history) that each patient has difficulty remembering The patient is trained in how to use the sentences in conversation and then in how to use the wallet to self-prompt factual personal information during conversations.

In a first study using a multiple baseline design, Bourgeois (1990) showed that three AD patients were able to learn the use of a memory wallet when conversing with their spouse and familiar partners, after caregivers were given intensive training in how to use the wallet. Coded transcriptions of conversations also revealed that the patients increased the number of on-topic and elaborated factual statements and decreased the number of ambiguous, perseverative, erroneous, and unintelligible statements produced in 5-min conversations. In addition, naive judges rated the conversational interaction of the patients as significantly improved when memory wallets were used. Treatment benefits remained at high levels after a 6-week delay. Improvements in conversation abilities when using the memory aid have also been demonstrated in other settings (such as an adult day care or a nursing home), with varying amounts of caregiver training (beneficial effects were still, seen even when caregiver training was not provided) and with a variety of conversation partners, such as members of the day-care staff or nursing assistants (Bourgeois 1991, 1993; Bourgeois & Mason, 1996; Hoerster et al., 2001).

Reducing Apathy. We recently described (Adam, Van der Linden, Juillerat, & Salmon, 2000) the intervention program that was conducted in the recently created day-care center of the University Hospital of Liège to reduce the generalized apathy observed in a 70-year-old AD patient (referred to as AM). This program aimed at restoring a leisure activity (knitting) at home by proposing several adaptations designed to minimize the impact of AM's cognitive deficits in knitting.

> The first stage of the intervention was to assess the semantic and procedural knowledge associated with the knitting activity. It appeared that the patient was able to explain verbally, and in detail, each of 10 knitting stitches (e.g., plain, purl, garter), which she was able to execute correctly (this was videotaped to allow detailed analysis), and she manipulated the knitting needles perfectly. Following this first assessment phase suggesting that AM had the basic knowledge to knit, a task that would motivate her had to be found. She suggested knitting a cardigan for her 2-year-old great granddaughter. The next step of the program aimed to identify the difficulties facing AM in this activity and to propose adaptations to reduce the impact of these deficits and to enable the patient to knit more independently. A first (videotaped) observation of the knitting activity in normal conditions revealed the existence of serious difficulties, which totally prevented work to progress. In fact, there was too much interfering information on the pattern, which was expected to guide the patient, and she had difficulties inhibiting this irrelevant information. Furthermore, AM had problems maintaining the relevant information in working memory when she had to pass from the pattern to the actual knitting. All these difficulties were consistent with what was observed in the neuropsychological examination. Consequently, a first adaptation of the

knitting pattern was made and consisted of suppressing the irrelevant information and enlarging the original pattern. In addition, the patient also displayed considerable difficulty in mentally planning the succession of diagrams designed to guide her in her knitting task (the diagram represents the pattern with the motif of the cardigan, with which the knitting task had to be realized). This operation involves substantial mental planning activity, a good problem-solving ability, and, more generally, central executive resources. In this context, considering AM's working memory and planning deficits, a second adaptation was proposed: The diagram was copied, cut out, and pasted according to the needs of each stage of the knitting. Because AM could not mentally plan the succession of diagrams, all the necessary information was visually presented to her. Following this adaptation, it was possible to make the first observations with regard to the concrete execution of the knitting task. In fact, until then, the patient was unable to follow the pattern, and, consequently, she was unable to knit. It appeared from these observations that the planning problems had been solved, but then other difficulties arose: The patient confused the diagram lines and jumped from one line to another (she actually also suffered from a slight cataract problem). A simple adaptation to compensate this deficit was to enlarge the diagram and, more specifically, to introduce a space between lines. Finally, when she was knitting, the patient had to manage several subtasks simultaneously or alternately: She had to count and to maintain in working memory the number of stitches to do, and she had to knit the stitches while memorizing the position on the diagram. This task was too difficult for AM considering her working memory (central executive) deficits. A last adaptation was suggested to reduce the demands on the central executive resources. First, the patient was encouraged to cross out the stitches already knitted (this assistance suppressed the position memory problem). Then, numbers were inserted in the diagram every time the number of stitches concerning one color block was superior to two. Thus, the patient did not have to count but simply to identify the number in a block of stitches. Following this last adaptation, AM's autonomy increased considerably; she made fewer mistakes and required less support. She was then encouraged to knit at home. Moreover, two postintervention assessments were made after 3 months of rehabilitation. Each consisted in observing during 30 min the patient's knitting activity and to identify both the errors and the number of stitches produced (with and without therapist intervention). In the first condition, the patient benefited from maximal assistance (the last adaptation). In the second assessment, the patient was confronted with a minimal assistance condition (she had the second diagram adaptation at her disposal). Results showed a decrease of AM's production when she was in the minimal assistance condition. She knitted 266 stitches in the maximal assistance condition, and she made only one mistake, which was corrected spontaneously. AM knitted 144 stitches in the minimal assistance condition and produced 11 errors (8 of which were self-corrected). Moreover, we also measured the number of hours devoted to knitting at home. It should be recalled that before the intervention, AM was completely unable to knit. After the last adaptation was made, in the 5th week, AM knitted for 18 hr (i.e., 2 hr, 30 min a day). Between Weeks 5 and 13, the knitting activity totaled approximately 90 hr at home (i.e., 1 hr, 20 min a day). Finally, a general evaluation was undertaken after 3 months of intervention. In summary, although an aggravation of her memory deficits was observed, the intervention significantly decreased AM's apathy and depressive mood as well as her husband's burden.

These data clearly show that a significant improvement can be induced in daily living activities in AD by adapting the realization conditions of these activities to decrease the impact of the patient's deficits. These findings also confirm that in some cases, negative mood symptoms could reflect a psychological reaction of subjects to the awareness of their autonomy loss in everyday activities (see Chen et al., 1999). They also indicate that decreasing the impact of functional deficits may have a positive effect on the mood state.

Rehabilitation of Topographical Disorientation in a Familiar Environment. Topographical orientation is frequently impaired in AD (see Rainville, Joanette, & Passini, 1994). However, very few studies have described AD patients with topographical disorders on the basis of a detailed theoretical model of the processes normally involved in the recognition and exploration of the environment. In a recent study, Rainville Passini, and Marchand (2001) confirmed the existence of a deterioration of wayfinding abilities in unfamiliar places for AD patients. They also suggested that these deficits are associated with a deterioration of planning and reasoning (see also Passini, Rainville, Marchand, & Joanette, 1995). In addition, Cherrier, Mendez, and Perryman (2001) indicated that a measure of egocentric and allocentric orientation ability was the best predictor of AD patients' performance on a novel Route Learning Test and, consequently, that episodes of topographical disorientation in AD may also occur secondary to poor spatial orientation. However, the ability to travel through an environment (familiar or unfamiliar) in a purposeful way involves the interaction of many cognitive components, which could be specifically affected by AD (see Aguirre & D'Esposito, 1999; Barrash, Damasio, Adolphs, & Tranel, 2000; Van der Linden & Meulemans, 1998).

> Let us consider the orientation in a familiar environment. First of all, a subject who wants to move from one location to another should be able to recognize buildings or landmarks and to appreciate the spatial relations between them. In addition, stored memories for previously experienced landmarks and for routes (spatial maps) are also necessary. Byrne (1982) distinguishes two types of stored maps that could apply to the same environment. A network map represents routes as a network of strings and locations along them as nodes, whereas vector maps encode horizontal information about directions and distances and are isomorphic with the real world as viewed from above. In addition, the ability to update one's current position and bearings on a route and to plan future movements requires some form of spatial working memory as well as working memory resources (Böök & Gärling, 1978; Riddoch & Humphreys, 1995).

Few neuropsychological studies have been conducted to reeducate topographical disorders in AD (see, however, Van der Linden & Seron, 1991; Van der Linden, Seron, & Juillerat, 2000, for a proposition of a global reeducation project that suggests different reeducation strategies adapted for each type of topographical disorder). In some early AD patients with sufficient cognitive resources and motivation, it might be possible to teach simple mnemonic techniques designed to increase the meaningfulness and association of the selected to-be-memorized route. For example, Davis and Coltheart (1999) used, in a nondemented patient presenting spatial disorientation, a mnemonic that consisted of a sentence including cues to the relative location of each street by referring to them in spatial order ("Dirty Howard and Russell kept Pip our lamb in the rocket" = Durham, Howick, Russell, Keppel, Piper, Lambert, and Rocket Streets). If a patient shows an impaired ability to update his or her current position and bearings on a route and to plan future movements due to a reduction of working memory resources, some general advice could be provided to the patient or the caregiver to limit the negative consequences of this resource reduction (e.g., to avoid getting involved in another activity while performing the task). Finally, external memory aids may also contribute to enhance the patients' topographical orientation ability.

An external memory aid has been recently used by Lekeu, Van der Linden, Adam, Laroi, and Salmon (2001) in the case of an 82-year-old early AD patient (referred to as ML), who presented severe difficulties in finding his way around his village. A neuropsychological assessment revealed verbal and visual episodic memory deficits, as well inhibition and switching difficulties. Furthermore, a detailed cognitive exploration of his topographical knowledge revealed that he had completely lost both vector and network map representations of his village. On the other hand, he showed no difficulties in recognizing landmarks, reading a map, and following spatial instructions and direction changes. The intervention exploited these preserved abilities to optimize the patient's spatial orientation in his village. More specifically, the therapist asked ML to use cards describing some routes, corresponding to walks and shopping activities the patient had the habit of doing before the disease (e.g., the route between ML's house and the pharmacy). These cards consisted of two parts: a visual representation of the route (including the landmarks) and a verbal description of the successive stages of the route. To limit the production of errors, ML was required to follow the routes, accompanied by the therapist, and to consult the card every time there was a direction change.

After 3 months of training, ML substantially increased his spontaneous walks and shopping activities; during the last 2 weeks of rehabilitation, he went for eight walks, whereas before training, he did not leave left home alone at all. In addition, he was again able to go shopping (an activity he had completely abandoned), without losing his way. A more standardized posttraining assessment revealed that with the help of the route cards, ML was able to go along either the routes he had practiced during training or new routes (all of which was completely impossible before training). More interestingly, without the help of cards, the patient was unable to go along new (unpracticed) routes but proved able to do so on the practiced routes. Nevertheless, no change was observed in vector and network map knowledge corresponding to his village. On the whole, these results suggest that the repeated practice of routes during training (by using assistance cards) favored the constitution of a procedural (or sensorimotor) knowledge specific to the practiced routes. However, it might be that as practice with routes accumulates, the patient will reacquire a cognitive map of his village. Besides the topographical intervention, ML also learned to use a mobile phone so that if he got lost during a walk, he could warn his family. The phone intervention consisted of pasting on the back of the phone a card describing each stage of its use. In addition, the use of the mobile was trained in the day-care center by using the spaced-retrieval method. ML easily learned to use the mobile phone, and he always took it with him during walks and shopping activities.

THE DAY-CARE CENTER: AN ADAPTED STRUCTURE FOR PATIENTS' REHABILITATION?

Adapted structures should be put into place for the cognitive interventions in early AD. A day-care center, which reproduces real-life premises (kitchen, workshop, vegetable garden, sewing room, etc.) and exists within local communities, appears to be an interesting development. Such day-care centers should be a place where optimization strategies are put into place before they are used at home, but they should also provide caregivers with support and ease the burden that the daily company of a demented patient represents.

Objectives of the Day-Care Center

A day-care center for early AD patients has several objectives. The first is to optimize the patient's daily living activities so as to increase his or her autonomy, maintain a good sociofamilial integration, and delay institutionalization. Such intervention occurs within a daily-life perspective: The neuropsychological analysis of strengths and weaknesses and defined goals of rehabilitation are directly related to the patient's daily life, within his or her specific environment.

Another goal of a day-care center is to serve as a meeting place and to propose satisfying (group and individual) everyday activities that fit the patients' level of competence. These activities may help to reduce patients' loss of confidence as well as depression and apathy. They may also contribute to maintain the patients' sense of personal identity, continuity, and coherence. Attending different group activities may help alleviate patients' loneliness, and patients may enjoy coming to the center and meeting other patients. Indeed, most AD patients dramatically decrease their social activities either because they are aware of their declining condition and the potential risky situations this may lead to or because they (or their family caregivers) dread that some embarrassing incidents may occur. In other words, instead of being limited just to offering a cognitive rehabilitation, the day-care center also has the opportunity to offer leisure-oriented activities and pursue a more immediate purpose—helping patients enjoy themselves and meet other people. Such moments of leisure may also allow the staff not only to observe the patients' difficulties but also, possibly, to detect some so far unsuspected preserved abilities. In addition, the leisure activities offered in the day-care center should not only have an occupational perspective but also should aim at developing knowledge that might prove useful with regard to everyday life or to train some specific abilities through play activities. Furthermore, the activities have to be adapted, bearing in mind the patients' commonly observed deficits.

In this perspective, Camp and his collaborators (Camp, 2001; Judge, Camp, & Orsulic-Jeras, 2000) found that adult day-care clients participating in a highly simplified memory bingo (which was part of larger project involving Montessori-based activities for both individuals and groups) showed significantly higher levels of constructive engagement (defined as motor or verbal behaviors in response to an activity) than control patients, who participated only in regular day-care programs. In addition, during the 9-month study, the patients who engaged in Montessori-based activities displayed less passive engagement (defined as passively observing an activity) than patients in regular activity programs. In another recent study, Romero and Wenz (2001) examined the effects in one group pretest-posttest design of a multicomponent self-maintenance therapy, in which satisfying everyday activities are associated with psychotherapeutic support aiming to help patients maintain a sense of meaningfulness, self-related knowledge training designed to maintain patients' memory-chosen biographical knowledge, and an intervention program for caregivers. The preliminary results showed a consistent improvement in patients' depression and other psychopathological problems (reported by the caregivers). Moreover, caregivers also felt less depressed, less mentally tired and restless, and more relaxed. However, more controlled studies are required to identify the factors responsible for the benefits and, more specifically, to examine the extent to which satisfying everyday activities specifically contribute, as hypothesized by the authors, to reduce behavioral and emotional disturbances consecutive to an incompatibility between patients' actual experiences and self-based expectations and preferences.

Finally, the day-care center should aim to provide the caregivers with psychological support, information, and counseling (especially by means of role playing), so they will be in a better position to interact with the patient and deal with his or her deficits. A social worker should also be available for administrative and social help (financial support, transportation facilities, home services, etc.). By welcoming the patient two to three times a week, the day-care center should also contribute to relieve the caregiver from the difficult task of caring daily for an AD patient. In addition to other interventions, support to caregivers has also proved useful in delaying patients' institutionalization (Flint, 1995; Lawton, Brody, & Saperstein, 1991).

The Liège and Geneva Day-Care Centers

Two day-care centers for the cognitive management of daily life activities in patients with mild to moderate AD were recently created at the University Hospital of Liège in Belgium (on the initiative of both the Neurology and the Neuropsychology University Departments) and the University Hospital of Geneva in Switzerland (on the initiative of the University Hospital's Department of Geriatrics). Both centers are located in the town and occupy an entire floor of a building; there is one secretariat, rooms for individual testing and treatment programs, one kitchen, one living/dining room, and rooms for other daily life activities and videotape analysis. Both centers are interdisciplinary (with neuropsychiatrists, neurologists, neuropsychologists, occupational therapists, and, in Liège, a social worker) and work in a relatively similar manner.

Patient Selection. All patients selected for the day-care center are diagnosed with AD at the University Hospital Memory Clinics. When the AD diagnosis is established, only patients with mild to moderate dementia are considered for the day-care center. Patients must be living at home, and their caregiver must be prepared to be involved in the daily activities of the patient and to ensure that proposed arrangements and strategies set up in the day-care center are correctly applied at home. The caregiver's collaboration is mandatory in selecting daily activities that need to be improved and in assessing the benefit of the intervention program at home. It is essential that the patient and relatives accept a diagnosis of probable or possible AD to understand the importance of a management program. They must, furthermore, accept a number of requirements, such as traveling to the day-care center, accepting the patient's cognitive difficulties, involving themselves in the program, and meeting other people with cognitive impairments. If patient and relatives are interested in a rehabilitation program, they are given written explanations on objectives, constraints, and the cost of day-care center activities.

Assessment at the Day-Care Center. There are two stages in patient evaluation at the day-care center. A large battery of tests, questionnaires, and scales, administered to both the patient and a relative, is used to determine preserved cognitive abilities, initial status concerning daily life activities, behavior and mood, and caregiver burden (e.g., Revised Memory and Behavior Checklist; Teri et al., 1992; Neuropsychiatric Inventory, NPI; Cummings et al., 1994; Geriatric Depression Scale; Sheikh & Yesavage, 1986; a caregiver burden scale; Zarit, Reever, & Bach Peterson, 1980; two scales assessing the patient's autonomy in basic everyday life activities; Gélinas, Gauthier, McIntyre, & Gauthier, 1999, and Teunisse & Derix, 1991). Interviews elicit precise details of previous and current interests and expertise, as well as principal needs and environmental constraints for each patient. All this information is used to define one or two primary (feasible) objectives, and a 3-month contract is signed to start an intervention program at the center.

A more individual assessment concerns activities that the patient and relatives would like to improve. The objective of this evaluation is to identify the nature of the difficulty and to find factors susceptible to optimize performance. In this perspective, a series of specific batteries are applied to explore different everyday activity domains, such as the processes and knowledge related to food, financial capacities (see Marson, Sawrie, et al., 2000), topographical orientation, walking, telephone use, and so forth.

Rehabilitation at the Day-Care Center. Therapeutic strategies may consist of rearranging the home environment and installing external cognitive aids or conducting individual neuropsychological rehabilitation. As mentioned earlier, the objectives of the cognitive rehabilitation are to improve cognitive performance by using optimizing factors, teaching specific knowledge (facts or skills) by adopting techniques (such as spaced retrieval, vanishing cues, or errorless methods, or both, which tap preserved cognitive systems.

Individual as well as group leisure activities are also proposed to the patients, according to their preferences, and support is provided to compensate for lost competence. Concerning the group leisure activities, several board games have been specifically developed. Some general principles govern all the adaptations made: The topics of the games are directed toward daily life activities or questions pertinent to the patients' everyday life. The questions are set so as to allow the AD patients to answer. Instead of letting the patients resort to free recall, which is usually severely defective, the answers are either cued or presented as a multiple choice quiz, so as to facilitate retrieval of information. The questions are organized into different difficulty levels, so that patients presenting slight differences in their cognitive level can still take part in the same game. The rules of the games are written on a cardboard paper which is set in front of each patient, and some of the patients are given a special cue so they can remember their pawn's color. Because several patients are trained to use external aids, such as diaries, questions sometimes address recall of recent events or information, which can be found in their memory aids. For information that may be particularly relevant for the patients (e.g., in a game modelled after Trivial Pursuit, knowing which emergency number to call after an accident), a mnemonic aid or learning by a specific technique (such as spaced retrieval or errorless learning) may be used. Patients' performances are recorded, and progress through the session is compared. A baseline is administered before and after the patients have participated in the game 12 times.

Among the proposed games at the Geneva and Liège day-care centers is one that resembles Trivial Pursuit. Patients have to move their pawns on squares according to the number of points indicated by the throw of a dice. The squares have different colors, which correspond to different themes: temporal and spatial orientation, health, daily living, news, and general knowledge. Each time an answer is correct, the patient gets a mark that has the square's color, and the goal is to get as many marks from different colors as possible during the game. Another game is played on a board that has a simplified map of the state of Geneva on it (most of the patients in the day-care center of Geneva are native to the area). Patients move (after throwing a dice) around the map, on which roads are traced from one town or one Geneva suburb to another. Squares are located in towns or suburbs and have different colors that correspond to themes related to daily life in Geneva: transportation and journeys, shopping areas, famous places, recent events, and annual celebrations. Here, answering a question is frequently the occasion for the patients to recall memories or anecdotes. A third game is based on social competencies. The patients move their pawns on a board on which there are three types of squares. On the first type, the patients have to make decisions about social situations that are described to them (e.g., "a sales representative rings at your door and wants to sell you an expensive watch, what do you do?"). On the second type, they have to do or say something to another participant ("You were just complimented, give a reply"), and on the third type, they have to do something related to their daily life, such as filling in a check or making an appointment at the hairdresser. The fourth game concerns use and management of money. The game board has thematic squares that represent places where money is used: grocery store, restaurant, post office, bank, movie theater, and so on. At the beginning of the game, each patient is given a purse with (fake) money in it, both in bills and small change. Each time a patient's pawn arrives on a square, the patient has to use this money, calculate an amount, make a decision about a purchase, make a check, and so on, according to his or her level of competency. If the task is successful, the patient receives a small sum that is added to his or her purse. The goal here is to have as much money as possible by the end of the game. Another game is called Europoly. The principle and rules of this game are inspired by the famous parlor game Monopoly, except that the money used is the new European currency, the Euro. The purpose of this leisure activity is to teach people with dementia how to use and manipulate this new currency and to operate a conversion calculator (by capitalizing on preserved procedural memory abilities in AD). In this game, patients are asked to execute some complex operations (e.g., converting Belgian francs into Euros or Euros into Belgian francs, making Euro transactions, manipulating the new Euro notes and coins).

Finally, socioeconomic data are recorded to determine individual difficulties and to help in administrative matters. Arrangements are proposed for traveling to the center, and the general practitioner is contacted when specific home care has to be provided.

A period of 3 months has been chosen to assess progress in daily life activities, to prove that therapeutic strategies are adequate, and to reconsider management objectives. The scales and questionnaires, given at the initial evaluation, are again used for evaluation after 3 months. To determine the patients' progress, specific activities assessed at baseline are reassessed in exactly the same conditions and videotaped for a precise rating. At 3 months, a decision can be made with the patient and relatives either to stop the rehabilitation program if no benefit is seen by either side, or, on the other hand, to modify, keep, or discuss new objectives.

CONCLUSIONS

Substantial progress has been made in the identification and comprehension of cognitive and behavioral deficits of early or very early AD patients, as well as of the consequences of these deficits on daily life and family caregivers' condition. Furthermore, an increasing number of studies have demonstrated the efficacy of various neuropsychological interventions on persons with early AD. However, numerous questions remain to be answered concerning the specific mechanisms responsible for the observed successes (or failures) of these interventions. A better understanding of these mechanisms should allow us to better identify the patients who will benefit most from a specific intervention.

In addition, as mentioned by Camp (2001; see also Phillips & Knopman, 1999), it is not sufficient to demonstrate that an intervention works under experimentally controlled conditions (i.e., the efficacy of the intervention); it is also necessary to show that the intervention can be successfully applied in less controlled real-world contexts (i.e., the effectiveness of the intervention) and largely diffused into caregiving systems. In this context, an intervention must be sufficiently robust to remain effective when applied in various clinical settings, must work with mixed dementias or dementias with comorbidities (all conditions that are common place), must be able to be administered by existing caregivers and professionals, must be adapted to the health care system parameters, and must be tied to reimbursement.

There exist some encouraging findings suggesting that these two transitions (from efficacy to effectiveness and from effectiveness to diffusion) can be realized in the AD patients' rehabilitation domain. For example, Camp and collaborators (see Camp, Foss, O'Hanlon, & Stevens, 1996) demonstrated the efficacy of the spaced-retrieval technique but also showed that this method can be incorporated into the daily environment of AD patients, disseminated in a variety of clinical settings, and used by different types of professionals. However, these initial findings clearly need to be strengthened and diversified.

From a more general point of view, it seems financially and pragmatically illusory to think that a great number of specialized neuropsychological day-care centers (such as those developed at the universities of Liège and Geneva) might be opened to fulfill the increasing needs concerning the assistance to AD patients and family caregivers. Put differently, the problem is to develop interventions that will be effective within neuropsychologist-free settings (Camp, 2001). It seems to us that a possible solution is to give to some (university) day-care centers a mission to be pilot centers involving clinical research (e.g., development of intervention programs and evaluation of their efficacy and effectiveness), diffusion of these intervention techniques, and organization of all the persons involved in caring for AD patients within a limited territory.

Because AD is characterized by a progression of neuropathological damage, the neuropsychological interventions have to be both flexible and modest. More specifically, they have to be continuously adapted to changes in the patient's condition and directly focused on daily life situations, with the purpose of short-term effectiveness (see Adam, Van der Linden, Juillerat, 2000; Clare & Woods, 2001). As far as progress being made in the cognitive analysis of everyday life activities in AD (a daily life cognitive neuropsychology) and in the identification of impaired and preserved cognitive processes and of optimization factors, we may hope that more theoretically articulated interventions will also be developed.

In the implementation of an intervention program in AD patients as well as in the evaluation of its effectiveness, it also seems more essential to include the perspective of the patients by allowing them to retain a capacity to maximize their cognitive abilities, to state specific preferences and needs, to provide information concerning their quality of life and emotions, and to make intervention-related decisions (a capacity that is still frequently denied to AD patients). More attention should be devoted to the range of feelings they may present (anger, fear, insecurity, and hopelessness), to the contribution of these feelings to many troublesome behaviors, and to the possibility of interventions to alleviate symptoms of depression and anxiety (Adam, Van der Linden, Juillerat, et al., 2000; Kasl-Godley & Gatz, 2000; Woods, 2001). It is also important to bear in mind that AD patients' difficulties may be due not only to the neuropathological process but also to the social context in which the patients interact. In this view, future research should address the role of the relationship between the caregiver and the patient as an important determinant of the caregiving context (Montgomery & Williams, 2001) and how the characteristics of the care system members (primary care physicians, family caregivers, and persons with dementia) and the quality of their interactions may affect the outcome of dementia care. Finally, an important challenge for the coming years will be to examine whether and how neuropsychological and pharmacological interventions may be combined to constitute a more efficient treatment strategy.

REFERENCES

Abrahams, J. P., & Camp, C. J. (1993). Maintenance and generalization of object training in anomia associated with degenerative dementia. *Clinical Gerontologist, 12,* 57–72.

Adam, S., Van der Linden, M., Juillerat, A. C., & Salmon, E. (2000). The cognitive management of daily life activities in patients with mild to moderate Alzheimer's disease in a day care center: A case report. *Neuropsychological Rehabilitation, 10,* 485–509.

Adam, S., Van der Linden, M., & Salmon, E. (2000). Controlled and automatic memory processes in Alzheimer's disease [Abstract]. *Consciousness and Cognition. An International Journal, 9,* 65.

Agnew, S. K., & Morris, R. G. (1998). The heterogeneity of anosognosia for memory impairments in Alzheimer's disease: A review of the literature and a proposed model. *Aging & Mental Health, 2,* 7–19.

Aguirre, G. K., & D'Esposito, M. (1999). Topographical disorientation: A synthesis and taxonomy. *Brain, 122,* 1613–1628.

Alberoni, M., Baddeley, A. D., Della Sala, S., Logie, R., & Spinnler, H. (1992). Keeping track of a conversation: Impairments in Alzheimer's disease. *International Journal of Geriatric Psychiatry, 7,* 639–646.

Almor, A., Kempler, D., MacDonald, M. C., Andersen, E. S., & Tyler, L. K. (1999). Why do Alzheimer patients have difficulty with pronouns? Working memory, semantics, and reference in comprehension and production in Alzheimer's disease. *Brain and Language, 67,* 202–227.

Anderson, M. C., & Spellman, B. A. (1995). On the status of inhibitory mechanisms in cognition: Memory retrieval as a model case. *Psychological Review, 102,* 68–100.

Anderson, S., & Tranel, D. (1989). Awareness of disease states following cerebral infarction, dementia, and head trauma: Standardized assessment. *Clinical Neuropsychologist, 3,* 327–339.

Arkin, S. (1992). Audio-assisted memory training with early Alzheimers' patients: Two single subjects experiments. *Clinical Gerontologist, 12,* 77–95.

Arkin, S. (1998). Alzheimer memory training: Positive results replicated. *American Journal of Alzheimer's Disease, 13,* 102–104.

Arkin, S. (2000). Alzheimer memory training: Students replicate learning successes. *American Journal of Alzheimer's Disease, 15,* 152–162.

Arkin, S. (2001). Alzheimer rehabilitation by students: Interventions and outcomes. *Neuropsychological Rehabilitation, 11,* 273–317.

Arkin, S., & Mahendra, N. (2001a). Insight in Alzheimer's patients: Results of a longitudinal study using three assessment methods. *American Journal of Alzheimer's Disease, 16,* 211–224.

Arkin, S., & Mahendra, N. (2001b). Discourse analysis of Alzheimer's patients before and after intervention: Methodology and outcomes. *Aphasiology, 15,* 533–569.

Arkin, S., Rose, C., & Hopper, T. (2000). Implicit and explicit learning gains in Alzheimer's patients: Effects of naming and information retrieval training. *Aphasiology, 14,* 723–742.

Bäckman, L., Josephsson, S., Herlitz, A., Stigsdotter, A., & Viitanen, M. (1991). The generalizability of training gains in dementia: Effects of an imagery-based mnemonic on face-name retention duration. *Psychology and Aging, 6,* 489–492.

Bäckman, L., Mäntilä, T., & Herlitz, A. (1990). The optimization of episodic remembering on old age. In P. B. Baltes & M. M. Baltes (Eds.), *Successful aging: Perspectives from the behavioral sciences* (pp. 118–163). Cambridge, UK: Cambridge University Press.

Bäckman, L., & Small, B. J. (1998). Influences of cognitive support on episodic remembering: Tracing the process of loss from normal aging to Alzheimer's disease. *Psychology and Aging, 13,* 267–276.

Baddeley, A. D. (1992). Implicit memory and errorless learning: A link between cognitive theory and neuropsychological rehabilitation? In L. R. Squire & N. Butters (Eds.), *Neuropsychology of memory* (2nd ed., pp. 309–314). New York: Guilford Press.

Baddeley, A. D., Baddeley, H. A., Bucks, R. S., & Wilcock, G. K. (2001). Attentional control in Alzheimer's disease. *Brain, 124,* 1492–1508.

Baddeley, A. D., & Wilson, B. A. (1994). When implicit learning fails: Amnesia and the problem of error elimination. *Neuropsychologia, 32,* 53–68.

Ballard, C. G., Cassidy, G., Bannister, C., & Mohan, R. N. (1993). Prevalence, symptom profile, and aetiology of depression in dementia sufferers. *Journal of Affective Disorders, 29,* 1–6.

Barrash, J., Damasio, H., Adolphs, R., & Tranel, D. (2000). The neuroanatomical correlates of route learning impairment. *Neuropsychologia, 38,* 820–836.

Benton, A. (1965). *Manuel pour l'application du test de rétention visuelle: Applications cliniques et expérimentales [Manual for the visual retention test administration: Clinical and experimental applications]* (2nd ed.). Paris: Centre de Psychologie Appliquée.

Berg, I. J., Koning-Haanstra, M., & Deelman, B. G. (1991). Long-term effects of memory rehabilitation: A controlled study. *Neuropsychological Rehabilitation, 1,* 87–111.

Bird, M. (2000). Psychosocial rehabilitation for problems arising from cognitive deficits in dementia. In R. D. Hill, L. Bäckman, & A. Stigsdotter Neely (Eds.), *Cognitive rehabilitation in old age* (pp. 249–269). Oxford, UK: Oxford University Press.

Bird, M. (2001). Behavioural difficulties and cued recall of adaptive behaviour in dementia: Experimental and clinical evidence. *Neuropsychological Rehabilitation, 11,* 357–375.

Bird, M., Alexopoulos, P., & Adamowicz, J. (1995). Success and failure in five case studies: Use of cued recall to ameliorate behavior problems in senile dementia. *International Journal of Geriatric Psychiatry, 10,* 305–311.

Bird, M., & Kinsella, G. (1996). Long term cued recall of tasks in senile dementia. *Psychology and Aging, 11,* 45–56.

Bird, M. J., & Luszcz, M. A. (1991). Encoding specificity, depth of processing, and cued recall in Alzheimer's disease. *Journal of Clinical and Experimental Neuropsychology, 13,* 508–520.

Bird, M.J., & Luszcz, M. A. (1993). Enhancing memory performance in Alzheimer's disease: Acquisition assistance and cue effectiveness. *Journal of Clinical and Experimental Neuropsychology, 13,* 921–932.

Bjork, R. A. (1988). Retrieval practice and the maintenance of knowledge. In M. M. Gruneberg, P. E. Morris, & R. N. Sykes (Eds), *Practical aspects of memory: Current research and issues* (pp. 396–401). New York : Academic Press.

Bond, J., & Corner, L. (2001). Researching dementia: Are there unique methodological challenges for health services research? *Ageing and Society, 21,* 95–116.

Böök, A., & Gärling, T. (1978). Processing of information about locomotion during locomotion: Effects of concurrent task and locomotion patterns. *Umea Psychological Reports,* 135.

Bourgeois, M. S. (1990). Enhancing conversational skills in patients with Alzheimer's disease using a prosthetic memory aid. *Journal of Applied Behavior Analysis, 23,* 29–42.

Bourgeois, M. S. (1991). Communication treatment for adults with dementia. *Journal of Speech and Hearing Research, 34,* 831–844.

Bourgeois, M. S. (1993). Effects of memory aids on the dyadic conversations of individuals with dementia. *Journal of Applied Behavior Analysis, 26,* 77–87.

Bourgeois, M. S., & Mason, L. A. (1996). Memory wallet intervention in an adult day-care setting. *Behavioral Interventions, 11,* 3–18.

Brodaty, H., McGilchrist, C., Harris L., & Peters, K. (1993). Time until institutionalization and death in patients with dementia: Role of caregiver training and risk factors. *Archives of Neurology, 50,* 643–650.

Brodaty, H., Roberts, K., & Peters, K. (1994). Quasi-experimental evaluation of an educational model for dementia caregivers. *International Journal of Geriatric Psychiatry, 9*, 195–204.

Brooks, B. M., McNeil, J. E., Rose, F. D., Greenwood, R. J., Attree, E. A., & Leadbetter, A. G. (1999). Route learning in a case of amnesia: A preliminary investigation into the efficacy of training in a virtual environment. *Neuropsychological Rehabilitation, 9*, 63–76.

Burgio, L. D., & Burgio, K. L. (1986). Behavioral gerontology: Application of behavioral methods to the problems of older adults. *Journal of Applied Behavior Analysis, 19*, 321–328.

Butler, R. N. (1963). The life review: An interpretation of reminiscence in the aged. *Psychiatry, 26*, 65–76.

Byrne, R. W. (1982). Geographical knowledge and orientation. In A. W. Ellis (Ed.), *Normality and pathology in cognitive functions* (pp. 239–264). London: Academic Press.

Camicioli, R., Howieson, D., Lehman, S., & Kaye, J. (1997). Talking while walking: The effect of a dual task in aging and Alzheimer's disease. *Neurology, 48*, 955–958.

Camp, C. J. (1989). Facilitation of new learning in Alzheimer's disease. In G. C. Gilmore, P. J. Whitehouse, & M. L. Wykle (Eds.), *Memory, aging and dementia* (pp. 212–225). New York: Springer.

Camp, C. J. (2001). From efficacy to effectiveness to diffusion: Making the transitions in dementia intervention research. *Neuropsychological Rehabilitation, 11*, 495–517.

Camp, C. J., Bird, M. J., & Cherry, K. E. (2000). Retrieval strategies as a rehabilitation aid for cognitive loss in pathological aging. In R. D. Hill, L. Bäckman, & A. Stigsdotter Neely (Eds.), *Cognitive rehabilitation in old age* (pp. 224–248). Oxford, UK: Oxford University Press.

Camp, C. J., & Foss, J. W. (1997). Designing ecologically valid memory interventions for persons with dementia. In D. G. Payne & F. G. Conrad (Eds.), *Intersections in basic and applied memory research* (pp. 311–325). Mahwah, NJ: Lawrence Erlbaum Associates.

Camp, C. J., Foss, J. W., O'Hanlon, A. M., & Stevens, A. B. (1996). Memory interventions for persons with dementia. *Applied Cognitive Psychology, 10*, 193–210.

Camp, C. J., Foss, J. W., Stevens, A. B., & O'Hanlon, A. M. (1996). Improving prospective memory task performance in persons with Alzheimer's disease. In M. Brandimonte, G. O. Eistein, & M. A. McDaniel (Eds.), *Prospective memory theory and applications* (pp. 351–363). NJ: Lawrence Erlbaum Associates.

Camp, C. J., Foss, J. W., Stevens, A. B., Reichard, C. C., McKitrick, L. A., & O'Hanlon, A. (1993). Memory training in normal and demented populations: The E-I-E-I-O model. *Experimental Aging Research, 19*, 277–290.

Camp, C. J., & McKitrick, L. A. (1992). Memory interventions in Alzheimer's-type dementia populations: Methodological and theoretical issues. In R. L. West & J. D. Sinnott (Eds.), *Everyday memory and aging: Current research and methodology* (pp. 155–172). New York: Springer-Verlag.

Camp, C. J., & Schaller, J. R. (1989). Epilogue: Spaced-retrieval memory training in an adult day-center. *Educational Gerontology, 15*, 641–648.

Camp, C. J., & Stevens, A. B. (1990). Spaced-retrieval: A memory intervention for dementia of the Alzheimer's type. *Clinical Gerontologist, 10*, 58–61.

Chase, W. G., & Ericsson, K. A. (1981). Skilled memory. In J. R. Anderson (Ed.), *Cognitive skills and their acquisition* (pp. 141–189). Hillsdale, NJ: Lawrence Erlbaum Associates.

Chemerinsky, E., Petracca, G., Sabe, L., Kremer, J., & Starkstein, S. (2001). The specificity of depressive symptoms in patients with Alzheimer's disease. *American Journal of Psychiatry, 158*, 68–72.

Chen, P., Ganguli, M., Mulsant, B. H., & DeKosky, S. T. (1999). The temporal relationship between depressive symptoms and dementia: A community-based prospective study. *Archives of General Psychiatry, 56*, 261–266.

Cherrier, M. M., Mendez, M., & Perryman, K. (2001). Route learning performance in Alzheimer's disease patients. *Neuropsychiatry, Neuropsychology, and Behavioral Neurology, 14*, 159–168.

Cherry, K., Simmons, S. S., & Camp, C. (1999). Spaced retrieval enhances memory in older adults with probable Alzheimer's disease. *Journal of Clinical Geropsychology, 5*, 159–175.

Clare, L., Wilson, B. A., Breen, K., & Hodges, J. R. (1999). Errorless learning of face-name associations in early Alzheimer's disease. *Neurocase, 5*, 37–46.

Clare, L., Wilson, B. A., Carter, G., Breen, G., Gosses, A., & Hodges, J. (2000). Intervening with everyday memory problems in dementia of Alzheimer type: An errorless learning approach. *Journal of Clinical and Experimental Neuropsychology, 22*, 132–146.

Clare, L., Wilson, B. A., Carter, G., Hodges, J. R., & Adams, M. (2001). Long-term maintenance of treatment gains following a cognitive rehabilitation intervention in early dementia of Alzheimer type: A single case study. *Neuropsychological Rehabilitation, 11*, 477–494.

Clare, L., & Woods, B. (2001). Editorial: A role for cognitive rehabilitation in dementia care. *Neuropsychological Rehabilitation, 11*, 193–196.

Coen, R. F., Swanwick, G. R. J., O'Boyle, C. A., & Coakley, D. (1997). Behaviour disturbance and other predictors of caregiver burden in Alzheimer's disease. *International Journal of Geriatric Psychiatry, 12*, 331–336.

Collette, F., Van der Linden, M., Bechet, S., & Salmon, E. (1999). Phonological loop and central executive functioning in Alzheimer's disease. *Neuropsychologia, 37*, 905–918.

Conway, M. A., & Pleydell-Pearce, C. W. (2000). The construction of autobiographical memories in the self-memory system. *Psychological Review, 107*, 261–288.

Coyette, F., & Van der Linden, M. (1999). La rééducation des troubles de la mémoire [Rehabilitation of memory disorders]: Les stratégies de facilitation. In Ph. Azouvi, D. Perrier, & M. Van der Linden (Eds.), *La rééducation en neuropsychologie: Etudes de cas [Rehabilitation in neuropsychology: Case studies]* (pp. 209–225). Marseille, France: Solal.

Cummings, J. L., Mega, M., Gray, K., Rosenberg-Thompson, S., Carusi, D. A., & Gornbein, J. (1994). The neuropsychiatric inventory: Comprehensive assessment of psychopathology in dementia. *Neurology, 44*, 2308–2314.

Cummings, J. L., Ross, W., Absher, J., & Gornbein, J. (1995). Depressive symptoms in Alzheimer disease: Assessment and determinants. *Alzheimer Disease and Associated Disorders, 9*, 87–93.

Davis, S. J. C., & Coltheart, M. (1999). Rehabilitation of topographical disorientation: An experimental single case study. *Neuropsychological Rehabilitation, 9*, 1–30.

Davis, R. N., Massman, P. J., & Doody, R. S. (2001). Cognitive intervention in Alzheimer's disease: A randomized placebo-controlled study. *Alzheimer Disease and Associated Disorders, 15*, 1–9.

Day, K., Carreon, D., & Stump, C. (2000). The therapeutic design of environments for people with dementia: A review of the empirical research. *The Gerontologist, 40*, 397–416.

Dick, M. B. (1992). Motor and procedural memory in Alzheimer's disease. In L. Bäckman (Ed.), *Memory functioning in dementia* (pp. 135–150). Amsterdam: Elsevier.

Dick, M. B., Andel, R., Bricker, J., Gorospe, J. B., Hsieh, S., & Dick-Muehlke, C. (2001). Dependence on visual feedback during motor skill learning in Alzheimer's disease. *Aging, Neuropsychology and Cognition, 8*, 120–136.

Dick, M. B., Andel, R., Hsieh, S., Bricker, J., Davis, D. S., & Dick-Muehlke, C. (2000). Contextual interference and motor skill learning in Alzheimer's disease. *Aging, Neuropsychology, and Cognition, 7*, 273–287.

Dick, M. B., Hsieh, S., Dick-Muehlke, C., Davis, D. S., & Cotman, C. W. (2000). The variability of practice hypothesis in motor learning: Does it apply to Alzheimer's disease? *Brain and Cognition, 44*, 470–489.

Done, D. J., & Thomas, J.A. (2001). Training in communication skills for informal carers of people suffering from dementia: A cluster randomized clinical trial comparing a therapist led workshop and a booklet. *International Journal of Geriatric Psychiatry, 16*, 816–821.

Earnst, K. S., Marson, D. C., & Harrell, L. E. (2000). Cognitive models of physicians' legal standards and personal judgments of competency in patients with Alzheimer's disease. *Journal of The American Geriatric Society, 48*, 919–927.

Earnst, K. S., Wadley, V. G., Aldridge, T. M., Steenwyk, A. B., Hammond, A. E., Harrell, L. E., & Marson, D. C. (2001). Loss of financial capacity in Alzheimer's disease: The role of working memory. *Aging, Neuropsychology and Cognition, 8*, 109–119.

Evans, J. J., Wilson, B. A., Schuri, U., Andrade, J., Baddeley, A. D., Bruna, O., Canavan, T., Della Sala, S., Green, R., Laaksonen, R., Lorenzi, L., & Taussik, I. (2000). A comparison of "errorless" and "trial-and-error" learning methods for teaching individuals with acquired memory deficits. *Neuropsychological Rehabilitation, 10*, 67–101.

Faure, S. (1995). L'évaluation des effets des prises en charge dans la maladie d'Alzheimer: Problèmes et méthodes. In A. Agniel & F. Eustache (Eds.), *Neuropsychologie clinique des démences: Evaluations et prises en charge* (pp. 251–266). Marseille, France: Solal.

Feher, E. P., Mahurin, R. K., Imbody, S., Crook, T., & Pirozzolo, F. J. (1991). Anosognosia in Alzheimer's disease. *Neuropsychiatry, Neuropsychology, and Behavioral Neurology, 4*, 136–146.

Feinberg, L. F., & Whitlatch, C. J. (2001). Are persons with cognitive impairments able to state consistent choices? *The Gerontologist, 41*, 374–382.

Fleischman, D. A., & Gabrieli, J. D. E. (1998). Repetition priming in normal aging and Alzheimer's disease: A review of findings and theories. *Psychology and Aging, 13*, 88–119.

Fleischman, D. A., & Gabrieli, J. D. E. (1999). Long-term memory in Alzheimer's disease. *Current Opinion in Neurobiology, 9*, 240–244.

Flint, A. J. (1995). Effects of respite care on patients with dementia and their caregivers. *International Psychogeriatrics, 7*, 505–517.

Fontaine, F. (1995). *Apprentissage de nouvelles connaissances chez les patients Alzheimer [Acquisition of new knowledge in Alzheimer patients]*. Montreal: Thèse de Doctorat, Département de Psychologie, Université de Montréal.

Fontaine, F., Van der Linden, M., Guyot, I., & Châtelois, J. (1991). *L'apprentissage de nouvelles connaissances conceptuelles chez une patiente Alzheimer [Acquisition of new semantic knowledge in an Alzheimer patient]*. Poster presented at the 59th ACFAS Congress, University of Sherbrooke, Québec, Canada.

Foss, J. W., Camp, C. J. (1994). *"Effortless" learning in Alzheimer's disease: Evidence that spaced-retrieval training engages implicit memory.* Poster presented at the 5th biennial Cognitive Aging Conference, Atlanta, GA.

Foster, N. A., & Valentine, E. R. (2001). The effect of auditory stimulation on autobiographical recall in dementia. *Experimental Aging Research, 27,* 215–228.

Gélinas, I., Gauthier, L., McIntyre, M. C., & Gauthier, S. (1999). Development of a functional measure for persons with Alzheimer disease: The Disability Assessment for Dementia. *American Journal of Occupational Therapy, 53,* 471–481.

Girelli, L., & Delazer, M. (2001). Numerical abilities in dementia. *Aphasiology, 15,* 681–694.

Girelli, L., & Seron, X. (2001). Rehabilitation of number processing and calculation skills. *Aphasiology, 15,* 695–712.

Glasgow, R. E., Zeiss, R. A., Barrera, M., & Lewinshon, P. M. (1977). Case studies on remediating memory deficits in brain-injured patients. *Journal of Clinical Psychology, 33,* 1049–1054.

Glisky, E. L., & Delaney, S. M. (1996). Implicit memory and new semantic learning in posttraumatic amnesia. *Journal of Head Trauma Rehabilitation, 11,* 31–42.

Glisky, E. L., Schacter, D. L., & Tulving, E. (1986). Learning and retention of computer-related vocabulary in memory-impaired patients: Method of vanishing cues. *Journal of Clinical and Experimental Neuropsychology, 8,* 292–312.

Godfrey, H. P. D., & Knight, R. G. (1988). Memory training and behavioral rehabilitation of a severely head-injured adult. *Archives of Physical Medicine and Rehabilitation, 69,* 458–460.

Goldenberg, G., & Hagmann, S. (1998). Therapy of activities of daily living in patients with apraxia. *Neuropsychological Rehabilitation, 8,* 123–141.

Goldstein, G., McCue, M., Rogers, J., & Nussbaum, P. D. (1992). Diagnostic differences in memory test based predictions of functional capacity in the elderly. *Neuropsychological Rehabilitation, 2,* 307–317.

Hamann, S. B., Monarch, E. S., & Goldstein, F. C. (2000). Memory enhancement for emotional stimuli is impaired in early Alzheimer's disease. *Neuropsychology, 14,* 82–92.

Harwood, D. G., Sultzer, D. L., & Wheatley, M. V. (2000). Impaired insight in Alzheimer disease: Association with cognitive deficits, psychiatric symptoms, and behavioral disturbances. *Neuropsychiatry, Neuropsychology, and Behavioral Neurology, 13,* 83–88.

Haut, M. W., Roberts, V. J., Goldstein, F. C., Martin, R. C., Keefover, R. W., & Rankin, E. D. (1998). Working memory demands and semantic sensitivity for prose in mild Alzheimer's disease. *Aging, Neuropsychology, and Cognition, 5,* 63–72.

Hayman, C. A. G., Macdonald, C. A., & Tulving, E. (1993). The role of repetition and associative interference in new semantic learning in amnesia: A case experiment. *Journal of Cognitive Neuroscience, 5,* 375–389.

Herrmann, D. J., & Palmisano, M. (1992). The facilitation of memory performance. In M. Gruneberg & P. Morris (Eds.), *Aspects of memory. Volume 1: The practical aspects* (pp. 147–167). London: Routledge.

Hill, R. D., Evankovitch, K. D., Sheikh, J. I., & Yesavage, J. A. (1987). Imagery mnemonic training in a patient with degenerative dementia. *Psychology and Aging, 2,* 204–205.

Hoerster, L., Hickey, E. M., & Bourgeois, M. S. (2001). Effects of memory aids on conversations between nursing home residents with dementia and nursing assistants. *Neuropsychological Rehabilitation, 11,* 399–427.

Huffman, J. C., & Kunik, M. E. (2000). Assessment and understanding of pain in patients with dementia. *The Gerontologist, 40,* 574–581.

Hunkin, N. M., & Parkin, A. J. (1995). The method of vanishing cues: An evaluation of its effectiveness in teaching memory-impaired individuals. *Neuropsychologia, 33,* 1255–1279.

Huppert, F. A., Johnson, T., & Nickson, J. (2000). High prevalence of prospective memory impairment in the elderly and in early-stage dementia: Findings from a population-based study. *Applied Cognitive Psychology, 14,* S63–S81.

Hutton, S., Sheppard, L., Rusted, J. M., & Ratner, H. H. (1996). Structuring the acquisition and retrieval environment to facilitate learning in individuals with dementia of the Alzheimer type. *Memory, 4,* 113–130.

Jacobs, D. H., Adair, J. C., Williamson, D. J. G., Na, D. L., Gold, M., Foundas, A. L., Shuren, J. E., Cibula, J. E., & Heilman, K. M. (1999). Apraxia and motor-skill acquisition in Alzheimer's disease are dissociable. *Neuropsychologia, 37,* 875–880.

Jacobs, M. R., Strauss, M. E., Patterson, M. B., & Mack, J. L. (1998). Characterization of depression in Alzheimer's disease by the CERAD Behavior Rating Scale for Dementia (BRSD). *The American Journal of Geriatric Psychiatry, 6,* 53–58.

Jacoby, L. L. (1991). A process dissociation framework: Separating automatic from intentional uses of memory. *Journal of Memory and Language, 30,* 513–541.

Jacquemin, A., Calicis, F., Van der Linden, M., Wijns, Ch., & Noël, M. P. (1991). Evaluation et prise en charge des déficits cognitifs dans les états démentiels [Assessment and rehabilitation of cognitive deficits in dementia]. In M. P. de Partz & M. Leclercq (Eds.), *La rééducation neuropsychologique de l'adulte [Neuropsychological rehabilitation of adult patients]* (pp. 137–151). Paris: Edition de la Société de Neuropsychologie de Langue Française.

Jacquemin, A., Van der Linden, M., & Feyereisen, P. (1993). Thérapie du manque du mot chez un patient bilingue présentant une maladie d'Alzheimer. *Questions de Logopédie, 27,* 91–96.

Josephsson, S., Bäckman, L., Borell, L., Bernspang, B., Nygard, L., & Rönnberg, L. (1993). Supporting everyday activities in dementia: An intervention study. *International Journal of Geriatric Psychiatry, 8,* 395–400.

Judge, K., Camp, C., & Orsulic-Jeras, S. (2000). Use of Montessori-based activities for clients with dementia in adult day care: Effects on engagement. *American Journal of Alzheimer's Disease, 15,* 42–46.

Juillerat, A. C. (2001). *Utilisation d'une stratégie d'imagerie et d'un agenda électronique dans la prise en charge d'un patient présentant une maladie d'Alzheimer à un stade débutant [Use of imagery mnemonics and electronic diary in the rehabilitation of early Alzheimer patients].* Manuscript in preparation.

Juillerat, A. C., Van der Linden, M., Seron, X., & Adam, S. (2000). La prise en charge des patients Alzheimer au stade débutant [Cognitive intervention in early Alzheimer's disease]. In X. Seron & M. Van der Linden (Eds.), *Traité de neuropsychologie clinique, tome 2* (pp. 269–289). Marseille, France: Solal.

Kaplan, E., Goodglass, H., & Weintraub, S. (1983). *Boston naming test.* Philadelphia: Lea & Febiger.

Kasl-Godley, J., & Gatz, M. (2000). Psychosocial interventions for individuals with dementia: An integration of theory, therapy, and a clinical understanding of dementia. *Clinical Psychological Review, 20,* 755–782.

Kazui, H., Mori, E., Hashimoto, M., Hirono, N., Imamura, T., Tanimukai, S., Hanihara, T., & Cahill, L. (2000). Impact of emotion on memory: Controlled study of the influence of emotionally charged material on declarative memory in Alzheimer's disease. *British Journal of Psychiatry, 177,* 343–347.

Kempler, D. (1995). Language changes in dementia of the Alzheimer type. In R. Lubinsky (Ed.), *Dementia and communication* (pp. 98–114). Philadelphia: B.C. Decker.

Kitwood, T. (1997). *Dementia reconsidered: The person comes first.* Buckingham, UK: Open University Press.

Kitwood, T., & Bredin, K. (1992). Towards a theory of dementia care: Personhood and well-being. *Ageing and Society, 12,* 269–287.

Koltai, D. C., Welsh-Bohmer, A., & Schmechel, D. E. (2001). Influence of anosognosia on treatment outcome among dementia patients. *Neuropsychological Rehabilitation, 11,* 455–475.

Komatsu, S., Mimura, M., Kato, M., Wakamatsu, N., & Kashima, H. (2000). Errorless and effortful processes involved in the learning of face-name associations by patients with alcoholic Korsakoff's syndrome. *Neuropsychological Rehabilitation, 10,* 113–132.

Kotler-Cope, S., & Camp, C. J. (1995). Anosognosia in Alzheimer's disease. *Alzheimer Disease and Associated Disorders, 9,* 52–56.

Lachman, M. E. (2000). Promoting a sense of control over memory aging. In R. H. Hill, L. Bäckman, & A. Stigsdotter Neely (Eds.), *Cognitive rehabilitation in old age* (pp. 106–120). New York: Oxford University Press.

Landauer, T. K., & Bjork, R. A. (1978). Optimal rehearsal patterns and name learning. In M. M. Gruneberg, P. E. Morris, & R. N. Sykes (Eds.), *Practical aspects of memory* (pp. 625–632). London: Academic Press.

Lawton, M. P., Brody, E. M., & Saperstein, A. R. (1991). *Respite for caregivers of Alzheimer patients: Research and practice.* New York: Springer.

Lekeu, F., Chicherio, C., Van der Linden, M., & Salmon, E. (2000). Prise en charge des difficultés de mémoire prospective dans la maladie d'Alzheimer [Rehabilitation of prospective memory deficits in Alzheimer's disease]. *Alzheimer, 3,* 17–20.

Lekeu, F., Van der Linden, M., Adam, S., Laroi, F., & Salmon, E. (2001). *Rehabilitation of topographical disorientation in Alzheimer's disease: A single case study.* Manuscript in preparation.

Lekeu, F., Van der Linden, M., Franck, G., Moonen, G., & Salmon, E. (2002). Exploring the effect of action familiarity on SPTs recall performance in Alzheimer's disease. *Journal of Clinical and Experimental Neuropsychology,* in press.

Leng, N. R. C., Copello, A. G., & Sayegh, A. (1991). Learning after brain injury by the method of vanishing cues: A case study. *Behavioural Psychotherapy, 19,* 173–181.

Lyketsos, C. G., Steele, C., Baker, L., Galik, E., Kopunek, S., Steinberg, M., & Warren, A. (1997). Major and minor depression in Alzheimer's disease: Prevalence and impact. *Journal of Neuropsychiatry, 9,* 556–560.

Marson, D. C., Earnst, K. S., Jamil, F., Bartolucci, A., & Harrell, L. E. (2000). Consistency of physicians' legal standard and personal judgments of competency in patients with Alzheimer's disease. *Journal of the American Geriatric Society, 48,* 911–918.

Marson, D. C., McInturff, B., Hawkins, L., Bartolucci, A., & Harrell, L. E. (1997). Consistency of physician judgments of capacity to consent in mild Alzheimer's disease. *Journal of the American Geriatric Society, 45,* 453–457.

Marson, D. C., Sawrie, S. M., Snyder, S., McInturff, B., Stalvey, T., Boothe, A., Aldridge, T., Chatterjee, A., & Harrell, L. E. (2000). Assessing financial capacity in patients with Alzheimer's disease: A conceptual model and prototype instrument. *Archives of Neurology, 57,* 877–884.

Mattis, S. (1973). *Dementia rating scale.* Windsor, UK: NFER-Nelson.

McCarthy, D. L. (1980). Investigation of a visual imagery mnemonic device for acquiring name-face associations. *Journal of Experimental Psychology: Human Learning and Memory, 6,* 145–155.

McGlynn, S., & Kaszniak, A. (1991). When metacognition fails: Impaired awareness of deficit in Alzheimer's disease. *Journal of Cognitive Neuroscience, 3*, 183–189.

McGlynn, S., & Schacter, D. (1989). Unawareness of deficits in neuropsychological syndromes. *Journal of Clinical and Experimental Neuropsychology, 11*, 143–205.

McKitrick, L. A., & Camp, C. J. (1993). Relearning the names of things: The spaced-retrieval intervention implemented by a caregiver. *Clinical Gerontologist, 14*, 60–62.

McKitrick, L. A., Camp, C. J., & Black, F. W. (1992). Prospective memory intervention in Alzheimer's disease. *Journal of Gerontology, 47*, 337–343.

Middleton, D. K., Lambert, M. J., & Seggar, L. B. (1991). Neuropsychological rehabilitation: Microcomputer-assisted treatment of brain-injured adults. *Perceptual and Motor Skills, 72*, 527–530.

Miller, E., & Morris, R. G. (1993). *The psychology of dementia*. Chichester, UK: Wiley.

Mittelman, M. S., Ferris, S. H., Shulman, E., Steinberg, G., & Levin, B. (1996). A family intervention to delay nursing home placement of patients with Alzheimer disease. *The Journal of the American Medical Association, 276*, 1725–1731.

Moayeri, S. E., Cahill, L., Jin, Y., & Potkin, S. G. (2000). Relative sparing of emotionally influenced memory in Alzheimer's disease. *Neuroreport, 11*, 653–655.

Moffat, N. J. (1992). Home-based cognitive rehabilitation with the elderly. In L. W. Poon, D. C Rubin, & B. A. Wilson (Eds.), *Everyday cognition in adulthood and late life* (pp. 659–680). New York: Cambridge University Press.

Montgomery, R. J. V., & Williams, K. N. (2001). Implications of differential impacts of care-giving for future research on Alzheimer care. *Aging and Mental Health, 5*, 23–24.

Moore, S., Sandman, C. A., McGrady, K., & Kesslak, J. P. (2001). Memory training improves cognitive ability in patients with dementia. *Neuropsychological Rehabilitation, 11*, 245–261.

Morris, P. E. (1979). Strategies for learning and recall. In M. M. Gruneberg & P. E. Morris (Eds.), *Applied problem in memory* (pp. 25–57). London: Academic Press.

Moye, J. (1999). Assessment of competency and decision making capacity. In P. A. Lichtenberg (Ed.), *Handbook of assessment in clinical gerontology* (pp. 488–528). New York: Wiley.

Neundorfer, M. M., McClendon, M. J., Smyth, K. A., Stuckey, J. C., Strauss, M. E., & Patterson, M. B. (2001). A longitudinal study of the relationship between levels of depression among persons with Alzheimer's disease and levels of depression among their family caregivers. *Journal of Gerontology, 56*, 301–313.

Ott, B. R., Lafleche, G., Whelihan, W. M., Buongiorno, G. W., Albert, M. S., & Fogel, B. S. (1996). Impaired awareness of deficits in Alzheimer's disease. *Alzheimer Disease and Associated Disorders, 10*, 68–76.

Palmer, C. V., Adams, S. W., Bourgeois, M., Durrant, J., & Rossi, M. (1999). Reduction in caregiver identified problem behavior in patients with Alzheimer disease post-hearing-aid fitting. *Journal of Speech and Hearing Research, 42*, 312–328.

Parkin, A. J., Hunkin, N. M., & Squires, E. J. (1998). Unlearning John Major: The use of errorless learning in the reacquisition of proper names following herpes simplex encephalitis. *Cognitive Neuropsychology, 15*, 361–375.

Passini, R., Rainville, C., Marchand, N., & Joanette, Y. (1995). Wayfinding in dementia of the Alzheimer type: Planning abilities. *Journal of Clinical and Experimental Neuropsychology, 17*, 820–832.

Patterson, M. B., & Bolger, J. B. (1994). Assessment of behavioural symptoms in Alzheimer's disease. *Alzheimer Disease and Associated Disorders, 8*, 4–20.

Pesenti, M., Seron, X., & Noël, M.-P. (2000). Les troubles du calcul et du traitement des nombres [Calculation and number processing deficits]. In X. Seron & M. Van der Linden (Eds.), *Traité de neuropsychologie clinique, tome* 2 (pp. 355–371). Marseille, France: Solal.

Phillips, C. D., & Knopman, D. S. (1999). Neurology "with the bark off": Tacrine, nursing home residents, and health services research. *Neurology, 52,* 227–230.

Powell-Proctor, L., & Miller, E. (1982). Reality orientation: A critical appraisal. *British Journal of Clinical Psychology, 26,* 83–91.

Prigatano, G. P., Fordyce, D. J., Zeiner, H. K., Roueche, J. R., Pepping, M., & Wood, B. C. (1984). Neuropsychological rehabilitation after closed head injury in young adults. *Journal of Neurological and Neurosurgical Psychiatry, 47,* 505–513.

Quayhagen, M. P., & Quayhagen, M. (2001). Testing of a cognitive stimulation intervention for dementia caregiving dyads. *Neuropsychological Rehabilitation, 11,* 319–332.

Quayhagen, M. P., Quayhagen, M., Corbeil, R. R., Roth, P. A., & Rodgers, J. A. (1995). A dyadic remediation program for care recipients with dementia. *Nursing Research, 44,* 153–159.

Rainville, C., Joanette, Y., & Passini, R. (1994). Les troubles de l'orientation dans l'espace dans la maladie d'Alzheimer [Spatial orientation deficits in Alzheimer's disease]. *Revue de Neuropsychologie, 4,* 3–45.

Rainville, C., Passini, R., & Marchand, N. (2001). A multiple case study of wayfinding in dementia of the Alzheimer type: Decision making. *Aging, Neuropsychology, and Cognition, 8,* 54–71.

Reed, B., Jagust, W., & Coulter, L. (1993). Anosognosia in Alzheimer's disease: Relationship to depression, cognitive function, and cerebral perfusion. *Journal of Clinical and Experimental Neuropsychology, 15,* 231–244.

Rey, A. (1964). *L'examen clinique en psychologie [Clinical assessment in psychology].* Paris: Presses Universitaires de France.

Riddoch, M. J., & Humphreys, G. W. (1995). 17 + 14 = 41? Three cases of working memory impairment. In R. Campbell & M. Conway (Eds), *Broken memories: Case studies in memory impairment* (pp. 253–266). Oxford, UK: Blackwell.

Riley, K. P. (1992). Bridging the gap between researchers and clinicians: Methodological perspectives and choices. In R. L. West & J. D. Sinnott (Eds.), *Everyday memory and aging: Current research and methodology* (pp. 182–189). New York: Springer-Verlag.

Rizzo, M., McGehee, D. V., Dawson, J. D., & Anderson, S. N. (2001). Simulated car crashes at intersections in drivers with Alzheimer disease. *Alzheimer Disease and Associated Disorders, 15,* 10–20.

Romero, B., & Wenz, M. (2001). Self-maintenance therapy in Alzheimer's disease. *Neuropsychological Rehabilitation, 11,* 333–355.

Rusted, J. M., Marsh, R., Bledski, L., & Sheppard, L. (1997). Alzheimer patients' use of auditory and olfactory cues to aid verbal memory. *Aging & Mental Health, 1,* 364–371.

Sabat, S. R. (1994). Excess disability and malignant social psychology: A case study of Alzheimer's disease. *Journal of Community and Applied Social Psychology, 4,* 157–166.

Sabat, S. R., & Collins, M. (1999). Intact social, cognitive ability, and selfhood: A case study of Alzheimer's disease. *American Journal of Alzheimer's Disease, 14,* 11–19.

Sabat, S. R., & Harré, R. (1992). The construction and deconstruction of self in Alzheimer's disease. *Ageing and Society, 12,* 443–461.

Salmon, D. P. (2000). Disorders of memory in Alzheimer's disease. In L. S. Cermak (Ed), *Memory and its disorders, Handbook of Neuropsychology* (2nd ed., pp. 155–195). Amsterdam: Elsevier.

Schacter, D., & Prigatano, G. (1991). Forms of unawareness. In G. Prigatano & D. Schacter (Eds.), *Awareness of deficits after brain injury* (pp. 258–262). New York: Oxford University Press.

Schacter, D. L., Rich, S. A., & Stampp, M. S. (1985). Remediation of memory disorders: Experimental evaluation of the spaced-retrieval technique. *Journal of Clinical and Experimental Neuropsychology, 7*, 79–96.

Schacter, D. L., Wagner, A. D., & Buckner, R. L. (2000). Memory systems of 1999. In E. Tulving & F. I. M. Craik (Eds.), *The Oxford handbook of memory.* Oxford, UK: Oxford University Press.

Schmand, B., Gouwenberg, B., Smit, J. H., & Jonker, C. (1999). Assessment of mental competency in community-dwelling elderly. *Alzheimer Disease and Associated Disorders, 13*, 80–87.

Schmidt, R. A. (1975). A schema theory of discrete motor learning. *Psychological Review, 82*, 225–260.

Schultz, R., Galagher-Thompson, D., Haley, W. E., & Czaja, S. (2000). Understanding the intervention process: A theoretical/conceptual framework for intervention approaches to caregiving. In R. Schultz (Ed.), *Handbook on dementia caregiving: Evidence-based interventions for family caregivers* (pp. 33–60). New York: Springer.

Selai, C. E., Trimble, M. R., Rossor, M. N., & Harvey, R. J. (2001). Assessing quality of life in dementia: Preliminary psychometric testing of the Quality of Life Assessment Schedule (QOLAS). *Neuropsychological Rehabilitation, 11*, 219–243.

Seron, X. (1997). Effectiveness and specificity in neuropsychological therapies: A cognitive point of view. *Aphasia, 11*, 105–123.

Seron, X. (2000). L'évaluation de l'efficacité des traitements. In X. Seron & M. Van der Linden (Eds.), *Traité de neuropsychologie clinique, tome 2* (pp. 39–62). Marseille, France: Solal.

Sheikh, J. A., & Yesavage, J. A. (1986). Geriatric Depression Scale (GDS): Recent findings and development of a shorter version. *Clinical Gerontologist, 5*, 165–173.

Smith, G., Della Sala, S., Logie, R. H., & Maylor, E. A. (2000). Prospective and retrospective memory in normal ageing and dementia: A questionnaire study. *Memory, 8*, 311–321.

Sohlberg, M. M., & Mateer, C. (1989). Training use of compensatory memory books: A three-stage behavioral approach. *Journal of Clinical and Experimental Neuropsychology, 11*, 871–891.

Souêtre, E., Thwaites, R. M. A., & Yeardley, H. L. (1999). Economic impact of Alzheimer's disease in the United Kingdoom. *British Journal of Psychiatry, 174*, 51–55.

Spector, A., Davies, S., Woods, B., & Orrell, M. (2000). Realty orientation for dementia: A systematic review of the evidence of effectiveness from randomized controlled trials. *The Gerontologist, 40*, 206–212.

Spector, A., Orrell, M., Davies, S., & Woods, B. (1998a). *Reality orientation for dementia: A review of the evidence for its effectiveness* [The Cochrane Library, Issue 4]. Oxford, UK: Update Software.

Spector, A., Orrell, M., Davies, S., & Woods, B. (1998b). *Reminiscence therapy for dementia: A review of the evidence for its effectiveness* [The Cochrane Library, Issue 4]. Oxford, UK: Update Software.

Spector, A., Orrell, M., Davies, S., & Woods, B. (2001). Can reality orientation be rehabilitated? Development and piloting of an evidence-based programme of cognition-based therapies for people with dementia. *Neuropsychological Rehabilitation, 11*, 377–397.

Squires, E. J., Hunkin, N. M., & Parkin, A. J. (1997). Errorless learning of novel associations in amnesia. *Neuropsychologia, 8*, 1103–1111.

Starkstein, S., Petracca, G., Chemerinski, E., & Kremer, J. (2001). Syndromic validity of apathy in Alzheimer's disease. *American Journal of Psychiatry, 158*, 872–877.

Starkstein, S., Sabe, L., Chemerinsky, E., Jason, L., & Leiguarda, R. (1996). Two domains of anosognosia in Alzheimer's disease. *Journal of Neurology, Neurosurgery, and Psychiatry, 61*, 485–490.

Ste-Marie, D. M., Jennings, J. M., & Finlayson, A. J. (1996). Process dissociation procedure: Memory testing in populations with brain damage. *The Clinical Neuropsychologist, 10*, 25–36.

Stevens, A., King, C. A., & Camp, C. J. (1993). Improving prose memory and social interaction using question asking reading with adult day care clients. *Educational Gerontology, 19*, 651–662.

Stevens, A., O'Hanlon, A., & Camp, C. (1993). The spaced-retrieval methods: A case study. *Clinical Gerontologits, 13*, 106–109.

Suhr, J., Anderson, S., & Tranel, D. (1999). Progressive muscle relaxation in the management of behavioural disturbance in Alzheimer's disease. *Neuropsychological Rehabilitation, 9*, 31–34.

Taylor, B. D., & Tripodes, S. (2001). The effect of driving cessation on the elderly with dementia and their caregivers. *Accident Analysis and Prevention, 33*, 519–528.

Teresi, J. A., Holmes, D., & Ory, M. G. (2000). The therapeutic design of environments for people with dementia: Further reflections and recent findings from the National Institute on Aging Collaborative Studies of Dementia Special Care Units. *The Gerontologist, 40*, 417–421.

Teri, L., Truax, P., Logdson, R., Uomoto, J., Zarit, S., & Vitaliano, P. P. (1992). Assessment of behavioral problems in dementia: The revised memory and behavior problems checklist. *Psychology and Aging, 7*, 622–631.

Teunisse, S., & Derix, M. M. (1991). Meten van het dagelijks functioneren van thuiswonende dementiepatiënten: Ontwikkeling van een vragenlijst [Measurement of functioning in daily life of dementia patients living at home: Development of a questionnaire]. *Tijdschrift voor Gerontologie en Geriatrie, 22*, 53–59.

Thornton, S., & Brotchie, J. (1987). Reminiscence: A critical review of the empirical literature. *British Journal of Clinical Psychology, 26*, 93–111.

Tulving, E. (1983). *Elements of episodic memory*. Oxford, UK: Oxford University Press.

Vaidya, C. J., Gabrieli, J. D. E., Monti, L. A., Tinklenberg, J. R., & Yesavage, J. A. (1999). Dissociation between two forms of conceptual priming in Alzheimer's disease. *Neuropsychology, 13*, 516–524.

Van der Linden, M. (1989). *Les troubles de la mémoire [Neuropsychology of memory deficits]*. Bruxelles: Mardaga.

Van der Linden, M. (1994). Neuropsychologie des syndromes démentiels [Neuropsychology of dementia]. In X. Seron & M. Jeannerod (Eds.), *Traité de neuropsychologie humaine* (pp. 282–316). Bruxelles: Mardaga.

Van der Linden, M. (1995). Prise en charge des troubles de la mémoire dans la maladie d'Alzheimer. [Rehabilitation of memory disorders in Alzheimer's disease]. In A. Agniel & F. Eustache (Eds.), *Neuropsychologie clinique des démences: Evaluations et prises en charge* [Clinical neuropsychology of dementia assessment and rehabilitation]. (pp. 267–282). Marseille, France: Solal.

Van der Linden, M., Ansay, C., Calicis, F., Jacquemin, A., Schils, J. P., Seron, X., & Wijns, Ch. (1991). Prise en charge des déficits cognitifs dans la démence d'Alzheimer [Rehabilitation of cognitive deficits in Alzheimer's disease]. In M. Habib, Y. Joanette, & M. Puel (Eds.), *Démences et syndromes démentiels: Approche neuropsychologique* (pp. 253–262). Paris: Masson.

Van der Linden, M., & Coyette, F. (1995). Acquisition of word processing knowledge in an amnesic patient: Implications for theory and rehabilitation. In R. Campbell

& M. Conway (Eds.), *Broken memories: Neuropsychological case studies* (pp. 54–80). Oxford, UK: Blackwell.

Van der Linden, M., Coyette, F., & Seron, X. (2000). La rééducation des troubles de la mémoire [Rehabilitation of memory disorders]. In X. Seron & M. Van der Linden (Eds.), *Traité de neuropsychologie clinique, tome 2* (pp. 81–103). Marseille, France: Solal.

Van der Linden, M., & Juillerat, A. C. (1998). Prise en charge des déficits cognitifs dans la maladie d'Alzheimer [Cognitive rehabilitation in Alzheimer's disease]. *Revue Neurologique, 154*, 137–154.

Van der Linden, M., & Meulemans, T. (1998). A cognitive neuropsychological approach to spatial memory deficits in brain-damaged patients. In N. Foreman & R. Gillett (Eds.), *Interacting with the environment: A handbook of spatial research, paradigms and methodologies* (pp. 33–58). Mahwah. NJ: Lawrence Erlbaum Associates.

Van der Linden, M., Meulemans, T., Belleville, S., & Collette, F. (2000). L'évaluation des troubles de la mémoire [Assessment of memory disorders]. In X. Seron & M. Van der Linden (Eds.), *Traité de neuropsychologie clinique, tome 1* (pp. 275–300). Marseille, France: Solal.

Van der Linden, M., Meulemans, T., & Lorrain, D. (1994). Acquisition of new concepts by two amnesic patients. *Cortex, 30*, 305–317.

Van der Linden, M., Meulemans, T., Marczewski, P., & Collette, F. (2000). The relationships between episodic memory, working memory, and executive functions: The contribution of the prefrontal cortex. *Psychologica Belgica, 40*, 275–297.

Van der Linden, M., & Seron, X. (1989). Prise en charge des déficits cognitifs [Cognitive interventions]. In O. Guard & B. Michel (Eds.), *La maladie d'Alzheimer* (pp. 289–303). Paris: Medsi/Mc Graw-Hill.

Van der Linden, M., & Seron, X. (1991). I disturbi dell'orientamento topographico: Proposte per un progetto terapeutico. In D. Grossi (Ed.), *La riabilitazione dei disturbi della cognizione spaziale* (pp. 99–119). Milano: Masson.

Van der Linden, M., Seron, X., & Juillerat, A. C. (2000). Evaluation et rééducation des troubles de l'orientation topographique [Assessment and rehabilitation of topographical disorders]. In X. Seron & M. Van der Linden (Eds.), *Traité de neuropsychologie clinique, tome 2* (pp. 105–116). Marseille, France: Solal.

Van der Linden, M., & Van der Kaa, M. A. (1989). Reorganization therapy for memory impairments. In X. Seron & G. Deloche (Eds), *Cognitive approaches in neuropsychological rehabilitation* (pp. 105–158). Hillsdale, NJ: Lawrence Erlbaum Associates.

Vanhalle, C., Van der Linden, M., Belleville, S., & Gilbert, B. (1998). Putting names on faces: Use of spaced retrieval strategy in a patient with dementia of Alzheimer type. *ASHA, American Speech & Hearing Association, Special Interest Division 2, Neurophysiology and Neurogenic Speech and Language Disorders, 8*, 17–21.

Vehey, F. R. J., Ponds, R. W. H. M., Rozendaal, N., & Jolles, J. (1995). Depression, insight and personality changes in Alzheimer's disease: Domain-specific differences and disease correlates. *Neuropsychiatry, Neuropsychology, and Behavioral Neurology, 8*, 26–32.

Wadley, V. G., & Haley, W. E. (2001). Diagnostic attributions versus labeling: Impact of Alzheimer's disease and major depression diagnoses on emotions, beliefs, and helping intentions of family members. *Journal of Gerontology, 56*, 244–252.

Watson, C. M., Chenery, H. J., & Carter, M. S. (1999). An analysis of trouble and repair in the natural conversations of people with dementia of the Alzheimer's type. *Aphasiology, 13*, 195–218.

Wechsler, D. A. (1987). *Manual: Wechsler Memory Scale-Revised.* New York: Psychological Corporation.

Wilson, B. A., Baddeley, A. D., & Cockburn, J. M. (1989). How do old dogs learn new tricks: Teaching a technological skill to brain injured people. *Cortex, 27,* 115–119.

Wilson, B. A., Baddeley, A. D., & Evans, J. (1994). Errorless learning in the rehabilitation of memory impaired people. *Neuropsychological Rehabilitation, 4,* 307–326.

Wilson, B. A., Baddeley, A. D., Evans, J., & Shiel, A. (1994). Errorless learning in the rehabilitation of memory impaired people. *Neuropsychological Rehabilitation, 4,* 307–326.

Woods, R. T. (2001). Discovering the person with Alzheimer's disease: Cognitive, emotional and behavioural aspects: *Aging and Mental Health, 5,* 7–16.

World Health Organization. (1980). *International classification of impairments, disabilities and handicaps.* Genoa: Author.

Yesavage, J., Brink, T., Rose, T., Lum, O., Huang, V., Adey, M., & Leirer, V. (1983). Development and validation of a geriatric depression screening scale: A preliminary report. *Journal of Psychiatric Research, 17,* 37–49.

Ylieff, M. (1989). Analyse et traitements comportementaux [Behavioral analysis and interventions]. In O. Guard & B. Michel (Eds.), *La maladie d'Alzheimer* (pp. 303–316). Paris: Medsi/McGraw-Hill.

Ylieff, M. (2000). Le traitement en milieu institutionnel [Rehabilitation of institutionalized patients]. In X. Seron & M. Van der Linden (Eds.), *Traité de Neuropsychologie Clinique, Tome 2* (pp. 291–302). Marseille, France: Solal.

Zanetti, O., Binetti, G., Magni, E., Rozzini, L., Bianchetti, A., & Trabucchi, M. (1997). Procedural memory stimulation in Alzheimer's disease: Impact of a training program. *Acta Neurologica Scandinavia, 95,* 152–157.

Zanetti, O., Vallotti, B., Frisoni, G. B., Geroldi, C., Bianchetti, A., Pasqualetti, A., & Trabucchi, M. (1999). Insight in dementia: When does it occur? Evidence for a nonlinear relationship between insight and cognitive status. *Journal of Gerontology, 54,* 100–106.

Zanetti, O., Zanieri, G., Di Giovanni, G., De Vreese, L. P., Pezzini, A., Metitieri, T., & Trabucchi, M. (2001). Effectiveness of procedural memory stimulation in mild Alzheimer's disease patients: A controlled study. *Neuropsychological Rehabilitation, 11,* 263–272.

Zarit, S. H., Reever, K. E., & Bach Peterson, J. (1980). Relatives of the impaired elderly: Correlates of feelings of burden. *Gerontologist, 20,* 649–655.

10

The Assessment of Functioning in Daily Life

Anne-Claude Juillerat
University Hospitals of Geneva

Martial Van der Linden
University of Geneva

The existence of a functional impairment that interferes with social or professional abilities or leads to a loss of autonomy in everyday life activities is an important component of the diagnosis of Alzheimer's Disease (AD), according to the most widely used criteria, such as the DSM-IV (American Psychiatric Association, 1994), the NINCDS-ADRDA (McKhann et al., 1984), and the ICD-10 (World Health Organization, 1993). In a recent study conducted on a large sample of early AD patients, Loewenstein, Ownby, et al. (2001) confirmed that specific assessment of functional abilities must complete the neuropsychological evaluation to maximize the accuracy of AD diagnosis. In addition, it has been shown that important dissociations can be found within some subjects between cognitive and functional measures and that the extent of changes of both measures may differ over time (Skurla, Rogers, & Sunderland, 1988; Teunisse & Derix, 1991), thus stressing the need for a specific evaluation of the functional domain in addition to cognitive functioning.

Other studies also demonstrated that evaluation of functional impairment is important to differentiate normal aging from depression and early dementia (Loewenstein & Mogovsky, 1999), to predict incident dementia (Agüero-Torres, Hillerås, & Winblad, 2001; Barberger-Gateau, Fabrigoule, Helmer, Rouch, & Dartigues, 1999; Morris et al., 2001), to characterize the disease's progression, and to determine the disease's severity, by using, for example, the Clinical Dementia Rating Scale (CDR; Hughes, Berg, Danziger,

Cohen, & Martin, 1982). Consequently, an evaluation of daily life functioning should be part of a systematic comprehensive assessment to diagnose dementia. The exploration of everyday activities is also very important for the clinical management of AD (see chap. 9 of this book); indeed, it will help determine the need for supervision and the objectives of the neuropsychological rehabilitation, for both the patients and family caregivers, as well as to assess the efficiency of intervention (either psychological or pharmacological).

This chapter discusses problems in the assessment of daily life activities in AD patients. The first part critically reviews current evaluation techniques (e.g., scales, simulation tasks, and objective measures). The second part examines theoretical models developed to understand functional impairment in patients with brain damage, which could be useful for both cognitive assessment and intervention in early AD. The few in-depth neuropsychological studies in this field carried out with AD patients are presented and discussed, and future research prospects are proposed. Finally, the impact of psychiatric symptoms and behavioral disturbances on everyday tasks in AD is evoked.

ACTIVITIES OF DAILY LIVING SCALES

To assess patients' daily functioning capabilities, several means have been used. Some of them depend on informant or self-ratings of behavior and are thus prone to a subjective perception of the situation (which is the case for most scales and questionnaires). More objective measures rely on observation, either in everyday life or in experimental simulations of everyday functional skills.

Because the agreement between self-report and actual functional abilities of patients suffering from cerebral lesions is highly variable, most scales used to assess daily living activities are administered to a caregiver or consist of a semistructured interview with a reliable informant. Such subjective reports take little time and are easy to administer. They can also be helpful when cognitive decline is such that a patient's self-assessments are no longer reliable. It must also be emphasized that comparison between informant and self-reports can provide clues about the patients' awareness of their abilities.

A difference between scales of daily living activities consists in the time range or the types of activities they cover: Some scales span the whole range of potential functional impairment, from the earliest to the latest stages, and are thus important for longitudinal follow-up because changes are expected with the disease's progression. When impaired functioning in everyday life is evaluated, a distinction is commonly made between two domains: basic physical activities, such as eating, dressing, toileting, and walking, referred to as activities of daily living (ADL) and more complex activities, such as using a telephone, taking medication, dealing with finances, and using public transportation referred to as instrumental activities of daily living (IADL). Because most scales were designed to evaluate all stages of dementia, they frequently integrate items related to both ADL and IADL. At the early stages, difficulties are normally limited to IADL but, as the disease progresses, a gradual increase in the functional disability is commonly observed. Other scales address in more detail specific domains, such as financial abilities (e.g., Loewenstein et al., 1989), or may allow separate analysis of different aspects of a task (e.g., initiation, sequencing, completion) and measurement of help needed.

Subjective Measures: Functional Scales and Questionnaires

The Functional Assessment Staging scale (FAST; Reisberg, 1988) and the Lawton's Instrumental Activities of Daily Living scale (Lawton & Brody, 1969) are among the most widely used functional scales specifically designed for patients with dementia. They permit a follow-up throughout the course of dementia because they include both IADL and ADL. The FAST is scored by the clinician after an interview with an informant, and the clinician rates functional changes in seven major stages (designed by numbers) and nine substages (designed by letters), which are hierarchically organized; scores range from 1 (*no impairment*) to 7f (*maximal impairment*). Each stage or substage corresponds to a description of the problems presented by the patient (e.g., Stage 2: complains of forgetting location of objects; Stage 5: requires assistance in choosing proper clothing; Stage 7d: unable to sit up independently; Stage 7f: unable to hold head up). Unfortunately, such an approach does not take into account the important heterogeneity of symptoms in AD. It is now well established that both the nature of the defective processes and the impairment progression can vary considerably from one patient to another (see chap. 3 of this book), and this will naturally impact differentially on daily living functioning. Such an ordinal description of the functional impairment has therefore little meaning, particularly at the early stages.

The Lawton's scale (Lawton & Brody, 1969) consists of items in different functional domains (ability to use telephone, shopping, food preparation, housekeeping, laundry, mode of transportation, responsibility for own medication, and ability to handle finances). Performance on each item is scored on a 3-, 4- , or 5-grade scale, a greater score implying a more impaired state of functional activity. Caregivers usually rate the scale, considering the patient's performance at home. Although it only taps a limited number of IADL domains and some of the items may be more suitable for assessment in women (e.g., cooking, doing the laundry), it has been used in large-scale epidemiological studies of dementia, such as the PAQUID study (a community study made in a random sample of 2,792 subjects age

65 and over, among which 1,500 had been followed since 1988). As part of this study, Barberger-Gateau et al. (1999) showed that a score summing up the number of dependencies at baseline on four items of Lawton's scale (ability to use telephone, mode of transportation, responsibility for own medication, and ability to handle finances), after elimination of physical reasons for impairment, is a strong predictor of the risk of being diagnosed with dementia in the 3 subsequent years. Also, if an increase in dependency was observed at the 3-year follow-up, it was correlated with a higher risk of dementia at the 5-year follow-up. Thus, the four scores can prove useful for screening dementia patients or those at risk for dementia, who should undergo careful and comprehensive neuropsychological evaluation, and identifying those patients who could benefit from an early intervention to maintain a good level of functioning for as long as possible.

An exhaustive review of the abundant literature of the existing scales is not the purpose of this chapter (larger reviews can be found in Burns, Lawlor, & Craig, 1999, or in Loewenstein & Mogosky, 1999). It nevertheless should be noted that some of the more recent scales, such as the Interview for Deterioration in Daily Living in Dementia (IDDD; Teunisse & Derix, 1991), the Disability Assessment for Dementia (DAD; Gélinas, Gauthier, McIntyre, & Gauthier, 1999), and the Cleveland Scale for Activities of Daily Living (CSADL; Patterson et al., 1992) not only cover both complex and self-care activities but also provide information regarding both initiation and completion of an activity (e.g., IDDD). Some even systematically separately rate initiation, planning and organization, and effective achievement (e.g., DAD, CSADL). Such distinctions can be helpful for early and differential diagnosis and therapeutic interventions.

However, although valuable, these approaches present several limitations:

- At a clinical level, such measures may be insensitive to subtle changes occurring in the early stages of the disease; they do not take into account the heterogeneity of AD; they can hardly give a precise picture of the patient's functioning within the community or at home; the scores may vary considerably due to differences between men and women and differences among the levels of education; and, finally, they give little information about the strategies used by the patients to complete a task.
- From a methodological point of view, lack of sensitivity, specificity, and interrater and test-retest reliabilities were described in the past (La Rue, 1987). However, good reliability and validity of both the DAD and the CSADL, when administered by trained examiners or caregivers, have been demonstrated more recently (Feldman et al., 2001; Patterson & Mack, 2001).
- Subjective scale scoring procedure is problematic because respondents are usually asked to rate overall ADL functioning, rather than

the patient's ability to perform one or more of the subtasks associated with each activity. Frequently, the scales allow a "all or none" type of answers, which does not allow a reflection of the gradual nature of the functional impairment. Moreover, answers to global questions depend on the caregivers' interpretations of the meaning of the question (e.g., "Can the patient use a phone ?" may be understood as the ability to search for a number, dial it, and correctly place the call, or simply answer the phone).

The use of questionnaires can help clinicians bypass the limitations of the functional scales. Questionnaires assess daily living situations to which a specific domain of cognitive functioning contributes. They present a list of items describing prototypical situations; either the patient or an informant has to determine how efficiently the patient is performing in these situations on a scale consisting of several anchors, which may refer either to the level of performance (e.g., "Compared with before the disease, is the patient's performance: *much improved, a bit improved, not much changed, a bit worse, much worse*") or the occurrence of the problems (e.g., *never, seldom, occasionally, often, always*). Though numerous questionnaires have been developed for neuropsychological purposes, few have been used for patients with dementia, but some explored the influence of memory problems on daily living activities (e.g., the Informant Questionnaire on Cognitive Decline in the Elderly; IQCODE; Jorm & Jacomb, 1989) and executive deficits (e.g., Lebert, Pasquier, Souliez, & Petit, 1998; Norton, Malloy, & Salloway, 2001). In the long run, a systematic use of questionnaires that assess specific domains could prove useful in establishing correspondences between functional and neuropsychological impairments.

Because all these scales are filled in either by the patients or their caregivers, it is clear that they are sensitive to significant subjectivity. Recent studies have clearly shown biases, both on the patients' and their caregivers' accounts. On the patients' side, it has been shown that they tend to rate their abilities significantly better than their caregivers do (McGlynn & Kaszniak, 1991). Furthermore, their ratings are influenced by socioeconomic factors, such as gender, marital status, level of education, and income. Female AD patients with a higher level of education report better functional abilities, and AD patients (both female and male) who perceive their financial situation as good report a better functional capacity (Rautio, Heikkinen, & Heikkinen, 2001).

Caregivers are hardly better in predicting the patients' functional abilities. Loewenstein, Argüelees, et al. (2001) demonstrated that a significant correlation between caregivers' reports and actual patients' performances was found only in cases where the patients did not evidence any objective functional deficit. More generally, caregiver biases have been repeatedly described. In particular, recent studies showed that informant report is influenced by:

- *Caregivers' characteristics.* Overestimation of disability is frequently related to the caregivers' stress or burden (La Rue, 1992; Zanetti, Geroldi, Frisoni, Bianchetti, & Trabucchi, 1999); informant ratings can also be disproportionally influenced by isolated events (e.g., patient involved in a traffic accident, responsible for a burnt dinner). However, spousal caregivers report more accurately than caregivers who are adult children of the patients. In general, caregivers living with the patient tend to overestimate deficits, whereas those who spend less than 20 hr a week in caregiving are more inclined to underestimate the problems (Loewenstein, Argüelees, et al., 2001).
- *Caregiver's expectations and attitudes.* For example, some caregivers might understate disability to prevent institutionalization.
- *Patients' characteristics.* The patient's characteristics also influence their caregivers' ratings. Patients' age (the younger they are, the better their caregivers estimate their functional abilities) and educational level (the higher, the better) affect ratings. Independently of their objective functional capacities on performance tests, patients with more intact cognitive abilities, more memory function, or both, may appear to their caregivers as better able to perform functional activities than may actually be the case (Bertrand & Willis, 1999; Loewenstein, Argüelees, et al., 2001).

It must be emphasized that ignoring the patient's self-assessment, especially in the early stages of dementia, may result in failure to identify critical information. Contrary to what was commonly believed, patients' self-reports reflect decline over time, suggesting that they are at least partly aware of the decline in their functional abilities, even if they generally tend to underestimate it (Bertrand & Willis, 1999). It is therefore essential to take the patients' perception of their competence into account for effective disease management to occur. Patient's self-ratings are also important because they may have implications for legal issues, such as decision making and competency assessment.

If only caregivers' reports were taken into account, patients' abilities could be underestimated, and the patients could be deprived of the stimulation generated by an active participation in daily living activities. In some cases rehabilitative strategies, such as implementation of simple household or cognitive interventions (e.g., labeling cabinets, providing a leisure activity, teaching a route) can be sufficient to give the patient an increased level of autonomy (see chap. 9 of this book). To avoid such discrepancies, a more neutral observation, or an external observer who can assess the patients' functional level, could then prove necessary.

Observational Measures

Direct Observation. To get a better picture of the handicap, a direct observation of patients in their natural environment could seem ideal. Unfortunately, this is hardly possible because most people would not accept such an intrusion in their private life and also because the presence of the examiner could influence the patients' performances (however, such an evaluation can easily be carried out if a patient lives in an institution).

An evaluation in the patient's habitual environment also raises several practical and methodological problems: The patient may not be confronted with situations in which he or she would experience trouble because they may just perform simple tasks or routine activities, or they may have been excused from the most difficult chores by caregivers. Identification of the problems in real-life situations may thus waste time. It might also be difficult to clearly see which strategies have been put into place by the patients to cope with their problems. And, finally, proximity of the caregivers may influence the patient's performance.

Diary and Checklist. Another approach could be the use of a diary or a checklist. The principle of the diary is to have the caregiver write in a notebook each problem met by the patient in his or her daily life for a defined period. This can either concern the global functioning of the patient or be limited to some type of activities (e.g., cooking, use of public transportation, hobbies). In the diary, the caregivers freely report their observations. In the checklist, the caregivers have to check the occurring trouble on a list of problems preestablished by the clinician.

In both cases, questions should be added to give a more precise picture of the problems (frequency and circumstances in which difficulties arise, time of day, physical or physiological state of the patient at the moment, etc.). However, it is important that the clinicians' preestablished lists appropriately reflect the problems faced by the patients in their everyday activities.

This approach also has limits. As seen before, the caregivers' reports on the patient's functioning can be highly subjective, but this misestimation of the impairments may be difficult to highlight. In addition, in the diary approach, the caregivers' descriptions strongly depend on their observation skills and accurateness; thus, it is necessary to explain to them what they are expected to do and train them by observing an activity prior to the actual everyday life observation. As for the checklist, it may be difficult to provide the caregivers with an exhaustive list that gives a precise picture of the actual activity. Therefore, it could be useful to compare patients' or caregivers' accounts of the everyday functioning with measures that are more objective, such as performance-based measures.

Simulation Tasks. To approach daily living activities in a more realistic way, other strategies have been developed. Several attempts were made over the past decade to develop ecologically valid, performance-based tests (see chap. 9 of this book), which could also allow objective assessment of the patient's abilities and the degree of autonomy in tasks simulating everyday activities. Such performance-based tests can also offer validation tools against which patient and caregiver ratings can be evaluated. Unfortunately, they often require a much longer administration time than subjective scales, and it can also be argued that an evaluation in the examiner's office is different from an evaluation at home.

To our knowledge, the Direct Assessment of Activities of Daily Living in Alzheimer's Disease (Skurla, Rogers, & Sunderland, 1988) constitutes a first attempt at developing a test that evaluates higher order daily living activities and interprets the performance as the consequence of the impairment of a specific cognitive domain, thus providing cues for management advice.

> Four experimental tasks, simulating ADL, were chosen to provide a direct measure of patients' performance. These tasks had to 1) be common to the daily life of older adults, 2) range from simple to more complex activities, and 3) be easily administered in a clinical setting. Selected categories of tasks that had potential for being problematic for individuals with cognitive impairment were dressing, preparing a meal, purchasing items, and using a telephone. As the chosen tasks were ranked from simple to complex on an a priori basis, the subjects had to successively select and put on clothes for a cold and rainy day; make a cup of instant coffee using an electric hot plate; simulate a purchase from the experimenter (buy both a food snack and appropriately sized winter gloves, using the correct amount of money); and place a telephone call to a drugstore to find out the pharmacy opening hours, using a telephone directory. Verbal, visual, or physical cues were given in case the subjects met difficulties. To establish the performance score, the tasks were subdivided into steps, allowing points to be given according to the degree of completion and assistance needed. The maximum score possible was 152. The time taken for completion was also measured.

A pilot study was conducted with 9 AD patients and 9 healthy elderly matched for sex, age, and educational level (see Table 10.1). In addition to the simulation tasks, a short mental status was administered to the patients (Short Portable Mental Status Questionnaire; Pfeiffer, 1975), and their Clinical Dementia Rating scale score (CDR) was calculated.[1] As expected, AD patients' performance was significantly different from controls'. A moderate relationship was also found between ADL and the CDR, with no association with the global mental status test, therefore stressing the need for separate evaluation of functional and cognitive domains when making patient care decisions. The authors also suggested that, in addition to providing the examiner with a direct observation and a way to verify impairment in ADL tasks, this approach could help to discern the nature of the impairment. For

---

[1]CDR ratings used to be 0 for people with no cognitive impairment, 0.5 for questionable dementia, and 1, 2, and 3, respectively, for mild, moderate, and severe dementia, but recent data suggest that patients with a CDR at 0.5 with memory impairment (0.5 or greater) and at least 3 of the 5 remaining CDR subscores (orientation, judgment and problem solving, community affairs, home and hobbies, and personal care) different from 0 all progress to dementia over a 9.5-year period (Morris et al., 2001).

TABLE 10.1

Example of a Task Analysis for the ADL Situational Test

Telephoning: Calling to Find Out Pharmacy Opening Hours
1. Attempts to use phone book.
2. Uses alphabetical headings to find pharmacies.
3. Selects number from appropriate category.
4. Picks up the receiver before dialing.
5. Holds receiver correctly.
6. Attempts to dial the number.
7. Dials the number correctly.
8. Begins conversation when connection is made.
9. Asks appropriately questions to find out pharmacy opening hours.
10. Reports correct information.
11. Places receiver down correctly.

Two scores are obtained for each ADL task. The performance score is derived from the level of assistance needed to complete each subtask. Performance of each subtask is scored 0 to 4 according to the following code: 4 = *completes subtask independently*, 3 = *requires verbal prompting*, 2 = *requires verbal and visual prompting*, 1 = *requires verbal, visual, and physical prompting*, 0 = *does not complete subtask*. The second score is the time required to complete each ADL task.

Note:. From "Direct Assessment of Activities of Daily Living in Alzheimer's Disease. A Controlled Study," by E. Skurla et al., 1988, Journal of the American Geriatrics Society, 36, 97-103. Copyright 1988 by the Journal of the American Geriatrics Society. Adapted with permission.

example, problems could be interpreted as resulting from immediate memory, sequencing, judgment, or volitional impairments. However, there was no indication as to how such an interpretation could be made with relation to a theoretical framework.

In 1989, Loewenstein et al. developed the Direct Assessment of Functional Status (DAFS; see Table 10.2) to evaluate functional capacities in dementia or suspected dementia.

> The DAFS consists of functional tasks and materials similar or identical to those used in the home environment, involving domains identified as important for functional assessment in the literature. The tested areas concern the skills of time orientation (e.g., telling time from progressively more difficult clock settings, giving the day of the week and month, naming the month and the year), communication (e.g., placing a phone call and mailing a letter), and transportation (e.g., identifying road signs), as well as financial (e.g., identifying currency, counting change, writing a check, and balancing a checkbook), shopping (e.g., selecting grocery items among others and re-

TABLE 10.2

Example of a Subscale of the DAFS

VI. Grooming

Maximum: 14 points

The patient is taken to the bathroom and asked to:

	Correct (2 points)	Incorrect (0 points)
Take cap off toothpaste	______	______
Put toothpaste on a brush	______	______
Turn on water	______	______
Brush teeth	______	______
Dampen wash cloth	______	______
Put soap on cloth	______	______
Clean face	______	______
Turn off water	______	______
Brush hair	______	______
Put on coat	______	______
Button	______	______
Tie	______	______
Zip	______	______

Note: From "A new scale for the assessment of functional status in Alzheimer's disease and related disorders" by D. A. Loewenstein et al. (1989), *Journal of Gerontology: Psychological Sciences,* p. P121. Copyright 1989 by the Gerontological Society of America. Adapted with permission.

membering them 10 min later), grooming/dressing (e.g., brushing teeth and hair, putting on a coat, demonstrating the ability to button, tie, and zip), and eating (e.g., correctly using utensils). One or 2 points are allowed for each item carried out or answered correctly, and a composite functional score (maximum 93 points) is derived from all the subscales, except for the transportation measure, which is used as an optional subscale (because some patients have never driven). The entire assessment takes approximately 30–35 min to administer.

Satisfactory interrater and test-retest performance have been established, and the instrument has shown good concurrent and discriminative validity. The DAFS also discriminates between depression and early dementia because mildly depressed patients, in contrast with early demented patients, do not differ from normal control with regard to functional capacity (Loewenstein et al., 1989). Rankin and Keefover (1998) performed an elaborated statistical treatment of the results with a group of demented patients (n = 107) and nondemented (n = 82) subjects on the DAFS. Their analysis revealed that the DAFS could be modified and shortened because performances on five items of the shopping skills (recall cereal, soup, tuna, and orange juice items; identify eggs) and six items of the financial skills (balance Check 1, make correct change, balance Check 2, write amount, identify dollar bill, count $12.17) best discriminated between demented and nondemented subjects. It could thus be used as a screening tool for dementia in a community-based study, especially because this type of instrument is less biased by education level than cognitive-based screening tests. However, although such an approach evaluates whether a person can perform a task, or what degree of assistance is needed, it does not provide information about the nature of the functional impairment or its underlying mechanisms.

With the aim to evaluate the cognitive processes that affect real-life task performance and to subsequently adapt management strategies, Baum and Edwards (1993) developed the Kitchen Task Assessment (KTA; see Table 10.3).

In this task, the patient has to cook a pudding from a commercial package. The test is scored according to the degree of assistance needed for completion of each of the following steps thought to reflect different cognitive processes: initiation, organization, inclusion of all steps, sequencing, safety, and completion of the task. During the validation procedure, 106 patients with very mild to severe dementia were tested. Some standard neuropsychological tests were also administered (Token Test short version; De Renzi, Pieczuro, & Vignolo, 1968; Trail Making Test; Armitage, 1946; Crossing-Off; Botwinick & Storandt, 1973), and the patients' Clinical Dementia Rating (CDR) and Blessed Dementia Scale (BDS) (Blessed, Tomlinson, & Roth, 1968) were estimated by a multidisciplinary team.

Results showed a relationship between the KTA and CDR, but the variation in observed performances within subjects sharing a similar CDR score indicated that knowledge of the disease's stage was not sufficient to predict a patient' abilities. Significant correlations were also found between the KTA and the neuropsychological measures; they were stronger for the more complex cognitive tests. Among the KTA items, strong correlations were observed between the obtained scores for each step of the task and the total score, suggesting that only one dimension may exist. To explore the internal structure of the variables, a principal component analysis was computed, which resulted in the identification of only one factor accounting for 84% of the variance. Unfortunately, the authors do not provide further interpretation of these results, arguing that the purpose of their study was mainly clinical. However, in a further study, Baum, Edwards, Yonan, and Storandt (1996) nevertheless examined more closely the relationship between classical neuropsychological tests (subtests of the Wechsler Memory Scale; Wechsler & Stone, 1973; subtests of the Wechsler Adult Intelli-

TABLE 10.3
The Kitchen Assessment Task Scoring Procedure

Component	*Independent*	*Required Verbal Cues*	*Required Physical Assistance*	*Not Capable*
Circle the number that corresponds to the level of support the individual required				
Initiation: Did he or she begin the task when asked to begin?	0	1	2	3
Organization: Did he or she gather the necessary items, tools, ingredients, etc. to do the job?	0	1	2	3
Performs all steps: Did he or she do everything that was necessary to complete the task?	0	1	2	3
Sequencing: Did he or she do everything in the order that made sense, given that task?	0	1	2	3
Judgment and safety: Was he or she safe and aware of potential dangers?	0	1	2	3
Completion: Did he or she recognize that the task was finished?	0	1	2	3

Note. From "Cognitive Performance in Senile Dementia of the Alzheimer's Type: The Kitchen Task Assessment," by C. Baum and D. F. Edwards, 1993, *The American Journal of Occupational Therapy, 47,* 431-436. Copyright 1993 by the American Occupational Therapy Association, Inc. Reprinted with permission.

gence Scale; Wechsler, 1955; Benton Visual Retention Test; Benton, 1973; Trailmaking Test part A; Armitage, 1946; Crossing-Off; Botwinick & Storandt, 1973; Boston Naming Test; Goodglass & Kaplan, 1973; and verbal fluency; Thurstone & Thurstone, 1949) and three functional tasks: use of actual objects, simulated activities of daily living, and the kitchen task. They demonstrated a substantial correlation between functional and neuropsychological tests (excepted for well-routinized motor activities) but found no meaningful association between any specific neuropsychological test and a specific functional measure. For the authors, both functional tasks and neuropsychological tests thus appeared to assess the same global cognitive deterioration that characterizes AD.

Other studies were carried out to assess better how impairments in specific cognitive skills can result in difficulties in everyday activity performance. These studies demonstrated that performance on ADL tasks is mainly associated with the neuropsychological domains of executive functions and memory (see, e.g., Nadler, Richardson, Malloy, Marran, & Hostetler-Brinson, 1993, who compared performance-based assessment of both IADL and ADL with the subscores of the Mattis Dementia Rating Scale, DRS; Mattis, 1988). On the basis of these results, they later examined the performance of an abbreviated and a neuropsychological battery—and particularly executive function and memory tests—to predict psychogeriatric patients' scores at performance-based IADL (Richardson, Nadler, & Malloy, 1995). Like Baum et al. (1996), they demonstrated a strong overall correlation between global neuropsychological and IADL performance (excepted for basic ADL, such as personal hygiene). In addition, a particularly significant relation was found between specific neuropsychological tests (the Hooper Visual Organization Test and verbal and visual memory tests) and the different tested ADL domains. The authors thus concluded that the use of specific neuropsychological tests could be helpful in making judgments about dependence in IADL. It has to be noted however that some traditional neuropsychological tests may not be adequate to identify precisely the cognitive processes implied in functional tasks. For example, verbal fluency has frequently been used in the previously mentioned studies to assess executive functioning but can hardly be considered appropriate to tap dimensions of executive functions, such as initiating, planning, organizing, inhibition, or dual-task coordination, particularly involved in ADL. Also, some functional tasks may have been too easy, therefore allowing the patients to perform the task in a routine way with a minimal demand on executive functions. These studies demonstrate the limits of correlational approaches in studying the relationship between neuropsychological deficits and impairment in everyday tasks. Again, an explanation for the paucity of such results could be that studies' design and performance interpretations were rarely based on a cognitive analysis and sound theoretical background.

Several assessment instruments or studies were developed with the aim to explore more specific areas of cognition functioning in daily living situations. Among them, the Rivermead Behavioural Memory Test (RBMT; Wilson, Cockburn, & Baddeley, 1985) was created to detect and evaluate everyday memory problems. Subtests of this battery specifically assess abilities to remember data or things to do (prospective memory) necessary to daily life mnemonic functioning: remembering a name or an appointment, recognizing pictures and faces, remembering to ask for a hidden belonging, following a route, and taking and delivering a message. In the validation procedure, a sample of healthy elderly was added to the original set of subjects because it was thought that memory problems—in particular, those related to autonomy in everyday life—were a common concern of elderly people and their caregivers. The RBMT can therefore be useful in an ecological diagnostic procedure because it helps to identify patients presenting with memory problems in daily life situations. It can also help assess the effect of rehabilitative intervention. However, although it can help orientate an intervention, it does not provide cues about the defective processes that should be restored: Results of different subtests only provide limited information and definitely can not explore in a satisfactory way the variables that can influence the performances in prospective memory, topographical orientation, and face or name recognition. Most certainly, the development of theoretically based—but still ecologically valid—evaluation tools would be needed to formulate a hypothesis about the defective processes.

Simulation tasks have also been used to explore other specific domains of everyday activities in demented patients. For example, Marson et al. (2000) developed a prototype psychometric financial capacity instrument (FCI) using 14 tasks of financial abilities (for a detailed description, see chap. 9 of this book).

Because of the limitations of subjective scales of daily living activities and questionnaires, performance-based measures are necessary, even though not sufficient, to give a more precise and objective picture of patients' everyday functioning. If several studies, as those mentioned previously, have opened new perspectives for functional assessment, their limits also stress the need for a more thorough reflection about the organization of action in everyday tasks, aspect which will be discussed in the following section.

TOWARD A NEUROPSYCHOLOGY OF DAILY LIVING ACTIVITIES

Most of the functional scales and performance-based tasks described previously were first developed as diagnostic tools, and they aimed to identify impairment in daily living activities. However, they evidence impairment without establishing its cause, they only provide limited information about the variables that can influence the performances, and they do not help in understanding the underlying processes responsible for the impairment. Therefore, they will not help establish theoretically based and adapted strategies for rehabilitation. To elaborate precise hypotheses about involved defective processes, it is necessary to develop examination tools that are based on theoretical models. In addition, simulation tasks must be as close as possible to daily situations and daily living activities to provide an appropriate prediction of action disorganization occurring at home or in social or work settings. The variables that may be part of the performance and their role have to be identified and specifically tested (e.g., planning abilities and executive functions, apraxia, working memory, episodic memory, semantic memory, memory for actions) with regard to a model of normal functioning. In other words, a cognitive neuropsychology of daily living activities is needed to provide patients with both accurate clinical assessment and adapted rehabilitative programs. Systematical studies started to focus on daily living activities impairment only recently, despite the impact of this impairment on patients' lives,

Despite a long history, and an accumulation of a large amount of empirical data, neuropsychological investigations of the action system were in most cases focused on the study of limb apraxia in a clinical-anatomical perspective. This led to much ambiguity at the conceptual level, as well as to inconsistencies in the terminology and classification (e.g., the confusion related to the terms ideomotor and ideational apraxia; see Tate, & McDonald, 1995). In AD, it was long believed that apraxia follows a homogeneous pattern of deterioration, from constructional apraxia at the earliest stages to ideomotor apraxia at the mild to moderate stages, and eventually to ideational apraxia at the most severe stages of the disease (de Ajuriaguerra, Richard, Rodriguez, & Tissot, 1966). However, several studies in the mid 1980s demonstrated the extreme heterogeneity of praxis disorders in AD (e.g., some patients present deficits at the early stages, whereas others do not until much later). Deficits in everyday activities may also be due to many different causes: impairment within the semantic system, gestural lexicon, working memory, and so on (see Roy, Black, Blair, & Dimeck, 1998). Moreover, research suggest that—as is the case for visual information—different subsystems may be implied in object-related actions, which depend on the intended type of action—for example, localization, identification, manipulation, or reaching (Jeannerod, & Decéty, 1994; Riddoch, Edwards, Humphreys, West, & Heafield, 1998). But most assessment tools hardly allow a comprehensive examination of gestural deficits, which in fact may prove to be very complex. As mentioned by Cooper and Shallice (2000), action control can be impaired in many different ways, such as grasping reflexes, anarchic hand syndrome, utilization behavior (in which a patient takes and uses objects that are obviously not appropriate to the current tasks), ideational apraxia, stereotyped behavior, and bradykinesia. This list is not exhaustive, and the relationship between some of these deficits, such as between ideational apraxia and Action Disorganization Syndrome (ADS), is far from being clear. Nevertheless, these disturbances raise problems that any model of action control should address. A better understanding of the level impairment and the nature of preserved abilities is also a prerequisite for the development of optimization strategies that will enhance the patients' autonomy.

Three Levels of Action

Human action organization can be analyzed at different levels. To clarify the situation, Cooper and Shallice (2000) suggested a categorization between low, high, and intermediate levels of action. At the lowest level, the carrying out of an action is routine, overlearned, and depends on the biomechanical bases of both the movements and the physical properties of the target. It has been suggested that such action is controlled by motor response schemas (Schmidt, 1975), which provide the spatiotemporal programs for simple functional movement sequences to motor systems; they are elaborated after abstraction of the relationship between similar movements, motor and sensory responses, and actions results. For some authors, these schemas are the subcomponents (sensorimotor mappings or gesture engrams) of larger skills (see Arbib, 1985; Jeannerod, Arbib, Rizzolatti, & Sakata, 1995; Schwartz & Buxbaum, 1997). For example, taking a glass of water means reaching, anticipating the shape, encompassing the glass, turning the forearm, selecting the number of fingers, and all of these may potentially be triggered from the object's affordances (name, size, or feel). At this level, individual subcomponents of action must be carried out in a precise manner, at specified moments, and must be strictly coordinated (no other action can take place in the meantime). They also strongly depend on both the surroundings and the effector system's physical characteristics and are usually performed automatically, with little attentional control.

The highest level can concern the organization of either well-learned activities, such as going to a restaurant or to the doctor, or of nonroutine or novel activities. These activities require greater attentional and executive resources (particularly problem solving, goal setting, and organization skills). Different concepts were developed to account for the organization of such activities: scripts (Schank & Abelson, 1977), memory organization packets (MOPs; Schank, 1982), or context-free managerial knowledge units (Grafman, 1995). According to Sirigu et al. (1995, 1996), a distinction should be made between a semantic component, which specifies the actions needed to achieve a goal, and a syntactic component, which specifies the temporal relations between these actions. At this level of action, and contrary to the lowest level of action, the different components of the global action can take place at different moments, they are not constrained to a precise order, and they can be separated by unconnected actions (e.g., purchasing a newspaper on the way to the doctor). Physical characteristics of the environment and the effector system are of no relevance here.

Between these two extremes, there is a full range of activities that involve sequences of movements that are well established through practice and that serve commonplace goals, such as preparing breakfast, brushing teeth, starting a car, dressing up, and so forth.

These skilled activities have been termed naturalistic action by Schwartz and Buxbaum (1997). Depending on their degree of familiarity, they require more or less attentional monitoring and problem-solving skills. In these situations, parallel execution of unconnected subactions is rare (though possible), and it seems probable that the different steps (subactions) of a goal (e.g., the subaction pouring water in a coffee cup as part of the goal preparing a cup of instant coffee) are represented as separated units at a cognitive level. From this point of view, the organization of these activities is very similar to the scripts or MOPs. But, as in reaching for a glass, both the timing of the subactions and the local characteristics of the environment must be taken into account but on a grosser grain (e.g., objects must be reachable, and things must be carried out before the environment changes much). Interruptions, though possible, can lead to a disorganization of the action and are thus not advised. For example, while preparing a cup of instant coffee, although one can delay or do something else between putting the coffee powder in the cup, pouring the water, and adding sugar or milk, it is generally not advisable.

This intermediate level has enough specificity to be considered as different from the others. In contrast to the inferior level, action at the intermediate level is not strictly dependant on the physical characteristics of the environment and the effector system and on the objects' affordances. Therefore, selection of which subaction is to be carried out may be subject to voluntary control, and this selection is crucial for a good execution of the action. In contrast to the highest level, all the subcomponents must be linked correctly over time in a rather short period and are usually nested under a single, higher level goal.

Thus, activities at the intermediate level of action require both an access to the component actions of a schema and a correct sequencing of these actions. Therefore, they depend on the implementation of multiple cognitive processes: retrieval processes from semantic memory about the objects' or actions' perceptual and functional properties, attention and working memory (to monitor which steps of the larger goal have been carried out, and which remain to be completed and to prevent repetition of action), and executive functions for the planning abilities, organization of the steps within the action, and problem-solving skills (Humphreys, Forde, & Riddoch, 2000).

In the following section, we will focus on the exploration of this level of action because it is closely related to the execution of most activities in everyday life, both ADL and IADL.

Lapses and Errors at the Intermediate Level of Action. The intermediate level of action is so complex that there is hardly any research on this subject in experimental psychology. However, there is evidence that the type of errors that occur at the intermediate level is specific, both in normal subjects and in brain-lesioned patients. Lapses in action are frequent in daily life. Reason published several diary studies (1979, 1984, 1990), in which healthy volunteers had to note all of their slips of actions in well-established, routine activities of everyday life, over a period of a few weeks. Participants reported on average almost one slip of action a day and mentioned misperceptions (spreading shaving foam instead of toothpaste on a toothbrush), insertions (switching on the light while entering a room in the middle of the day), omissions (forgetting to put tea into a teapot before adding water and noticing it only when seeing the color of the liquid). Reason suggested that slips of action occur primarily in highly practiced, overlearned routines that are completed automatically and only monitored intermittently at critical points in the sequence. As the errors described by normal subjects were quite systematic, Reason attempted to develop an error classification, which appears to be particularly relevant to the intermediate level of action control (1979, 1984, 1990; see also Norman, 1981):

> *Omission:* A step or a subaction is forgotten within an action sequence, with no intention to omit this step or subtask (e.g., not undressing before getting into the shower or forgetting to put tea in the teapot before pouring water).
>
> *Anticipation:* This occurs when a subtask is carried out earlier than it's supposed to within an action sequence (e.g., wrapping a gift box without placing the gift inside).
>
> *Perseveration:* This is the unintentional repetition of a step or a subtask (e.g., adding sugar for the second time in a cup of coffee).
>
> *Object substitution:* An intended action is carried out with a wrong object (e.g., place shaving foam instead of toothpaste on the toothbrush).
>
> *Capture:* This is the substitution of an intended action against a nonintended one due to unintended triggering of strong habit schemas by environmental cues (e.g., putting on fishing boots when entering the garage instead of getting a shovel).

These categories are neither totally separated nor definitive, and it can be difficult to use them to classify some action sequences (in particular, it can be difficult to classify an error as an omission or an anticipation; an anticipative error could be analyzed as the omission of a preceding step or subtask). Nevertheless, as errors from each category occur in the normal functioning of unimpaired action selection systems, any modelization attempt of the intermediate level of action should be able to account for these errors.

The Action Disorganization Syndrome (ADS)

The analysis of brain-lesioned patients' performances in daily living activities can be of both clinical and theoretical relevance; a better understanding of the mechanisms that underlie the occurrence of action errors can open prospects to rehabilitative interventions, and the consequences of brain lesions on daily life's activities can help to specify the networks involved in action realization.

So far, disorders of skilled action control have mostly been described in patients with severe closed head injury (CHI), who often demonstrate action control problems in previously learned everyday tasks. These problems may appear as an exaggerated form (both in quality and in quantity) of the lapses committed by the normal subjects and have mostly been interpreted as aftereffects of prefrontal or underlying white-matter lesions, which are frequent in CHI. For example, a formerly autonomous patient may experience problems in shopping (forgetting items to buy) or cooking (starting a meal too early or too late; overcooking a roast). These tasks depend on the activation and serial organization of numerous subgoals and, because the complete execution of a task may take time, on the maintenance of the goal and on resistance to interferences.

In the past, these disorders in everyday action have been studied and interpreted within the frame of apraxia (see, e.g., what Luria termed frontal apraxia, 1966). More recent accounts rather refer to contemporary theories of the frontal lobes, for which a system of attentional control (located within the frontal structures) plays a key role in action planning and organization, working memory, and inhibition abilities. It thus seems plausible to attribute CHI patients' difficulties in complex daily living activities to an impairment of this attentional control system (or executive functions). But how could such an impairment account for dysfunctional abilities in more simple tasks, such as brushing one's teeth or preparing a cup of coffee, which have been observed in several clinical observations (Buxbaum, Schwartz, Branch Coslett, & Carew, 1995; Schwartz et al., 1995)? Frontal lobe theories cannot explain such a sensitivity to errors. The previously mentioned activities are considered as routines, which benefit from procedural memory and thus minimize the need for deliberate planning and attentional resources. Because these activities are mostly short and triggered by context, they should also be less dependant on working memory for the maintenance of goal representations. However, the automaticity of these routine tasks can be questioned. As seen previously, normal subjects are also prone to errors in these simple tasks. This suggests a contribution, though minimal, of executive functions and their control resources. An obvious way to evaluate this hypothesis is to test patients with focal frontal lobe lesions. But so far, almost no study of daily living activities impairment has been conducted in patients with lesions strictly limited to the frontal lobes. A specific evaluation of a patient with left frontal damage (Humphreys & Forde, 1998) showed that he did not make many errors on simulation of daily living tasks, suggesting that frontal lobe damage is not sufficient to cause significant problems on everyday activities. Hence, it seems highly probable that the patients with frontal lesions described by Luria (1966) or by Schwartz et al. (Schwartz et al., 1995; Schwartz, Reed, Montgomery, Palmer, & Mayer, 1991), who showed impairments of everyday activities, suffered from more extensive lesions.

Errors in clinical tests of simple daily living activities are also a defining characteristic of ideational apraxia, which is usually associated to lesions of the left inferior parietal lobule (De Renzi & Lucchelli, 1988; Poeck & Lehmkühl, 1980). It is thus intriguing to understand how ideational apraxia can be linked to the difficulties demonstrated by "frontal" patients. Schwartz et al. (1991), based on the interpretation of a case study, suggested that deficits in activities of daily living result from a faulty activation of high-level schemas (goals) toward lower-level schemas (actions). The observation of a second case (Schwartz et al., 1995) led the authors to postulate a possible defect in the action routines that are determined by the objects' affordances. This interpretation is similar to the ones developed by De Renzi and Lucchelli (1988), Ochipa, Gonzalez Rothi, and Heilman (1989), and Schwartz and Buxbaum (1997). For these authors, defects in the knowledge of objects' or tools' properties (what has been termed ideational apraxia) is bound to a defect in action execution. It is nevertheless unclear what type of knowledge is necessary for accurate tool use in naturalistic action. For Roy and Square (1994), access to semantic knowledge about the objects or tools is essential, whereas Riddoch and Humphreys (1987) suggest that representation of the structural description for objects or tools is sufficient to activate an appropriate gesture schema. For Ochipa et al. (1989), two systems of tool or object knowledge are necessary for a correct execution of everyday actions. One system specifies the function (how) and the other specifies the lexical and perceptual associations of the objects or tools (what).

Numerous questions have thus been raised, but there have been relatively few theoretical accounts that aim to explain how the frontal lobe or the conceptual system might be involved in controlling everyday behavior and what the nature of the control processes might be. The most significant of these attempts will be described in the following section.

Empirical Studies of Naturalistic Action. Over the past decade, a few studies have explored ADS in patients (Buxbaum, Schwartz, & Montgomery, 1998; Humphreys & Forde, 1998; Schwartz et al., 1991; Schwartz et al., 1995, 1998, 1999) with the goal to understand how the pattern or type of action errors produced in everyday actions relate to the patients' neuropsychological deficits.

In their first study, Schwartz et al. (1991) extensively studied a patient (referred to as HH) with a bilateral frontal lesion due to a pericallosal artery aneurysm's rupture. Researchers observed HH while he prepared coffee on his breakfast tray and while he brushed his teeth during his morning wash. His performance was videotaped to allow a detailed scoring of his errors (e.g., object substitution, sequencing errors, omissions) and the authors developed a specific coding system to systematically describe and quantify his ability to carry out these everyday tasks.

> This coding system is based on an event hierarchy from the bottom up. The tasks are first divided into minimal units of action called A-1 steps, which are defined as the "smallest component of a behavioural sequence that achieves a concrete, functional result or transformation, describable as the movement of an object from one place to another or as a change in the state of an object." The A-1s are then grouped together into larger units, A-2s, that realize task subgoals or subroutines (according to the norms for a given task, the subject's habits, and the environment affordances). Crux actions are also defined as the basic operations that are invariably essential to the completion of a subgoal. Having described the patient's performance at the A-1 and A-2 levels, the authors obtain a detailed, quantitative measure of disorganization and impairment, which takes into account the action errors (such as those described by Reason, 1979), the crux actions omissions, the proportion of independent A-1s (i.e., those that did not lead to the accomplishment of a task subgoal), and the serial order of A-2s.

This coding system proved useful not only in describing the patient's performance but also in monitoring its improvement. For example, the number of independent A-1s gradually decreased over time from 80% to 20% of HH's actions. At this level of the basic operations, HH demonstrated problems that were consistent with frontal apraxia, that is, errors consistent with faulty sequential organization (omissions, anticipations, and perseverations) and errors triggered by external stimuli. For example, HH might spoon butter or oatmeal into his coffee or pour coffee grinds into his orange juice. With regard to the errors of place, object substitutions or objects misuse, where the action was appropriate but one of its arguments was incorrectly filled, virtually everything on the breakfast tray was subject to misuse. HH committed object, tool, and action or gesture substitution errors, such as using the wrong utensils to eat and stir, while displaying no evidence of agnosia.

To account for these deficits, Schwartz et al. (1991) drew on theories of skilled action, which postulate ensembles of schemas arranged in a hierarchical control structure as described by Norman and Shallice (1986). Norman and Shallice (1986) suggested a hierarchical framework to explain how both routine and nonroutine actions operate: Most everyday actions are done in a routine way, for which lower-level action schemas are stored. These schemas provide the motor system with the spatiotemporal programs for simple movement sequences. They can either be activated above their threshold by triggering stimuli from the environment or by the activation from a higher level schema, which serves a more general goal. When a conflict arises between several routines activated at the same time, it is managed by a contention-scheduling mechanism, which automatically allows the activation of the relevant action schemas and the inhibition of the irrelevant ones. This system thus requires little attentional control. On an other hand, a supervisory attentional system (SAS) is responsible for translating goals and intentions into actions (here, larger action units are represented within higher level schemas). The SAS can directly activate or inhibit activation from the lower level, arrange the low-level schemas into temporal sequences, monitor the behavior when errors occur, and thus prevent behavior from being solely driven by the environment. It allows behavioral planning and organization, especially in novel or potentially dangerous situations, and can be considered as mainly executive. According to Baddeley (1986), the SAS corresponds to the central executive component in his model of working memory.

Skilled actions thus depend on preexisting connections that support the activation of low-level schemas by the high-level schemas and are carried out in an automatic mode of control once the schemas at the highest levels are activated (which corresponds to the contention-scheduling mode of action control). In HH's case, Schwartz et al. (1991) postulated a loss of top-down control in frontal apraxia, thus preventing high-level schemas to pass information or activation values reliably to the low-level schemas and resulting in a variety of errors. But this hypothesis addresses neither the question of the etiology of the top-down activation difficulties (general executive resources or routine action planning processes) nor the potential role of defective bottom-up activation (which may be due to impaired perceptual or semantic processing).

In a subsequent study, Schwartz et al. (1995) described another patient, referred to as JK, who developed severe ADS after a closed head injury. Just as for HH, JK's routine task performances were carefully described and analyzed, but he was also administered a detailed neuropsychological battery, which assessed the status of his visual processing and semantic knowledge. This assessment revealed an amazing preservation of visual processing and semantic knowledge of functional attributes and also defective results on some semantic tests and on gesture production, even when the patient was given the necessary object (implement) for the action. Because these defects led to a disruption of the automatic online access to low-level schemas (faulty activation of the movement engrams by the visual and tactual cues afforded by the implement), it was hypothesized that this disruption could play a significant role in the action planning. Nevertheless, this alone could not account for the severity of JK's everyday-action disorder because the literature confirms the preservation of routine action production in patients with more severe gestural and semantic deficits. It was therefore assumed that the supervisory attentional system, which supports action planning when automaticity fails, was also deficient. On the other hand, an isolated disorder of the supervisory attentional system also would not be sufficient to cause frontal apraxia because patients with dysexecutive syndrome or focal frontal lesions are able to perform simple, overlearned tasks appropriately.

These observations led Schwartz et al. (1995) to develop their unified hypothesis. It postulates that ADS results from a combination of two impairments: a disruption of routine action planning (the fast, automatic retrieval of information from semantic or gestural memory stores, or both, relevant to action planning) and a reduction of the SAS and working memory resources.

Isolated action disorders (such as ideomotor or ideational apraxia) are not sufficient to cause ADS because it can be compensated by executive functions. As long as executive functions are unimpaired, this recourse to a controlled mode of action will not have any effect on everyday activities. Defective executive control is also not sufficient because it leaves routine activities, which are usually automated, intact. But if an impairment also affects action production schemas, this will lead to a nonautomated mode of execution and thus aggravate the consequences of the dysexecutive syndrome on daily living functioning. The severity of the defects will then vary according to the demands of the task and the degree to which it was automated.

Because both a defective executive control and an impairment in the action production schemas must be present to cause ADS, the neurological conditions that predispose one to such a disorder are those that produce widespread or multifocal damage, involving both anterior and posterior cortices, as in closed head injuries or AD.

However, in their most recent studies, Schwartz and her collaborators significantly modified their point and largely confuted their initial unified hypothesis, as stated (Buxbaum, Schwartz, & Montgomery, 1998; Schwartz et al., 1999; Schwartz et al., 1998). In these studies of ADS, Schwartz's group focused on the exploration of deficits in a larger group of patients suffering from CHI (Schwartz et al., 1998) or from right or left cerebrovascular accidents (Buxbaum et al., 1998; Schwartz et al., 1999). To assess systematically familiar naturalistic action performance, Schwartz et al. (1998) used the Multi-Level Action Test (MLAT; Buxbaum, Schwartz, & Carew, 1997).

> The MLAT is built on three primary tasks: making toast with butter and jam, wrapping a present, and packing a lunchbox. These tasks are performed under four conditions that manipulate the presence of distractor objects and the number of tasks to be performed (solo vs. Dual conditions), with the aim of eliciting certain types of errors (e.g. substitutions) in patients vulnerable to them: 1) solo-basic: all and only the materials needed are presented in the array; 2) solo-distractors: functionally related (and, frequently, visually similar) distractors items are also presented; 3) dual-basic: the participant performs one primary task and another, secondary task in any order (e.g., preparing a toast and wrapping a present); and 4) dual-search: some of the target items and a variety of distractor objects are presented in a closed drawer.

The MLAT can thus be administered under various environmental conditions with increasing levels of difficulty. In a study of 30 CHI patients and 18 control subjects, Schwartz et al. (1998) demonstrated that patients obtained lower scores and committed more errors in all conditions, including in the completion of single tasks with no distractors, but in particular in dual-task conditions. Analysis of errors demonstrated that CHI patients committed more omission errors than control subjects but that otherwise their pattern of errors was very similar to that of control subjects. It must be noted that the presence of distractors among the object array did not cause a decline in the performances.

Subjects who performed within the normal range on the MLAT were also asked to perform the same tasks under a more demanding condition so that the effects of increasing attentional demands on naturalistic action could be observed. This test condition was modeled after Shallice and Burgess's Six Elements Test (1991): The subjects had to complete six tasks while following a number of rules imposed by the examiner (the three different tasks each consisted of two parts and had to be carried out in a fixed period of time, but the subject was not allowed to do the two subtasks of the same type one after the other). Under this condition, the CHI patients, who so far had performances within the range of normal controls, made significantly more errors but still had a pattern of errors that was strikingly similar to the control group's. On the whole, this finding showed that, depending on the environmental context, even mildly impaired CHI patients would commit action errors.

The same tasks were administered to patients with left cerebrovascular lesions (Buxbaum, Schwartz, & Montgomery, 1998). As a group, patients with left hemispheric lesions (LHL) were not more prone to errors than CHI patients or patients with right hemispheric lesions (RHL) and presented a similar error profile. Buxbaum et al. (1998) also compared the performances of a patient with a severe ideational apraxia with those of two patients with RHL. Not only did the apraxic patient have normal performances in executive functions and working memory, but also there was an important similitude in the errors committed by all three patients. Hence, LHL are not responsible for specific disturbances in complex everyday actions (however, it must be pointed out that RHL and LHL patients were only classified according to the side of their lesions, not by lobar localization).

Schwartz et al. (1999) also tested a group of patients with RHL on the MLAT and compared them to normal controls. Although they showed a similar profile of errors, patients with RHL committed significantly more errors than both control subjects and the CHI patients tested in the 1998 study. It was thus hypothesized that a reduction of attentional resources, in which the right hemisphere may play an important role, could explain these results.

Based on these observations, Schwartz et al. (1999) rejected previous theories of naturalistic action, which postulated a hierarchical framework to account for action control (Norman & Shallice, 1986; Schwartz et al.,

1991) as well as their own previously developed unified hypothesis (Schwartz et al., 1995). Their line of argument can be summarized as:

1. Theories of frontal lobe systems (Norman & Shallice, 1986) were inappropriate to account for the results mentioned previously: The impairment of top-down (volitional) activation should lead to an increase of sensitivity to bottom-up interferences (automatically triggered by the environment), and a greater number of errors should occur under conditions where distractors are present (because action schemas would be activated in parallel by perceptual stimuli and compete for selection), but this was not the case. The patients did not demonstrate a higher rate of errors when they performed the MLAT tasks in the presence of distractor objects (Schwartz et al., 1998, 1999).
2. The SAS hypothesis failed to explain the high rate of errors committed by the patients under the most simple condition.
3. The working memory hypothesis was not supported. Deficits in working memory are supposed to cause difficulties in sustained activation of a goal schema, and thus patients' performances should be worse if environmental cues are not present to trigger the appropriate behavior. But results showed no difference in error pattern with the presence of environmental cues.

To provide an alternative explanation to their findings, the authors suggested that the observed impairment could best be explained by a limitation in attentional resources: Normal subjects commit errors if they do not allocate enough attention to the task realization, and patients have less attentional resources to devote to the planning, execution, and monitoring of the tasks, especially under more demanding conditions, and thus commit more errors.

Thus, limitation in resources could explain the positive relationship between the increase in attentional demands and the rise in omission errors. It can also lead to an inability to solve the competition for schema activation and thus cause failure to activate the appropriate schema above threshold.

To summarize, Schwartz et al. (1991, 1995) first suggested that action disorganization resulted from a loss of automaticity in the execution of action schemas, which had to be compensated by executive functions (scripts, semantics). If executive functions were also impaired, this would lead to a defective compensation and to the occurrence of difficulties in everyday activities. However, on the basis of their most recent studies, the authors (Buxbaum et al., 1998; Schwartz et al., 1998, 1999) now hypothesize that a reduction in attentional resources could lead to omissions (because the activating schemas were not sufficiently activated). This reduction could also explain why no specific error patterns were found in patients when compared with normal subjects and why normal subjects would also commit errors under certain conditions.

Humphreys and Forde (1998) also attempted to assess factors that could contribute to ADS, especially those related to frontal lobe lesions. They examined the performances of normal subjects and 4 neurological patients on a range of everyday tasks, on long-term memory for action knowledge, on general sequencing abilities, and on performance of novel or nonroutine tasks. Two of the patients presented marked ADS, and two others were matched for deficits within those domains of cognitive abilities that are thought to be necessary for successful performance in everyday tasks (working and episodic memory, as well as inhibition of overlearned responses to stimuli by the Stroop test). One of the matched control patients was amnesic after carbon monoxide poisoning, and the other presented left frontal damage. Neither of these two made many errors in the routine tasks, indicating that neither frontal lobe damage nor severe long-term memory impairment are sufficient to cause significant problems on everyday tasks. On the contrary, ADS patients were selectively impaired in carrying out everyday activities, such as making toast, wrapping a gift, and posting a letter and tended to make the same kind of errors as other ADS patients (e.g., Schwartz et al., 1995). They were also poor at describing how a particular task should be carried out or at ordering the actions within a task with the subactions written on labels. These data thus suggested that ADS was due to a faulty activation of learned action schemas, rather than impaired episodic memory or executive functions. Part of this study demonstrated, nevertheless, that the latter are involved in nonroutine actions, as stated by Norman and Shallice (1986). Comparison with the frontal control patient showed that damage limited to the frontal lobe (and to the SAS) did not produce a large number of errors in everyday activities; problems only occurred when semantic distractors were present. This may reflect a competition in selection of action between objects that could each be used for the task. Still, if not sufficient, damage to the SAS may be necessary for ADS to occur. Resuming Schwartz et al.'s unified hypothesis (1995), Humphreys and Forde suggested that the combination of SAS and routine action schemas' impairments could result in disturbances in routine actions. Nevertheless, these authors also suggested that dysexecutive problems could be split as dissociations were observed in the ADS patients' pattern of performances. These differences could reflect impairments in at least two different processes involved in the maintenance of appropriate temporal order for sequential actions: a process of automatic rebound inhibition once a subaction has been performed (thus hindering the repetition of this action) and an active process of error monitoring. Moreover, impaired action schemas may partly be compensated for by bottom-up triggering from the properties of the objects or from the environmental conditions of the task.

Everyday Tasks and AD

Though functional impairment and everyday action disorders are frequent in AD, they have so far rarely been approached from a cognitive point of view. Yet, AD is most often characterized by lesions in the posterior cortical areas (considered as essential for action schema selection because lesions in these areas often cause apraxia) and by an early disconnection between associative cortical areas, particularly between frontal and posterior associative areas, thus causing impairment of executive functioning (see chap. 3 of this book). In light of what has been discussed previously, all conditions are thus met to cause ADS. It is therefore astonishing that this has not been more frequently evoked in the neuropsychological literature on AD, especially because deficits in episodic and semantic memory and agnosia (which are frequent in AD) can also contribute to difficulties in ADL.

There are probably several reasons for this neglect. First, classical dementia assessments and commonly used neuropsychological tests cannot predict functional handicap, and examination settings hardly allow a good evaluation of daily living activities (e.g., through simulation tasks). Second, some deficits may not be obvious; even though ADL can no longer be performed in an automatic mode, they can be carried out by the intermediate of controlled processes (which depend on executive functions). However, because a dysexecutive syndrome commonly appears early in dementia, some typical errors in ADL performances should occur (see Schwartz et al., 1998). Third, AD patients may use different types of information to compensate for specific actions schema selection defects. For example, contextual cues, such as sight or touch of objects in real life, can provide information relevant to actions' spatiotemporal programs, thus compensating for the loss of action schemas (Riddoch et al., 1998; Riddoch, Humphreys, & Edwards, 2000).

Moreover, it has been demonstrated that AD patients have much better performances when they have to recall a motoric (rather than verbal or visual) information or to perform an action themselves (Bird & Luszcz, 1993; Dick, 1992; Dick, Kean, & Sands, 1989). Action memory may also benefit from the hierarchical and logical nature of action sequences, which provide a structure for organizing recall of actions to achieve a goal (Mandler, 1984). In other words, it may be that deficits in ADL at the early stages may not be evident because of a redundancy between neural systems responsible for the selection of action schemas necessary to completion of everyday tasks, which can partly compensate for each other. It would thus prove particularly interesting to study the presence of ADL impairment at different stages of the disease and to identify the nature of the impairment. However, and rather surprisingly, most reports of AD patients who failed to perform routine activities remained at a very general level of observation or were anecdotal, and most of them concerned patients who were already at mild to severe stages of the disease.

Rusted, Ratner, and Sheppard (1995) examined the performances of an AD patient at preparing a cup of tea at home (one of the few daily living activities he was still able to perform independently) over a 2-year period.

> The patient's tea-making routine, which involved 26 actions divided into three subgoals, was analyzed. The patient was tested under three conditions: 1) he had to make a cup of tea as he normally did (patient enactment); 2) he had to give very detailed instructions so as to help the experimenter—who is observed by the patient—to make a cup of tea (patient-guided enactment); and 3) he had to recall his method of making tea with as much detail as possible (verbal recall). Rusted et al. (1995) found that verbal recall was significantly lower than patient or patient-guided enactment of the task, throughout the follow-up. Interestingly, verbal recall scores correlated significantly with MMSE scores, whereas performance scores did not. However, no relationship was found between the type of committed errors and the global performance or the MMSE scores, and the errors also differed from those committed by healthy elderly persons. Moreover, at the early stages, the patient was able to complete the task and perform almost all of the actions, even though the maximal length of correct consecutive sequences within a subgoal rapidly decreased. As the disease progressed to the moderate to severe stages, omission errors increased, and the first significant difficulty was a selective loss of the initial subgoal, which suggested a hierarchical organization of activity memory and a highly systematic breakdown in retrieval. Moreover, the equivalence of the patient and patient-guided enactment suggested that, at least for this patient, contextual cues and observation of observable outcomes were more important determinants of accurate recall than actual activation of motor programs.

This preliminary work remains largely anecdotal, especially because the results from the cognitive test (MMSE) are not very informative. An evaluation procedure designed to assess the various cognitive functions potentially underlying the tea preparation (such as working memory, gestural and planning abilities, script knowledge of the tea-making procedure, etc.) would have been much more useful because it could have helped to identify which components are essential to keep a relative autonomy in the task execution. However, it raises interesting questions, especially with regard to the understanding of the processes behind the functional consequences of cognitive decline. Single case studies are necessary to understand the heterogeneity of performances in AD patients; however, these studies should be based on a detailed neuropsychological assessment.

Another interesting analysis of dressing performance has been carried out by Feyereisen, Gendron, and Seron (1999) in 25 patients suffering from moderate to severe AD. Performance was assessed by means of the Action Coding System of Schwartz et al. (1991, 1995), which analyzes complex activities of consecutive sequences, and a modified version of Optimage.

Optimage is a qualitative tool based on behavioral observation that assesses autonomy in four activities and encourages the emergence of potential abilities with different levels of prompts (Gendron & Lévesque, 1993). The study confirmed the frequency of dressing impairment in dementia, which correlated with severity as assessed by the Global Deterioration Scale (GDS) (Reisberg, Ferris, de Leon, & Crook, 1982) and the MMSE. However, it also observed exceptions to this rule. Some severely demented patients were still able to dress alone, and moderately demented patients were having unexpected difficulties. The authors also carried out a qualitative analysis of the problems to identify mechanisms underlying the deficit. Unsatisfactory executions and incorrect choices were the most common errors when performance was only mildly impaired, whereas passivity, scattered gestures, and irrelevant verbalizations were frequent in the more severely impaired subjects. However, no clear pattern of association emerged, and the same kind of failure (e.g., omission) could be observed in patients with different cognitive symptoms. The authors argued that a thorough analysis of errors together with a more appropriate neuropsychological examination are needed to support Schwartz's hypothesis (1991, 1995) that impairments in everyday actions result from a combination of multiple separate deficits. They also suggested that other factors, such as context and the caregiver's social behavior (e.g., frequency of smiles, relaxed attitude), should be taken into account because they may influence the patients' performances.

Buxbaum et al. (1997) also published two detailed case studies of naturalistic action in demented patients. One patient suffered from semantic dementia (referred to as DM); the other one from AD (referred to as HB). The authors particularly investigated the relationship between semantic knowledge and naturalistic action. The MLAT (Buxbaum et al., 1997) was administered to both patients. Despite a degradation of semantic knowledge demonstrated by different neuropsychological tests, DM's performance on the MLAT did not reflect the significant semantic knowledge impairment he showed on neuropsychological testing, and he appropriately used objects and tools within the context of action. In contrast, HB performed quite well on semantic and praxis tests but presented a significant impairment on executive functioning. On the MLAT, his performance was significantly impaired, and he committed many errors (sequence, omission, action addition, semantic substitution, object misuse), even under the simpler MLAT conditions, and his pattern of errors was similar to that of the patient HH's mentioned previously (Schwartz et al., 1991).

Executive function thus appears to be essential for error-free action, and a seemingly preserved semantic network is not sufficient to guide an action to an effective and efficient completion of the task. On the other hand, a defective activation of the semantic network seems to be compensated by a bottom-up activation of action schemas triggered by contextual cues and, particularly, sensorimotor information received from the manipulation of tools and objects. It is also probable that a top-down activation from the goals (parent schemas) represented at the highest level can play a role in this compensatory process.

Further evidence for the role of executive function in naturalistic action impairment in AD is provided by a study led by our group with a small group of patients (Juillerat, Peigneux, Van Hoecke, Lekeu, & Van der Linden, 1999). We examined the performances of 12 patients suffering from mild to moderate AD and matched controls in sequential and complex daily living activities requiring multiple objects use (e.g., prepare a sandwich or wrap a gift). A score was attributed to each task, according to the number of actions completed correctly, and the errors were classified after the MLAT error taxonomy (Schwartz & Buxbaum, 1997; Schwartz et al., 1998):

Omission: For example, fail to put a stamp on a letter.

Sequence: Anticipation-omission (e.g., seal thermos before filling; stir mug of water before filling).

Object substitution: For example, stir coffee with fork, place coffee pot on burner.

Action addition: Action not a necessary part of the task, includes utilization behavior and anomalous actions (e.g., cut gift box).

Gesture substitution: Correct object used with incorrect gesture (e.g., use scissors as a knife).

Grasp-spatial misorientation: Misorientation of the object relative to the hand or to another (reference) object (e.g., grasp wrong end of scissors, place stamp on envelope sideways).

Spatial misestimation: Spatial relationship between two or more objects incorrect (e.g., cut paper too small for gift wrap).

Tool omission: For example, spread mustard with finger instead of knife.

Quality: Inappropriate or inexact quantity (spatial or volume; e.g., fill thermos with juice until it overflows).

Analysis of the errors showed that both patients and control subjects committed a range of errors, which are included in Schwartz's taxonomy. Patients committed more errors of omission, sequence, action addition, spatial misestimation, or quality, but there was no difference for object or action substitution, grasp-spatial misorientation, or tool omission. A greater amount of errors was committed in the most demanding tasks (those with more steps and more objects to manipulate). Globally, time for completion was significantly increased in AD patients, and there was a significant correlation between the total time for completion and the DRS (Mattis, 1988), particularly with the memory, executive (concepts and initiation), and attentional subscores. It must nevertheless be noted that no correlation was found between the total score at the tasks and the MMSE or DRS scores and that an important heterogeneity was observed within the patients.

These results are globally in accordance with the findings that an increased level of complexity leads to more selection competition (and thus to more omissions) and that deficits of AD patients are due to a combination between a loss of automaticity in the selection of action schemas and a reduction of processing capacities (Humphreys & Forde, 1998; Schwartz et al., 1998); however, this data is still preliminary, and a detailed analysis is in progress with a larger sample of patients and more detailed neuropsychological testing, assessing in particular working memory, gestural abilities, and executive functions.

It thus appears, both from case and group studies, that a careful assessment of naturalistic action performance carried out simultaneously with a targeted neuropsychological examination (including, in particular, a thorough evaluation of working memory, executive functions, and conceptual knowledge) could lead to a better understanding of the relationship between functional impairment in daily living activities and cognitive processes. Because working memory and executive functioning deficits are among the first signs of AD (see chap. 3 of this book), it is of the utmost importance to be aware of their potential consequences on patients' autonomy in their activities of daily living. Conversely, functional loss in complex daily living activities could be among the earliest signs of dementia, even though cognitive impairment would still appear globally unnoticed (see Barberger-Gateau et al., 1999).

Because of the large heterogeneity of symptoms at the early stages of the disease, AD patients may also present selective impairment of cognitive processes, such as semantic system, working memory, gestural lexicon, or executive functioning. Careful assessment of their performance on both neuropsychological tests and naturalistic action tasks such as the MLAT could be useful to test empirically the hypotheses derived from theoretical models or to develop new theoretical interpretations to account for the observed performances. However, it could also have considerable implications regarding legal issues in daily life activities. Among them, a particularly important challenge confronting the neuropsychologist concerns the exploration of driving capacity. Indeed, special concerns may be raised about driving safety associated with AD.

> Studies of automobile accident frequency among drivers with AD have provided conflicting results. Nevertheless, on the basis of a large review of the literature, Dubinsky, Stein, and Lyons (2000) found that driving is mildly impaired in those drivers with probable AD at a CDR severity of 0.5. However, this impairment is no greater than that tolerated in drivers aged 16 to 21 and those driving under the influence of alcohol at a blood alcohol concentration less than 0.08%. On the other hand, drivers with AD at a CDR severity of 1

were found to have a substantially increased accident rate and driving performance errors. This increased risk is derived from crash statistics, performance studies of drivers with AD, and testing of components of the driving task. Considering this evidence, the authors recommend that patients and their families should be informed that patients with AD whose CDR severity is 1 or more should not drive a car and that patients with possible AD with a 0.5 severity of CDR pose a significant traffic safety problem when compared with other elderly drivers. Consequently, referral of these patients for a driving performance evaluation by a qualified examiner should be considered, as well as a 6-month follow-up assessment of dementia severity and driving abilities.

However, Foley, Masaki, White, Ross, and Eberhard (2001) rightly emphasized that cessation of driving is difficult to enforce in drivers with cognitive impairments and that appropriate testing facilities are woefully lacking. Dubinsky et al. (2000) also indicate that further research is needed to determine if there are subsets of AD patients with a CDR 1 severity of who can drive safely, or who can drive safely with some restrictions (e.g., driving within a limited area). Other questions that need to be addressed or explored more deeply in AD concern crash rates, taking into account driving exposure, crash type, and severity; driving limitations or technological solutions, which could decrease crash risk; reliable predictors of unsafe driving; efficacy of frequent assessments of driving; effects of driver retraining programs; and ethical and practical implications of managing demented drivers.

Recently, some interesting data have been published that throw light on the question while adding some confusion. Foley, Masaki, Ross, and White (2000) studied over 3 years the prevalence of driving in elderly men diagnosed with incident dementia in the Honolulu-Asia Aging Study, a population-based longitudinal study of AD and other dementias. They found that the prevalence of driving declines dramatically with the level of cognitive functioning. Only 22% of the incident cases of AD or other dementia with a CDR of 1 were still driving at the time of their evaluation, compared with 46% of those with a CDR of 0.5. They also estimated that approximately 4% of men ages 75 years and older who were still driving (about 175,000 persons) had very mild or mild dementia (CDR < 2) and that men who had moderate or more severe stages of dementia were rarely still driving.

In a pilot study based on a 5-year retrospective analysis of state-recorded crash data and crash characteristics, Carr, Duchek, and Morris (2000) observed that drivers with very mild (CDR = 0.5) or mild (CDR = 1) AD who continued to drive seemed to have crash rates similar to those of the cognitively intact age-matched controls, even when adjusting for driving exposure. In addition, patients with mild AD reported less roadway exposure than drivers with very mild AD or controls. Finally, no statistical differences were found between the causes and consequences of crashes involving drivers with AD when compared with the control subjects. The role of awareness in self-imposed driving restrictions has been evidenced by Cotrell and Wild (1999). They showed in particular that a deficit of awareness for attention was significantly associated with an absence of self-imposed driving restrictions, such as avoiding unfamiliar routes. Moreover, Bedart, Molloy, and Lever (1998) found that cognitively impaired patients, allowed to drive alone, were more likely to have been involved in crashes than patients not driving alone. However, it remains to identify the nature of this effect to establish whether the presence of a codriver represents a safe strategy to extend driving privileges in cognitively impaired elderly drivers.

Concerning the assessment of driving capacity, there exists presently no consensus on the best method to detect cognitively impaired drivers. Several standardized road tests have been developed (e.g., Hunt et al., 1997), but there still exist some problems with this type of test (see Hunt & Weston, 1999). In particular, it is essential to inform the patients and their families that the road driving part of the assessment may need to be repeated due to performance fluctuations in the disease. Another problem with road tests is due to unpredictable traffic situations. Thus, real driving ability may be difficult to interpret due to, for example, the presence, at an intersection, of visual cues arising from the performance of other drivers, which can help the patient's own driving behavior (cues that will be not necessarily present in other driving situations). Moreover, even if patients drive poorly on a road test, they frequently disagree with the recommendation to stop driving and argue, for example, that they were driving a car different from their own. It should be noted that this argument may have some validity because operating a new car probably requires more attentional resources than operating a familiar car, and, considering the dual-task coordination problems frequently observed in AD patients, it might be difficult for the patient to coordinate effortful car operations (e.g., finding the indicator lights, horn) and appraising an intersection situation. Finally, there is the safety issue: Operating conditions must be constrained to minimize risks of crash in road tests, and this consequently reduces assessment sensitivity. In other words, road tests in limited driving conditions are likely to emphasize relatively overlearned skills (procedural memory), which are not predictive of challenge-related driving performance (Bieliauskas, Roper, Trobe, Green, & Lacy, 1998). For all these reasons, the use of neuropsychological assessment and of simulated driving environment may constitute an interesting alternative or complement to road tests. Recently, Rizzo, McGehee, Dawson, and Anderson (2001) tested AD patients with mild to moderate AD on the Iowa Driving Simulator and discovered that 6 of 18 drivers with AD (33%) had crashes when the driver's approach to an intersection triggered an illegal incursion by another vehicle, versus none for 12 nondemented drivers of similar age. These findings are globally consistent with those of an earlier study using rear-end collision avoidance scenarios (Rizzo, Reinach, McGehee, & Dawson, 1997), in which 6 of 21 AD patients (29%) had crashes, versus none of 18 controls. However, it should also be noted that most AD drivers (15 of 21) did not crash and showed fair vehicular control (15 of 21 patients in the rear-end collision study and 12 of 18 patients in the intersection study). By combining both studies, Rizzo et al. (2001) also showed that neuropsychological predictors of crashes included visuospatial impairment, disordered attention, reduced processing of visual motion cues, and overall cognitive decline. These data suggest that driving appraisal (and manipulation of task demands) in a safe and controlled environment as well as neuropsychological evaluation may be useful in assessing the fitness of AD patients to drive. In particular, a simulated environment permits the creation of information flows that identify specific reaction and safety errors in crash avoidance situations, which would be hazardous, not to say unethical, on the road (Rizzo et al., 2001). It should be added that drivers with dementia who continue to drive appear to perform worse on traffic-sign recognition than normal elderly drivers (Brashear et al., 1998; Carr, LaBarge, Dunningan, & Storandt, 1998). This suggests that a traffic-sign naming test may be a useful component of driving ability assessment Finally, for those patients who lost driving privileges and who depend mainly on informal transportation (such as rides from families and friends; see Taylor & Tripodes, 2001), it seems essential to develop transportation policies and to improve the range of alternative transportation options.

The problem with the evaluation of driving abilities illustrates how crucial it is to develop theoretical models to better assess patients' competencies and account for their performances. However, such issues must also be addressed within the framework of a more comprehensive assessment, which should include, for example, the driving exposure and the conditions in which the patient drives (e.g., time of the day, traffic conditions), the potential for rehabilitative strategies, or the ethical and legal implications of driving authorization or limitation. In this sense, the assessment of the AD patients' autonomy in daily living activities is not only a question of assessment but also a concern of society, its values, and the role of the healthy and sick elderly living within this society in general.

Thus, a better understanding of the relationship between functional impairment in daily living activities and cognitive processes is particularly important for cognitive rehabilitation prospects. Detailed illustrations of how the interpretation of handicaps in everyday tasks, based on a theoretical model, can prove helpful to rehabilitation are discussed in chapter 9 of this book. This chapter also underlines the need for interventions in AD patients, taking into account multiple dimensions, such as cognitive, psychosocial, conjugal, economical, and behavioral aspects. Regarding the latter, it is well established that, in addition to physical handicap due to concomitant illness (see Salazar Thomas & The Canadian Study of Health and Aging, 2001), neurobehavioral disturbances can also influence functional autonomy. Recent attempts to examine the relationship between these disturbances and ADL are discussed in the following section.

IMPACT OF NEUROPSYCHIATRIC SYMPTOMS ON FUNCTIONAL ABILITIES

As described in chapter 7 of this book, AD patients frequently manifest symptoms such as anxiety, depression, delusions, hallucinations, wandering, aggression, purposeless activity, and so on. At a general level, Rigaud, Bayle, Forette, Buteau, and Fagnani (2000) showed a significant correlation between the presence of neuropsychiatric symptoms (assessed by the Neuropsychiatric Inventory, NPI; Cummings et al., 1994) and both a scale of IADL (Lawton & Brody, 1969) and a scale of caregiver's burden (Zarit, Orr, & Zarit, 1985). Similarly, Tekin, Fairbanks, O'Connor, Rosenberg, and Cummings (2001) showed that IADL were sensitive to both neuropsychiatric disturbances (assessed with the NPI) and cognitive impairment.

Analyzing the most prominent psychiatric and behavioral symptoms in a group of 114 AD patients, Harwood, Barker, Ownby, and Duara (2000) showed that specific signs and symptoms (e.g., hallucinations, night/day rhythm disturbances, delusions, wandering, and purposeless activity) were significantly associated with a functional impairment (evaluated by the Blessed Dementia Scale; Blessed et al., 1968). Rapoport et al. (2001) also found that hallucinations were related to impaired basic ADL, even if depression and apathy were controlled for. However, other authors did not replicate these findings. For example, Paulsen et al. (2000) and Green et al. (1999) failed to demonstrate a relationship between psychotic symptoms or behavioral impairment and self-care abilities.

Given that dysfunction in executive functioning has frequently been associated with impairment in ADLs, Norton et al. (2001) put forward the hypothesis that behavioral measures related to executive or frontal lobe dysfunction may also serve as predictors of functional impairment. They assessed 30 dementia patients with the DRS (Mattis, 1988) and administered to their caregivers an ADL and IADL scale (a modified version of the Activities of Daily Living Questionnaire; Lawton, & Brody, 1969), the NPI, and the FLOPS (Frontal Lobe Personality Scale; Grace, Stout, & Malloy, 1999). The FLOPS is a questionnaire designed to measure specific behaviors subserved by the frontal lobe systems. It is administered to an informant who is asked to rate different behaviors with regard to their frequency of occurrence, both before evidence of brain disease and over the weeks preceding the administration of the questionnaire. It consists of 46 items that comprise three subscales: executive dysfunction, disinhibition, and apathy. Each item is rated on a 5-point scale, which ranges from *almost never* to *almost always*.

The authors demonstrated by a hierarchical regression analysis that if the Initiation/Perseveration subscale of the DRS accounted for a significant part of the variance in IADLs, the FLOPS executive dysfunction subscale accounted for an additional 25% of the variance. On the other hand, the NPI failed to make an additional significant contribution to the regression equation. For the ADLs, the FLOPS apathy subscale was the strongest predictor of failure, and it was demonstrated that this effect was not due to depression.

Chen, Sultzer, Hinkin, Mahler, and Cummings (1998) also associated executive dysfunction with specific neuropsychiatric symptoms and an inability to perform daily living activities. These authors used the Neurobehavioral Rating Scale[2] (NRS; Sultzer et al., 1992) to assess psychiatric and behavioral symptoms and an adapted version of the Blessed Dementia Scale (Davis, Morris, & Grant, 1990) to evaluate the functional impairment of 31 AD patients. These authors reported that agitation and disinhibition correlated with both impairment in executive skills (Controlled Oral Word Association FAS subtest; Benton & Hamsher, 1976; Wisconsin Card Sorting Test; Nelson, 1976; DRS Conceptualization and Initiation subscales; Mattis 1989) and functional disability. Considering that both executive functioning and many neuropsychiatric disturbances are mediated through frontal-subcortical circuits, the authors postulated that underlying neurobiological correlates may be the basis for this relationship.

Among the neuropsychiatric signs that are frequent in AD, the role of depression in functional impairment is also debated. Studies examining whether depression is related to increased impairment reported mixed and inconsistent results. For example, Pearson, Teri, Reifler, and Raskind (1989) suggested that the diagnosis of depression was related to functional status beyond what could be accounted for by cognitive impairment. Fitz and Teri (1994) also suggest that, though functional ability in AD patients is multifactorial, depression can explain part of the variance in performances (33% for ADL items and 40% for IADL functioning). According to these authors, this impact of depression can vary according to the degree of dementia severity (more important at the earliest stages). However, other studies failed to find depression to be significantly associated with ADL functioning (Harwood et al., 2000).

More studies are needed to analyze the controversial relationship between neuropsychiatric symptoms and ADL in dementia patients. Most studies suggest that both cognitive and behavioral symptoms can influence the functional abilities of AD patients, but important differences in the results are probably due to methodological aspects and design limitations within studies (the range of examined ADL/IADL items differed, ADL and IADL were only assessed through short questionnaires filled in by the caregivers, criteria for behavioral symptoms were variable, there were differences in the construction of the behavioral scales, etc.).

To identify the consequences of neuropsychiatric symptoms on everyday life (e.g., autonomy, lifestyle, business' management), it is obvious that ADL/IADL scales and brief cognitive screenings instruments are not comprehensive enough and that performance-based measures (such as

[2]The NRS is a 28-item observer-rated assessment of cognitive and noncognitive factors in dementia. A principal component analysis has revealed six NRS factors: agitation/disinhibition, anxiety/depression, behavioral retardation, psychosis, cognition/insight, and verbal output disturbances. The NRS total neuropsychiatric score represents the sum of 20 items measuring noncognitive symptoms. Each item is scored on a scale of 0 (*non present*) to 6 (*extremely severe*).

simulations of daily living activities) and detailed neuropsychological assessments are needed. Thus, further studies should aim to better understand the relationship between specific neuropsychological deficits (e.g., episodic or working memory, executive functions) and neuropsychiatric problems, identify potential shared underlying mechanisms, and investigate the impact of cognitive and pharmaceutical treatment on functional disability. For example, as suggested by Norton et al. (2001), interventions that reduce behavioral disturbances or enhance cognitive functioning may be expected to improve adaptive functioning, reduce caregiver burden, and delay the need for higher levels of care.

CONCLUSIONS

Functional assessment is not only essential for an accurate diagnosis of AD but also an indicator of the course of the disease, an outcome measure for therapeutic interventions (both cognitive or pharmaceutical), and a good indicator of the type and degree of support needed from both the patients and their families. Unfortunately, assessment of ADL is so far largely unsatisfactory because classical scales of ADL are insensitive to early or subtle changes and biased by a number of factors. On the other hand, classical neuropsychological tests do not allow a prediction of the patients' competences in everyday life, particularly at the early stages of the disease.

To have an accurate picture of an individual's level of overall autonomy it is necessary—though not sufficient—to add performance-based tests that reproduce everyday life situations to subjective scales. Such measures can document how independently a person can perform a task and with what degree of assistance, but they do not provide information about the nature of the functional impairment or its underlying mechanisms.

To clarify what cognitive processes could be involved, attempts were made to relate functional evaluation with neuropsychological test performances (Baum et al., 1996; Nadler et al., 1993; Richardson et al., 1995), but the results remained unsatisfactory. In particular, these studies neither allowed prediction of functional impairment according to the observed cognitive deficits nor gave cues to rehabilitation possibilities.

These problems can be explained by the limits of the neuropsychological investigations of the action system, which long remained focused on the study of limb apraxia. Further studies demonstrated that other cognitive processes or subprocesses than those involved in single gesture production were also implied, depending on the action type. This stressed the need for a better specification of the studied level of action and for an identification of the involved cognitive processes based on theoretical models of normal functioning. The development of such explanatory models was initially based on observation of lapses in action selection in healthy subjects (Reason 1979, 1984, 1990) and single-case studies of neurological patients (Schwartz et al., 1991, 1995). Later, both case and group empirical studies were led with appropriate evaluation tools of naturalistic action, error classification systems, and precise exploration of implied cognitive processes (gestural lexicon, working memory and attentional resources, knowledge of perceptual and functional properties of objects and actions, and executive functions). In other words, a cognitive neuropsychology of daily living activities was born, thus opening ways to provide patients with both accurate clinical assessment and adapted rehabilitative programs.

Though it is clear that activities at the intermediate level of action (i.e., activities that involve sequences of movements that are well established through practice and that serve commonplace goals) depend on the implementation of multiple cognitive processes, the hypotheses raised to account for the role of these different processes are still under discussion. Norman and Shallice (1980) initially developed the contention-scheduling approach of action control, which suggests that most routine actions are planned online and usually triggered in response to environmental conditions. The contention-scheduling mechanism allows both the automatic activation of relevant action schemas and, if needed, the automatic inhibition of the irrelevant schemas. A supervisory attentional system intervenes as an additional influence when action schema selection is not sufficient—for example, when decision-making or planning abilities are needed, when two distinct activities are performed simultaneously, or when a novel or dangerous situation arises. A recent computational model of contention-scheduling parameters different cognitive domains (such as action schemas, object representations, resources, and selection process) and their integration in action control through excitatory and inhibitory mechanisms (Cooper & Shallice, 2000). This model can imitate disturbances in action control observed in both normal subjects and neurological patients.

On the other hand, Schwartz et al. (1991, 1995) developed a unified hypothesis based on detailed empirical studies to account for everyday action disturbances, a model which was also adopted, though in more detail, by Humphreys and Forde (1998). This hypothesis assumes that ADS results from a combination of both a disruption of routine action planning and a reduction of the supervisory attentional system and working memory. However, on the basis of their subsequent studies, Schwartz et al. (1998, 1999; Buxbaum et al., 1998) put forward the hypothesis that a limitation in resources could explain the positive relationship between an increase in attentional demands and a rise in omission errors.

Though different, these theoretical propositions to account for everyday action disturbances share the idea that multiple cognitive processes, which are hierarchically organized, are involved in action control.

Because AD is characterized by widespread lesions that impinge on multiple cognitive functions, it is not surprising that these patients commonly present with impairment in action organization. So far there have been few in-depth studies of this problem, despite its consequences on the patients' autonomy and quality of life. Moreover, most neuropsychological studies of daily living impairment failed to take into account the clear superiority of motor abilities over verbal ones in AD patients (Bird & Luszcz, 1993; Dick, 1992; Dick et al., 1989; Grinstead & Rusted, 2001) and did not consider the redundancy between neural systems responsible for the selection of action schemas necessary to everyday task completion, which could allow a defective process to be compensated by another system.

Studies with early AD patients were carried out recently to understand the complex interaction between the different cognitive processes implied in the realization of everyday action and to provide cues for possible targets of rehabilitative intervention (Buxbaum et al., 1997; Feyereisen et al., 1999; Juillerat et al., 1999). They assessed diverse dimensions of cognition (e.g., semantic knowledge, gestural aspects, working memory, and executive functions) and looked at their connections with a thorough observation of the performance of specifically designed tasks of daily living activities. These studies globally confirm the hypothesis of a relationship between a decrease in everyday performances and the combination of a loss of automaticity in the selection of action schemas and a reduction in processing resources. However, impairment patterns remain to be identified and connected with precise cognitive processes or subprocesses because problems that are usually merged under a single label (e.g., dysexecutive syndrome or semantic impairment) can certainly be divided into different forms of dysfunctions.

In addition, the impact of behavioral problems—and particularly the role of depression and apathy—on everyday tasks must be considered and investigated. Not only do they have a significant impact on the patients' and their caregivers' quality of life, but their relationships with both functional and cognitive abilities are far from being clear.

Because of the consequences of functional problems as a real-life handicap, it seems obvious that there is a need for performance-based measures and comprehensive neuropsychological and neurobehavioral assessments instead of ADL/IADL scales and brief cognitive or neuropsychiatric screenings.

Comprehensive assessment should not only help in understanding the relationship between different types of impairments and potential common underlying mechanisms, but it should also investigate how both cognitive and pharmaceutical interventions may ameliorate the patients' autonomy and quality of life (Adam, Van der Linden, Juillerat, & Salmon, 2000).

REFERENCES

Adam, S., Van der Linden, M., Juillerat, A.-C., & Salmon, E. (2000). The cognitive management of daily life activities in patients with mild to moderate Alzheimer's disease: The role of a day-care centre. *Neuropsychological Rehabilitation, 10,* 485–509.

Agüero-Torres, H., Hillerås, P. K., & Winblad, B. (2001). Disability in activities of daily living among the elderly. *Current Opinion in Psychiatry, 14*, 355–359.

American Psychiatric Association. (1994). *Diagnostic and statistical manual of mental disorders* (DSM-IV). Washington DC: Author.

Arbib, M. A. (1985). Schemas for the temporal organisation of behaviour. *Human Neurobiology, 4*, 63–72.

Armitage, S. G. (1946). The analysis of certain psychological tests used for the evaluation of brain injury. *Psychological Monograph, 60*, 1–48.

Baddeley, A. D. (1986). *Working memory*. Oxford, UK: Clarendon Press.

Barberger-Gateau, P., Fabrigoule, C., Helmer, C., Rouch, I., & Dartigues, J.-F. (1999). Functional impairment instrumental activities of daily living: An early sign of dementia? *Journal of the American Geriatrics Society, 47*, 456–462.

Baum, C., & Edwards, D. F. (1993). Cognitive performance in senile dementia of the Alzheimer's type: The kitchen task assessment. *The American Journal of Occupational Therapy, 47*, 431–436.

Baum, C., Edwards, D. F., Yonan, C., & Storandt, M. (1996). The relation of neuropsychological test performance to performance of functional tasks in dementia of the Alzheimer type. *Archives of Clinical Neuropsychology, 11*, 69–75.

Bedart, M., Molloy, D. W., & Lever, J. A. (1998). Factors associated with motor vehicle crashes in cognitively impaired older adults. *Alzheimer Disease and Associated Disorders, 12*, 135–139.

Benton, A. L. (1973). *The revised visual retention test: Clinical and experimental applications*. New York: Psychological Corporation.

Benton, A. L., & Hamsher, K. (1976). *Multilingual aphasia examination*. Iowa City: University of Iowa.

Bertrand, R. M., & Willis, S. L. (1999). Everyday problem solving in Alzheimer's patients: A comparison of subjective and objective assessments. *Aging & Mental Health, 3*, 281–293.

Bieliauskas, L. A., Roper, B. R., Trobe, J., Green, P., & Lacy, M. (1998). Cognitive measures, driving safety, and Alzheimer's disease. *Clinical Neuropsychologist, 12*, 206–212.

Bird, M., & Luszcz, M. (1993). Enhancing memory performance in Alzheimer's disease: Acquisition assistance and cue effectiveness. *Journal of Clinical and Experimental Neuropsychology, 15*, 921–932.

Blessed, B. E., Tomlinson, B. E., & Roth, M. (1968). The association between quantitative measures of dementia and senile change in cerebral gray matter. *British Journal of Psychiatry, 114*, 797–811.

Botwinick, J., & Storandt, M. (1973). Speed functions, vocabulary ability, and age. *Perceptual and Motor Skills, 36*, 1123–1128.

Brashear, A., Unverzagt, F. W., Kuhn, E. R., Glazier, B. S., Farlow, M. R., Perkins, A. J., & Hui, S. L. (1998). Impaired traffic sign recognition in drivers with dementia. *American Journal of Alzheimer's Disease, 13*, 131–137.

Burns, A., Lawlor, B., & Craig, S. (1999). Activities of daily living. In *Assessment scales in old age psychiatry* (pp. 127–162). London: Martin Dunitz.

Buxbaum, L. J., Schwartz, M. F., Branch Coslett, H., & Carew, T. G. (1995). Naturalistic action and praxis in callosal apraxia. *Neurocase, 1*, 3–17.

Buxbaum, L. J., Schwartz, M. F., & Carew, T. G. (1997). The role of semantic memory in object use. *Cognitive Neuropsychology, 14*, 219–254.

Buxbaum, L. J., Schwartz, M. F., & Montgomery, M. W. (1998). Ideational apraxia and naturalistic action. *Cognitive Neuropsychology, 15*, 617–643.

Carr, D. B., Duchek, J., & Morris, J. C. (2000). Characteristics of motor vehicle crashes of drivers with dementia of the Alzheimer type. *Journal of the American Geriatrics Society, 48,* 100–102.

Carr, D. B., LaBarge, E., Dunningan, K., & Storandt, M. (1998). Differentiating drivers with dementia of the Alzheimer type from healthy older persons with a traffic sign naming test. *Journal of Gerontology: Psychological Sciences, 53,* 135–139.

Chen, S. T., Sultzer, D. L., Hinkin, C. H., Mahler, M. E., & Cummings, J. L. (1998). Executive dysfunction in Alzheimer's disease: Association with neuropsychiatric symptoms and functional impairment. *The Journal of Neuropsychiatry and Clinical Neurosciences, 10,* 426–432.

Cooper, R., & Shallice, T. (2000). Contention scheduling and the control of routine activities. *Cognitive Neuropsychology, 17,* 297–338.

Cotrell, V., & Wild, K. (1999). Longitudinal study of self-imposed driving restrictions and deficit awareness in patients with Alzheimer disease. *Alzheimer Disease and Associated Disorders, 13,* 151–156.

Cummings, J. L., Mega, M., Gray, K., Rosenberg-Thompson, S., Carusi, D. A., & Gornbein, J. (1994). The neuropsychiatric inventory: Comprehensive assessment of psychopathology in dementia. *Neurology, 44,* 2308–2314.

Davis, P. B., Morris, J. C., & Grant, E. (1990). Brief screening tests versus clinical staging in senile dementia of the Alzheimer type. *Journal of the American Geriatrics Society, 38,* 129–135.

de Ajuriaguerra, J., Richard, J., Rodriguez, R., & Tissot, R. (1966). Quelques aspects de la désintégration des praxies idéomotrices dans les démences du grand âge [Some aspects of ideomotor apraxia within great age dementias]. *Cortex, 2,* 438–462.

De Renzi, E., & Lucchelli, F. (1988). Ideational apraxia. *Brain, 111,* 1173–1185.

De Renzi, E., Pieczuro, A., & Vignolo, (1968). Ideational apraxia: A quantitative study. *Neuropsychologia, 6,* 41–52.

Dick, M. B. (1992). Motor and procedural memory in Alzheimer's disease. In L. Bäckman (Ed.), *Memory functioning in dementia* (pp. 135–150). Amsterdam: Elsevier Science Publishers B.V.

Dick, M. B., Kean, M. L., & Sands, D. (1989). Memory for action events in Alzheimer-type dementia: Further evidence of an encoding failure. *Brain and Cognition, 9,* 88–108.

Dubinsky, R. M., Stein, A. C., & Lyons, K. (2000). Practice parameter: Risk of driving and Alzheimer's disease (an evidence-based review). Report of the Quality Standards Subcommittee of the American Academy of Neurology. *Neurology, 54,* 2205–2211.

Feldman, H., Sauter, A., Donald, A., Gélinas, I., Gauthier, S., Torfs, K., Parys, W., & Mehnert, A. (2001). The disability sssessment for dementia scale: A 12-month study of functional ability in mild to moderate severity Alzheimer disease. *Alzheimer Disease and Associated Disorders, 15,* 89–95.

Feyereisen, P., Gendron, M., & Seron, X. (1999). Disorders of everyday actions in subjects suffering from senile dementia of Alzheimer's type: An analysis of dressing performance. *Neuropsychological Rehabilitation, 9,* 169–188.

Fitz, A. G., & Teri, L. (1994). Depression, cognition, and functional ability in patients with Alzheimer's disease. *Journal of the American Geriatrics Society, 42,* 186–191.

Foley, D. J., Masaki, K. H., Ross, G. W., & White, L. R. (2000). Driving cessation in older men with incident dementia. *Journal of the American Geriatrics Society, 48,* 928–930.

Foley, D. J., Masaki, K. H., White, L. R., Ross, G. W., & Eberhard, J. (2001). Practice parameters: Risk of driving and Alzheimer's disease. *Neurology, 56*, 695.

Gélinas, I., Gauthier, L., McIntyre, M. C., & Gauthier, S. (1999). Development of a functional measure for persons with Alzheimer's disease: The disability assessment for dementia. *American Journal of Occupational Therapy, 53*, 471–481.

Gendron, M., & Lévesque, L. (1993, March/April). Evaluating the functional autonomy of persons with Alzheimer's disease: A tool for observing four activities of daily living. *The American Journal of Alzheimer's Care and Related Disorders and Research*, 24–35.

Goodglass, H., & Kaplan, E. (1973). *Boston Naming Test scoring booklet*. Philadelphia: Lea & Febiger.

Grace, J., Stout, J., & Malloy, P. (1999). Assessing frontal behavioral syndromes with the Frontal Lobe Personality Scale. *Assessment, 6*, 269–284.

Grafman, J. (1995). Similarities and distinctions among current models of prefrontal cortices functions. *Annals of the New York Academy of Sciences, 769*, 337–368.

Green, C. R., Marin, D. B., Mohs, R. C., Schmeidler, J., Aryan, M., Fine, E., & Davis, K. L. (1999). The impact of behavioral impairment of functional ability in Alzheimer's disease. *International Journal of Geriatric Psychiatry, 14*, 307–316.

Grinstead, K., & Rusted, J. (2001). Do people with Alzheimer's disease have a disproportionate deficit in functional knowledge? Verbal versus motoric access to semantic memory. *Aging and Mental Health, 5*, 295–300.

Harwood, D. G., Barker, W. W., Ownby, R. L., & Duara, R. (2000). Relationship of behavioral and psychological symptoms to cognitive impairment and functional status in Alzheimer's disease. *International Journal of Geriatric Psychiatry, 15*, 293–400.

Hughes, C. P., Berg, L., Danziger, W. L., Cohen, L. A., & Martin, R. L. (1982). A new clinical scale for the staging of dementia. *British Journal of Psychiatry, 140*, 226–231.

Humphreys, G. W., & Forde, E. M. E. (1998). Disordered actions schemas and action disorganisation syndrome. *Cognitive Neuropsychology, 15*, 771–811.

Humphreys, G. W., Forde, E. M. E., & Riddoch, M. J. (2000). The planning and execution of everyday actions. In B. Rapp (Ed.), *The handbook of cognitive neuropsychology* (pp. 565–589). Philadelphia: Psychology Press.

Hunt, L. A., Murphy, C. F., Carr, D., Duchek, J. M., Buckles, V., & Morris, J. C. (1997). Reliability of the Washington University Road Test: A performance-based assessment for drivers with dementia of the Alzheimer type. *Archives of Neurology, 54*, 707–712.

Hunt, L. A., & Weston, K. (1999). Assessment of driving capacity. In P.A. Lichtenberg (Ed.), *Handbook of assessment in clinical gerontology* (pp. 585–605). New York: Wiley.

Jeannerod, M., Arbib, M. A., Rizzolatti, G., & Sakata, H. (1995). Grasping objects: The cortical mechanisms of visuomotor transformation. *Trends in Neurosciences, 18*, 314–320.

Jeannerod, M., & Decéty, J. (1994). From motor images to motor programs. In J. Riddoch & G. W. Humphreys (Eds.), *Cognitive neuropsychology and cognitive rehabilitation* (pp. 225–243). Mahwah, NJ: Lawrence Erlbaum Associates.

Jorm, A. F., & Jacomb, P. A. (1989). The Informant Questionnaire on Cognitive Decline in the Elderly (IQCODE): Socio-demographic correlates, reliability, validity and some norms. *Psychological Medicine, 19*, 1015–1022.

Juillerat, A.-C., Peigneux, P., Van Hoecke, I., Lekeu, F., & Van der Linden, M. (1999). Activités de la vie quotidienne et maladie d'Alzheimer [Daily living activities and Alzheimer's Disease]. [Abstract] *Revue de Neuropsychologie, 9*, 291.

La Rue, A. (1992). *Aging and neuropsychological assessment.* New York: Plenum Press.

Lawton, M. P., & Brody, E. M. (1969). Assessment of older people: Self-maintaining and instrumental activities of daily living. *The Gerontologist, 9,* 179–186.

Lebert, F., Pasquier, F., Souliez, L., & Petit, H. (1998). Frontotemporal behavioral scale. *Alzheimer Disease and Associated Disorders, 12,* 335–339.

Loewenstein, D. A., Amigo, E., Duara, R., Guterman, A., Hurwitz, D., Berkowitz, N., Wilkie, F., Weinberg, G., Black, B., Gittelman, B., & Eisdorfer, C. (1989). A new scale for the assessment of functional status in Alzheimer's disease and related disorders. *Journal of Gerontology: Psychological Sciences, 44,* 114–121.

Loewenstein, D. A., Argüelles, S., Bravo, M., Freeman, R. Q., Argüelles, T., Acevedo, A., & Eisdorfer, C. (2001). Caregiver's judgement of the functional abilities of the Alzheimer's disease patient: a comparison of proxy reports and objective measures. *Journal of Gerontology: Psychological Sciences, 56B,* P78–P84.

Loewenstein, D. A., & Mogosky, B. J. (1999). The functional assessment of the older adult patient. In P. A. Lichtenberg (Ed.), *Handbook of assessment in clinical gerontology* (pp. 529–554). New York: Wiley.

Loewenstein, D. A., Ownby, R. L., Schram, L., Acevedo, A., Rubert, M., & Argüelles, T. (2001). An evaluation of the NINCDS-ADRDA neuropsychological criteria for the assessment of Alzheimer's disease: A confirmatory analysis of single versus multi-factor models. *Journal of Clinical and Experimental Neuropsychology, 23,* 274–284.

Luria, A. R. (1966). *Higher cortical functions in man.* New York: Basic Books.

Mandler, J. (1984). *Stories, scripts and scenes: Aspects of schema theory.* Hillsdale, NJ: Lawrence Erlbaum Associates.

Marson, D. C., Sawrie, S. M., Snyder, S., McInturff, B., Stalvey, T., Booth, A., Aldridge, T., Chatterjee, A., & Harrell, L. E. (2000). Assessing financial capacity in patients with Alzheimer disease. *Archives of Neurology, 57,* 877–884.

Mattis, S. (1989). *Dementia Rating Scale.* Odessa, FL: Psychological Assessment Resources.

McGlynn, S. M., & Kaszniak, A. W. (1991). When metacognition fails: Impaired awareness of deficit in Alzheimer's disease. *Journal of Cognitive Neuroscience, 3,* 183–189.

McKhann, G., Drachman, D., Folstein, M. F., Katzman, R., Price, D., & Stadlan, E. M. (1984). Clinical diagnosis of Alzheimer's disease: Report of the NINCDS-ADRDA work group under the auspices of the Department of Health and Human Services task force on Alzheimer's disease. *Neurology, 34,* 939–944.

Morris, J. C., Storandt, M., Miller, P., McKeel, D. W., Price, J. L., Rubin, E. H., & Berg, L. (2001). Mild cognitive impairment represents early-stage Alzheimer disease. *Archives of Neurology, 58,* 397–405.

Nadler, J. D., Richardson, E., Malloy, P., Marran, M. E., & Hostetler-Briston, M. E. (1993). The ability of the Dementia Rating Scale to predict everyday functioning. *Archives of Clinical Neuropsychology, 8,* 449–460.

Nelson, H. E. (1976). A modified card sorting test sensitive to frontal lobe defects. *Cortex, 12,* 313–324.

Norman, D. A. (1981). Categorisation of action slips. *Psychological Review, 88,* 1–15.

Norman, D. A., & Shallice, T. (1980). *Attention to action: Willed and automatic control of behaviour* [Chip report 99] San Diego: University of California.

Norman, D. A., & Shallice, T. (1986). Attention to action: Willed and automatic control of behaviour. In R. Davidson, G. Schwartz, & D. Shapiro (Eds.), *Consciousness and self regulation: Advances in research and theory* (Vol. 4; pp. 1–18). New York: Plenum.

Norton, L. E., Malloy, P. F., & Salloway, A. (2001). The impact of behavioral symptoms in activities of daily living in patients with dementia. *American Journal of Geriatric Psychiatry, 9,* 41–48.

Ochipa, C., Gonzalez Rothi, L. J., & Heilman, K. M. (1989). Ideational apraxia: A deficit in object selection and use. *Annals of Neurology, 25,* 190–193.

Patterson, M. B., & Mack, J. L. (2001). The Cleveland Scale for Activities of Daily Living (CSADL): Its reliability and validity. *Journal of Clinical Geropsychology, 7,* 15–28.

Patterson, M. B., Mack, J. L., Neundorfer, M. M., Martin, R. J., Smyth, K. A., & Whitehouse, P. J. (1992). Assessment of functional ability in Alzheimer's disease: A review and a preliminary report on the Cleveland Scale for Activities of Daily Living. *Alzheimer Disease and Associated Disorders, 6,* 145–163.

Paulsen, J. S., Ready, R. E., Stout, J. C., Salmon, D. P., Thal, L. J., Grant, I., & Jeste, D. V. (2000). Neurobehaviors and psychotic symptoms in Alzheimer's disease. *Journal of the International Neuropsychological Society, 6,* 815–820.

Pearson, J. L., Teri, L., Reifler, B. V., & Raskind, M. A. (1989). Functional status and cognitive impairment in patients suffering from AD with and without depression. *Journal of the American Geriatrics Society, 37,* 1117–1121.

Pfeiffer, E. A. (1975). A short portable mental status questionnaire for the assessment of organic brain deficit in elderly patients. *Journal of the American Geriatric Society, 23,* 433.

Poeck, K., & Lehmkühl, G. (1980). Das Syndrom des ideatorische Apraxie und seine Localisation [The syndrome of ideational apraxia and its lovcalization]. *Nervenartz, 51,* 217–225.

Rankin, E. D., & Keefover, R. W. (1998). Clinical cutoffs in screening functional performance for dementia. *Journal of Clinical Geropsychology, 4,* 31–43.

Rapoport, M. J., Van Reekum, R., Freedman, M., Streiner, D., Simard, M., Clarke, D., Cohen, T., & Conn, D. (2001). Relationship of psychosis to aggression, apathy and function in dementia. *International Journal of Geriatrics Psychiatry, 16,* 123–130.

Rautio, N., Heikkinen, E., & Heikkinen, R.-L. (2001). The association of socioeconomic factors with physical and mental capacity in elderly men and women. *Archives of Gerontology and Geriatrics, 33,* 163–168.

Reason, J. T. (1979). Actions not as planned: The price of automatization. In G. Underwood & R. Stevens (Eds.), *Aspects of consciousness* (pp. 67–89). London: Academic Press.

Reason, J. T. (1984). Lapses of attention in everyday life. In W. Parasuranam & R. Davies (Eds.), *Varieties of attention* (pp. 515–549). Orlando, FL: Academic Press.

Reason, J. T. (1990). *Human error.* Cambridge, UK: Cambridge University Press.

Reisberg, B. (1988). Functional assessment staging. *Psychopharmacology Bulletin, 24,* 653–659.

Reisberg, J. T., Ferris, S. H., de Leon, M. J., & Crook, T. (1982). The Global Deterioration Scale (GDS) for assessment of primary degenerative dementia. *American Journal of Psychiatry, 139,* 1136–1139.

Richardson, E., Nadler, J. D., & Malloy, P. (1995). Neuropsychological prediction of daily living skills in geriatric patients. *Neuropsychology, 9,* 565–572.

Riddoch, M. J., Edwards, M. G., Humphreys, G. W., West, R., & Heafield, T. (1998). Visual affordances direct action: Neuropsychological evidence from manual interference. *Cognitive Neuropsychology, 15,* 645–683.

Riddoch, M. J., & Humphreys, G. W. (1987). Visual object processing in a case of optic aphasia: A case of semantic access agnosia. *Cognitive Neuropsychology, 4,* 131–185.

Riddoch, M. J., Humphreys, G. W., & Edwards, M. G. (2000). Neuropsychological evidence distinguishing object selection from action (effector) system. *Cognitive Neuropsychology, 17,* 547–562.

Rigaud, A. S., Bayle, C., Forette, F., Buteau, L., & Fagnani, F. (2000). Les patients atteints d'Alzheimer à domicile: Coût et retentissement de la maladie [Alzheimer's patients at home: Cost and effect]. *Gérontologie, 115,* 17–23.

Rizzo, M., McGehee, D. V., Dawson, J. D., & Anderson, S. N. (2001). Simulated car crashes at intersections in drivers with Alzheimer disease. *Alzheimer Disease and Associated Disorders, 15,* 10–20.

Rizzo, M., Reinach, S., McGehee, D., & Dawson, J. D. (1997). Simulated car crashes and cash predictors in drivers with Alzheimer's disease. *Archives of Neurology, 54,* 545–551.

Roy, E., Black, S. E., Blair, N., & Dimeck, P. T. (1998). Analyses of deficits in gestural pantomimes. *Journal of Clinical and Experimental Neuropsychology, 20,* 628–643.

Roy, E., & Square, P. (1994). Neuropsychology of movement: Sequencing disorders and apraxia. In D. W. Zaidel (Ed.), *Neuropsychology* (pp. 183–218). San Diego, CA: Academic Press.

Rusted, J., Ratner, H., & Sheppard, L. (1995). When all else fails, we can still make tea: A longitudinal look at activities of daily living in an Alzheimer patient. In R. Campbell & M. A. Conway (Eds.), *Broken memories. Case studies in memory impairment* (pp. 397–410). Oxford, UK: Blackwell.

Salazar Thomas, V., & The Canadian Study of Health and Aging. (2001). Excess functional disability among demented subjects? *Dementia and Geriatric Cognitive Disorders, 12,* 206–210.

Schank, R. C. (1982). Dynamic memory: A theory of reminding and learning in computers and people. Cambridge, UK: Cambridge University Press.

Schank, R. C., & Abelson, R. (1977). *Scripts, plans, goals and understanding.* Hillsdale, NJ: Lawrence Erlbaum Associates.

Schmidt, R. A. (1975). A schema theory of discrete motor skill learning. *Psychological Review, 82,* 225–260.

Schwartz, M. F., & Buxbaum, L. G. (1997). Naturalistic action. In L. G. Gonzalez-Rothi & K. M. Heilman (Eds.), *Apraxia: The neuropsychology of action* (pp. 269–289). East Sussex, UK: Psychology Press.

Schwartz, M. F., Buxbaum, L. J., Montgomery, M. W., Fitzpatrick-De Salme, E. J., Hart, T., Ferraro, M., Lee, S. S., & Branch Coslett, H. (1999). Naturalistic action production following right hemispheric stroke. *Neuropsychologia, 37,* 51–66.

Schwartz, M. F., Montgomery, M. W., Buxbaum, L. J., Less, S. S., Carew, T. G., Coslett, H. B., Ferraro, M., Fitzpatrick-De Salme, E. J., Hart, T., & Mayer, N. H. (1998). Naturalistic action impairment in closed head injury. *Neuropsychology, 12,* 13–28.

Schwartz, M. F., Montgomery, M. W., Fitzpatrick-De Salme, E. J., Ochipa, C., Coslett, H. B., & Mayer, N. H. (1995). Analysis of a disorder of everyday action. *Cognitive Neuropsychology, 12,* 863–892.

Schwartz, M. F., Reed, E. S., Montgomery, M. W., Palmer, C., & Mayer, N. H. (1991). The quantitative description of action disorganisation after brain damage: A case study. *Cognitive Neuropsychology, 8,* 381–414.

Shallice, T. (1982). Specific impairments of planning. *Philosophical Transactions of the Royal Society of London, B298,* 199–209.

Shallice, T., & Burgess, P. (1991). Deficits in strategy application following parietal lobe damage in man. *Brain, 114,* 727–741.

Sirigu, A., Zalla, T., Pillon, B., Grafman, J., Agid, Y., & Dubois, B. (1995). Selective impairments in managerial knowledge following pre-frontal cortex damage. *Cortex, 31*, 301–316.

Sirigu, A., Zalla, T., Pillon, B., Grafman, J., Agid, Y., & Dubois, B. (1996). Encoding of sequence and boundaries of scripts following prefrontal lesions. *Cortex, 32*, 297–310.

Skurla, E., Rogers, J. C., & Sunderland, T. (1988). Direct assessment of activities of daily living in Alzheimer's disease. A controlled study. *Journal of the American Geriatrics Society, 36*, 97–103.

Sultzer, D. L., Levin, H. S., Mahler, M. E., High, W. M., & Cummings, J. L. (1992). Assessment of cognitive, psychiatric, and behavioral disturbances in patients with dementia: The Neurobehavioral Rating Scale. *Journal of the American Geriatric Society, 40*, 549–555.

Tate, R., L., & McDonald, S. (1995). What is apraxia? The clinician's dilemma. *Neuropsychological Rehabilitation, 5*, 273–297.

Taylor, B. D., & Tripodes, S. (2001). The effect of driving cessation on the elderly with dementia and their caregivers. *Accident Analysis and Prevention, 33*, 519–528.

Tekin, S., Fairbanks, L. A., O'Connor, S., Rosenberg, S., & Cummings, J. L. (2001). Activities of daily living in Alzheimer's disease. *American Journal of Geriatric Psychiatry, 9*, 81–86.

Teunisse, S., & Derix, M. M. A. (1991). Interview to determine deterioration in daily functioning in dementia. *Tijdschrift voor Gerontologieen-Geriatrie, 22*, 53–59.

Thurstone, L. L., & Thurstone, L. G. (1949). *Examiner manual for the SRA Primary Mental Abilities Test.* Chicago: Science Research Associates.

Wechsler, D. (1955). *Manual: Wechsler Adult Intelligence Scale.* New York: Psychological Corporation.

Wechsler, D., & Stone, C. P. (1973). *Manual: Wechsler Memory Scale.* New York: Psychological Corporation.

Wilson, B. A., Cockburn, J. M., & Baddeley, A. D. (1985). *The Rivermead Behavioural Memory Test.* Bury St. Edmunds, UK: Thames Valley Test Company.

World Health Organization. (1993). *The ICD-10 classification of mental and behavioural disorders. Diagnostic criteria for research.* Geneva: Author.

Zanetti, O., Geroldi, C., Frisoni, G. B., Bianchetti, A., & Trabucchi, M. (1999). Contrasting results between caregiver's report and direct assessment of activities of daily living in patients affected by mild and very mild dementia: The contribution of the caregiver's personal characteristics. *Journal of the American Geriatrics Society, 47*,196–202.

Zarit, S. H., Orr, N. K., & Zarit, J. M. (1985). *The hidden victims of Alzheimer's disease: Families under stress.* New York: New York University Press.

11

The Role of Caregivers in Assessment and Intervention

Francine Fontaine
Brigitte Gilbert
Karine Morasse
Institut Universitaire de Gériatrie de Montréal

In the course of the last 15 years, several studies in cognitive neuropsychology have profoundly changed our understanding of the early phases of Alzheimer's Disease (AD). These studies provided evidence of the heterogeneous nature of the onset and progression of AD, of selective deficits with preservation of certain cognitive functions, and of the presence of general factors that can potentially optimize the cognitive abilities of AD patients (see chaps. 3 and 9 of this book). Based on detailed analysis of neuropsychological profiles of individual patients, it thus became possible to develop strategies of cognitive intervention that tap residual abilities and minimize the negative impact of the disease on activities of daily living (see chaps. 9 and 10 of this book).

The present chapter describes how persons close to patients may contribute significantly not only to cognitive assessment but also to the elaboration and application of certain interventions in the early stages of the disease. Given the special problems of each patient, frequent contact between the patient's family and the neuropsychologist is necessary to establish a structured setting that is sufficiently flexible to allow for adjustments to a constantly changing reality. The sooner such a relationship is established, the greater its benefits to the patient and the family.

THE ROLE OF THE CAREGIVER IN COGNITIVE ASSESSMENT

Better Understanding for Better Intervention

A better understanding of the caregiver implies better daily intervention (Lévesque, Roux, & Lauzon, 1990) and is a general rule that all persons working in rehabilitation have frequently experienced. This principle is equally applicable to patients suffering from an irreversible degenerative disease.

Thus, the first step to follow when initially dealing with families of AD patients is to inform them of the neuropsychological assessment results. The initial diagnosis of AD is often like a bomb on the morale of the patient and family members. It is perceived as the immediate end of everything and the prospect of a bleak future. However, we have often experienced that taking sufficient time with the family to inform them of the specific cognitive functions that have been affected and unaffected by the disease has in itself a reassuring effect on the family. This step is thus considered a precondition to any proposal of intervention. Furthermore, we avoid using the term dementia because of its popular association with insanity and loss of control. Rather, we refer to the patient's problem as a degenerative illness and attempt to focus the family's attention on the patient's present mental status.

This approach is particularly relevant for AD patients in the early stages of the disease (early AD) because they still possess numerous preserved cognitive capacities at this stage. Early AD patients are capable of assuming social, domestic, and sometimes professional responsibilities, though to a lesser extent than previously maintained. Memory problems are principally limited to the recall of recent events, though the extent of these deficits may vary across patients. The patient may better recall information in situations where there are cues for recall and meaningful levels of encoding. The patient's semantic knowledge is normally well preserved, and, despite the presence of word-finding difficulties, the patient still maintains functional language skills. Although early AD patients are usually aware of their diminished skills, they may be unable to adequately assess the consequences of their deficits.

Explaining the neuropsychological evaluation to the patient's family is a critical moment in establishing confidence between the caregiver (who is normally a family member), the patient, and the neuropsychologist. In situations where the caregiver is open to the possibility of participating in further interventions (which is not always the case), the caregiver may help in measuring the effects the disease on the patient's daily life. Indeed, experiences with interdisciplinary interventions, notably those of occupational therapists, speech therapists, and social workers, have repeatedly indicated that the causal relation between the patient's deficit, as revealed by neuropsychological evaluation, and it's impact on a day-to-day basis, is not always evident. It is thus important to maintain a sufficiently personalized intervention program that incorporates the internationally recognized concept of handicap (World Health Organization, 1980).

Identifying Daily Problems

Two patients with similar cognitive profiles may suffer from very different consequences of their deficits, depending on environmental challenges, expectations, daily habits, and attitudes of family members. This is why the role of the family is so crucial for identifying the patient's daily problems. The caregiver shares daily experiences with the patient and is thus a main witness of the cognitive deficits manifested by the patient. In addition, the caregiver usually has known the patient for many years, sometimes for several decades, prior to the onset of the disease. The caregiver is thus familiar with the patient's habits, tastes, desires, and manners of dealing with daily problems. This information is precious in understanding and helping the patient.

During the interview with the caregiver, the clinician has to listen and to interpret appropriately what the caregiver says, while asking questions that take into consideration information provided by the neuropsychological assessment. We usually begin by asking general questions, such as "What is wrong?" "What is changed from before?" "What worries you?" However, responses to these questions will be reconsidered and further pursued by the clinician because the caregiver rarely emphasizes the patient's important problems at this stage, afraid of worsening the clinical diagnosis (see chap. 12 of this book). It is therefore necessary "to take the time to take the time" at each moment of the relationship with the family.

Use of Rating Scales, Diaries, and Checklists

By asking the patient's relatives specific questions about the daily functioning of the patient, the clinician establishes a portrait of the patient's abilities and disabilities. Rating scales, diaries, and checklists can help systematize this data collection and identify the behaviors or activities requiring more precise investigation.

Rating scales are lists of broad questions about behaviors or activities that are usually completed by the neuropsychologist interviewing the caregiver. Rating scales generally require quantifying the behaviors (e.g., on a scale from 0 to 5). Many scales are available. Although there is no perfect rating scale to quantify the everyday functioning of the patient, some can be of great help in orienting the interview with the caregiver. A list of some well-known rating scales is found in Table 11.1.

Because memory problems are often the major complaint of patients with early AD, it is important to pay particular attention to this domain.

TABLE 11.1

Some Questionnaires to Help Structure Interviews With Caregivers

Instrument	*Number of Items*	*Functions Assessed*
IADL Scale (Instrumental Activities of Daily Living Scale; Lawton & Brody, 1969)	8 items	IADL
SAILS (Structured Assessment of Independent Living Skills; Mahurin, Bettignies, & Pirozzolo, 1991)	50 items	ADL/IADL; developed for direct observation
DAFS (Direct Assessment of Functional Status; Loewenstein et al., 1989)	7 items	ADL/IADL; developed for direct observation
IQCODE (Informant Questionnaire on Cognitive Decline in the Elderly; Jorm & Korten, 1988)	26 items	Cognitive decline (in the past 10 years); translations and short 16-item version available
GERRI (Geriatric Evaluation by Relatives Rating Instrument; Schwartz, 1983)	49 items	Cognitive functioning, social functioning, affect
CBRS (Cognitive Behavior Rating Scale; Williams, 1987)	116 items	Cognition, behavior, affect
CAMDEX (Cambridge Mental Disorders of the Elderly Examination; Roth et al., 1986)	Formal testing and interview	Memory, intellect, drive, personality, behavior
PFQ (Present Functioning Questionnaire; Crockett, Tuokko, Koch, & Parks, 1989)	65 items	Memory, language, everyday tasks, self-care, personality
FRS (Functional Rating Scale; in Crockett et al., 1989)	8 items	Cognition, affect, activities and hobbies, personal care
QAM (Questionnaire d'auto-évaluation de la mémoire; Van der Linden et al., 1989)	66 items	Memory (in French)
Echelle d'évaluation comportementale et instrumentale (Eustache et al., 1993)	14 items	Perception, cognition, behavior, affect (in French)

We administer the memory auto-evaluation questionnaire (QAM; Van der Linden, Wijns, Von Frenkel, Coyette, & Seron, 1989) to the spouses, although it was originally created for patients. The QAM allows the neuropsychologist to evaluate the manifestations and frequencies of different types of memory deficit in everyday activities of AD patients. The questionnaire is structured in such a way that its different components reflect different aspects of memory problems elucidated on the basis of a cognitive model of memory (episodic memory, procedural memory, working memory, semantic memory), as well as other factors that may affect memory performance. Jointly used with the patient and caregiver, this questionnaire provides a considerable degree of precision about the patient's anosognosia.

Subsequently, personalized diaries or checklists might be used to record the profile of psychological problems that were identified with the caregiver and the circumstances in which they occur. The problematic behaviors, such as memory problems or inappropriate behaviors in social situations, are noted in the diary. The caregiver is then asked to record each occurrence of the problematic behaviors in everyday functioning. Caregivers should include a description of the circumstances in which the problem happened and other important information, such as the emotions shown by the patient. Like the diary, the checklist also consists of a predetermined list of behaviors. However, the behaviors are more specific than those found in the diary, and the caregiver simply checks off at different times of the day those that are relevant (Meulemans, 1995). These behaviors may include, for example, social disinhibition or forgetting appointments or a person's name.

The use of a diary can be illustrated in the following example. Working memory deficits are known to be associated with early AD. In daily life, this problem can manifest itself in a difficulty to encode an information while simultaneously doing something else (such as being informed by someone of the impending visit of a friend while listening to the TV). Such problems are usually not described by the caregiver in this manner but rather may be stated as "My wife forgets everything I say to her" or "My father doesn't pay enough attention." A diary can be useful to trace the profile of forgotten information. To do this, the caregiver notes the specific circumstances in which the patient received information. Was the patient doing something else when the information was given? Was the patient listening or did the patient seem to be inattentive? Was there any background noise when the information was provided? Thus, these notes will help identify circumstances in which forgetting is more likely to occur and also evaluate the frequency of the problem. Such observations will help the caregiver to discern particular situations that induce memory problems as well as provide the neuropsychologist with a clearer profile of the difficulties.

Checklists are also important in establishing a performance baseline before intervention. Sohlberg, Glang, and Todis (1998) have developed an ecological approach, emphasizing the role of the caregiver: once a problem is identified, the process of collecting data for baseline performance is completed with the caregiver's help. Observations are recorded using a checklist, which is adapted to the problematic situation. Interestingly,

Sohlberg et al. (1998) showed that caregivers may even identify their own methods to improve the patient's desired behavior.

Although rating scales, diaries, and checklists can be of great help to the clinician, they also have some inconveniences. For instance, the patient may feel spied on, and this might lead to conflicts with family members. If the patient is conscious of his or her cognitive problems, it is important that the patient understand the purpose of documenting his or her behavior. If the patient is not aware of such cognitive or functional difficulties, the caregivers will need to use diplomacy and have patience. It must be emphasized that the observations should always reflect the caregiver's desire to help the patient and must never be done with the intent of finding faults.

Other Important Information

The caregiver may also give information about domains of activities for which the patient has preserved or expert knowledge (e.g., bird watching, playing golf). This information is important because it may well be instrumental in patient intervention. Moreover, the clinician has to evaluate the way in which the caregiver deals with the patient's deficits. Are there adaptive strategies used to deal with the patient's behavioral problems? Does the caregiver adopt a childish attitude with the patient? Does the caregiver already adopt some general strategy to help the patient retrieve information from long-term memory? The caregiver can also inform the clinician about the environmental settings that can be modified to help the patient. Finally, habits of the patients that might be beneficial for intervention can be elucidated—for example, the use of an agenda or specific notation method.

The caregiver's observation of the patient's difficulties in everyday activities is also important for establishing the focus of the cognitive intervention program. What activities or situations are compromised by the cognitive decline? What are the behaviors that the caregiver considers stressful?

Comprehensive information gathering will provide the clinician with good knowledge of the impact of cognitive deficits on the patient's functioning. As a consequence of the understanding of stress factors, the clinician will be better able to establish intervention priorities. The clinician will learn how the caregiver already intervenes with the patient in the patient's environment, routines, and habits. Unfortunately, this ideal intervention scenario does not always develop as planned, for one reason or another.

However, the information gathered can be influenced by the manner in which the caregivers deal with the disease and with their sick relative (see chap. 12 of this book). Indeed, when using formal instruments, clinicians should never forget that they are dealing with suffering people and must use their clinical judgment to conduct the interview and interpret the information provided by the caregivers. Caregivers may either exaggerate or minimize aspects of the patient's behavior. We have often been surprised by the variability in tolerance levels across families: One level of incapacity may be well accepted in some families but regarded as totally unacceptable in others.

As an example, a patient's deficit of attentional resources or executive functions are frequently misunderstood. Difficulties in making decisions or finishing activities may be interpreted as signs of depression or laziness, a view that reflects the caregiver's perception that the patient has abandoned responsibility or refuses to plan activities in advance. For some caregivers, the problems are explained solely by an accentuation of certain negative personality traits of the patient. It is the responsibility of the clinician to take the time to explain and refute these false beliefs.

Understanding the Cognitive Basis of Everyday Difficulties

Once the clinician is able to identify the specific difficulties of the patient in everyday activities with the help of the caregiver's information, he or she will have to understand in greater detail the nature of the underlying causes of the cognitive deficits before intervention measures can be proposed.

Because the intervention concerns patients in the early stage of the disease, the neuropsychologist's attention will be focused on activities that are more complex than those of the daily routine (i.e., activities of daily living or ADL). Some of these include instrumental activities of daily living (IADL), such as the ability to use the telephone, to shop, to prepare meals, to do housekeeping, to do the laundry, to take public transportation, to take medication correctly, or to handle finances (Lawton & Brody, 1969). Other activities concern those involving problem solving, learning, or social interactions. Each of these activities may involve more than one cognitive deficit: long-term or working memory problems, deficits of executive functions, poor motivation, or even depression. A complete neuropsychological assessment is therefore necessary to understand the exact cause of the patient's daily problems.

With the help of the caregiver, the neuropsychologist may be able to grasp the general cognitive deficit by fragmenting problematic activities into their more distinct functional components. For example, the preparation of a meal requires a variety of cognitive skills, each of which may be impaired separately. If the patient no longer takes the initiative to prepare meals, it may be because he or she cannot mentally initiate such an activity, is depressed or disorientated in time, or believes that the demands of the task are too great. Alternatively, the patient might be able to carry out the elementary preparatory actions (e.g., peeling potatoes, cooking a steak) but may have difficulties organizing these actions into a coordinated and appropriate sequence. The patient may be unable to read or understand

and follow a recipe because of problems with abstract thinking or language comprehension. A patient with working memory problems can have difficulties monitoring several food items that are cooking at the same time or be unable to focus on the task at hand because he or she is distracted by a TV show or a ringing telephone. This person may leave items cooking on the stove, which can result in potentially dangerous situations. A problem with long-term memory might jeopardize the preparation of a meal if, for instance, the patient forgets that salt was already added to the recipe or that a cake is in the oven. The patient may even forget the ingredients of recipes he or she previously knew by heart. These problems might be aggravated by the possibility that the patient is not aware of them; the patient might underestimate the risks involved in these activities.

Analyzing the daily activities together with the caregiver is crucial because it establishes a clearer picture of the situation and reassures the family that not all the patient's psychological abilities have been lost. We thus minimize possible catastrophic reactions, while promoting a better understanding of the problem by the caregivers.

The information gathered by the clinician together with the neuropsychological assessment will allow the caregiver to be directly implicated in the intervention program.

THE ROLE OF THE CAREGIVER IN COGNITIVE INTERVENTION

The intervention program is based on a detailed analysis of the cognitive functions related to the handicap identified situations. The intervention program may aim to optimize residual abilities, to acquire specific domains of information, or to implement the use of external aids. Given the progressive nature of the illness, the intervention program will have to exploit maximally the patient's preserved abilities at each stage of the disease, according to each patient's specific condition.

The role of the caregivers may have several facets: familiarizing themselves with certain general factors of performance optimization and, with the help of the clinician, applying them in the patient's daily life; ensuring that the patient uses external aids; and recognizing and encouraging the use of the patient's preserved abilities and, in certain cases, collaborating with the clinician in the development of special rehabilitation strategies.

The proposed intervention program must take into account several factors: the cognitive deficits and preserved abilities that are relevant for the intervention, the actual handicap situation, patient and family expectations, and their family's level of understanding and their availability. The family must perceive their role and implication as a helping element, rather than an added burden. The approach taken must be tailored to the individual needs of the family, and requires small steps to be taken at a time in order to maintain the motivation of the patient and the family. At the St-Luc Revalidation Hospital in Brussels the clinicians establish a therapeutic contract with the family, which defines the objectives and duration of the intervention program. This allows the clinician to evaluate periodically the pertinence of continuing the program (Jacquemin, Calicis, Van der Linden, Wijns, & Noel, 1991). The importance of priorities for the patient should not be underestimated, and, once again, the caregiver's observations are important when establishing the priorities. For instance, a patient's incapacity to pay monthly bills (due to forgetfulness) does not need to be part of an intervention if both spouses have agreed that the caregiver can take care of this responsibility.

Priority should be devoted to the explanation of anosognosia, if this deficit is revealed by the neuropsychological evaluation. It is important to discuss this aspect of cognition with the family members. Has the caregiver noticed that the patient underestimates his or her memory problems? How well does the patient evaluate the impact of the cognitive deficits in his or her daily life? As the disease progresses, anosognosia will become more important and may limit any rehabilitation effort (Van der Linden et al., 1991). In the presence of anosognosia, the caregiver's attitude will have to be modified if they wish to improve the patient's cognitive abilities. First, the caregiver has to be convinced of the presence of anosognosia. Factual information provided by the caregiver about the patient's memory problems may be used. That the patient forgets appointments may be used to demonstrate the problem. In interviews conducted with both caregiver and patient, anosognosia can be demonstrated to the caregiver by asking the patient questions about his or her memory and appointments. How is the patient describing personal strategies to retain new information? How does the patient manage appointments? Are some of them missed? This interview should be done with diplomacy, the goal being the confrontation of the caregiver's perception with reality. Having convinced the caregiver of the presence of anosognosia, the next step will be to offer ways of coping with it. The caregiver should avoid discussions with the patient about the existence and degree of cognitive problems, adopting instead a more directive attitude with the patient. For instance, more time and supervision will have to be invested in this case to implement the use of external aids because the patient will not find these tools necessary.

Becoming Familiar With the Daily Use of Optimizing Factors

The clinician should address general methods of optimizing cognitive functions. The goal of this approach is to apply research findings to the family setting. Our experience has taught us that it is insufficient to simply discuss matters with the caregiver. Rather, it is essential to allow the caregiver to observe the clinician interacting with the patient, to simulate various real-life situations with the patient, and to use role playing (see

Jacquemin et al., 1991, for relevant examples). To optimize the beneficial effects of such activities, examples should be taken from the patient's daily life, chosen from the information the clinician has previously gathered.

For instance, the caregiver should be informed that the patient can be helped by the use of probe or multiple-choice questions (these are more formally referred to as cued recall or recognition tasks) if open questions are too difficult. Questions such as "what was your main activity today?" may be too general for the patient to provide details on events that took place during the day. The caregiver must learn to ask more specific questions.

It also happens frequently that the caregiver misinterprets the patient's word-finding difficulties (especially for proper names) as manifestations of a memory problem. This may cause some frustration on the part of the patient and the caregiver. In such situations, the clinician may attempt to explain the distinction, but it may be more appropriate to train the caregiver at producing initial word sounds to help the patient find a word or to encourage the patient to provide semantic or gestural cues to facilitate communication (see chap. 9 of this book).

Moreover, the caregiver should learn that retention of a new information will improve, if the patient is allowed more time to process this information. Verbal information presented orally should be told slowly, with many pauses, and repeated several times if necessary. If the patient has to retain either written or nonverbal information, he or she should be encouraged to reread or to look carefully at the presented material.

It should also be pointed out that information encoded by different sensory modalities has a greater likelihood of being retained by the patient. For example, if the patient is verbally informed that there is an invitation to play bridge the following Saturday, the invitation will be better remembered if the patient writes it down in a calendar. The to-be-recalled information could also be performed, as well as verbally provided (e.g., placing a newly bought compact disc on a shelf in the presence of the early AD patient). Recall will probably be even better if the patient performs the given information himself (e.g., storing the compact disc the caregiver bought). Because the recollection of motor actions and sequences seem to be unaffected in early AD, these capacities should be exploited as much as possible as mnemonic cues.

Minimizing memory errors is also of great importance (Baddeley & Wilson, 1994) because they tend to be repeated (either verbally or in action). To prevent such errors, the patient should not be put in situations where he or she is required to guess information. For instance, we know that new information has a greater likelihood of being forgotten because the patient is suffering from an anterograde memory deficit. If the patient hesitates when confronted with a question relating to recent facts, the answer should be given to the patient. If the patient gives a wrong answer, the best way to minimize the likelihood of repeating the error is to correct the response and, if necessary, use a spaced retrieval technique (see chap. 9 of this book) to ensure that the correct information will be encoded.

Early AD patients frequently manifest lower attentional resources (Belleville, Peretz, & Malenfant, 1996). The caregiver should therefore be told to avoid placing the patient in situations that demand divided attention. Conversations should occur when the patient is not focusing on another activity, such as listening to the TV, preparing a meal, writing, or carrying out a physical activity. Each of these situations requires the full attentional capacity of the patient. Additional stimuli will simply prevent the patient from correctly performing an ongoing activity and reduce the chances of retaining what has been said to him or her. Background noise, such as music, will also interfere with the information encoding. Once again, it may be necessary to establish a checklist to evaluate the impact of the intervention.

Another general guideline concerns the importance of routine activities and environmental stability. Changing the locations of common objects (clothing, keys, etc.) should be avoided because the patient is still able to remember familiar settings. The patient will not search for objects that were usually put in a specific place. If, for instance, the telephone book is suddenly placed in the library instead in the familiar telephone desk, the patient will continue to look in the desk's drawer every time the book is needed. Weekly activities that are already part of a well-established routine for the patient should also be maintained and extended. This is also true of new activities that eventually can become part of the patient's routine.

These recommendations and general guidelines should not be underestimated and special care and time should be devoted to ensure that such principles will be understood and applied by the caregiver. As mentioned before, observation of the clinician's interaction with the patient and role playing might also teach the caregiver to cope better with the patient's cognitive deficit.

Assisting the Patient Through the Use of External Aids

External aids may be seen as memory prosthesis for early AD patients. The caregiver should be encouraged to exploit such aids that are already successfully used by the patient. It is known that routine activities or procedures are better preserved in the memory of early AD patients. Is the patient already using an agenda? If so, the caregiver should encourage its use by reminding the patient to keep it with him or her all the time and to note immediately important information as well as appointments, even if they may seem unimportant (e.g., a friend's invitation to supper). The caregiver can then cue the patient to look at the agenda when checking appointments, preferably at similar time periods each day.

The caregiver should also be informed that other external aids can be used to compensate for memory, language, or attentional problems. West (1985) provides many examples of what she refers to as daily memory places, which can constitute external memory aids. For example, common objects (e.g., keys, glasses) may be better found by the patient if they are always put in places that are well in view (e.g., a table in the hall). Other aids include notepads with a pen near the telephone, a blackboard on which to write things to do, an alarm clock, or a pill aid. The caregiver should know that these aids are particularly useful in the early stages of the disease.

However, these aids will only become efficient after their systematic use has been acquired, with the assistance of the caregiver. A new routine is more likely to be integrated by the patient if it is followed systematically. To achieve this, the caregiver has to supervise and enhance the use of the tool. To help the caregiver to take the responsibility of implementing the use of external aids, a checklist may be used. The caregiver can note each time the patient has to be reminded to use the aid. This will indicate the extent to which the patient is learning to use these aids independently over time.

Sometimes, a memory book is more appropriate than an agenda. This aid is an extension of the agenda with new and personalized sections (e.g., phone numbers, things to do, names of newly met people; Sohlberg & Mateer, 1988). Although the neuropsychologist will first implement the memory book in a clinical setting, the caregiver's help will rapidly become essential. The caregiver plays an important role in initially maintaining the beneficial effects of this technique during the time intervals between rehabilitation sessions, eventually ensuring the generalization of such effects on a long-term basis. The caregiver can also be implicated in developing and implementing a communication book (Jacquemin et al., 1991).

Recognizing and Favoring the Maintenance of Preserved Capacities

Gathering information with the caregiver about the patient's daily functioning will likely result in identifying preserved functions (functional language, absence of significant visuoperceptive problems) and maintained levels of capacities or expertise in various domains. Recent research has shown the existence of intact abilities (e.g., those related to playing musical instruments, card games, or constructing puzzles) among AD patients, even those in advanced stages of their illness. It is in the best interest of the patient that such abilities are consistently practiced with the help of the caregiver. Unfortunately, family members focus too often on the patient's deficit, ignoring the remaining existing potential talents.

A typical example is the tendency of caregivers to perform tasks for the patient to speed up activities, thus ignoring completely or partially preserved abilities. Daily activities should be maintained and encouraged, even if some of the behavioral elements required by any given activity are disrupted by the disease. For instance, patients may lose their ability to drive a vehicle, but there should be no reason why the patient should not be allowed to participate in the vehicle's maintenance (e.g., filling up with gas, clearing of snow). Indeed, once components of the deficit that interfere with the completion of tasks are identified, the family should integrate the patient step-by-step into daily activities. The caregiver becomes the patient's supervisor, by assisting the patient in only those activities that he or she is unable to perform completely alone. Indeed, the patient will likely have demonstrated a sufficient level of preserved semantic memory and motor skills to participate in such activities.

The following examples might illustrate this point. One of our patients exhibited important episodic memory problems. The patient, a highly cultured and socially active professor, had to give up his job because he was no longer able to remember what he had taught in the previous lectures and was unable to maintain a stream of thought if a student interrupted him with a question. However, an arrangement with the family was made to enable him to continue giving short lectures to a small group of students at home. During each presentation, an assistant was present to ensure the continuity of his lectures. With his family's collaboration, he was able to use his preserved knowledge, expertise, and teaching skills to pursue a productive activity in a manner that was symbolically related to his sense of self-esteem.

Another progressively amnesic patient, who had maintained good social and conversational skills, was able to maintain his job as a visual artist and teacher. In this case, the family became involved by helping the patient organize his agenda and academic activities and by preparing the material necessary for the lessons.

Furthermore, a patient's well-established semantic knowledge (e.g., world war history) can be used as a topic of discussion or as a cue for recalling new information. A visit to a museum may be better recalled if the caregiver establishes links between different elements of semantic knowledge that the patient has successfully maintained. An exhibited work of art, for instance, can be compared (in terms of similarities and differences) to others that are well known by the patient. Moreover, if the patient was an expert in painting, works of art can be related to particular schools of aesthetic thought.

Collaborating for the Application of Specific Rehabilitation Strategies

Studies have shown that mnemonic techniques (e.g., spaced-retrieval and vanishing cues strategies) can be applied with success among AD patients for the learning of item-specific knowledge (see chap. 9 of this book). The use of such learning methods requires time, a very structured setting, and a certain level of experience on the part of the neuropsychologist. When such specific training is possible, the caregiver may indicate the domains of knowledge that could be trained. Item-specific knowledge can cover a wide range of items, such as phone numbers, names of people, things to do, and so forth. For instance, if the patient has been recently admitted to a day hospital, the therapists' names can be taught with these techniques. However, the caregiver has to be motivated and persistent in making sure that the patient attends the learning sessions regularly (which is not always easy, given the number of times the patient must travel to these meetings).

The caregivers should be familiarized with the strategic memory methods to apply them in daily situations. They should be informed that the spaced-retrieval technique yields more effective results for active long-term memory retrieval (see chap. 9 of this book). For instance, a patient may remember televised news events better (a topic for discussion at meetings with friends) if asked to discuss at them at different, expanded time intervals. Moffat (1992) has documented the positive outcome of this technique in a situation where a moderately impaired patient was required to learn the names of common objects, with the help of family members. Specific techniques can thus help the patient to acquire new information, and the caregivers can be trained by using a role-playing approach.

Another method, known as the fading or vanishing cues method, has been used successfully with severe DTA patients in conjunction with the spaced-retrieval technique (Bird, Alexopoulos, & Adamowicz, 1995). It was also shown that this method yields long-term memory maintenance effects on acquired information (Fontaine, 1995). Consider, for instance, a situation in which the caregiver has bought a new sophisticated telephone that dials a pre-specified telephone number by pressing a button. The caregiver may teach the patient how to use the telephone, using step-by-step instructions. Progressively (after a few trials), the caregiver may eliminate later steps in an attempt to see whether the patient can execute them. If so, the patient is asked to repeat the complete procedure with the instructions provided only for the first steps. Further demonstrations may involve eliminating more steps and so on, until the patient is able to use the telephone autonomously.

Family members are the privileged persons to promote, maintain, and generalize the patient's cognitive training. However, some patients are less cooperative with a family member than with the clinician. Furthermore, some caregivers have neither the energy nor the patience to take part fully in this training. Clinical judgment is needed to determine whether it is appropriate to spend time teaching mnemonic strategies to the caregiver.

SUMMARY AND CONCLUSION

Family members that are close to AD patients play an important role in the evaluation and intervention of cognitive deficits. The neuropsychologist must establish a relationship of confidence with the caregiver and maintain a constant interaction with this person throughout the entire therapeutic process. To achieve this goal, the caregiver has to be thoroughly informed of the results of the neuropsychological evaluation. The caregiver may then help to identify the handicap situations in the daily life of the AD patient. Certain instruments, such as rating scales, diaries, and checklists may be jointly used to collect additional information. On the basis of the received information and the neuropsychological test results, the clinician attempts to understand the underlying cause of the functional deficit by breaking it up into elementary cognitive components. Finally, intervention programs may be proposed. The caregiver will have to apply optimalization factors, encourage the use of external aids, and favor the maintenance of preserved knowledge of the patient. In some cases, the caregiver may also collaborate in applying specific reeducation strategies.

Thus, the caregiver is an essential partner to the neuropsychologist during the process of intervention. This alliance is even more important in the early stages of the disease, when these interventions can be applied with a maximum gain. However, it is evident that the personal characteristics of the patient and the caregiver have to be taken into account. Only by using an individualized and flexible approach that takes into account the heterogeneous profiles of AD and the needs and limits of the patient, can cognitive intervention yield appropriate and efficient results.

REFERENCES

Baddeley, A. D., & Wilson, B. A. (1994). When implicit memory fails: Amnesia and the problem of error elimination. *Neuropsychologia, 32*(1), 53–68.

Belleville, S., Peretz, I., & Malenfant, D. (1996). Examination of the working memory components in normal aging and in dementia of the Alzheimer type. *Neuropsychologia, 34*(3), 195–207.

Bird, M., Alexopoulos, P., & Adamowicz, J. (1995). Success and failure in five case studies: Use of cued recall to ameliorate behaviour problems in senile dementia. *International Journal of Geriatric Psychiatry, 10*, 305–311.

Crockett, D., Tuokko, H., Koch, W., & Parks, R. (1988). The assessment of everyday functioning using the Present Functioning Questionnaire and the Functional Rating Scale in elderly samples. *Clinical Gerontologist, 8*(3), 3–25.

Eustache, F., Agniel, A., Dary, M., Viallard, G., Puel, M., Demonet, J-F., Rascol, A., & Lechevalier, B. (1993). Echelle d'évaluation comportementale et instrumentale: Sériation chronologique des symptômes comportementaux [Instrumental and behavioral assessment scale: Chronological ordering of behavioral symptoms]. *Neuropsychologie, 3*, 37–61.

Fontaine, F. (1995). Utilisation de la méthode d'apprentissage par estompage auprès de sujets avec des troubles mnésiques progressifs [Use of the vanishing cues technique with subjects presenting progressive memory deficits]. Thèse de doctorat, Département de Psychologie, Université de Montréal.

Jacquemin, A., Calicis, F., Van der Linden, M., Wijns, C., & Noel, M.-P. (1991). Evaluation et prise en charge des déficits cognitifs dans les états démentiels [Assessment and management of cognitive deficits in dementias]. In M.-P. de Partz & M. Leclercq (Eds.), *La rééducation neuropsychologique de l'adulte* (pp. 137–151). Paris: Editions de la Société de Neuropsychologie de Langue Française.

Jorm, A. F., & Korten, A. E. (1988). Assessment of cognitive decline in the elderly by informant interview. *British Journal of Psychiatry, 152*, 209–213.

Lawton, M. P., & Brody, E. M. (1969). Assessment of older people: Self-maintaining and instrumental activities of daily living. *The Gerontologist, 9*, 179–186.

Lévesque, L., Roux, C., & Lauzon, S. (1990). *Alzheimer comprendre pour mieux aider.* Montréal: ERPI.

Loewenstein, D. A., Amogo, E., Duara, R., Guterman, A., Hurwitz, D., Berkowitz, N., Wilkie, F., Weinberg, G., Black, B., Gittelman, B., & Eisdorfer, C. (1989). A new scale for the assessment of functional status in Alzheimer's disease and related disorders. *Journal of Gerontology: Psychological Science, 44*(4), 114–121.

Mahurin, R. K., De Bettignies, B. H., & Pirozzolo, F. J. (1991). Structured assessment of independent living skills: Preliminary report of a performance measure of functional abilities in dementia. *Journal of Gerontology: Psychological Science, 46*(2), 58–66.

Meulemans, T. (1995). L'évaluation écologique des démences [Ecological assessment of dementia]. In F. Eustache & A. Agniel (Eds.), *Neuropsychologie clinique des démences: Évaluation et prise en charge* (pp. 235–247). Marseille, France: Edition Solal.

Moffat, N. J. (1992). Home-based cognitive rehabilitation with the elderly. In L. W. Poon, D. C. Rubin, & B. A. Wilson (Eds.), *Everyday cognition in adulthood and late life* (pp. 659–680). New York: Cambridge University Press.

Roth, M., Tym, E., Mountjoy, C. Q., Hippert, F. A., Hendrie, H., Verma, S., & Goddard, R. (1986). CAMDEX: A standardized instrument for the diagnosis of mental disorder in the elderly with special reference to the early detection of dementia. *British Journal of Psychiatry, 149*, 698–709

Schwartz, G. E. (1983). Development and validation of the geriatric evaluation by relatives rating instrument (GERRI). *Psychological Reports, 53*, 479–488

Sohlberg, M. M., Glang, A., & Todis, B. (1998). Improvement during baseline: Three case studies encouraging collaborative research when evaluating caregiver training. *Brain Injury, 12*, 333–346.

Sohlberg, M. M., & Mateer, C. (1988). Training use of compensatory memory books: A three stage behavioral approach. *Journal of Clinical and Experimental Neuropsychology, 11*, 871–891.

Van der Linden, M., Ansay, C., Calicis, F., Jacquemin, A., Schils, J. P., Seron, X., & Wyns, C. (1991). Prise en charge des déficits cognitifs dans la démence d'Alzheimer [Management of cognitive deficits in Alzheimer's Disease]. In M. Habib, Y. Joanette, & M. Puel (Eds.), *Démences et syndromes démentiels: Approche neuropsychologique* (pp. 253–262). Québec: Edisem.

Van der Linden, M., Wijns, C., Von Frenkel, R., Coyette, F., & Seron, X. (1989). *Un questionnaire d'auto-évaluation de la mémoire [A memory auto-assessment questionnaire].* Bruxelles: Editest.

West, R. L. (1985). *Memory fitness over forty.* Gainesville, FL: Triad Publishing.

Williams, J. M. (1987) *Cognitive behavior rating scales.* Odessa, FL: Psychological Assessment Resources.

World Health Organization (1980). *International classification of impairments, disabilities, and handicaps.* Genève: Author.

12

Taking Care of the Caregivers

Louise Lévesque
Université de Montréal
Centre de recherche de l'Institut Universitaire de Gériatrie de Montréal

Marie Gendron
Centre de recherche de l'Institut Universitaire de Gériatrie de Montréal

Family caregivers who take care of a relative with dementia at home are exposed to numerous stressful events of long duration, such as the management of difficult behaviors, the provision of constant supervision, and the lack of an intimate relationship with the sick relative. Numerous studies have shown that caring for a relative with dementia has deleterious effects on the psychological well-being of family caregivers and leads to social isolation (Schulz, O'Brien, Bookwala, & Fleissner, 1995). One option often used to alleviate these effects is to offer support groups to the caregivers. These support groups are usually of short duration (six to eight meetings) and focus on the following three elements: information about Alzheimer's Disease (AD), development of skills to deal with the relative's behaviors, and mutual support through expression of emotions among the group members (Lavoie, 1995). However, critical reviews of outcomes studies have indicated that the positive effects of support groups on the caregivers' well-being are quite modest, although caregivers generally appreciate them (Bourgeois, Schulz, & Burgio, 1996; Knight, Lutzky, & Macofsky-Urban, 1993; Lavoie, 1995; Lévesque & Lauzon, 2000). The same critical reviews report that apart from some methodological limits of the outcomes studies (e.g., small sample size), there is a lack of theoretical underpinnings to guide the development of support group interventions, and their short duration precludes deep discussion on the various topics covered during the sessions. Moreover, according to a meta-analytic review (Knight et al., 1993), individual interventions seem to be more effective than group interventions with regard to the caregivers' well-being. There is also a recent trend to develop multimodal interventions that incorporate family meetings in addition to group or individual encounters (Mittelman et al., 1995; Zarit, Anthony, & Boutselis, 1987) because it is well recognized that the entire family system is affected by caregiving. Evaluative studies of these programs reveal positive effects on the caregivers' well-being (Mittelman et al., 1995; Whitlach, Zarit, & von Eye, 1991).

Taking into account these various observations, we developed a multimodal (individual/family/group sessions) intervention to promote the well-being of the caregivers living with a demented relative.[1] A pilot study focusing on the intervention process was then conducted to examine its acceptability—that is, the caregivers' reaction to the key elements of the intervention. This examination was considered a necessary step before conducting a large evaluative study of the impact of the intervention on caregivers' well-being. Within the limits of this chapter, only the individual mode of intervention is presented. The chapter has been intentionally written from a clinical perspective so that we can share those features of the pilot project that might be helpful to clinicians. The key characteristics of the individual mode of intervention are described in the first part of the chapter. In the second section, the intervention process is presented through clinical observations, and in the third part contains a critical look at the intervention.

KEY CHARACTERISTICS OF THE INDIVIDUAL INTERVENTION

Theoretical Model

The intervention is based on the stress and coping theoretical model of Lazarus and Folkman (1984). According to that theory, stress is defined as a transaction between the person's environment that is appraised as exceeding the person's resources and endangering his or her well-being. More specifically, it is not the mere presence of objective stressors or of potentially stressful demands of daily living that is related to well-being but the cognitive appraisal of these demands (primary appraisal) and of the coping resources available (secondary appraisal). If a demand is perceived as stressful, a coping response emerges to face the demand, and its effect on the demand is then assessed (reappraisal). Folkman et al. (1991) have in-

[1]This intervention has also been tried with caregivers of a schizophrenic relative. Nicole Ricard (Université de Montréal) was the principal investigator responsible for the intervention with these caregivers.

tegrated the theoretical elements of this model into an intervention framework (see Fig. 12.1). Based on their work, our intervention encompasses two components.

Components

The first component, cognitive appraisal, is about the identification of specific stressors and of their changeable/unchangeable nature. Caregivers often perceive their whole caregiving situation as stressful. They are therefore invited to shift their attention from a global stressor to specific stressors (see Fig. 12.1). The next task is to distinguish between changeable and unchangeable aspects of the stressors. This distinction influences the choice of coping strategies. There should be a match or a fit between the ap-

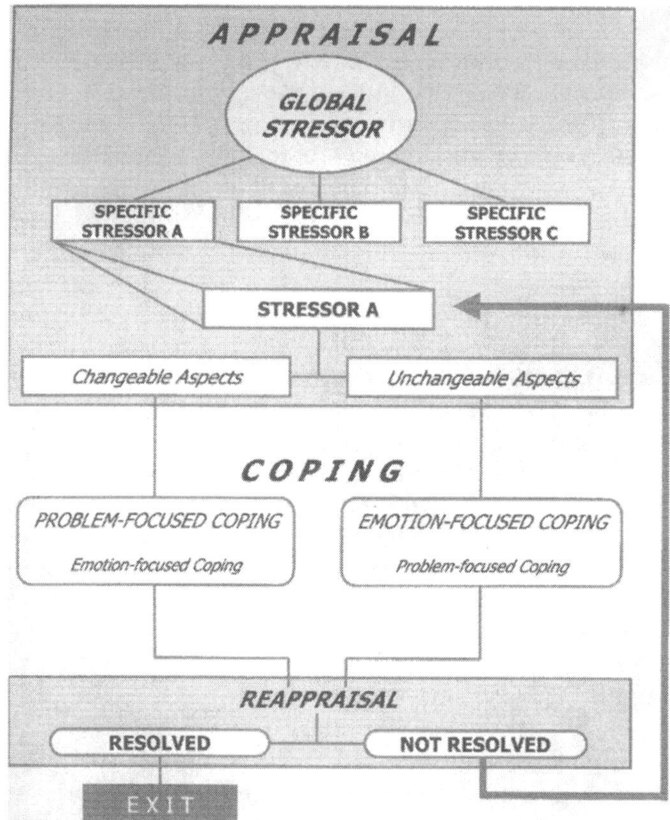

FIG. 12.1. Appraisal and coping model. From "Translating coping theory into an intervention," by S. Folkman et al., 1991. In J. Eckenrode (Ed.), *The social context of coping* (p. 246). New York: Plenum. Copyright 1991 by Plenum Publishing Corporation. Reprinted with permission.

praisal of changeability and the focus of coping: problem-focused or emotion-focused coping.

The second component concerns coping *strategies*, that is, cognitive or behavioral efforts to deal with a stressful encounter. Our intervention includes three well-known coping strategies. The first one, problem solving (problem-focused coping), is considered appropriate for altering the changeable aspect of a stressor (e.g., agitated behaviors of the relative during bathing). The second strategy is reframing the meaning of a stressor (emotion-focused coping). It is directed toward managing the emotional response related to the unchangeable aspect of a stressor (e.g., sadness due to the loss of the relative as an active confident). The third strategy is seeking social support; it can be helpful either to focus on the problem (e.g., advice seeking) or the emotion (e.g., finding a confident).

The Approach

The exploration of the stress and coping process is centered on the caregiver's personal daily reality. Indeed, the same source of stress can be cognitively appraised as stressful by one caregiver, but not perceived as such by another caregiver. Therefore, the clinician must be attentive to their emotional reactions. To do this, the clinician has to accompany the caregivers building an alliance with them as they unfold their unique experience. Openness to listen—nonjudgmental listening—is most important in such an alliance.

Flexibility is also required and is shown by respecting the readiness of the caregivers to reveal their experience and to attempt either of the three coping strategies. Within that perspective, the choice of the order of presentation of the three coping strategies varies according to the caregiver's readiness and particular stressful situations. Rather than simply suggesting a solution for an ad hoc problem, the intent is to focus on teaching these strategies, helping the caregivers to an awareness of their existing abilities as well as of potential ones. Therefore, information and practical suggestions are given when relevant. Assignments that the cargivers do alone at home or with the clinician and role playing are means through which coping strategies are learned and practiced.

Modalities

The two components of the intervention were covered during an average of 13 individual sessions (weekly or twice-weekly intervals), instead of the 9 that were foreseen at the beginning of this pilot project. Two nurses acted as the clinicians responsible for the implementation of the intervention with a caregiver, who was invited to telephone to them between sessions if they wished. Taping of the 2-hour sessions (using audiocassettes) proved essential in preparing subsequent sessions. For example, situations that lent themselves to the coping strategy of reframing were identified and used later as examples when that strategy was discussed in detail. At the end of each session, the clinician kept a diary about how the encounter had gone. The clinical observations reported in the following part of this chapter come from the transcription of the tapes, together with the diary.

Participants

Five primary caregivers living with their relatives took part in the intervention: 3 wives, 1 husband, and 1 daughter. The caregivers' average age was 65 (range between 59 to 75), and the average years of formal education were 11 (range between 4 and 18). Four of them had already participated in a support group offered by the Alzheimer Society; it was felt that to exclude them from the pilot study would be unethical. The relatives were all diagnosed with AD; they were at a moderate stage and required nearly constant supervision.

THE INTERVENTION PROCESS THROUGH CLINICAL OBSERVATIONS

Cognitive Appraisal

Identification of Specific Stressful Situations. At the beginning of the intervention process, the clinician's first responsibility is to listen attentively to the caregivers to become familiar with their perception of their experience, and of any stressful situations, and to encourage the expression of emotions. Such moments are precious to the caregivers because they often have no other place where they can be themselves without feeling judged. Questions from the clinician facilitate the revealing of emotions and difficult situations—for example, "Looking after a sick relative must seem hard for you at times; are there situations that affect you particularly? You said that you have been taking care of your relative for several years; is there anyone who takes care of you?"

The caregivers usually recount their situation with considerable emotion but in rather vague terms. The following statements taken from the tapes illustrate global situations: "I have bouts of nostalgia"; "I'm hurting inside"; "I feel empty." Does the nostalgia perhaps refer to the intimacy the couple had enjoyed before the onset of the illness? Or is it retirement dreams that the spouse's illness has forced the caregiver to give up? Does *hurting* mean that the caregiver is angry, despairing, helpless? When the caregiver talks of *feeling empty,* is it great physical fatigue? Or the loss of significant communication with the sick relative?

As the caregivers express their overflow of emotions, the clinician gradually helps the caregivers to make more precise statements and explains that too-broad situations are usually ambiguous, complex, and therefore difficult to manage. The process of breaking down a global situation into specific ones often helps caregivers become aware that something can be done. As one caregiver said: "You can behave better when you carve up the situation in small pieces."

The caregivers are then invited to choose four or five specific situations that they would like to change and to place each specific situation on a scale of 0 (*not stressful*) to 10 (*extremely stressful*). This assessment serves as a baseline; when the caregivers try out a coping strategy, they can observe the results. Does it work or not? Throughout the sessions, those chosen situations serve as reference points for presenting the key concepts of the intervention, thus facilitating their understanding and integration by the caregivers. However, these situations may become less stressful as the care-givers use appropriate coping strategies; hence, there is an opportunity to show them their abilities. Table 12.1 exposes some stressful events identified by caregivers and how stressful they seemed before and after their use of a coping strategy or strategies.

Identification of Changeability. Many situations seem nonchangeable to the caregivers because they are convinced they have already tried everything possible. Beginning with the list of identified specific stressful situations, the clinician points out that a stressful situation usually encompasses changeable and nonchangeable aspects, and the way of managing the situation differs according to its changeability. The clinician helps the caregivers to pinpoint which aspects of the situations are changeable or unchangeable. The notion of changeability is presented simply and rather briefly because there are many opportunities throughout the intervention to return to the link between the changeability of the stressors and the choice of problem-focused coping or emotion-focused coping.

Coping Strategies

The first situation that caregivers choose to work on is usually the one with the highest score of stressfulness. Depending on the nature of the situation, one of the three coping strategies selected for this intervention is then proposed.

Problem Solving

As mentioned earlier, the problem-solving coping strategy is directed at altering the changeable aspect of a stressful situation. This strategy, which encompasses six steps, is most useful when the stressful situation concerns difficult behavior by the demented person. The first step is to observe and to identify when the difficult behavior occurs, the circumstances that trig-

TABLE 12.1

Tool Used to Identify Stressful Situations

Stressful situations	*On Stressfulness Scale (0 to 10) at Beginning of Program*	*Coping Strategies (problem solving, reframing, seeking social support)*	*On Stressfulness Scale (0 to 10) at the end of Program*
M. spends his time vacuuming and that irritates me.	10		2
The sons don't want to hear about their father's illness.	9		6
M. moves the dishes around in the cupboard and does not use the right towel to dry the dishes.	9		3
I'm physically worn out because I'm the only caregiver.	8		3
As his wife, I feel very lonely; our communication as a couple is not what it once was; we used to make a close couple.	10		7
My relationship with my friends is more difficult because of M's illness.	6		2
My communication with my relative is no longer what it used to be; we were such a great pair.	10		7

ger the behavior, how often it happens, and the consequences of the behavior. Using a tool developed by the authors, the clinician invites the caregivers to keep a brief record of their observations. Caregivers often declare that no single event has provoked the behavior; however, one can be identified most of the time, if not always. One caregiver often reported, "I still haven't said what I mean; my relative[2] gets angry and becomes hostile." When the caregiver role plays the circumstances that provoked the hostility, the clinician realizes that the caregiver's tone of voice already reflected impatience. Impatience is certainly picked up by the relative!

The examination of the consequences is also important to determine the recipient of the consequences (the sick relative, the caregiver, or both of them) and the nature of those consequences. For example, for several weeks a relative had been in the habit of emptying every pocket anywhere at all and scattering handkerchiefs all over the house, something never done before. This caused frequent daily quarrels between the caregiver and the relative. During the analysis of the consequences, the caregiver realized that the main concern was really about what visitors might say, thus dramatizing the situation because, in reality, the actual consequences were somewhat trite.

Another caregiver reported that mealtime was very stressful. This caregiver usually asked the relative to help with certain recipes that required a long preparation time. The relative not only had trouble cutting certain vegetables but also made many comments (e.g., the way of cooking the food, the amount of seasoning). While working on the problem-solving strategy, the caregiver decided to separate the activity into two steps: preparing the food with the relative, but doing the actual cooking when alone. To the caregiver's surprise, the relative preferred to rest in the rocking chair while the caregiver did the cooking, and from then on the atmosphere was much more agreeable.

The other five steps of problem solving are to generate alternative solutions without censoring (i.e., brainstorming); select a solution, pros, and cons; plan and mentally rehearse implementing the strategy (i.e., the caregivers mentally anticipate problems they might encounter when implementing the chosen solution); try out the solution; and evaluate the outcome (Lévesque, Roux, & Lauzon, 1990; Zarit, Orr, & Zarit, 1985).

Reframing

Reframing (an emotion-focused form of coping strategy) refers to finding a different way to think about the situation, or creating an alternative meaning for it, so that the emotion generated by the unchangeable aspects

[2]In reporting verbatim, the term *relative* is used to designate the demented person; it does not specify a particular kinship (wife, husband, etc.) or a gender.

of a stressful event may be more easily managed. Reframing is based on the cognitive approach, according to which emotions are often engendered by thoughts (Beck, Rush, Shaw, & Emery, 1979; Burns, 1980). Four different ways of reframing are discussed with caregivers.

The first way concerns the caregivers' misunderstanding or misinterpretation of the demented relative's difficult behaviors. Indeed, some caregivers attributed the relative's difficult behaviors to a deliberate lack of cooperation and interpreted them as personal insults. Some questions can let the clinician check the caregivers' knowledge and understanding of the effects of their relative's disease: "In your opinion, how has your relative's illness changed him (or her)? According to you, what makes the sick person behave the way he (or she) does?" One caregiver reported the following:

> My relative argues with me constantly. I spend my time repeating everything for him; he says he understands but in fact he has understood nothing. I give him all the explanations he needs, but nothing helps [the caregiver believed that explaining more would compensate for the relative's memory loss]. He hides papers from me. I don't want to play his game; if I do, he will be the one to have the big end of the stick. He agrees to going out, but when it comes time to leave he pretends he knows nothing about it; he shows no respect for me when he lies to me like that, and I feel very aggressive.

Upon hearing the above, the clinician discussed the effect of AD on the sick person's behaviors. The clinician proposed a different perspective by reframing the meaning of difficult behaviors as a consequence of dementia. However, in doing so, there is a risk that the caregiver will think that nothing can be done to change the behaviors. It is therefore important that caregivers learn that the problem-solving coping strategy may be helpful to decrease the frequency of the difficult behaviors.

This example also illustrates that when an inaccurate meaning is given to a behavior because of a lack of knowledge, it can inadvertently aggravate the behavior. It also shows that the caregivers tend to rely on a rational style of communication (e.g., reasoning, arguing) to obtain cooperation. The use of a rational style has been found to be associated with negative feelings about the caregiving role (Lévesque, Cossette, & Lachance, 1998; Lévesque, Cossette, & Laurin, 1995). Indeed, caregivers who rely on this pattern of communication may experience frustration and feel impatient or incompetent because a rational approach has little, if any, chance of improving the relative's behavior caused by the cognitive impairment. Therefore, the clinician must help the caregiver to practice an appropriate way of communicating with the sick relative and to rely on an affective style of communication (e.g., telling the relative that he or she can feel safe, asking if the relative feels anxious or worried); this has been found to be associated with positive feelings about the caregiving role and a positive affect (Lévesque et al., 1995, 1998). During the intervention, the caregiver quoted previously changed the interpretation of the relative's behaviors as well as some personal verbal and nonverbal behaviors, realizing that they had an impact on those of the relative.

> I am the one who controls my relative's humor by the way I talk to him. I focus on his self-esteem rather than on reprimanding him. I no longer announce in advance what I will do, since he forgets as soon as I've finished speaking. When I see that something we have begun to do together is too much for him, instead of criticizing or blaming him, I pretend to be too hot or too tired to continue and I begin again when I'm alone. Now I am the master of the situation, and I feel less aggressive.

Certain caregivers have reported that giving up the reasoning and arguing is more difficult because their relative shows no physical signs that indicate a communication difficulty. Learning that this problem is not unique (i.e., recognition of the universality of the situation) is helpful. The clinician reminds the caregivers that it would be exceptional if they never used reasoning and never felt impatient especially because their pattern of communication before the illness had frequently been a rational one.

The second way of reframing is relevant, especially when the painful feelings are associated with essentially unchangeable situations, such as the irreversible character of AD and the inevitable decline of the loved person. The caregivers experience various feelings: sadness, disarray, anger, and revolt. These painful feelings often reflect the caregivers' response to the loss of the intellectually and socially active person they once knew and who had been their confidant. Experiencing painful feelings is normal in this situation, and such sentiments should not be denied. Can reframing help with such painful feelings? In such a situation, it is imperative to take time to listen to the caregivers and to acknowledge their feelings. Depending on each caregiver's readiness, the clinician invites the caregiver, in a subtle and gentle manner, to begin the long and painful process of accepting daily losses and of focusing on their relative as that person is now—that is, with some impairments but also with some abilities, however small. The clinician has to support the caregivers in their effort to develop a new perspective. According to Park and Folkman (1997), "in circumstances that are not amenable to problem solving, the stressful impact of the problem may be buffered by responses that control the meaning of the problem" (p. 124). One caregiver tried to focus on the 5% of the sick relative's past behaviors that were fortunately still part of her repertory. Two other caregivers realized that they had to focus on the "new" sick relative, the one for whom they were now caring.

> I became aware during the intervention that I had to grieve the loss of the relative I once knew. I am now trying to appreciate the relative that is here, now, in this house. I'm learning to love him in a different way ... love is taking on a different color. All that helps me to appreciate the fact that I still have him

with me. I try to enjoy everything I can with my relative, to see him as he is now, not as he was before his illness.

A third way of reframing is to think about the satisfying aspects of the caregiving role. Some authors have criticized the predominant focus on the burden of care (Nolan, Grant, & Keady, 1996), whereas Cartwright, Archbold, Stewart, and Limandri (1994) have proposed the concept of caregiving enrichment (e.g., the pleasant feeling caregivers experience when they can manage to diminish their relative's unhappiness). The invitation to recognize any satisfying or gratifying aspects usually surprises caregivers, who have rarely questioned themselves about such things. Some caregivers reply that they are merely doing their duty and that, if they were the ones with the disease, their spouse would do the same for them. Such oft-heard statements lead one to believe that caregivers have a tendency to minimize the value of the work they do. It is helpful if the clinician points out that although the work may seem quite ordinary to the caregiver, it is really rather extraordinary because the relative needs it so much. Caring can be seen as a source of self-esteem (Nolan et al., 1996). Caregivers develop personal qualities, such as greater tolerance and a deep sense of achievement. Following are some of the caregivers remarks: "I find that I have grown because of the illness; I feel less angry. I am less and less afraid and I can move forward slowly, even though it's hard; I couldn't do that before. I never felt equal to the situation; now I have more self-confidence, more maturity."

The fourth way of reframing is to invite the caregivers to examine some common dysfunctional thoughts (i.e., a cognitive distortion leading to misinterpretation of facts and events) that increase the risk of experiencing negative feelings and therefore affect well-being. Dysfunctional thoughts are, of course, not peculiar to caregivers; everyone has some kind of cognitive distortions. However, it was assumed that it would be helpful for caregivers to be aware of some common forms of dysfunctional thoughts, the link between such thoughts and painful emotions, and the power a person has to change such thinking. Concrete examples of dysfunctional thoughts observed clinically in caregiving situations are then discussed: jumping to conclusions, overgeneralization, magnification (catastrophizing) or minimization, all-or-nothing thinking, "should" statements, and personalization leading to guilt feelings, (for a definition, see Burns, 1980). The caregivers are invited to pinpoint the ones they use most often and to refer to their list of stressful situations to realize that some aspects of these situations may be amplified by dysfunctional thoughts. The task for the clinician is to help the caregiver understand the link between dysfunctional thoughts and painful emotion and to replace the dysfunctional thoughts with more helpful and rational ones.

The tool in Table 12.2 is used to help caregivers restructure the nonhelpful thinking; certain questions help them with the process of reframing (Burns, 1980). Reframing is also facilitated when the caregiver

TABLE 12.2

Tool Used for Reframing

What situation provokes a painful feeling?	What part of my thinking is unhelpful?	Intensity of feeling (0 to 10)	1) To have more helpful thinking, ask myself: • Do I help myself by this thinking? Could I see things differently? • Am I asking too much of myself? • What evidence do I have for thinking this way? 2) What more helpful thoughts might replace my distorted thinking?	Intensity of feeling (0 to 10)
When I put away my relative's clothes at bedtime.	All my life I've had high standards and I'm going to maintain them. I never give up.	10	The little bit of free time I have is in the evening. Is it that important the house be in perfect order? Is my well-being not more important than putting clothes away?	4

learns to step back from a stressful situation and to find time every day for a pleasant activity, even if only for a short time. Some examples of caregivers' dysfunctional thinking are as follows: "I'm a perfectionist and my relative's illness shouldn't make me change that"; "I feel guilty about not having enough patience with my relative"; "I think only of the negative aspects of the day"; "My sign is Aries and I'm too stubborn to change."

Seeking Social Support

The aim of this coping strategy is to reinforce or to broaden the caregivers' social support. Based on the work of Folkman et al. (1991) and Lévesque and Bergeron (1997), this part of the intervention considers the caregivers' reluctance to seek support, the skills required to identify the support they need, and the mobilization and maintenance of that support.

Reluctance to Seek Support. The clinician's first task is to explore the caregiver's many and varied objections to asking for support:

> Some family members will think I'm not capable if I ask them for help; they wanted me to place my relative in an institution, but I told them I could manage.... My friends should see that I need help and offer it without waiting to be asked.... I'm so afraid of being told "no" ... I'm afraid people will think they have to say "yes." ... I don't want to place a burden on the children ... I've never been one to complain and I'm not going to start now.... My relative needs help more than I do ... It's humiliating to ask for help.... I'm discouraged by the red tape in the health care system; I'd rather go without it.... My relative will not allow anyone else to come and replace me for a few hours.

Reframing can help caregivers overcome such reluctance. For example, to the caregiver who thinks that seeking help is a form of selfishness, the clinician may reply that everyone has the right to some time off during the long period of caregiving. Taking care of oneself does not mean neglecting the other one; it is not a synonym for selfishness. It may also be relevant to remind the caregiver that requesting help from someone can be seen as a sign of confidence in that person and that family members often feel sad and helpless because they do not know what practical help they can offer; they would appreciate a clear request. Caregivers' beliefs about the caregiver role may come into play and can be gently challenged. In some cases, it may be helpful to point out that the sick relative might even benefit from seeing other people.

Identification of the Needed Support and the Supportive Person. Once the caregivers have become aware of their reluctance, they are invited to identify clearly their need for support as well as the type of support required in a specific situation. Various types of support are discussed with the caregivers: emotional (e.g., moral comfort), material (e.g., physical tasks), social (e.g., visiting) and informative (e.g., advice). There should be a narrow fit between the caregivers' need of support and the type of support required.

The next task is to ensure a fit between the type of support required and the best person to provide it. To do so, the notion of a support network is exposed to the caregivers. They are invited to identify the people in their informal network (family members, friends, etc.) or the formal resources of community services that are best able to offer the support required. They are asked to think about the pros and cons of seeking help from the persons or the resources identified. The notion of reciprocity or symmetry in the exchange of support is then discussed. A lack of symmetry is most often seen in caregivers' feelings of indebtedness toward the potential helper and such feelings can hamper their self-esteem. When this makes the caregivers uncomfortable, the clinician points out to them that they have already helped their sick relative a great deal, that they have probably helped, in the past, the person from whom they are now requesting help or will one day have the opportunity to do so. The caregivers may also reduce their discomfort by telling the potential helper about their feelings of indebtedness.

Mobilization and Keeping the Support. Once the previous steps are completed, the clinician accompanies the caregiver in planning a request for support. Role playing allows the caregivers to identify any reluctance as well as to evaluate the precision of the request (type of support, frequency, duration, place, etc.) and the ways to deal with a refusal. Following that is a discussion about ways of maintaining the support obtained: expressing appreciation to the resource person, watching for signs of fatigue in that person, and offering regular feedback about the support received.

While considering the coping strategy of seeking support, one caregiver stated clearly how difficult it was to ask for help from anyone, but especially from two sons. The caregiver had often asked them for help in the past, but always in vain. However, the caregiver came to realize that the request had never clearly stated the type of help that was expected from the sons. The caregiver had always used vague words and, as well, had spoken in a joking fashion. Once the needs to which the sons could respond were identified, the caregiver was afraid that they could not be expressed clearly without seeming hostile and too emotional. The caregiver taped the requests and practiced making them. This was the same caregiver who also taped all the sessions and listened to them when needed. While listening to the tapes, the caregiver picked up certain signs of hostility that were not to be passed on to the two sons.

A caregiver had assumed that the sick relative would be unhappy in a day-care center. Realizing that the assumption was not based on facts, the caregiver took the necessary steps for a trial experience in such a center and found that the relative liked being there very much. Other caregivers made a request to community services to receive more help, such as increased hours of respite at home or day care. Another caregiver decided to speak to the daughter of the family about the help she provided, thinking that it was too much for her. The results were surprising: "It really opened my eyes. I saw her capacity for tolerance, her concern for me and her lack of frustration." The intent of the tool in Table 12.3 is to help the caregivers to practice the strategy of seeking support.[3]

A CRITICAL LOOK AT THE INTERVENTION

This critical look at the intervention is based on the information gathered during an open interview with each of the caregivers at the end of the individual intervention. The interview was carried out by an interviewer who had not taken part in the implementation of the pilot study.

All of the caregivers greatly appreciated that they were able to express their innermost emotions and worries. The close alliance felt between them and the clinician greatly facilitated this process and helped them feel less emotionally upset, more calm, more confident, and in better control of the situation. The following comments reflect some of the caregivers' remarks:

> Without this intervention, I would have continued in my own wretched way. I felt like a train rushing toward a precipice and, without help, I would not have been able to stop.... The intervention is very deep—as well as practical. I had already taken a group program that helped me by making me see that I was not alone in my situation, but I never said certain private things that I did in this intervention.... I was able to work on with the clinician and thus remove my blinders.... Now, when faced with a difficult situation, I think

[3]The individual sessions were followed by two family meetings to examine the exchange of support between the caregiver and the family members while being attentive to conflicts among the family members about how the care is provided and to allow each member to discuss their perception of the relative's illness and any difficult aspects of the caregiving situation. This part of the intervention was largely based on Zarit's et al. work (1985; see also, Zarit & Zarit, 1998). The family meetings were followed by three group meetings of all the caregivers who had participated in the individual sessions. The objectives were to help caregivers benefit from the recognized therapeutic properties of bringing together people living a similar experience, such as mutual support, and socialization (Yalom, 1975); to reinforce the caregivers' new knowledge and skills learned during the intervention, having been exposed to similar concepts in the individual sessions; and to create a new support network that may remain in place after the intervention has been completed. This last objective was not met, mainly due to the summer vacation period.

TABLE 12.3

Tool Used for Seeking Help

Need: Find someone to stay with X one afternoon a week.		Kind of support: Material
People in my personal network who could help: 1. Claude 2. Julie 3. ___	Positive facts about this person: 1. Always in good humor. 2. The person who best understands my situation. 3. ___	Disadvantages to asking this person: 1. He is very busy with three children. 2. She sometimes seems a little fragile. 3. ___
Community resources that could help: 1. ___ 2. ___ 3. ___	What pleases me about the resources: 1. ___ 2. ___ 3. ___	Disadvantages of the resource: 1. ___ 2. ___ 3. ___
My plan for requesting help: 1. I'll phone Julie Friday evening. 2. ___ 3. ___	If it is someone in my personal network, could it be a give and take of helping? If so, how? 1. I was an important support for her at the time of her divorce. 2. ___ 3. ___	Is the help received satisfactory? If I get help from someone in my personal network, what can I do to maintain that help? 1. ___ 2. ___ 3. ___

> about our meetings and that helps me.... The meetings seemed to help me develop a second nature; a spark was kindled.

The theoretical notions underlying the intervention appear quite easy to grasp by the caregivers, and the intervention being geared to their own daily reality facilitated their understanding of the key concepts. The notion of shifting from a global stressor to a specific one as well as the notion of changeable and unchangeable aspects of a stressor appeared relevant to the caregivers for it helped them to better understand their stressful situations.

Concerning the three coping strategies, all of the caregivers except one (referred to as Mrs. X) applied these strategies and consequently felt better equipped to continue caregiving. These caregivers found it useful to learn the strategy of problem solving because it resulted in reducing the frequency of some of the relative's behaviors that were difficult to tolerate.

> Now I analyze things a lot more, instead of saying "that's the way it is" and then doing nothing. If you get into the habit of thinking, you do it in other situations.... I have more control when I analyze things.... When I'm in a difficult situation I ask myself if it can be changed or not. I take the time to think before speaking or acting.... What has helped me is putting a name on what I'm doing.... Now I understand why I am doing it.

> These caregivers were also attentive to the coping strategy of reframing, one that is often new to them. They found this strategy very helpful in changing their perspective; reframing brought them to question themselves and to examine their values and beliefs and the meaning given to their caregiving experience: "You have done more than just give out information. The intervention touches the human dimension of caring; it includes a higher level than that of discussing the fact that my relative has wet his pants.... The intervention touches our human values."

As well, it is during the sessions on reframing that caregivers increasingly realize that the entire intervention process is meant to promote their personal well-being.

> Until now I had the impression that my relative was getting more attention than I am [referring to problem-solving], but now I see that this attention is really for me [referring to reframing].... This part of the intervention has helped me in all my relationships—with my children and with my friends. They often remark how much I have changed.... The situations have not changed but I feel better prepared to face them and reframing changes my way of looking at them.

Although these four caregivers did make a request for help or for more help, it became clear that the coping strategy of seeking social support is not an easy one to use. As mentioned earlier, the caregivers were reluctant to ask for support, informal or formal. Moreover, this part of the intervention sometimes awakened painful emotions, in particular when a caregiver sees that, although surrounded by people, there is no confidant. Community health practitioners often encourage caregivers to use their informal network because of the limited community-based services. Before doing so, they should be aware that help seeking is a complex coping strategy.

Although the foregoing comments provide information about the acceptability of the intervention, it had a different result in the case of Mrs. X, who participated in 14 sessions. Indeed, Mrs X made almost no attempt to practice the coping strategies. She very much appreciated her relationship with the clinician, she expressed a great deal of emotion, and her situations were appraised as most stressful. However, with regard to coping strategies, she stated that it was a question of months before she was ready to use them. The problem was not one of failing to understand the coping strategies. It was as though her emotional distress had blocked her readiness or impeded the cognitive and behavioral efforts that are necessary if coping strategies are to be acquired and used (Folkman & Lazarus, 1988; Lazarus, 1991; Nolan et al., 1996). Based on the work of Edwards and Cooper (1988), Nolan et al. (1996) point out that "Coping may in itself be stressful, in which case the stressful condition to be dealt with itself provokes further stress in the coping response required" (p. 55). It might therefore be important to offer the program to caregivers before they become too worn out; thus, they would be better equipped to continue their caregiving experience. Another possibility is that other coping strategies not included in the intervention might have been more appropriate for this caregiver. Mrs. X was also the only caregiver who did not attend a support group. The other four caregivers had an earlier experience of support group, which may have started them on some kind of a reflective process about their caregiving experience and thus made them more open to the intervention in this study. However, it was not possible to disentangle the influence of a previous support group for these caregivers.

Taking into account the comments of the caregivers, it appears to the research team that the relational aspect of the intervention is just as important as its content. As mentioned in the first section of the chapter, a relationship within which the clinician accompanies (the term *accompany* comes from the Latin word *companio* meaning "he who shares bread") the caregivers and forms an alliance with them is essential. Although this alliance requires openness, the clinicians are, at the same time, exposed to a whole gamut of painful emotions and situations. This difficult confrontation with reality may overwhelm the clinicians and call into question their own value system. To maintain openness, the clinicians have to be aware that their own values may influence their interpretation of the caregiver's statements and thus prevent them from exploring the latter further. It has also been observed that flexibility or respect for the caregiver's readiness is vital. To change takes time. The clinicians have to remind themselves that a strategy that seems disarmingly simple to them may be a mountain to a caregiver.

As for the content of the program, the theoretical framework provides an overall vision of the intervention and of the reference points that must be well understood by the clinicians if they are to make the necessary linkages between the various concepts of the intervention and the caregiver's particular caregiving experience and daily reality. However, a well-integrated knowledge of the intervention does not, by itself, suffice. The intervention also requires sound clinical judgment. For example, when the clinicians realize that the caregiver's situation requires the mobilization of more than one adaptive strategy, the formers' clinical judgment, based on their knowledge of the caregiver, guides them in proposing the strategy with which to begin. The following remark describes this: "I felt that the intervention was solid. I was not sure of where I was going, but the clinician never lost her way. She made the detours I needed. When we went over the content of our sessions, I recognized everything—my weeping, what she said to me, the work we did together, the exercises she had me do."

CONCLUSIONS

In this chapter, we attempted to share our experience regarding the care of family caregivers of a relative with dementia. However, one must remember that this pilot intervention was implemented with only five caregivers; no other follow-up interview (besides the one at the end of the project) was carried out with the caregivers to see if they continued to refer to the key elements of the intervention and to use the coping strategies. Moreover, the impact of this intervention on caregivers' well-being has not yet been evaluated. Still, it is hoped that some features of this individual intervention, which is one part of a multimodal program (see footnote 3), may shed some light on the practice of community health workers. Based on the stress and coping paradigm of Lazarus and Folkman (1984), the main objective of this intervention is to enhance the caregiver's abilities to cope with the stressful demands of caring. Within that paradigm, the caregiver is considered an active, meaning-giving person in his or her process of transaction with these stressful demands. This process is integrated in the personal history of the caregiver and of the sick relative as well as the relationship between them and the family members. With Nolan et al. (1996), the authors believe that this paradigm has a heuristic value for guiding intervention. It helps researchers to go far beyond the notion that the deleterious effects of caregiving are mainly related to the tasks in providing care.

Family caregivers are an essential but fragile resource. It is rather disturbing that although there is now great empirical evidence that the caregivers' well-being is jeopardized, community-based services are becoming scarce in the current economic context. It is imperative that the caregivers be provided with helping conditions if they are to fulfill their supportive role for their ill relative. Actually, there is a danger that the caregivers' degree of participation in caregiving will be determined by formal resources made available to the caregivers, rather than by themselves and their needs. The risk is great that caregivers will be seen as resources, rather than people who themselves need resources.

ACKNOWLEDGMENTS

This research was funded by the Conseil Québécois de la Recherche sociale (RS-2746 095). Louise Lévesque, RN, MSc, and Nicole Ricard, RN, PhD, were the principal investigators. The research assistants were Janique Beauchamp, RN, PhD candidate, Marie Gendron, RN, PhD, and Hélène Plourde, RN, BSc.

REFERENCES

Beck, A. T., Rush, A. J., Shaw, B. F., & Emery, G. (1979). *Cognitive therapy of depression*. New York: Guilford Press.

Bourgeois, M. S., Schulz, R., & Burgio, L. (1996). Interventions for caregivers of patients with Alzheimer's disease: A review and analysis of content, process, and outcomes. *International Journal of Aging and Human Development, 43*(1), 35–92.

Burns, D. D. (1980). *Feeling good*. New York: New American Library.

Cartwright, J. C., Archbold, P. G., Stewart, B. J., & Limandri, B. (1994). Enrichment process in family caregiving to frail elders. *Advances in Nursing Science, 17*(1), 31–43.

Edwards, J. R., & Cooper, C. L. (1988). Research in stress, coping and health: Theoretical and methodological issues. *Psychological Medicine, 18*(1), 15–20.

Folkman, S., Chesney, M., McKusick, L., Ironson, G., Johnson, D. S., & Coates, T. J. (1991). Translating coping theory into an intervention. In J. Eckenrode (Ed.), *The social context of coping* (pp. 239–260). New York: Plenum Press.

Folkman, S., & Lazarus, R. S. (1988). Coping as a mediator of emotion. *Journal of Personality and Social Psychology, 54*, 466–475.

Knight, B. G., Lutzky, S. M., & Macofsky-Urban, F. (1993). A meta-analytic review of interventions for caregiver distress: Recommendations for future research. *The Gerontologist, 33*, 240–248.

Lavoie, J.-P. (1995). Support groups for informal caregivers don't work! Refocus the groups or the evaluations? *Canadian Journal on Aging, 14*, 580–595.

Lazarus, R. S. (1991). Cognition and motivation. *American Psychologist, 46*, 352–366.

Lazarus R. S., & Folkman, S. (1984). *Stress, appraisal and coping*. New York: Springer.

Lévesque, L., & Bergeron, R. (1997). L'arrimage entre le soutien social et les besoins des aidants familiaux dont le parent est atteint de démence [Congruence between social support and needs of family caregivers of a demented relative]. In R. Hébert, K. Kouri & G. Lacombe (Eds.), *Vieillissement cognitif normal et pathologique* (pp. 163–172). Actes du congrès scientifique de l'Institut universitaire de gériatrie de Sherbrooke. St-Hyacinthe, Québec: Edisen.

Lévesque, L., Cossette, S., & Lachance, L. (1998). Predictors of the psychological well-being of primary caregivers living with a demented relative: A one-year follow-up study. *The Journal of Applied Gerontology, 17*, 240–258.

Lévesque, L., Cossette, S., & Laurin, L. (1995). A multidimensional examination of the psychological and social well-being of caregivers of a demented relative. *Research on Aging, 17*, 322–369

Lévesque, L., & Lauzon, S. (2000). L'aide familiale et le soin d'un proche atteint de démence [Family caregiving and the care for a demented relative]. In P. Cappeliez, P. Landreville & J. Vézina (Eds.), *Psychologie clinique de la personne âgée* (pp. 217–238). Ottawa, Canada: Les Presses de l'Université d'Ottawa.

Lévesque, L., Roux, C., & Lauzon, S. (1990). *Alzheimer, comprendre pour mieux aider.* Montréal: Éditions du Renouveau Pédagogique.

Mittelman, M. S., Ferris, S. H., Shulman, E., Steinberg, G., Ambinder, A., Mackell, J. A., & Cohen, J. (1995). A comprehensive support program: Effect on depression in spouse-caregivers of AD patients. *The Gerontologist, 35*, 792–802.

Nolan, M., Grant, G., & Keady, J. (1996). *Understanding family care.* Philadelphia: Open University Press.

Park, C. L., & Folkman, S. (1997). Meaning in the context of stress and coping. *Review of General Psychology, 1*(2), 115–144.

Schulz, R., O'Brien, A. T., Bookwala, J., & Fleissner, K. (1995). Psychiatric and physical morbidity effects of dementia caregiving: Prevalence, correlates, and causes. *The Gerontologist, 35*, 771–791.

Whitlach, C. J., Zarit S. H., & von Eye, A. (1991). Efficacity of interventions with caregivers: A reanalysis. *The Gerontologist, 31*(1), 9–14.

Yalom, I. D. (1975). *The theory and practice of group psychotherapy.* New York: Basic Books.

Zarit, S. H., Anthony, C. R., & Boutselis, M. (1987). Interventions with caregivers of demented patients: Comparison of two approaches. *Psychology and Aging, 2*, 225–232.

Zarit, S. H., Orr, N. K., & Zarit, J. M. (1985). *The hidden victims of Alzheimer's disease.* New York: University Press.

Zarit, S. H., & Zarit, J. M. (1998). Family caregiving. In S. H. Zarit & J. M. Zarit (Eds.), *Mental disorders in older adults, fundamentals of assessment and treatment* (pp. 290–319). New York: Guilford Press.

Author Index

Note: Page numbers followed by a *t* indicate a table.

B

C

G

H

I

L

M

N

O

P

Q

R

S

X

Y

Z

Subject Index

Note: Page numbers followed by a *t* indicate a table.

A

B

C

D

E

N

O

P

T

V

W